STOCKWELL OF MINNEAPOLIS

Stockwell of Minneapolis

A Pioneer of Social and Political Conscience

William P. Everts, Jr.

NORTH STAR PRESS OF ST. CLOUD, INC.

Library of Congress Cataloging-in-Publication Data

Everts, William P., 1918-
   Stockwell of Minneapolis : a pioneer of social and
political conscience / William P. Everts.
   446 p. 23 cm.
   ISBN 0-87839-103-7 (pbk. : alk. paper)
   1. Stockwell, Sylvanus A. 2. Legislators—Minnesota
—Biography. 3. Minnesota. Legislature—Biography.
4. Social reformers—Minnesota—Biography. 5. Minnesota
—Politics and government—1858-1950. I. Title.
F606.S87 1996
977.6'04'092--dc20
[B]   96-41286
               CIP

Cover photo: Looking north on Nicollet Avenue from Sixth Street, ca. 1910. (Courtesy of the Minnesota Historical Society)

Printed in Canada

ISBN: 0-87839-103-7

Published by: North Star Press of St. Cloud, Inc.
        P.O. Box 451
        St. Cloud, Minnesota 56302

Dedication

FOR MY SONS,
HAMILTON, JOHN, ROB, AND TED

Author's Note

I am profoundly grateful to the many people who contributed to this project. First and foremost is the late Janet Salisbury. I first met Janet in 1984 in Minneapolis. A retired editor at the University of Minnesota Press, she soon became interested in the Stockwell undertaking, joined in the research, gave encouragement and shared ideas until her death in 1995. In a very real sense, she was "a spiritual right hand." Without her, this book would not exist in its present form.

Also in 1984, author Priscilla McMillan gave valuable help. I thank her for the guidance she gave at my request. Another whom I thank is historian Carl Chrislock, always supportive and generous with his time during the days when we were both at work in the old Minnesota Historical Society building.

I thank the staff of the Minnesota Historical Society for their help in the production of this book. Russell Fridley, former director, and his young research historian, Mark Haidet, gave me a running start in 1984. Mark has been a friend and adviser ever since. I received help from the entire staff at the society and am especially grateful to Patricia Harpole, Allissa Rosenberg, Steve Nielsen, Toni Anderson, Faustino Avaloz, Ruth Bauer Anderson, Dallas Lindgren, Brigid Shields, and Sharon Cleveland. Recently, Patricia Harpole and Sue E. Holbert performed magnificently as a team to create the book's index. A crucial ingredient, and I am most grateful.

I now have strong allegiance to William Mitchell College of Law in St. Paul. Dean Hogg, members of the faculty, the library staff, and all the student body have been gracious, welcoming, and a pleasure to be with. Work in the Warren E. Burger Library, open nearly every day from 8:00 A.M. to 12:00 midnight, was and remains a joy. I was made to feel like a professor emeritus, and I thank Peggy Birk, graduate and former faculty member, for suggesting it as a place to work.

Don Fraser and Ross Corson, President of the Minnesota Independent Scholars Forum, never failed to respond when asked to lend a hand. I thank them both.

I am deeply grateful to Ellen Green for her sound judgment and excellent, insightful editing of the manuscript. And I thank her husband Ken for his assistance in rounding up illustrations, gaining clearance for their use, and in many other ways.

Priscilla Palm and Dee Berglund, ever faithful, showed infinite patience as typists and displayed the rare knack of reading illegible scrawl on a yellow pad, then typing it to become a manuscript. I thank them both, and also Betty Chatham for her recent, high caliber secretarial assistance.

It has been a joy having John Chafee on board for this project. From faraway Washington, he added timely humor and lifted one's spirits when down. Surely it was a singular act of friendship on his part to write the preface of this book, faced daily as he is with a mountainous pile of work while serving in the most demanding of posts. I thank him for taking it on.

Janet Salisbury introduced me to many of her friends who, in their younger days, knew the Stockwells personally or were knowledgeable about their activities. These friends became my friends; their recollections and insights were extremely valuable, and I thank them for sharing those memories. I also thank Violet Sollie, a remarkable letter writer who became a good friend. She knew the Stockwells intimately as a neighbor and was herself active in the Farmer-Labor Party.

Among relatives whose personal recollections have been vital are Leon Hamlet and his wife, Charlotte, Stockwell's niece. They now live in Milwaukee. I thank them and their son, John, for ongoing help in the project.

And to many others, I am thankful for ideas, advice, encouragement and other wide-ranging efforts on my behalf that have not only furthered the project but made it more rewarding and great fun: Dorothea Guiney, Mark Gleason, Jane Cunningham, Jean A. Brookins, Dave Wood of the *Star Tribune*, Khoren Arisian of the First Unitarian Society of Minneapolis, Natasha Kurchanova, Paul Rosenthal, Jack N. Birk, Nancie Litin, Don Vande Sand, Mona Brown, and R.W. "Bud" Gurney. I also thank Rita and Corinne Dwyer, who have been such a pleasure to work with at North Star Press and who have contributed greatly to the finished product.

Above all, there is my family: sons Hamilton, John, Rob, and Ted; my brother Stocky and my late, dear sister, Libby, all of whom have played a larger part and helped in more ways than they can possibly realize. And I thank my wife, Kit, who graciously accepted my extended preoccupation with the Stockwell biography, kept house and home together during my many absences, and who has, with high good spirits and unfailing patience, been a strong support throughout.

William P. Everts, Jr.

Contents

Preface

Certain periods in our nation's history have had great fascination for Americans: the Colonial Era and the giants who founded our country; the Civil War and Lincoln, Lee, and Grant; World War II, and Franklin D. Roosevelt and Truman.

We have remained relatively unfamiliar with the period between shortly after the end of the Civil War and the start of World War II. We know that railroads were built to span our nation and that there were governmental scandals; then came the jazz age and a period of great athletes such as Bobby Jones, Babe Ruth, and Bill Tilden. In the 1930s, we know there was a terrible Depression. But not much else stands out from those years at the end of the nineteenth and the first several decades of the twentieth centuries.

Yet those were extremely turbulent years for our country. The story of the life of S. A. Stockwell is about those years—1890 to 1940. To understand Stockwell, it is necessary to understand what was taking place in the United States during his lifetime.

Stockwell was born into a society where laissez faire was the order of the day: Build those railroads, dig those mines, electrify the cities and the streetcars. Those who were not strong got out of the way of those who were. There were no child labor laws, no employer liability insurance, no eight-hour work days. U.S. senators were elected by state legislatures that were frequently dominated by large corporations such as the mining, gas, railroad, or electric companies. Women did not have the right to vote; their place was in the home.

Stockwell believed much was wrong with such a society and devoted his life to doing something about it. The causes for which he battled ran the gamut from the parochial (protective cabs to shield Minneapolis street car operators from wintery weather) to the international (opposition to the Boer War and freedom for the Philippines) and most everything in between.

Stockwell possessed those character traits that are absolutely necessary for individuals who seek to change an often-unwilling society: total dedication to his goals, incredible persistence, unflagging energy, the capacity to absorb disappointments, and intellectual and physical courage.

Many of the great events of Stockwell's time are shrouded in the mists of history: Henry George and his single tax; Free Silver and William Jennings Bryan; World War I and the American Neutrality Society; the furor over teaching evolution in public schools; the Sacco-Vanzetti trial and executions. This biography of Stockwell brings those events and others to life.

It is clear that Stockwell was considerably ahead of his time and suffered the same disregard and occasional disdain that other prophets have endured. In 1891, he introduced legislation giving women the right to vote. It wasn't until a national constitutional amendment passed twenty-eight years later in 1919 that women achieved that right.

Early in this century, Stockwell was demanding protection for Minnesota's forests and an end to pollution of its lakes and rivers so that they might be enjoyed by future generations.

In 1929, it was the efforts of an outraged Stockwell that gained admission for a fully qualified young black woman to the University of Minnesota's School of Nursing. It was logical for the young woman's family to turn to Stockwell for help because he had long fought against discrimination of Blacks in insurance rate settings, employment, housing, and other areas.

Some issues with which Stockwell wrestled nearly one hundred years ago are still subject to vigorous debate today: the deterrent effect of capital punishment, state ownership of public utilities, and the initiative and referendum.

The mere longevity of Stockwell's crusading spirit inspires awe. First elected to the Minnesota legislature in 1890 and last elected in 1938, he enjoyed election victories and defeats in the intervening forty-eight years, sometimes winning by handsome margins, sometimes barely losing, as in 1892 when he lost by fifty-four votes, and sometimes getting trounced, as in the Teddy Roosevelt landslide of 1902.

It would be easy to dismiss Stockwell as a persistent gadfly enjoying the notoriety that comes in being a lonely dissenter. Such would be a totally inaccurate appraisal of his career.

He wanted victory, not just a cause. In order to foster more liberal thinking, he helped launch the Saturday Lunch Club in Minneapolis, and it became an extremely popular forum for the presentation of new and bold ideas.

For years, the annual cornfests he put on at his farm were large gatherings for both socializing and to hear speeches by leading liberal politicians and an occasional iconoclast.

His public embracing of unpopular positions was not without dangers and cost. During World War I, his antiwar stance led to the ransacking of his office and the termination of an office lease he had had for twenty years.

Blessed with Maud, a wife who had every bit the courage and dedication Stockwell had, he never faltered in pursuit of the right as he saw it. If he had a fault, it was his occasional inability to acknowledge that seeking the perfect is sometimes the enemy of achieving the good. Compromise wasn't easy for him. He was aptly described as "Wanting the Kingdom of Heaven Right Away!"

There are wide differences in our fifty states. Some are marked by a demand for a very high level of rectitude in its public servants, some are willing to innovate and experiment in how better to deliver governmental programs, some are anxious to have first-class education and social programs and are willing to pay for them. Minnesota has long been a leader in every one of those areas. It is a progressive state in the very best sense of the word. This wasn't preordained, nor did it just happen to come about on its own. Minnesota is the state that it is because of a series of courageous individuals who have been willing to go into the arena, to enter the fray, to join in the battle for better government instead of standing on the sidelines.

A shining star in that galaxy of dedicated public servants is Sylvanus Albert Stockwell.

John Chafee
U.S. Senator

Sylvanus A. Stockwell

STOCKWELL OF MINNEAPOLIS

Chapter 1

Looking Westward

T he Stockwell name is English, but William Stockwell, who brought the name to America, was born in Scotland about 1650. According to family tradition, William was enticed as a youth aboard a vessel setting sail for America. After a voyage normally taking about six weeks, he reached New England, probably landing at Boston Harbor. In an extension of the practice whereby immigrants from England voluntarily traded seven years of labor in return for passage, William was indentured on arrival.[1]

Although the work William performed and its location is not known, there are some clues. In 1646, John Winthrop, the younger son of the first governor of the Massachusetts Bay Colony, opened what became the first successful colonial ironworks in Saugus (then part of Lynn), north of Boston and south of Salem. In addition to employing a nucleus of skilled ironworkers from England, from the beginning the ironworks retained involuntary indentured labor. Sixty-one Scots, taken prisoner in 1650 by the forces of Oliver Cromwell in the closing stages of the English Civil War, were deported to Massachusetts Bay Colony and so employed. William Stockwell, who ultimately settled not far from Saugus, may have toiled as an unskilled laborer or learned a trade at the ironworks, which is now restored as a national historic monument.[2]

After William Stockwell served his indentured term, he began a normal life in the land to which he had been forcibly introduced. Initially he took to the sea, though he did find time to court Sarah Lambert, a second-generation American whose father, William Lambert, had sailed to New England from London on the *Susan and Ellen* in 1655. William and Sarah were married on April 14, 1685, in Ipswich and made it their home.[3]

The Stockwells had five sons and three daughters, all born and raised in Ipswich: William, Jr. (b.1685/86), John (b.1686/87),

Sarah (b.1688), David (b.1693/1695), Mary (b.1698), Jonathan (b.1700), Ebenezer (b.1702), and Elizabeth (b.1705).

In 1700 William gained a seat in the town meeting house, but, late in life, William, Sarah, William, Jr., and John (and the rest of the family afterwards) migrated to an unpopulated new settlement, the town of Sutton, about seventy-five miles west and south of Ipswich between Worcester and Providence. Their westward migration parallels that of other settlers who fanned into western Massachusetts, Connecticut, Rhode Island, and New Hampshire in the late-seventeenth and early-eighteenth centuries, but the move is nevertheless surprising. Most of those pushing to the interior were later arrivals. William Stockwell was an elderly lover of the sea with roots in Ipswich. Why leave one of New England's loveliest towns for an area described in the deed to the township (purchased in 1684 by nine Boston businessmen from John Wampus and his tribe of Nipmug Indians) as "a tract of waste land eight miles square . . . embracing within its limits an Indian reservation of four miles square called Hassanimisco"?[4]

William Stockwell, Jr., the eldest son, led the exodus. He was the pioneer, and his fortunes affected the whole family. In 1712, William, Jr., and his family moved to the so-called Middle Precinct of Salem (now the separate community of Peabody) during a time of considerable interest in Boston and Salem in a proposed new town called Sutton. Mabel Stockwell Kennedy in *The Stockwell Genealogy* gave this account:

> Where he had lived just prior to this is not certain although he was definitely very familiar with Salem as he had married a girl [Elizabeth Shaw] from that town just a few years before. He was warned out of town on August 2, 1712 which would indicate that he had moved there about May, 1712 (The warning read: "Whereas Information is given to ye Selectmen yt one William Stockwell has Intruded himself into this towne without lease of the towne or Selectmen thereof and is resident at ye house where William Shaw Jun. lately lived, order yt ye towne Clerk give forth a Warrant for ye warning him out of towne as ye law directs. Warrant went forth August 2, 1712, to Const's Locker.") . . . Salem, like most other Massachusetts towns, sent warnings to newcomers within three months after their arrival in compliance with a provincial law to the effect that newcomers entertained in a town three months and not "warned out" and their names returned to the Court of Quarter Sessions were considered as inhabitants, and the town would be responsible for them in the event that they should become public charges. The warning to William Stockwell, Jr., also states that he was

2

living at the house where William Shaw, Jr., (his brother-in-law) lately lived. Since William Shaw had died just a short time before, leaving a wife and six children, this is no doubt the reason for William Stockwell moving there.

At Salem Middle Precinct the Stockwells were close neighbors of the King, Marsh, Waters, and Walden families, all of whom were to become closely connected with the settlement of Sutton. Probably what precipitated their interest in the town was an opportunity to receive free land there just as a reward for being a settler.[5]

Sutton's town charter, signed by Governor Joseph Dudley of the Massachusetts Bay Colony on May 15, 1704, had provided that thirty families and a minister must forthwith be settled in Sutton. No families of sufficient boldness and enterprise to pioneer the town presented themselves "forthwith." In view of the ongoing Queen Anne's War (1702-1713), second in a series of French and Indian wars fought between Great Britain and France for control of the continent, the proprietors were granted up to seven years after the close of hostilities to meet the settlement requirement.[6]

In 1716, the families of Benjamin Marsh, Elisha Johnson, and Nathaniel Johnson braved the risks and moved to Sutton. They built cabins near the center of town, stacked firewood, stored provisions, and readied for winter. The great snowstorm in late February that year must have made them question their decision.

On the morning the snow began falling, Elisha left his family to obtain supplies in Marlborough. He was seen on his way by a friendly Indian, who, when the storm subsided, started on snowshoes for the tiny settlement. The Indian found the Johnson cabin by the hole the fireplace smoke had made through the snow. The family would "doubtless have perished had it not been for the kind forethought of this friendly Indian." Mrs. Johnson said "no human voice ever sounded half so sweet as did that."[7]

In spite of the perils, later in 1717, other families accepted the offer of a farm for the taking. By year's end, the thirty families to whom a grant of four thousand acres had been made, and for whom house lots of forty acres each had been laid out, were on the ground. Among them were the families of William, Jr., his father, and his brother John.

The Stockwells may have left Massachusetts' north shore for another reason. Salem was a town in agony in the 1690s and thereafter. Witchcraft, along with murder and sodomy, was punishable by death in seventeenth-century America. During the Salem witchcraft trials of 1692, twenty persons were executed and scores more arrested on suspicion of being witches—"persons who hath conference with the devil, to consult with him and/or do his bidding," in the words of England's great jurist, Lord Coke. Many fled to other regions to avoid persecution; some fled the country. The population of Salem decreased, its business suffered; its economy may never have fully recovered. While the trials ended in Salem in 1692 and many in the community came to rue the excesses they had encouraged, belief in witchcraft continued to flourish. As late as 1720, three children in Littleton, near Concord, accused a woman of bedeviling them. She died before the alarmed community hauled her into court.[8] Perhaps the Stockwells welcomed the opportunity to leave Salem even if not to seek refuge.

Although the purchasers' deed describes Sutton as a wasteland, historians William A. Benedict and Hiram A. Tracy gave a far more favorable view in their *History of the Town of Sutton, Massachusetts, 1704-1876*:

> The tract of land included in the grant was with the exception of here and there a cleared space, on which the Indians raised their corn, and a few marshes, called meadows, an unbroken forest, heavily wooded with pine, oak, hickory, chestnut, birch and maple. In its physical aspect it presented many attractive features, and was a favorite resort of its native owners, who reserved a home within its limits. Its surface is uneven and hilly, and, though none of its hills rise to a great height, yet many of them are of sufficient elevation to reveal from their summits scenes of quiet beauty unsurpassed in any other portion of New England. The soil is varied, in the southern and eastern part being of a sandy and gravelly nature, while in the northern and western parts much of it is a clayey loam. In the main it is well adapted to agriculture, though some portions, particularly in the southern part, are too rocky to be brought under cultivation, and none of it was subdued and made productive without much patient toil.[9]

The first houses were small, rude dwellings, often log cabins. John Stockwell's home—fifteen feet by ten—was large enough to hold the first town meeting on December 3, 1718. Every dwelling had a huge fireplace. Within a few years, the settlers cleared away large portions of the unbroken forest and fenced in fields for cultivation. The women and girls engaged in domestic labor, spinning wool and weaving it into cloth on their handlooms. At the end of a day, each could see what he or she had accomplished.

The early settlers were unschooled and attached little importance to schooling. Authors Benedict and Tracy did not fault them for their priorities:

When we consider that the early settlers of this town had had only the most limited advantages of schools, and some of them none at all, we are not surprised that so little interest was at first manifested in education. There is no mention of a school [in the annals of the town] until 1725, and then only in connection with a proposed sale of the school land—two hundred acres—which had been given by the proprietors in accordance with the conditions of the grant of the general court confirming the purchase of the township from the Indians.

The children may have had instruction in private schools but no action seems to have been taken by the town in the matter of the establishment of a public school previously to 1730, when it was voted that a school should be kept for four months in four places, at the discretion of the selectmen, one month in a place . . .

No record can be found of an appropriation for the support of a school until 1732. The name of John Smith appears upon the treasurer's book as the schoolmaster for this year. The school was kept at the house of Mr. John Gibbs, who was paid fifteen shillings for its use. About this time the town was presented at the court for failure to employ a schoolmaster as the law required, and a fine was imposed, notwithstanding the remonstrances of Dea. Percival Hall, Robert Goddard, John Stockwell, and John Bound who appeared in behalf of the town as defendants.[10]

John Stockwell, also known as Ensign John and Captain John from service in Queen Anne's War, was named a defendant because he was a selectman (councilman) in 1718, 1719, 1731, and 1732. The responsibilities of this town office, its holders chosen annually to manage the concerns of the town, were wide-ranging and included matters of church, state, law, education, economics, and finance. John was also frequently chosen at town meetings for committee assignments. On December 3, 1718, he was named to a committee chosen to build and furnish a meeting house. On March 17, 1719, he was named to a three-man "committy to get a minister, by the second Sabbath in May, and so on for three months." At a town meeting the following year, the committee was empowered to "discors" Reverend John McKinstry about the opening. At an adjourned meeting on March 21, 1720, McKinstry was "chosen to be settled in Sutton aforesaid, and to have sixty pounds per annum for his yearly sallery." In the fall of 1720, John was one of ten persons to sign a covenant leading to the founding of the First Congregational Church of Sutton, a condition imposed when purchase of the township was approved. On

5

August 16, 1725, when the town voted to sell surplus school land, "reserving the thirty acre lot and the money to be put out for the benefit of a school in Sutton forever," John Stockwell was asked to serve on the committee to sell the land.[11]

Reverend McKinstry did not succeed as initial pastor of the First Congregational Church. He found the profaneness and other vicious practices of the people unmanageable. Religion in Sutton under his stewardship "was in a low and languishing condition, and wicked men abounded." McKinstry was dismissed in 1728, and John Stockwell was asked to serve on a committee to find a new minister. Reverend David Hall, whose diary was to become a valuable record of Sutton's history, was chosen to take his place.[12]

At a town meeting held March 26, 1729, John Stockwell was named to serve on a fiscal committee with near sovereign power:

> Voated that Lieut. Elisha Johnson, Insing John Stockwell, mr John Sibley should be a Comitty to Judg upon the Present value of Paper Money in Pursuant to our forth voats last March ye 26 1729.

The committee reported on September 8, 1729:

> Wee, the Com'ttee. chosen by the Town May the 20th 1729 to judg upon the valley of Paper Money, met together in pursuance of s'd voat in order there to. we the Committy declared as followeth—1. That sixteen shillings of Paper money is adjudged to be equivalent to an ounce of silver. 2. that as to day labour it will in general answer at three and six pence per day. 3. that it will in generall purchess as followeth, beof three pence half penny per pound, porc at five pence per Pound. 4. That it purchase Indian Corn at four shillings; and Rye at six and wheat at eight shillings per bushil, as witness our hands.
>
> Elisha Janson
John Stockwill
John Sibley[13]

The population of Sutton grew steadily in the eighteenth century. Descendants of William Stockwell added significantly to the total: Stockwell became a household name. The number of families in town rose from thirty in 1717 to about eighty families and nearly four hundred inhabitants when Reverend Hall became pastor in 1728. But the infant mortality rate was high, and lives were frequently cut short by epidemics, as in the case of Rachel Stockwell, wife of Jonathan Stockwell, head of what has come to be known in family history as the Jonathan line, of which S. A. Stockwell was a seventh-generation member. The diary of Reverend Hall gives this account:

May 1760. A time of sickness. Many taken with a fever; two died in one week. John Holton and Jona. Stockwell's wife. Many more sick. June 5th. Sickness still prevailing deaths multiplied.[14]

The colonial wars also took their toll. The Seven Years War (1756-1763), last and decisive final phase of the French and Indian Wars leading to France's relinquishment of all military and political power in North America, drew 336 officers and enlisted men from Sutton; Absalom, Benajah, Daniel, Jeremiah, John, Jonathan, Jr., Stephen, and William Stockwell were among those who served.[15]

Twelve years later came the American Revolution (1775-1781). Asa H. Waters described Sutton's response to the call to arms in spirited terms:

On the breaking out of the revolutionary war, few towns in the Commonwealth rallied to the cause with such spirit and unanimity as the town of Sutton. The first gleaming ray from the torch of liberty kindled to a flame the whole surrounding region, and volunteers flocked to its standard in great numbers. Long before the battle of Lexington, they had formed a band of "minute men," well mounted and armed, and under the command of Col. Jonathan Holman, who had been a veteran in the British service in Canada during the old French war.

As soon as the news of that fight reached them, they sprang to their saddles, and, riding with all speed through the whole night, reached Concord just as the enemy were retreating to Boston.

It was not thirty days after that fight before Sutton and the neighboring town had raised a full regiment of ten companies, all volunteers, and they were on the march to the field of action.

They were organized under the command of Col. Ebenezer Larned of Oxford; marched to Roxbury, where they arrived more than two months before Washington came to take command of the army . . .

Soon after the arrival of Col. Larned's regiment at Roxbury, occurred the famous battle of Bunker Hill, "all of which it saw, a part of which it was," although it was not actually engaged in the fight on the hill. It formed a part of the right wing of the army, under command of Gen. John Thomas, which was stretched round from Dorchester through Roxbury to Boston line, to prevent the enemy from breaking through and making a flank movement.

Quite a number of casualties occurred in this regiment. Whether these men were killed or wounded by shot and shell from the enemy's ships, whose cannon swept the surrounding region, or whether they were volunteers from the ranks who rushed into the fray, which many did, can now never be known.[16]

Jonathan Stockwell, Jr., saw four of his sons march off to war. Aaron, the eldest, was a private in Capt. Samuel Sibley's company. On his initial tour of duty, Aaron advanced as far as Braintree on April 21, 1775, in response to the alarm sounded by Paul Revere. Eli and Solomon saw intermittent service.[17] Reuben enlisted May 1, 1775, in Col. Ebenezer Larned's regiment, which marched directly to Boston to engage the British at Bunker Hill. He survived the conflict but did not return home. *The Stockwell Genealogy* contains this report:

> Sutton, Mass. vital records state: A son of Jonathan Stockwell died July 13, 1775, I suppose not 20 years old in ye army with ye camp disease. The diary of Rev. David Hall of Sutton . . . states, "July 19, 1775," (relating the events of the past week) "Thursday" (July 13, 1775) "Next day went to visit Reuben Stockwell and prayed with him and others at Jamaica Plains, sd Rueben died yt day & next day (I) went about 4 miles to his funeral."[18]

When the war was over, Aaron, Eli, Solomon, and their fellow townsmen returned home for good, to a growing manufacturing center. The impetus for manufacturing in America coincided with the impetus for independence. For a long period, England had discouraged manufacturing in the colonies to increase the demand for her own products. As relations between England and the colonies deteriorated, it became evident something must be done to stimulate home manufacturing. The first provincial congress of Massachusetts took the matter in hand at a meeting in Salem on October 5, 1774. Appealing to the patriotism of the people, the congress strongly recommended the production of wool, the raising of flax and hemp, the making of nails, steel, tin plate, firearms, saltpeter, gunpowder, paper, glass, buttons, salt, combs, cards, and "the establishment of all such arts and manufactures as might be useful to the people."[19]

The citizens of Sutton were fully in accord, having adopted a like resolution at a town meeting as early as March 1768. Their township's excellent facilities for manufacturing made easier the achievement of these ends. Benedict and Tracy stressed an important natural advantage:

> There are within its limits several natural ponds fed largely by hidden springs whose outlets afford fine water privileges.

The principal of these are Dorothy Pond in the north part of town, Ramshorn in the northwest, Crooked Pond near the centre, and Manchaug Pond in the southwest. Blackstone River—called by the Indians Kittatuck—has its rise in Ramshorn Pond, and passes through the town from northwest to southeast. This river furnishes valuable water power. So also does Mumford River, the outlet of Manchaug Pond. Mill Brook, the outlet of Crooked Pond (now called Singletary Lake), has in the distance of a mile a fall of 175 feet, and affords seven water privileges.[20]

By 1793, a paper mill, a printing office, an oil mill, ten grist-mills, six sawmills, seven trip hammers, five scythe-and-ax shops, a hoe-maker, six plants for manufacturing potash, and several nail-makers were in operation. The industrial revolution begun in England earlier in the century had reached central Massachusetts.

And so it continued. In 1822 a factory was built for broad-cloth, and, for the first time in Sutton, cloth was woven by power looms. The ease with which wool could be worked into cloth by machinery astonished the townspeople. Gradually the spinning of wool by hand, except that of yarn for knitting, ceased. By midcentury, Manchaug Village, on the north branch of Mumford River and earlier recognized by Rhode Island investors as ideally suited for manufacturing, became a textile center with three large mills.[21]

About this time Silvanus Stockwell came of age. Son of Peter Stockwell, grandson of Solomon, Silvanus was born in Sutton on March 23, 1824, the year John Quincy Adams was elected sixth president of the United States and one year before completion of the Erie Canal. Peter Stockwell built Silvanus a house in 1850 just as Solomon had for Peter, years earlier. But Silvanus was restless. Perhaps Sutton was getting too crowded for him. Perhaps he disliked the stench from Burbank's paper mill. Had polluted effluent from the textile mills in Manchaug Village driven bass and perch from Mumford River, leaving only horned pout for the fishermen? Or had Silvanus been thrown from his horse, frightened by the sudden clap of a trip hammer? Whatever the reasons, Silvanus Stockwell and others in town looked westward. Some Woodburys and Putnams, in fact, were thinking about moving as far away as the Territory of Minnesota. Silvanus would not be alone. Hundreds of young men and women his age were leaving the East Coast and heading inland.

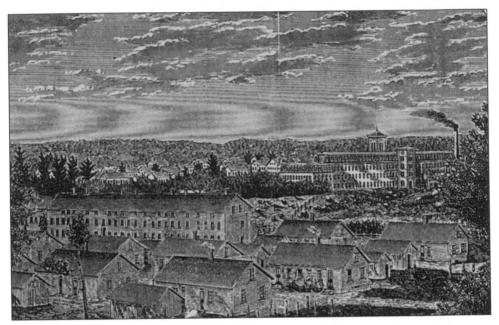

Manchaug Village (Sutton) about 1850. (Photo from Benedict and Tracy, *History of Sutton*)

References

1. Mabel Stockwell Kennedy, *The Stockwell Genealogy* (Lebanon, New Hampshire: New Victoria Printers, Inc., 1983), p. 3.

2. See Mary Stetson Clarke, *Pioneer Iron Works* (Philadelphia: Chilton Book Company, 1968), and Stephen P. Carlson, *The Scots of Hammersmith* (No city: Eastern National Park and Monument Association in cooperation with Department of the Interior, National Park Service: 1976). Ralph W. Gurney, a current resident of Sutton and local historian, reported to the author that a number of early members of the Stockwell family lived in Saugus and were employed at the ironworks.

3. Kennedy, *Stockwell Genealogy*, p. 8.

4. William A. Benedict and Hiram A. Tracy, *History of the Town of Sutton, Massachusetts, 1704-1876* (Worcester: Sanford & Company, 1878), pp. 9-12. Reprinted 1966 and 1970 by Commonwealth Press.

5. Kennedy, *Stockwell Genealogy*, pp. 11-12.

6. Benedict and Tracy, *History of Sutton*, pp. 9-12.

7. Benedict and Tracy, *History of Sutton*, p. 18.

8. David Freeman Hawkes, *Everyday Life in Early America* (New York: Harper & Row, 1980), p. 160-67; Arthur Meier Schlesinger, *Birth of the*

Nation (New York: Alfred A. Knopf, 1968), p. 79. See also Marion L. Starkey, *The Devil in Massachusetts* (Garden City, New York: Doubleday & Company, 1969), a re-creation of the witchcraft scare in Salem. Ralph Gurney reported to the author that witch hunts were a factor in emigration from Salem to his region.

9. Benedict and Tracy, *History of Sutton*, pp. 12-13. The authors conceded that the godforsaken, southeastern sector of the town, called Purgatory, was aptly named. See pp. 14-15.

10. Benedict and Tracy, *History of Sutton*, pp. 498-99.

11. Benedict and Tracy, *History of Sutton*, pp. 23-32; 427-28.

12. Benedict and Tracy, *History of Sutton*, pp. 436-37.

13. Benedict and Tracy, *History of Sutton*, pp. 38-39.

14. Benedict and Tracy, *History of Sutton*, p. 81. The diary of Reverend David Hall is in the possession of the Massachusetts Historical Society. Many of the Stockwells were buried in a private cemetery west of Manchaug Pond on Douglas Road. This cemetery was destroyed by vandals. The name Stockwell, often misspelled, appears on many gravestones in other cemeteries in Sutton.

15. Benedict and Tracy, *History of Sutton*, pp. 778-80.

16. Benedict and Tracy, *History of Sutton*, pp. 771-72.

17. Maud Stockwell Kennedy in *The Stockwell Genealogy* (p. 412) states that Solomon Stockwell "served in the Revolutionary War 1775-1781. He was 6 feet tall with light complexion." Her conclusion is supported in vols. 12 and 15, Secretary of the Commonwealth, *Massachusetts Soldiers and Sailors in the War of the Revolution* (Boston: Wright and Potter Printing Company, 1907), an official publication based on master rolls, payrolls, and other documents of the Revolutionary War, and in the Continental regiment books numbering twenty-one volumes. of individual pay accounts. There is confusion, however, as to the commands in which Solomon, son of Jonathan, Jr., served. William M. Olin, secretary of the Commonwealth of Massachusetts researched the question in 1911 and concluded in a letter (in the possession of the author) to Walter L. Stockwell dated February 21, 1911, that two Solomon Stockwells from Sutton took part in the war. Walter was the great grandson of Solomon and the youngest brother of Sylvanus A. Stockwell.

18. Kennedy, *Stockwell Genealogy*, p. 409.

19. Benedict and Tracy, *History of Sutton*, pp. 85-87, 524.

20. Benedict and Tracy, *History of Sutton*, p. 13.

21. Benedict and Tracy, *History of Sutton*, pp. 538-64.

Chapter 2

Anoka

In 1856 at age thirty-two, Silvanus Stockwell and his young bride, Charlotte Bowdish Stockwell, left Sutton, Massachusetts, to settle in the Territory of Minnesota. They joined throngs from New England, as the 1850s saw dramatic emigration from east to west in the United States. Land was the magnet—fertile land free of boulders. Land cost nothing if one squatted, $1.25 per acre for up to 160 acres if acquired under preemption laws. Newspaper reporters, advertisers, land speculators, and promoters described the West in glowing terms, imploring Easterners to leave their homes and settle there. New Englanders were especially responsive to pleas to settle in the region of the upper Mississippi Valley.

Minnesota was established as a territory in 1849, with boundaries extending as far westward as the Missouri River. Population of the new territory was fewer than 7,000. By 1852 the population had more than tripled. The census of 1860 showed a total population of 172,023. The American-born citizens among them (not including Indians) numbered 113,295. New England had sent 18,822. Theodore C. Blegen, in *Minnesota: A History of the State*, summarized the contribution New Englanders were to make:

> The Yankee element lent special character and color to institutions . . . The tough-fibered people directly or by stages out of New England made basic contributions in this foundation era. They built farms, started towns, opened business places, invested money, speculated, pioneered professions, launched newspapers, schools and churches, engaged in politics and government, and left the imprints of their leadership on numerous institutions.[1]

Statehood came in 1858. St. Paul, lying on the east side of the Mississippi River, became the capital of the country's thirty-second state. The Red River, flowing north to the Hudson Bay, marked the western boundary. In 1858 Chippewa (Ojibwe) Indians occupied lands in the northern and eastern parts of the state, while the Sioux (Dakota) occupied the south and west. Fort Snelling had been established as a military outpost in 1819 at the confluence of the Mississippi and Minnesota rivers. At mid-century, the white settlers in the territory, including entrepreneurs and the military, were mainly centered in the Fort Snelling-St. Paul area.

The Falls of St. Anthony, lying above St. Paul at Minneapolis, played a key role in the growth of the region because travelers going north or south on the Mississippi River were required to portage before navigation could be resumed. The falls became "the practical head" of river navigation. Indians congregated there; fur traders built there; the U.S. Army built Fort Snelling there. The availability of waterpower at the Falls of St. Anthony and at Stillwater on the St. Croix River led to the development of two of Minnesota's major industries—lumber and flour milling.

Far-reaching improvements in transportation primarily explain the swift growth of the region. Better canals, steamboats on the Great Lakes, roads and railroads, and fleets of vessels on the Mississippi River all played a part:

> By 1854, it became possible to travel all the way from New York to Rock Island, Illinois, by railroad, with transfers to steamboats headed for St. Paul. Steamboat arrivals at St. Paul, in excess of 100 in 1855, rose to nearly 300 two years later, and to more than 1,000 in 1858. Intending settlers poured onto the wharves at St. Paul. One packet company alone brought in more than 30,000 people in the summer of 1855, most of whom could find no inns where they could sleep in the capital city before they made their way to villages and farmlands. Settlement customarily was a matter of individual and family action, but not a few groups of people banded together in colonization plans, migrating as communities, hunting—often after advance agents had been sent out in their behalf—for lands favorable to farming and to the building of towns of their own.[2]

Among the early settlers was Silvanus Stockwell and his young wife, Charlotte Polly Bowdish Stockwell. Born February 8, 1830, in Decatur, Oswego County, New York, Charlotte had attended one of New York's early academies, majoring in French. Upon graduation she became a certified teacher, and, at age fourteen, she began teaching in the grammar schools of New York.

Charlotte's parents were William Bowdish, a Methodist minister in central New York, and Phoebe Stanton Bowdish. Two daughters and five sons lived to maturity. The sons all became

Charlotte Bowdish Stockwell, mother of S. A. Stockwell. (Family Photo)

Methodist ministers, three with churches around and in New York City. Two sons served for a time as chaplains in the Civil War. On February 15, 1853, when Silvanus and Charlotte were married in New York City, Charlotte's uncle, the Reverend Leonard Bowdish, performed the ceremony.

Silvanus, at first going against the tide of westward movement, brought Charlotte Bowdish Stockwell back to Sutton. They moved into a house that Peter Stockwell had built for them across the road from his own.[3] From there they made their plans to move west. Silvanus would leave first. In the spring of 1856, traveling alone, he proceeded first by train to Prairie du Chien, Wisconsin, on the Mississippi River, and then by steamboat north to St. Paul. From St. Paul he took the stage to Anoka, a pioneer settlement thirty miles farther north, where the Rum River flowing southward joins the Mississippi. Silvanus reached Anoka on May 31, 1856. Others from Sutton, including Simon Woodbury and George Putnam, were already living there.[4]

Anoka, located near the line dividing Dakota from Chippewa territory, was like a buffer of neutral ground. The settlement was comparatively safe from Indian warfare and proved decidedly favorable for the French fur traders; there the traffic of both tribes could be secured while neither was apt to occupy the land for any length of time. The first of these traders were brothers, Peter and Francis Patoile. They established a trading post in 1846, erecting a small building on the east side of the mouth of the Rum River.[5] Someone named the settlement Anoka for a Dakota word meaning "on both sides" or "from both sides" and a Chippewa word meaning "laborer," "labor," or "work."[6] Because of emigrants from eastern states like Stockwell and others from Sutton, Anoka became known as the second New England town in Minnesota, Stillwater being the first.

On October 31, 1854, A. W. Giddings, M.D., just out of medical school, wrote to his brother in Williamsfield, Ohio, of the town the Stockwells had chosen:

> The city was owned and laid out by a company from Maine— energetic men who had laid out $40,000 erecting saw and grist mills, planing machine, lath factory, etc., etc. Now we have two public houses, one larger and furnished as well as any in Williamsfield [the Farnham House]. The other accommodates fifteen boarders and two families of six each. The landlady is a half breed. One boarding house, sixteen dwelling houses, one stable, all in the short space of three months. There are about three families in each house. This is pioneering—move the family onto the ground and build the house around them as lumber can be procured. But for my own part I am as pleasantly situated as I could wish. I am boarding at Mr. Shaw's—very kind new Englanders. The old gent is a very refined, inquisitive old Yankee. His son and wife, two men and one maid servant compose the family. The house is made of logs hewed, two storys high, with a dining room and kitchen back, parlor in front. All the rooms except the kitchen are papered and carpeted. There is a nice piano in the parlor; indeed the house is as richly furnished as any in your own town. But a very different state of things exists from what one might suppose. All are getting rich. People make nothing of doubling their property once in five or six months. Everything is very high here—enough to frighten one at first; but I have become accustomed to the charges, which are equal to those in any of our eastern cities. One dollar per day for board at the hotel—horse three dollars per week.[7]

Maine continued to figure prominently in the town's development. Not only did the founders come from Maine, but so also did a high percentage of settlers who followed. Experienced in lumbering, these men moved to Anoka because lumbering in Maine was on the wane and their skills were in great demand in the region. One proud lumberjack, when asked where he came from, "hitched up his pants and took another chaw of tobacco and said, 'I'm from the Penobscot, b'God.'"[8]

Silvanus Stockwell probably lived in a boardinghouse or a public house during that first summer. He soon found a job as a butcher and remained one for three years before turning full time to farming. That summer he purchased a building lot in the center of town on Jackson Street, directly east of the later site of a large Catholic Church. In September Charlotte joined him. He met her

Ferry across the Rum River at Anoka, from *Harper's*, August 1860, p. 293. (Courtesy of the Minnesota Historical Society)

in St. Paul and they took the stage back to Anoka, "the trip consuming the better part of a day."

In the spring of 1857, the Stockwells built a house on their land. Their four children were born in that Jackson Street house: Sylvanus Albert on June 8, 1857; William Wellington on March 11, 1859; Walter Lincoln on January 12, 1868; and Charlotte Susie on June 22, 1870.[9] The Stockwells took in boarders while space permitted. Their kitchen became one of Anoka's earliest schools, with Charlotte as teacher. More pupils came in the second year. The kitchen became too crowded, so Charlotte moved her class to the parlor.

Charlotte Stockwell improved the Jackson Street property by planting trees that "grew to a towering height and remained standing until well into the next century." Years later her son Sylvanus, called Albert by most who knew him, followed her lead on his property in Minneapolis, when he planted an elm in the front yard upon the birth of each of his daughters—Ruth, Charlotte, and Beth. (In 1984, the trees were gone.)

While Dr. Giddings saw "all" around him getting rich, the Stockwells were not among them. But they did survive. Then came a setback for the whole region:

> The boom had been at high tide in 1856 and 1857. Business expanded, speculation was rampant, the currency of the time was one of the wildcat variety issued by banks in distant states, and prices of land and property went skyward. Businessmen sought to enlarge their capital and draw on credit as far as they could, and the pioneer banks of Minnesota were pushed to the extreme for loans. By 1857 there were some thirty banks in the territory . . . Speculation in Minnesota was bad enough, but the troubles that beset the territory in the summer and autumn of 1857 were national. Because of interrelations with eastern banks and increasing money stringency, Minnesota's banks were soon in serious difficulty. Only a few banks survived. The real estate boom was deflated. Business companies failed; many people left the territory; merchants could not dispose of their stocks or meet their debts. Minnesota, on the eve of statehood, found itself in an economic chaos.[10]

Silvanus Stockwell was party to a dollar exchange typical of the day. He bought a yoke of oxen from a man named Nichols, paying him $110.00 in "Glencoe" money. Nichols succeeded in passing the money, but the Bank of Glencoe, which had issued it, shortly was reported as wholly without assets, and its bills became worthless. The Blodgetts, who were boarders at the Stockwell home and whose first child was born there, had a similar experience. Harry Blodgett bought a cow from Jack Milliman for thirty-five or forty dollars, and before Milliman could get to town to spend the money, the bank failed and he could not buy his dinner with the entire amount. S. C. Robbins, a teacher in a nearby town, had the worst of it. He taught the full winter of 1857-1858 and in the spring got his entire winter's pay in money valuable only for kindling.[11]

17

Trade took the form of barter, and merchants found themselves forced to trade their goods for farm products. If Silvanus Stockwell had needed a harness for his team of oxen, he would have purchased it with produce from his land.

Growth in the town was nevertheless rapid. In 1855 the population hit 150; by 1860 the number had quadrupled. Anoka had emerged from a sprawling settlement of uncertain future—a frontier trading post for itinerant pioneers and covered wagon trains heading farther west—to a village of 656 people putting down roots in a new land. By 1868 there were 1,600 settlers.[12]

The St. Paul and Pacific was the first railroad to open for traffic in Minnesota. In June 1862, the train began operation with a run between St. Paul and St. Anthony. In January 1864, the line was extended to Anoka. Passenger trains were comprised of three passenger cars, one baggage car, and a caboose. The seats were upholstered; kerosene lamps and a wood burning stove were standard features. The locomotives burned wood, and trains sped along at thirty miles per hour. A traveler from Anoka to St. Paul could depart at 8:55 a.m. and reach St. Paul at 10:15 a.m., after stops at Fridley (9:30 a.m.) and St. Anthony (9:55 a.m.). When railroad service began, the *Anoka Star* on January 9 proclaimed:

> Our people have reason for self-gratulation. Those who were the pioneers here and have experienced the trials, hardships and privations incident to such a life must feel that the change is great. We are now placed at once in the midst of advantages and comforts of civilization. No longer in the back woods or wild prairie. No more Indian scares. No longer poor, seedy, rough, dull, stupid or behind times in things that constitute life, beauty, respectability and social attraction. Hurrah for The Railroad.

The town was not for the timid or the lazy. Settlers recognized that most necessities of life would have to be produced right there; they responded with hard work, public service, long hours, and volunteering. In keeping, Silvanus Stockwell served as coroner and deputy sheriff. He was the first treasurer of Anoka County to be elected by the people after Minnesota's admission to the union. He served as treasurer from 1859 to 1861 and was alderman of the City of Anoka from 1885 to 1887. Charlotte Stockwell also plunged into community life right from the start. In addition to teaching school in her home, Charlotte, true to the Bowdish calling, for many years taught a girls' Sunday School class at Anoka's Methodist-Episcopal Church. Her Methodist activities never abated. Neighbor James Peet in his diary took note of her activities and those of others in the small but caring community.

Wedding photo of James Peet and Harriet Evans, with Harriet's sister Lucy standing behind them. 1854. (Courtesy of the Minnesota Historical Society)

James Peet had come to live in Anoka at the close of the Civil War. A chaplain in the Union Army at Vicksburg, Mississippi, he contracted a serious pulmonary disease (probably tuberculosis) and was granted a medical discharge. He chose Anoka as home for his family.

The Stockwells and the Peets became friends as well as neighbors. The parents were about the same age and so were their children. They attended the same church; they were attended to by the same doctor; they were readers and encouraged their children to read; they were lifetime abolitionists who strove to help those freed after the Civil War. They helped each other. James Peet's diary describes the last two years of his life:

> August 26, 1865. I heard Bro. Bowdich [Rev. C. G. Bowdish] preach and attended the Sunday School . . . The custom is to board with other families while building one's house in Anoka.
>
> October 7, 1865. The Sunday School is in a most flourishing condition, superintended by E. T. Alling.
>
> October 14, 1865. I called Dr. Giddings to see our sick child . . .
>
> October 19, 1865. James Warren Peet died on October 19, 1865, aged 17 months and 22 days.
>
> November 12, 1865. The ME [Methodist Episcopal] Church at Anoka appears to be in a prosperous condition, Sunday School especially, E. T. Alling, Supt.

November 18, 1865. I am this day 37 years old. Oh! How little I have accomplished during my life time.

December 10, 1865. At church took collection for Freedmen of $17.04.

December 27, 1865. PM-At Sister Stockwell's at the Sewing BEE for Freedman Aid Society. Bot $13.15 cheap material to make up. Eve at home.

December 28, 1865. Olin commenced reading *Uncle Tom's Cabin* to the family.

December 29, 1865. My family attended the Methodist Meeting Sunday School as usual which is the best Sunday School for the size I was ever connected with.

January 3, 1866. Mrs. Peet gone to the Sewing Bee to make up clothing for the colored freed people South. Thank God I live to the time when there is not a single slave, legally, in the U.S., the last having been emancipated by the late ratification of the constitutional amendment.

January 4, 1866. Everyone at home listening to the reading of *Uncle Tom's Cabin* by my son Olin. The children are of course much interested in it as well as us older ones.

January 5, 1866. Evening at home sewing with a machine and listening to the reading of *Uncle Tom's Cabin* by my son Olin.

January 7, 1866. The Sunday School numbers about 100 and for its size is, I think the best Sunday School I ever saw. Parents, teachers, and all take an active interest in it . . . Being unable to teach a class myself because of partial loss of voice (bronchitis), I am a scholar in Bro. Lathrop's Bible class.

January 8, 1866. P.M At Sister Stockwell's looking over and helping about packing the box of clothing for the freedmen valued at $91.50 contributed by the ME Church Congregation of Anoka.

January 9, 1866. *Uncle Tom's Cabin* read in the family.

January 10, 1866. *Uncle Tom's Cabin* was read in the family.

January 15, 1866. Paid $200 back to George Putnam having received some back pay from the U.S. Government.

March 3, 1866. I made a practical matter of such proverbs or sayings as "Better wear out than rust out." I have often wished to "cease at once to labor and live" but now I live unable to labor.

March 15, 1866. I weigh 128 pounds.

July 9, 1866. 80 of the 170 Red River carts returned this A.M. on road by our house.[13]

July 14, 1866. Cistern finished up today. 1 foot of sawdust to 8 or 10 inches dirt over the plank and I think it is proof against freezing in the winter.[14]

[Entries by James's wife, Harriet Peet:]

Harriet Alling's Sunday school class, Anoka, ca. 1875. The second boy below S. A. Stockwell (initialed) is Olin F. Peet, son of James Peet. (Courtesy of the Minnesota Historical Society)

November 9, 1866. Sister Sterling came and helped me cut out my sewing and the ladies are going to meet at Mrs. Stockwell's and sew for me tomorrow. It will be a great relief to me to get my sewing done. James is steadily failing.

November 14, 1866. James talks of his departure with as much composure as he would were it a journey he is about to take . . .

November 26, 1866. Death of James Peet.

January 1, 1867. My earnest prayer is now that if my boys are spared to grow up they may at least be as good as their father was.[15]

There were many callers during James Peet's last days. Friends carried him to church, cut wood, sewed, and contributed money. Mr. Colton "made us a present of a half ton of hay." Dr. Giddings took James for rides in his carriage. Those who made the coffin would not take pay. Son Olin Peet was especially good at taking care of his father.

Olin was spared, but the reprieve was brief. He died at age twenty-six from a puzzling, undiagnosed disease. Robert Charles Peet, born October 1857, died December 29, 1859. Ed L. Peet was the only son to lead a full life. Harriet Peet remarried and lived forty-eight years more.[16]

In 1880, Charlotte Stockwell wrote the obituary of another Methodist Church member, one Ellen Coleman. Charlotte's "glowing tribute" carried a religious flavor, "distinctly Methodist, typical of the Protestant thinking of that time":

Methodist Sunday School teachers and officers, Anoka, ca. 1872. Charlotte Bowdish Stockwell stands directly to the right of the superintendent. (Courtesy of the Minnesota Historical Society)

She had been a Christian 28 years, and was conscientious, earnest and devout. Her Christian graces showed a maturity that only comes from a constant study of the "Book" and an intelligent use of means.

She is missed in Sunday School, where she was a devoted teacher, and in the Women's Foreign Missionary Society of which she was a model secretary for eight years.[17]

Charlotte Stockwell's religious faith, however, was not that of Silvanus. Walter wrote of his father:

He was a farmer. So far as I know he was never seriously troubled with a surplus of the world's goods, though there was nothing of poverty. We always had plenty to eat and were warmly clad . . . Our home was always an inviting one, though not elaborately or elegantly furnished . . . My father was a good man, honorable, courteous, dignified, but rather reserved, not much given to sentiment. In fact, he was a Puritan. He lacked the abiding Faith which was my mother's. He lived twenty-one years after her passing.

In April 1875, Silvanus and Charlotte Stockwell traded their Jackson Street house for a larger one built by Moses Frost on the avenue one block north of the St. Paul and Pacific Railway tracks. The new house was about a mile from the center of town—"a fine farm located in Section 6 near the railroad station."[18] The farm comprised some fifteen acres of land; farming far beyond the subsistence level became possible. On Jackson Street, the Stockwells lived mostly off the animals on the farm and the crops they raised. Anything sold was extra. At the new place they produced enough to sell to others in significant quantity. The soil was suitable for growing small fruits, vegetables, corn, oats, barley, and potatoes, but butter and eggs were their principal products for marketing.

Operating a farm on this larger scale made family participation crucial. Each member of the Stockwell family was called upon to do his or her share. Walter recalled one of his regular duties:

I frequently drove my mother to Minneapolis to market her excellent dairy, butter, and other farm products. These trips meant an early start with the horse and buggy. A daylight start in the morning brought us into Minneapolis sometime before the gas lights were out. It was an all day trip to go down, deliver butter and eggs to her customers, purchase the supplies and get home.

One trip in particular stood out:

We had driven to Minneapolis the morning of Saturday, July 2, 1881. We left Minneapolis after noon and had gotten out to what was then Shingle Creek, now Camden Place, when the news of Garfield's assassination reached us. The feeling of horror which I had is hard to describe.

His recollection of earlier trips was happier:

> My mother and father took my sister and me to the wonderful celebration of July 4, 1876. It was a great event. The parade was marvelous as I think of it. I believe this was one of the first times I rode on a railway train. The old St. Paul and Pacific, now the Great Northern Railway, at that time ran as far as St. Cloud . . . That year my mother and father with my sister went east, visited relatives, and attended the Centennial Exposition [the first world exposition in America] at Philadelphia. I think there had been some money received from the estate of my mother's uncle, Rev. Leonard Bowdish . . . Much was said at the exposition about an instrument through which people could talk . . . It was about this time that silver coins—25 and 50 cent pieces— came into use. The resumption of specie payment was about to go into effect following the era of the Civil War.

Charlotte's mother, Phoebe Stanton Bowdish, came to live with the family after the move to the larger house. In failing health, she died in 1878 and was buried in Oakwood Cemetery in Anoka.

These were times when a woman was supposed to be entirely absorbed in her home and family; she became an object for criticism if she pursued interests outside her home. But Charlotte Stockwell would have none of that. She was "early interested in the movement for women's suffrage," she was an active member of the Women's Foreign Missionary Society, and she marched in picket lines with other members of the Women's Crusade, forerunner of the Women's Christian Temperance Union, in the fight against saloons. Charlotte's remarks delivered before the Women's Foreign Missionary Society in a speech entitled, "Sane Reasons Why Women Should Be Engaged in the Woman's Missionary Work," disclose an activism of the highest order:

> They owe it to themselves. The life and work of the majority of women is in a very circumscribed sphere. There are cares and duties in our own homes that cannot be ignored and must not be neglected, and however much we say of the importance of those duties and however keenly we may feel the necessity of performing them as "unto the Lord," still there is so much of monotony and sameness in them that, if permitted to engross all our thoughts, will certainly make us narrow in our ideas and be dwarfing to the life and activity of the mind. The ruts made deep and long into which the wheels of domestic care drop us are by no means a stimulant to mental action.

This fact is patent to anyone who has occasion to listen to the conversation of the average woman of any company. The complaints of those fortunate enough to employ servants as to the wonderful trials had with them; the small talk about styles and shapes and costume of those who make personal adornment the sum of living; the unkind and bitter sayings of those who set themselves up as critics of others' conduct. All these show that women need something to lift them out of themselves and set all these active brains, and talking tongues, and willing hands upon a higher plane of living and thinking. The condition of the enslaved millions of heathen women appeals to us all to train ourselves to unselfish labor for their elevation.

We would not arrogate to our sex too much, but it is conceded that woman's nature is more sympathetic than man's and here is a field for her most enlarged sympathy. When as wives we take our seat in our homes the equal of the husband, and at our tables as the hostess of the house, we may well pity the vast multitudes who must stand while the husband sits and must wait until this appetite is satisfied before partaking herself of food, and may not even have a right to his individual love but is liable at any moment to be displaced even in the menial place she holds if the husband's interest or fancy wills it. These are only a few of the sorrows of women of heathen lands. The women of Christian lands, more if possible than the men, should be earnest Christians. The light of the glorious gospel of the son of God gives to her all she enjoys. The sweet ties of home and husband and children and friends are all the fruit of the teachings of the Bible, so that the principle of common honesty demands that we be earnest and persistent in our endeavors to send the same light to those who sit in the region and shadow of death.

A woman seated in her palanquin with all the appointments of the better class of women in India was brought to the door of the dispensary where Mrs. Julia Lane McClure is the physician. "Oh, Dr., do cure me, do cure me quick for if I am sick long, and grow pale and poor, my husband will get a young wife." That is the heathen woman. Contrast that with the Christian woman. There is no expense too great if it be possible to save a wife, and if continued ill health is the misfortune it does seem that the weaker the wife is the more tender is the devotion of husband and child, and wrinkles and gray hairs and continued years bind closer the heart who in the glad morning of youth plighted each to the other their love and loyalty . . .

The women of the church need this work of the missionary society to increase their activity in all departments of church work. It is those who see least to do in the world that do the least. "Lift up your eyes and behold the fields already white for harvest" and this lifting up the eyes to consider the need of the world is the first step toward doing for the world's need. We go bent over the daily routine of our lives and unless an effort is made to lift up the eyes and see, all our time and energy may be spent in the little world of our own homes.

The Women's Foreign Missionary Society, called into being in a most providential manner and sustained as it is for the most part by women, gives but small sums yearly, but that small amount given regularly and surely carries on a work that is immense in its operations and results . . .

I have looked over the ladies of the church and it is my honest conviction that we might each raise at least $1 per year and in no way distress ourselves in the matter of money. "There is that which giveth and yet increaseth and there is that which holdeth more than is meet and it tendeth to poverty."

To be a co-worker with noble men and women in any good cause is of itself ennobling. How much more when we can be, and are called to be co-workers with Christ in hastening the day when "the heathen shall be given his for an inheritance and the utmost part of the earth for a possession."

Albert would not have been present to hear his mother's speech, but he certainly knew what she was about. The religious atmosphere his mother created doubtless strengthened inborn qualities—his idealism and sense of justice.

Another cause outside the home in which Charlotte Stockwell enlisted was the Women's Crusade. Saloons were key establishments in Anoka from its beginning. The rigors of frontier life did not make for abstinence, and alcohol was currency for business with the Indians. With the arrival of permanent settlers, however, and the emergence of churches, opposition to the sale of liquor grew. Methodist women led the charge.

The *Anoka County Union Centennial*, September 1965, described the conflict:

The temperance movement in Anoka was a constant crusade in the early days . . . Down through the years the sale of hard liquor has been a controversial issue in Anoka—the cause of vigilance committee raids, women's praying crusades, election battles, and mass meetings.

The Empire Saloon was a principal target of the Women's Crusade. On May 11, 1859, it mysteriously caught fire. Two months later the Methodist Church caught fire. The town saw it as revenge.

Fifteen years later a pastor opened a temperance meeting of one hundred persons by praising the women who were willing to

Women crusaders against a legalized saloon in Anoka in 1873. The woman in the window, looking down, wife of the saloon keeper, threw water on the women while they were praying. Sometimes beer was emptied on the sidewalk so the crusaders couldn't kneel. (Courtesy of the Minnesota Historical Society)

act in the work of praying for saloonkeepers' souls and for the closure of all saloons. One newspaper covering the event carried a picture of the ladies praying in front of a saloon and billiard hall. The editor wondered whether the women were praying for the saloonkeepers' souls or praying the saloonkeepers would get out of town.

Walter stood firmly if not totally with his mother on the saloon issue:

> My mother was a member of the Crusaders, the forerunner of the W.C.T.U. She with other good women of Anoka was engaged in the fight against the saloon. One day when I was five or six years old, I went with other children (I think my sister was with me) down to the foot of Jackson Street and saw—at least the incident is firmly impressed upon my memory—my mother with

other Crusaders before the hotel saloon of Jim McLaughlin . . . These good women were forced off the sidewalk into the street. My fear for my mother and my indignation then was such as to rouse in me a lasting hatred for the saloon as an institution, and while I have not been a total abstainer, I have ever fought the saloon and its influence. Whether it was at this time or later, my mother and other women were arrested for disturbing the peace. I recall my consternation at the thought that my mother might have to go to jail. I think the case was never pushed, but as far back as I can remember and for years after I left home, the license and no-license fight was waged in Anoka. My mother and father were always to be found fighting on the no-license side. They found it difficult to think any good of one who favored the licensing of the saloon.

Late in her life, Charlotte Stockwell was elected one of the first two women members of the Board of Education of Anoka. When her youngest child graduated in 1888, she was board president, and she had the pleasure of presenting a diploma to her own daughter. Her remarks were brief:

Your teacher has said, "These whom we present to you have faithfully performed the tasks set for them." This is a high encomium. To be faithful in "that which is least" is but a prophecy of faithfulness in tasks and duties that are sure to come to you all in your future course. You have by a slow process commencing in the nursery and continuing through the different grades furnished by our excellent schools come to this happy hour, and as you step from this platform to higher and more taxing employments may we not hope that faithfulness in the tasks that shall come to you may be your watchword.

It is with pleasure that I now present to you these diplomas.

Charlotte died of tuberculosis on May 17, 1889, after a long illness. She too was buried in Oakwood Cemetery in Anoka. Her son, Sylvanus Albert, said of her years later:

I had the good fortune to be born of a noble mother, and nursed abolition milk. I was taught from youngest infancy that the chief duty of a citizen was to do his part, and do it honestly and nobly. It has been my good fortune to have all my life been in a good home. My mother was a noble woman of fine quality, a farmer's wife, hitched to a churn the most of her life, and yet with time enough to be a mother to every motherless and fatherless child the whole countryside around. I early learned from her lips the idea that woman was the equal of man before the law, or ought to be. She was a devoted doer of every good thing. One of the earliest recollections I have of her, and one of the dearest, is seeing her kneeling on the snow in front of Sam Leland's saloon in the old Women's Crusade.[19]

References

1. Theodore C. Blegen, *Minnesota: A History of the State* (Minneapolis: University of Minnesota Press, 1979), p. 175.

2. Blegen, *Minnesota*, p. 180.

3. Walter Lincoln Stockwell was state superintendent of public instruction in North Dakota. His *Memories and an Appreciation of My Mother Charlotte Bowdish Stockwell* affords information about the Stockwell family history. Much of this chapter is taken from his tribute privately published at Fargo, North Dakota, on February 8, 1930, the hundredth anniversary of her birth. Copies are in the collections of the Newberry Library, Fargo, and the University of Minnesota.

4. Benedict and Tracy, *History of Sutton*, 81, pp. 307-08.

5. "Tracks," *Anoka in 1889* (Anoka: G. H. Goodrich, 1889), p. 7. Reprinted by the Anoka Historical Society in 1976 as a bicentennial project.

6. Albert M. Goodrich, *History of Anoka County* (Minneapolis: Hennepin Publishing Company 1905), pp. 50-56.

7. Goodrich, *Anoka County*, pp. 60-62.

8. Blegen, *Minnesota*, p. 321.

9. Neither Sylvanus Albert nor William had sons. Walter had one son, Walter Lincoln, Jr., born in North Dakota on March 6, 1897. He was killed at age thirty-seven when a train struck the tractor he was driving, leaving a widow but no children. With his death, the Stockwell family name as descending from Silvanus came to an end.

10. Blegen, *Minnesota*, pp. 208-09.

11. Goodrich, *Anoka County*, pp. 79-88.

12. *Anoka County Union Centennial*, September 1965.

13. Trade between Red River settlements to the north and west and Fort Snelling and St. Paul to the south began as early as 1822. Goods were carried on primitive, two-wheeled Red River carts made entirely of wood and drawn by a single ox or pony. No axle grease was used, and creaking wheels could be heard for miles. Caravans comprised of hundreds of carts left Pembina with buffalo robes, pemmican, dried meat, and furs. Return trips carried merchandise "as miscellaneous as the stock of a country store." A trail on the east side of the Mississippi River crossed the Rum

River at Anoka where there were several fording places. See William Watts Folwell, *A History of Minnesota*, rev. ed. (St. Paul: Minnesota Historical Society, 1956), 1:226.

14. Cisterns were reservoirs or tanks for storing or holding water. Virtually every home had a cistern built under the house or alongside it. Rainwater was carried by gutter and pipe to the cistern. The water was soft, but, because of dirt washed from the roof, it was dark-colored until the dirt settled. A cistern required a good cleaning "at least once a year." See Harlan Thurston, *Life in Anoka-1900* (Anoka: Anoka Historical Society, 1972).

15. *Diary of James Peet*, Volumes 11 and 12, Minnesota Historical Society, St. Paul.

16. Edward L. Peet to William P. Everts, February 22, 1992.

17. Edward L. Peet, son of Ed L. Peet, and himself a Methodist minister, characterized Charlotte Stockwell's prose as typical of then-Protestant thinking. Edward L. Peet recently retired as minister of Glide Memorial Church in San Francisco, where he served with distinction for many years.

18. N. W. Winchell, Edward D. Neill, and J. Fletcher Williams, *History of the Upper Mississippi Valley* (Minneapolis: Minnesota Historical Company, 1881), p. 248.

19. Stockwell, *Memories and an Appreciation*. The good women of Anoka also believed the name of the Rum River should be changed to something more upstanding. They were never able to accomplish the change.

Chapter 3

The Wider World

The Women's Crusade was not the only reform movement Albert Stockwell would know. Often because the conditions calling for remedy were most acute on the urban seacoast, the East had taken the early lead in education, the antislavery movement, municipal reform, public health, and better care for criminals and the insane. There the population was denser; the wealth and cooperation necessary for progress were available. And the area was in closest contact with Europe, from which much was borrowed for improvement of the democratic experiment. The leaders of thought in the new world compared ideas with leaders of the old through correspondence and acquaintance. These ideas eventually crystallized into action.[1] But the West was not less interested in the welfare of the common man.

Before the Civil War, western idealism may have produced fewer movements than in the East, but this was because the westerner's idealism was supported by his individualism; his idealism was his individualism—God helped him who helped himself. But during the thirty years after the war, when the bulk of suitable, available land in the West was spoken for, westerners—those born in the United States and those from other countries who streamed to the region—suffered economically. And the westerner came to believe that reliance solely upon self was not enough.[2]

Advances in agriculture made possible by new machinery such as the McCormick reaper had not proved entirely a blessing. Farmers incurred indebtedness with the purchase of heavy farm equipment. Storage facilities were costly or inadequate, and grain surpluses often forced farmers to sell crops at a loss. While farmers in the 1860s were unanimous in their clamor for more railroad construction and (naively) thought competition between railroads would keep rates low, the time would come when their enthusiasm for railroads would turn to open distrust or hatred. Prohibitive rates, higher charges for a short haul than a long haul, and discrimination against persons and places coupled with price-fixing between the railroads intensified farmers' wrath. They were frustrated by the high charge of middlemen and a lack of proper credit facilities. Overproduction and an unscientific tariff have since been suggested as more basic causes for agricultural distress, but those were unmanageable problems. Dissatisfaction more readily found vent against tangible obstacles to prosperity. Rural wealth had fallen far behind urban prosperity, and farmers came to believe they were being tricked by an antagonistic capitalism. The work ethic was not enough. The farmers were coming to the view that legislators, state and federal, must come to the rescue.[3]

A feeling of rural inferiority added to the farmers' woes. Psychological stress—perhaps the lowest blow of all and of little concern in New England—became endemic in the vast reaches of the West, where provisions of the Homestead Act required purchasers to live on their land, making it difficult to keep in touch with friends. Loneliness prevailed. The westerner's schooling was below eastern standards, and the tiller of the soil became a figure for the humorist. Little wonder western farmers suffered from an acute inferiority complex. Their state of mind, as well as their economic grievances, accounted for a series of revolts soon to occur.

The Grange movement was the most important uprising of the immediate postwar period. Disillusioned farmers joined an organization known as the Patrons of Husbandry, or Grange, founded in 1867 by Oliver H. Kelley. Born in Boston in 1826, Kelley headed west as a young man, and, in 1849, he took up land in Minnesota at Elk River, about six miles from Anoka. He founded the Patrons of Husbandry for the purpose of relieving the monotony of rural social life. A man of enormous energy, Kelley developed his organization into one of national scope, with state and local branches known as granges. Local granges fostered picnics, lectures, Saturday get-togethers, and educational meetings. At first nonpolitical, the members soon put themselves behind legislators sympathetic to the plight of the farmer.

In the upper Mississippi Valley, discontent was greatest because of a growing exhaustion of soil—rotation of crops was yet to come. State legislators sought to regulate both the railroads and grain elevators, and several states established maximum rate laws and railroad commissions with the power to fix rates or recommend reductions. These laws failed for three main reasons: crudeness of form, inviting rejection on legal grounds; ongoing railroad propaganda; and the panic of 1873, in which some railroads fell into bankruptcy.[4]

Grange activity declined steadily between 1875 and 1880. Growth had been too swift, resulting in unwieldiness; political failure had discredited the organization. The Grange had started cooperatives to eliminate the cost of the middleman, but for the most part they proved unsuccessful.

In its long-term results, however, the Grange was not a failure. Through its efforts, a principle was established in the courts that still has not been altered: that the public has the right to control corporations clothed by the public interest.

Coinciding with the growth of the Grange was the growth of young Albert Stockwell. He attended Anoka's common schools but, according to his brother Walter, did not graduate from high school "probably because there were no high schools as we know them."[5] The lack of formal higher education did not bar him from becoming a teacher, however. He began teaching in nearby Sherburne County in 1875 at the age of eighteen. Later he taught in the village schools of Anoka, Hennepin, and other counties, living at home or boarding in the community where he taught. He remained a teacher for three years. Oliver Kelley's farm was nearby, and Kelley was a voluminous contributor to the agricultural press. No doubt Stockwell, who had an inquiring mind and was familiar with farmers' woes from firsthand experience, heard Kelley's message. In discussions engendered by the Grange, Stockwell became increasingly interested in the fundamentals of democracy.

While teaching, Stockwell got his first taste of politics:

> When he was but nineteen he began active work in political campaigns, he and another young man organizing and conducting a campaign for the mayoralty of Anoka against Captain [O. L.] Cutter in opposition to the saloon interests, their candidate being easily elected.[6]

In 1878 Stockwell began fourteen years employment with the American Railway Express Company. The family farm, located slightly farther from town than the St. Paul and Pacific Railway depot, made it was easy enough to stop by and ask whether the company could use a good man. Stockwell served as a railway express agent first in Anoka and then for a time in Winnipeg. Walter visited his brother in Winnipeg (population 3,700 in 1873, the year it incorporated), finding it "a straggling town along Main Street."

In 1882 Stockwell was transferred to Minneapolis, where he became railroad train messenger. Whether he requested the trans-

S. A. Stockwell as a young man.
(Courtesy of the Minnesota Historical Society)

fer or whether it was for the convenience of American Express is unknown. In any case, the move was part of what Arthur Schlesinger has called the most striking national phenomenon from 1860 to 1890—the movement to the cities. During this period, Minneapolis grew from a village of 2,564 to a city of 164,967. Immigration contributed to national urbanization, but the underlying cause was deeper. A mass exodus from country to city was occurring throughout the world, mainly because of the economic and social advantages of city life.

If the choice to move was Stockwell's, what was his motive? Did he see Minneapolis as an area where someone concerned with the public good might aim higher and achieve more? Whatever the motive, if he had not made the move to Minneapolis, he would not have met and married Maud Conkey.

Maud was the daughter of DeWitt Clinton Conkey, who was born July 10, 1824, near Plattsburgh, New York, on the shore of Lake Champlain. His forebears had settled in Pelham, Massachusetts, not far from Sutton. DeWitt attended country schools and then graduated from Clinton County Academy. His two older sisters had gone west—Elizabeth to Kansas and Ellen to Burlington, Wisconsin. DeWitt taught in the country schools of upstate New York, then followed his sisters west. He joined Ellen and her husband in Burlington, but not before he had become engaged to Antoinette Kingsley, whom he had met at the academy.

Antoinette was a teacher in Beekmantown, New York. When she was two years old, her father, traveling from Plattsburgh to Montreal with a valuable load of merchandise, had "met a tragic death." According to Elizabeth Stockwell Everts (the author's mother), he was murdered. Antoinette was adopted by an uncle, Owen Tennant Roberts, at Beekmantown. Antoinette's mother, Almira Roberts Kingsley, became a nurse. Known and loved for miles around as Aunt Myra, she lived a busy if childless life, caring for sick and invalid neighbors as well as keeping house for her father, a justice of the peace.

In the fall of 1851 DeWitt surprised Antoinette when he burst into her classroom without notice to say he had returned to marry her. He wanted to take her back to Burlington, Wisconsin, to live. She agreed, and on October 16 they were married at her uncle's farm.

To reach Burlington they traveled from Plattsburgh by boat on Lake Champlain to Ticonderoga, by train to Albany, by canalboat to Buffalo, by steamboat to Milwaukee, and then by stagecoach to Burlington. DeWitt worked as a bookkeeper in the flour and woolen mills owned by Ellen's husband, Pliny Perkins. DeWitt and Antoinette subsequently moved to Racine, then to Milwaukee, and, after sixteen years in Wisconsin, to Minneapolis.

DeWitt and Antoinette Conkey had seven children: Ellen, born in 1852, lived one day. George, born in 1853, lived but three years. (Antoinette had taken him and his baby brother, Charles, to Beekmantown to see her family, and he died during the visit.) Charles Clinton, born in 1855, grew up to become an employee of the *Minneapolis Tribune*, but he died of tuberculosis at age twenty-four. Ida, born in 1858, died at age four, victim of a diphtheria epidemic that swept through Milwaukee. Maud, born in 1862, was the last of the children born in Wisconsin. Mabel, born in 1867, mar-

DeWitt and Antoinette (Kingsley) Conkey, parents of Maud Conkey Stockwell. (Author photo)

ried Eugene Day in 1896. (Their children were Eugenia, Kingsley, and John.) Lucius James, born in 1871, for many years was engaged in railroad construction work in British Columbia. (He married Josephine Champagne in 1933; their son, C. C. Conkey, lived in California until his death in 1992.)

Maud Conkey moved with her family to Minneapolis in 1867 when she was five years old. Her father had taken a position at the North Star Woolen Mill. The Conkeys belonged to the Universalist Church and attended the Church of the Redeemer in Minneapolis. For most of his life, DeWitt was a staunch Republican, but in later years he leaned toward the Democratic party, considering it more sympathetic to the general welfare. (He died in 1907, Antoinette in 1913.)[7]

When the family arrived, Minneapolis was a village of ten thousand, sharing the waterpower of the Falls of St. Anthony with the village of St. Anthony. The availability of water determined the sites of the two settlements and a suspension bridge connected the otherwise separate villages. Minneapolis grew more rapidly, expanding westward into a region of lakes, small streams, and wooded hills.

In *Early Minneapolis Memories*, Maud Stockwell wrote of her childhood:

> The only conveyances for hire in the 70s and 80s were hacks which were found at livery stables and at the railroad stations. When visitors came from out of town, Father would sometimes engage a hack, load us all in, by placing footstools for the children, and gaily we would drive first to Minnehaha Falls, then to Fort Snelling, where we inspected the old Round Tower with its slits in the side for rifle firing, then drove down, down the rough, winding road to the Ferry Boat Landing on the Mississippi side of the Fort. The ride across the river never ceased to thrill us, and then came the slow climb to the top of the bluff on the St. Paul side . . . The drive home would be by way of St. Anthony, with an inspection of the famous flour mills, the woolen mills, and the falls.[8]

Maud Conkey began her education at the Jackson School at a time when there were so few buildings in the school district that the superintendent, W. O. Hiskey, had time to visit every classroom. At age seventy-eight, she still recalled her fright and humiliation when he asked her to spell the word "bread" and she spelled it phonetically. The mistake was not fatal to her progress, and in 1880 she was a member of the first class to graduate from the new Minneapolis Central High School. Always a keen reader—perhaps she also read *Uncle Tom's Cabin* to her family—she became an active member of the Literary Club in Minneapolis. Her parents thought her "awfully forward" for going alone to evening meetings, though she always came back "in the company of a young man."[9]

Maud Conkey taught school in Minneapolis for five years. Somewhere along the way she met Albert Stockwell. He was smitten by the young teacher and later recalled his rejected proposal as one of life's most embarrassing moments: "It was 1886 out in Excelsior, on the banks of Minnetonka, under a box elder tree . . . A friend always but nothing stronger." Later, she changed her mind, and they were married, on October 4, 1887. The following year they bought a large lot in the southeastern part of Minneapolis, where they built a two-story, eight-room house. This

Class of 1880, Central High School (the only high school) in Minneapolis. The young woman in the middle row, second from the left is Maud Conkey. (Unidentified newpaper clipping)

was farm country, and theirs was one of the first houses built that far out of town. They moved into the house on August 31, 1888. A large sunporch was added later, and they lived at 3204 East Fifty-first Street until October 1937, when they took an apartment on Garfield Avenue.

Stockwell left American Railway Express in 1892 to enter the life insurance business as an agent for the Provident Life and Trust Company. Why did he choose life insurance? A daughter, Ruth, was born in 1889; Charlotte followed in 1891, and family expenses were mounting. Did the life insurance business hold promise of higher income? Were the hours of an insurance agent more flexible, freeing time for work on the farm and pursuit of other interests? Or had Stockwell discovered a possible conflict of interest? He had been elected to the legislature in 1890 and served in the 1891 session. Was it best to sever all railway connections? In the view of many, the railroads corrupted and controlled the Minnesota legislature.[10]

Stockwell remained with Provident Life and Trust Company for four years. Then, in 1896, the Pennsylvania Mutual Life Insurance Company asked him to become its general agent for Minneapolis. He accepted and remained with Penn Mutual for the next thirty years. With these posts came independence and a free hand to act on the missionary zeal imparted to him by his mother. Standing on high, moral ground, Charlotte Bowdish Stockwell had urged Albert by example to do what he could to help the less fortunate. He decided to follow her lead.

Maud Conkey as a young woman. (Author photo)

Stockwell was positioned geographically as well as morally to join the ranks of reformers. Most reformers of the day, as Schlesinger pointed out, thought less about agrarian problems than about rapidly growing urban evils. These men and women sprang from three main blocks: former abolitionists, immigrant radicals, and progressives of the younger generation. Those longest on the stage were the abolitionists, most of whom had been interested in many reforms besides the abolition of slavery. With emancipation achieved, they attacked wide-ranging abuses in the 1870s and 1880s. Thus Wendell Phillips of Massachusetts, an abolitionist, devoted himself after the Civil War to the advocacy of moral causes including prohibition, reform in penal methods, concessions to the Indians, Negro education, votes for women, and the labor movement. William Lloyd Garrison did the same. And Gerrit Smith of New York worked in the cause of Sunday observance, opposed the use of tobacco and alcohol, advocated vegetarianism, joined the cause of women's suffrage, and worked for the abolition of capital punishment.[11]

The immigrant radicals were socialists or anarchists who sought to remake society. Socialism arrived in the United States about 1850. Proponents believed that the possibility for amassing colossal fortunes was the root of society's troubles, and they sought fundamental changes in society through the socialization of important industries; the people should collectively own these enterprises and operate them for the common good. The Socialist-Labor party, formed in 1892 on a national basis, lacked appeal because, by and large, Americans were not ready to give up on the capitalist system. Rather, they wanted a fair chance to succeed. But socialist panaceas did stimulate native-born humanitarians.

Anarchism met with even less success in America. The anarchists proposed replacement of all political government with loosely federated groups, each following its own way of life while owning the means of production and exchanging goods within the confederation. Anarchists advocated the employment of force, if necessary, as a means of bringing about change, a tenet repelling many who were otherwise sympathetic. In the 1880s, Germans in the Chicago area constituted the bulk of anarchist membership.

Reformers of the younger generation—including Albert Stockwell—were idealistic young men and women shocked by the cruelty of the factory system and the inequities of capitalism. They wanted to do something. Typically they entered the ministry, the field of journalism, or public life. Unanimously, they recognized how capitalism introduced evils into American life. All deplored the commercialization and corruption of politics and saw democracy in grave danger. E. L. Godkin, Irish-born founder and editor of *The Nation*, who later became editor of the *New York Evening Post*, and George W. Curtis of *Harper's Weekly* took the lead in pointing out the dangers. Tammany Hall was a hated target.

The rise of cities between 1860 and 1890 had far-reaching effects on the national economy. Cities were indispensable as financial centers, trade centers, and reservoirs of labor. Leaders of manufacturing and finance and developers of railroads were urban dwellers. Most had risen from humble circumstances, and they thought not in terms of national needs but of profit. It was easy for Cornelius Vanderbilt, Jay Gould, James J. Hill, John D. Rockefeller, Andrew Carnegie, and Charles Schwab, all vigorous and ruthless men, to think that prosperity for them would benefit all. America was still steeped in individualism and laissez faire. These men, unhindered by the government, were seen as cornerstones of society. Godkin, for all his dismay at corruption, was more dismayed at the idea of government regulation of business.[12]

But the glitter of huge fortunes simply accentuated city slums. Workers were not getting their fair share. The increased number of factory workers after the Civil War gave impetus to the labor movement. While in 1860 there were approximately one million factory workers in the country, by 1890 there were some four million, a rate of increase far outstripping that of the population.[13] Formerly employed in cottage industries or small factories, wage earners lost much of their former independence. Typically, the employer was absent and the relationship impersonal. The workday tended to grow longer, the factories more dangerous and gloomy. To the worker the ballot seemed a hopeless means of relief, and labor leaders promoting unionism found eager listeners, their organizing facilitated by the massing of workers within city limits.

The Knights of Labor was the first all-encompassing, national body of organized workers. Founded in 1869, it attempted to unite the workers of the United States into one union under centralized control. Membership was open to all—men and women, white and black, skilled and unskilled, laborers and capitalists, merchants and farmers. Only liquor dealers, professional gamblers, lawyers, and bankers were excluded.[14] Growth of the organization was extraordinary, reaching seven hundred thousand in 1885—testimony to its leadership and the workers' desire to organize. The stated objective of the Knights of Labor was to:

> secure to the toilers a proper share of the wealth they create; more of the leisure that rightfully belongs to them; more societary advances, more of the benefits, privileges, and emoluments of the world; in a word, all the rights and privileges necessary to make them capable of enjoying, appreciating, defending and perpetuating the blessings of good government.

More specifically, the Knights of Labor sought higher wages, an eight-hour work day, arbitration of industrial disputes, and recognition of the right to form unions. Their creed was neither revolutionary nor anti-capitalist. They merely wanted larger opportunities. Employers saw matters differently. Typically they saw wages as an operating expense; labor's contribution was small compared to managerial ability and to the cost of plant investment.

The consequence was a series of costly conflicts. An era of gigantic strikes began with the depression of 1873. Employers often hired private forces to put down strikers. The 1892 strike at the Homestead works of Carnegie Steel Company was a chilling example of that tactic. A fierce battle between workers and three hundred armed Pinkerton detectives resulted in ten deaths and the injury of over sixty workers. Workers found that strikes conducted during economic depressions were unsuccessful; employers simply shut down.

By far the most serious disturbance—and one hastening decline of the Knights of Labor—was the Haymarket Riot of 1886. The country was prosperous and business was flourishing. The Knights of Labor, trade unions, and socialist unions combined in a massive strike for the eight-hour day. The dispute at McCormick Harvester Company culminated in a riot on May 3 in Chicago in which the police killed one and wounded several other labor demonstrators. A mass meeting was held the next day in protest of this massacre. As the police broke up the meeting, someone threw a bomb into their midst. Seven persons, including a policeman, were killed, and over sixty people were injured. Though the perpetrator could not be found, Judge Joseph E. Gay of the Cook County Criminal Court determined that those inciting the deed by word or action were equally as guilty as those who committed the act. Under such instructions, the jury found eight anarchists guilty of murder and sentenced one to life imprisonment and seven to death. Of these seven, one committed suicide, four were hanged, and the others had sentences commuted to life imprisonment. Later, finding that the judge had "conducted the trial with malicious ferocity," Governor John Peter Altgeld pardoned the three anarchists still serving prison sentences. Although there was no doubt of the innocence of these men, Altgeld was denounced from coast to coast as an aider and abettor of anarchy. The Knights of Labor, in no way responsible for the Haymarket Riot, became victim of the popular revulsion against radical organization of any kind. Its influence began to wane, and by 1890 the Knights had practically disappeared. Indiscriminate strikes, mismanagement, and the difficulty of holding skilled and unskilled workers in the same union caused the downfall of the organization.[15]

The newly formed American Federation of Labor, a coalition of trade unions made up of workers of the same craft or skill, was to become the dominant force in the labor movement.

Stockwell was witness to the injustices occurring around the labor movement, and, to him, Governor Altgeld was a hero. The rendering of assistance to men imprisoned because of political views would become a lifetime commitment. Two other injustices disturbed Stockwell as deeply: the plight of blacks in the South and of Indians in the West.

The blacks' acceptance as equals plainly had not followed emancipation. The Civil War had left open the matter of the adjustment of two races. Blacks were a badge of southern defeat, making them disliked or detested and making adjustment more difficult. They had no training for work beyond menial tasks or for freedom's responsibilities. Northern meddling increased the blacks' unpopularity in the South, where, for a time during reconstruction, they were able to vote and hold office. This situation continued at varying levels in different southern states until the withdrawal of federal troops by President Rutherford B. Hayes in 1877. With troop withdrawal, federal authorities ceased intervening on the blacks' behalf; the North turned to problems of its own.

Blacks, unprotected, struggled with ignorance and poverty. Lynchings were not uncommon. Blacks were allowed to pursue livelihoods—to walk in the white man's direction—so long as they kept to themselves. But the color line was drawn at social and political equality. States passed laws providing for separate schools and prohibiting intermarriage. In 1881 Tennessee passed the first Jim Crow law, specifying separate train coaches for blacks. Other states followed. Blacks were separated in public conveyances, hotels, restaurants, and places of amusement. Even hotels in Minneapolis and St. Paul turned them away.

The Indian problem involved fewer persons—native Americans numbered about two hundred sixty thousand in the 1880s while blacks numbered over six million—but it was no less tragic. A period of almost incessant conflict between Indians and whites had begun in 1863, highlighted by outbreaks such as Custer's last stand in 1876 when Sioux and Cheyenne Indians killed 260 soldiers on the banks of the Little Big Horn in southern Montana. By the turn of the century, Indians were reduced to dependent status—a defeated, disembodied people rebuffed from their own domain. In the words of Samuel Eliot Morison and Henry Steele Commager in *The Growth of the American Republic*:

Those who once ruled undisputed the American continent were now settled on government reservations, eking out an existence on government doles, cut off from the free life of an earlier day, disintegrating morally and physically, pitiful and tragic representatives of the race which helped the white man to adjust himself to the American scene, of the Hiawathas and the Pocahontases who for so long fired the imagination of the American people.[16]

The cause of blacks and native Americans became another of Stockwell's lifetime commitments.[17]

References

1. Arthur M. Schlesinger, Sr., professor of American history at Harvard University for three decades beginning in 1924, achieved special distinction in the field of social and intellectual history as distinguished from political history. Much of the material following is based on his course History 63. See also his *The Rise of Modern America: 1865-1951* (New York: The MacMillan Company, 1951); and Samuel Eliot Morison and Henry Steele Commager, *The Growth of the American Republic* (New York: Oxford University Press, 1940).

2. For further discussion, see William P. Everts, Jr., "E. L. Godkin: On Trial in the West," honors thesis, Harvard University, 1939.

3. Everts, "E. L. Godkin."

4. Solon J. Buck, *The Granger Movement* (Cambridge: Harvard University Press, 1913), p. 101.

5. Some sources indicate he attended and graduated from high school in Anoka; others refer to common schools only. The latter seems correct.

6. *Compendium of History and Biography of Minneapolis and Hennepin County, Minnesota*, R. I. Holcombe and William H. Bingham, eds. (Chicago: Henry Taylor & Co., 1914), p. 495.

7. Maud Conkey Stockwell, *A Sheaf of Kingsley—Conkey Family History*, November 1947; *History of Minneapolis and Hennepin County*, p. 271. Maud Stockwell's history of the Kingsley-Conkey family, never published, was written for her niece and nephews, Eugenia, Kingsley, and John Day. A copy is in the possession of the author.

8. *Early Minneapolis Memories*, a booklet reprinted by the First Unitarian Society in 1981, was written by Maud Stockwell for her family in 1945.

9. *Minneapolis Morning Tribune*, May 16, 1949.

10. Morison and Commager, *Growth of the Republic*, 2:74.

11. Schlesinger, *Rise of Modern America*, p. 107.

12. Everts, "E. L. Godkin."

13. Schlesinger, *Rise of Modern America*, p. 93.

14. Morison and Commager, *Growth of the Republic*, 2:155.

15. Morison and Commager, *Growth of the Republic*, 2:155-156; Schlesinger, *Rise of Modern America*, p. 102. For a tribute to Governor John Peter Altgeld, see John F. Kennedy, *Profiles in Courage* (New York: Harper & Brothers, 1961), pp. 233-234.

16. Morison and Commager, *Growth of the Republic*, 2:85.

17. As early as 1856 the *New York Tribune* had nearly three thousand subscribers in Minnesota, more than any other territorial newspaper. In the 1880s the *Minneapolis Tribune* and the *St. Paul Pioneer Press*, among other newspapers, brought world and national problems to the newsstands in Minneapolis. See Blegen, *Minnesota*, p. 203. Stockwell thirsted for news of the issues of the day, and his reading was fervid and extensive. Helen Hunt Jackson's widely read *A Century of Dishonor* (Boston: Roberts Brothers, 1888) protesting the wrongs inflicted on American Indians was almost certainly on his reading list.

Chapter 4

Finding Henry George

Socialism and anarchy proposing abolishment of capitalism and other radical panaceas surfaced to address the ills of capitalism, but the great middle class, steeped in Horatio Alger, was too comfortable to respond. Wage earners, for all their hardship, shared this optimism. For the most part they were less class-conscious than wage-conscious and simply wanted the door of opportunity to remain open.

The first significant American solution for the country's ills was that of Henry George. Where other answering philosophies would abolish capitalism, his would save it.

Henry George was born in Philadelphia in 1839 of middle-class parents. As a student, he was only fair, and his father allowed him to quit high school where, he said later, for the most part he had been idle. He held several jobs on land and sea before setting sail through the Straits of Magellan for the West Coast in 1859.[1]

Henry George. (From the Oil Portrait by Henry Thurston See in *Progress and Poverty*. Courtesy of the Robert Schalkenbach Foundation)

Employment at publishing and printing houses in San Francisco led nowhere for George. Though penniless, he married Annie Fox in 1861, borrowing clothes for the wedding. Heart-breaking years of impoverishment began, and two children were born amidst the couple's destitution. But from these depths, Henry George gained a burning, personal knowledge of poverty that gave impetus and meaning to all he wrote and did thereafter. In an upward turn in the spring of 1865, he began a program of self-improvement in writing. His career took new direction, and he won employment as a newspaper reporter, editorial writer, and then managing editor for the *San Francisco Times*.

In 1868, when the first transcontinental railroad neared completion, George wrote a piece for the *Overland Monthly* about the railroad's impact, taking the view that increased population and business activity would result in greater wealth for the few and greater poverty for the many. He attributed California's pioneer prosperity to "the natural wealth of the region which was not yet monopolized—great opportunities were open to all." Later that year he traveled to the East Coast on behalf of the *San Francisco Herald*. In New York, expecting to find the height of civilization and social adjustment, he was struck by the "shocking contrast between monstrous wealth and debasing want." Why did poverty follow progress? He resolved to devote his life to finding out.

George returned to California in 1869, just before completion of the railroad from Sacramento to Oakland. Land speculation was rampant. One day, while riding horseback through the hills of Oakland, he stopped to talk to a passing teamster who told him about the exorbitant price of agricultural land. Suddenly it came to him that here was the answer to the question he had asked in New York. He saw then that

> with the growth in population, land grows in value, and the men who want it must pay more for the privilege. I turned back, amidst quiet thought, to the perception that there came to me, and has been with me ever since.[2]

George spent the rest of his life explaining and proclaiming in the United States about what he had learned. He had seen that relatively few people in California owned most of the land. This denied other Californians the right to acquire it, even though they might need it for their very existence. Land, like air and water, should belong to all people. Landlords exacted excessively high rents, and this was robbery. To cure this condition it should not be necessary to distribute land, he said; rather, the solution was to abolish all taxes on individuals and income, placing instead a single tax on basic land values. All land is not equally valuable because of location, the presence of minerals, and such differences as climate and fertility. A single tax would level off the artificial advantages, doing away with what came to be known as the unearned increment of land. Improvements on land would not be taxed because they were the work products of the owner. Establishment of a single tax would curb land speculation as well as the

47

Sketch of Henry George. (Courtesy of the Henry George Foundation of America)

practice of allowing valuable city lots to remain empty or to be put by the owner to only minimum use, George thought.

Progress and Poverty was George's masterpiece. Published in 1880, it reached a worldwide audience. In the United States, George's thesis held greater appeal for industrial workers than for farmers, as farmers hoped to benefit from rising land values. Intellectuals like Clarence Darrow, George Bernard Shaw, Leo Tolstoy in Russia, and Sun Yat Sen in China were among the converts, along with thousands from all walks of life throughout the world. According to Morison and Commager:

> Over two million copies of his book were sold, and on the dusty plains of Kansas, in the slums of Liverpool and of Moscow, on the banks of the Ganges and of the Yangtze, poor men painfully spelled out the message of *Progress and Poverty* to grasp a new vision of human society.[3]

In 1880 Henry George moved to New York City. He ran for mayor in 1886, finishing second behind the Tammany candidate but polling eight thousand more votes than Theodore Roosevelt, who came in third. George died in New York in 1897. An estimated hundred thousand persons passed before his bier.

S. A. Stockwell, on the banks of the Mississippi, discovered *Progress and Poverty* as a young man. If he did not commit the book to memory, he knew it chapter and verse. George's work formed the centerpiece of Stockwell's economic and political philosophy, and Stockwell furthered the single-tax cause in every possible way. His first opportunity came in the 1880s when he was a member of mixed Assembly 805, a local unit of the Knights of Labor, during a period when local assemblies held frequent discussions on economic subjects and such matters as strikes and labor disputes.[4] In the Minnesota legislature, he pressed for measures that would enable the people to vote on the question; he organized single-tax clubs, brought national speakers to Minneapolis, and arranged many, many meetings throughout the state, all in the interests of the single tax.

In 1927, A. W. Rankin, called upon to describe his friend Stockwell as a politician, envied his commitment:

> Now a single taxer cannot be what is ordinarily known as a politician, because he has a vision. I always envy and admire a man who can see clearly to the end and satisfy himself that there is a

panacea, a cure all for the ills that we are heir to, and Stockwell has stood a faithful single taxer through all these years. I think he would tell us tonight that the economic ills of this country can be settled only when the single tax principle is adopted.[5]

Nothing changed his commitment, held also by Maud Stockwell, who had heard Henry George speak at the Exposition Building in Minneapolis when she was a young woman. In 1939, Albert and Maud Stockwell gave their grandson (this author) a copy of *Progress and Poverty* with this inscription:

> For Bill,
>   When democracy flowers, the truth expressed in these pages will be recognized and followed.
>   One of the great joys of life has been personal contact with Henry George and scores of women and men who have been glad to spread the truth.
>   We pass the torch to you.
>
>   Albert
>   Nanna[6]

References

1. The discussion here and in the following paragraphs is based largely on Schlesinger, *Rise of Modern America*; Morison and Commager, *Growth of the Republic*; and *Dictionary of American Biography* (New York: Charles Scribner's Sons, 1964), volume 4.

2. *Dictionary of American Biography*, 4:213.

3. Morison and Commager, *Growth of the Republic*, 2:368; *Minneapolis Journal*, July 4, 1894.

4. Henry George, Jr., to Albert Dollenmayer, April 23, 1887.

5. Remarks, Complimentary Birthday Dinner, June 8, 1927.

6. Many advocates of the thinking of Henry George are currently active in an association known as Common Ground/USA, an educational, non-profit organization with offices in Columbia, Maryland, that is devoted to the economic principles of Henry George. Henry George Schools of Social Science are to be found in New York City with extensions in numerous other cities in the United States as well as some seven foreign countries. "Public collection of rent" is now seen by most proponents as a better name than "the single tax," suggesting as it does that the public is only collecting what rightfully belongs to it and is not at all imposing improperly upon the people. Nicolaus Tideman, Professor of Economics, Virginia Polytechnic Institute and State University, to William P. Everts, January 14, 1994.

Chapter 5

Hastening the Kingdom of Heaven—1891

W illiam Watts Folwell (1833-1929), historian and first president of the University of Minnesota, wrote of S. A. Stockwell in a letter to William E. Leonard on June 8, 1927: "I have long been an admirer of Mr. Stockwell . . . I have sympathized with his hopes and labors for a better and fairer social life, but his pace has been swift for my tardy feet. He wants the Kingdom of Heaven right away." Folwell may have been thinking of the influx of proposals to correct faults and evils in society submitted by Stockwell in the 1891 (and later in the 1897) Minnesota legislative session. Stockwell's bills, motions, and resolutions—his votes for and against—displayed freshman urgency; they were an immediate disclosure of the nature of the man and his priorities.

Left to right: William W. Folwell, Cyrus Northrop, George Edgar Vincent, and Marion Leroy Burton. (Courtesy of the Minnesota Historical Society)

In 1890 Stockwell, at age thirty-three, entered politics. Until 1888 he had been a Republican, but the party of Abraham Lincoln had changed. The corruption the country had suffered under President Ulysses S. Grant in the 1870s still blemished the Grand Old Party. James G. Blaine, defeated Republican candidate for president in 1884, was a grafter in the eyes of many honorable Republicans. The Republican party had not been sympathetic to farmers or wage earners or even capable of understanding the reasons for their discontent. Grover Cleveland, renominated by the Democrats for a second term in 1888, had proven himself a man of integrity and courage. A fiscal conservative, he had opposed the protective tariff and strongly supported civil service reform. Neither major party was ready to embrace Henry George's single tax. Unlike Stockwell, Cleveland did not view government as an instrument for social reform. Stockwell saw the Democratic party as the more congenial home.

The Minnesota legislature consisted of a house of representatives and a senate. It met biennially. Senators served four-year terms, members of the house two-year terms. Stockwell's residence was in the thirty-third (legislative) district, which included the seventh, eleventh and twelfth wards of Minneapolis and the towns of Excelsior, Eden Prairie, Bloomington, and Richfield to the south. He decided to run for the house as a Democrat. His long-standing membership in mixed Assembly 805 of the Knights of Labor, his stand for laws protecting the health of workers, his opposition to child labor, and his support of tax reform all endeared him to labor. His determination to help the farmers with their endless problems was known.

Democrats in Minnesota battled not only their opponents but also a tradition of Republicanism in the 1890 campaign. All of the governors and other elected state officers had been Republican since 1860. Occasionally a Democrat won a seat in Congress but that was the exception; Republicans had enjoyed a comfortable majority in both houses of Minnesota's legislature for thirty years.

During the summer of 1890 hopes ran high in the ranks of the opposition for an end to Republican domination. For one thing, the opposition had been significantly strengthened by the emergence of the Farmers' Alliance, an echoing voice of agrarian protest across the South and Midwest. The conditions giving rise to the Grange still existed. The Farmers' Alliance turned to political action, calling for an inflationary monetary policy and the invocation of state police power and federal authority to control freight rates and marketing and lending practices.[1]

In July 1890, the Farmers' Alliance was organized as a third party in Minnesota to participate in the fall elections. Sidney Owen, widely respected editor of a farm journal, was named the standard-bearer in the race for governor. Others rose to run for legislative seats as Alliance party candidates. In many instances the party endorsed Democratic or Republican candidates sympathetic to its cause. Stockwell gained their endorsement.

The Minnesota elections of November 1890 brought an abrupt halt to thirty years of Republican party control in the state. Republican losses were traceable to voter dissatisfaction with pro-tectionism, as exemplified by the unpopular McKinley tariff of 1890, tight money policies, and the party's failure to adopt reform measures sought by farmers and wage earners. Such measures were promised by the Alliance party and liberal Democrats. While the Republican candidate for governor, William R. Merriam, was reelected, he won by the narrowest of margins and received only forty percent of the popular vote. Sidney Owen polled nearly twen-ty-five percent of the vote. For the legislature, Democratic and Alliance candidates succeeded as never before. Hennepin County was entitled to twenty-one seats—Democrats won nineteen. Among the nineteen sworn in on January 6, 1891, was S. A. Stockwell, who finished second among eight candidates in District 33, with 2,406 votes. James Huntington, also a Democrat, received 2,571.[2]

Neither the Democrats nor the Alliance alone could organize the house or senate. Disagreements emerged about such matters as the selection of speaker and choice of committee chairmen. Stockwell was named chairman of the Committee on Labor and Labor Legislation—an assignment certainly to his liking—and appointed to the Appropriations, Education, Engrossment, and Geological and Natural History Survey committees.

Another obstacle to cooperation between Democrats and the Alliance was the attitude of the longtime Democratic boss, Michael Doran, who was extremely conservative and not happy about pro-posed Alliance solutions to societal problems. The Democrats and the Alliance did finally succeed in jointly organizing the house and the senate, but not without loud Republican protest.

Difficulty in agreeing on procedural matters foreshadowed differences on substantive issues that would surface upon the introduction of legislative measures. The differences were not just between the Democrats and the Alliance but between factions in all three parties. Carl H. Chrislock in "The Alliance Party and the Minnesota Legislature of 1891," described one of the trouble spots:

> Some Democratic legislators were not responsive to Doran's lead-ership, but this did not automatically make them sympathetic to the Alliance party. For example, in the Hennepin County delegation

several Minneapolis Democrats were advocates of Henry George's single tax. A few were enthusiastic supporters of employer liability legislation, the eight-hour day, factory inspection, and prohibition of child labor. Leading the latter group was S. A. Stockwell, then at the beginning of his phenomenally long career in the Minnesota legislature. These issues, however, offered a slender base for cooperation with the Alliance party. Its members were, on the whole, suspicious of the single tax. Alliance platforms had given endorsement to labor's most important demands, but rank-and-file Alliance members were at best lukewarm supporters of the measure. No doubt many of them feared that the eight-hour day and bans on child labor might be applied to agriculture.[3]

Organizational matters out of the way, Stockwell wasted no time in pressing forward with matters of substance. On January 14, he introduced HF14, a bill for an act to regulate the employment of peace officers. The anti-Pinkerton measure aimed to curtail the vicious strike-breaking practices used by some employers. It would require all recognized legal officers to be residents of the state of Minnesota; outside officials would have no authority. The measure further provided that it was unlawful to institute or keep any private detective office for the purpose of keeping or letting out any armed force for hire, or for any person or corporation to keep or let any armed force for hire. Rather, all armed forces should be subject to the police authorities created by law and under the control of the state or municipality. Stockwell's bill was unanimously adopted by the house on April 17 and became law as Chapter 16, General Laws of Minnesota, 1891.[4]

On January 14, Stockwell also introduced HF13, a bill for an act to provide for the weekly payment of wages by corporations. Biweekly or monthly payment of wages was the usual practice. Referred to the Committee on Labor and Labor Legislation, the bill progressed slowly, and no action was ever taken by the full house.

On January 15 Stockwell introduced HF23, a bill for an act to provide free textbooks and school supplies for students in the public schools of Minnesota. The bill was read and referred to the Committee on Education. Little progress was made on the measure in the 1891 session, but Stockwell successfully fought it through later. The *Minneapolis Labor Review* commended him:

> In those days of low pay before trade unions were so powerfully organized, many a Minnesotan who later rose to fame would have been denied an education but for the free textbooks the Stockwell law made available, for the penniless conditions of many families then made the purchase of textbooks impossible.[5]

On January 23, Stockwell introduced HF124, a bill for an act limiting the employment of children. Referred to the Committee on Labor and Labor Legislation, it was indefinitely postponed.

Carl. J. Buell. (Courtesy of the Minnesota Historical Society)

HF125, also introduced by Stockwell on January 23, required all healthy children to attend school. This measure was referred to the Committee on Education. Indefinite postponement followed.

For Stockwell in his freshman year to sit back and learn what he could about the systematics of lawmaking without working day and night at the capitol would have been an easy matter: If he reached home in time for supper,[6] young Ruth would be there to welcome him; Maud was expecting a second child any day (Charlotte was born on February 25, 1891). But Stockwell opted to deliver firsthand to Minnesotans the message Henry George was delivering around the world.

On the evening of January 29, 1891, Stockwell remained in St. Paul with his friend Carl J. Buell, and a representative of labor, to attend a public meeting of farmers gathered in the senate chamber. The *St. Paul Pioneer Press* covered the meeting the next day:

> A brace of single tax agitators named Buell and Stockwell and an ultra labor agitator, with single tax proclivities, named Martin, came down from Minneapolis last evening to capture the meeting of the farmers at the Senate Chamber. Buell got the floor and talked for forty-five minutes and, to all appearances, would have talked until the Chamber was wanted by the Senate this morning had not Chairman McGee called him down. The farmers, with few exceptions, listened to him with dreary patience, and his many good things fell flat—with the exception that he smiled at them himself, and was assisted in the effort by four or five sympathizers.
>
> Sergeant-at-Arms [Henry] Plowman of the House, who is a plowman by the trade, got the floor and commenced to shoot hot shot into the camp of the single tax men. But Buell, not at all squelched by the chairman's hint, bobbed up every few minutes to make a speech of five minutes or so in reply to the rural gentleman. This just suited Mr. Plowman, and it took him but a few minutes to prove to the audience that a country man could be more than a

match for a city talker. Mr. Plowman took the ground that the interests of the farmers demanded that all a man's personal and real property should be taxed. He thought that mortgages should be taxed in the place where they are recorded.

The agitator urged that taxing personal property was a mere farce, as the owners of such property would not make correct returns. Stockwell arose and presented a list of wealthy Minneapolis people who are now deceased who in their lifetime had returned to the assessor as their personal effects mere nominal sums. The probate judge had found these men to have been possessed of effects worth many thousands of dollars.

Mr. Plowman replied that the assessor was to blame for all that . . . At the close of a reading of a resolution to be heard at a later meeting calling for the taxation of all property, both personal and real, Buell was on his feet again. But the meeting adjourned promptly, and the speech he did not make was probably put on ice for the next occasion.

Buell and Stockwell were lifelong friends. Their faith in the teachings of Henry George coincided. Buell's views on the single tax, as outlined in the senate chamber on January 29, 1891, were later published in his *Minnesota Legislature of 1923*:

Our present system is the real underlying cause of landlordism—the taking of profit by the mere holding of land. Landlordism, in all its varied forms and ramifications, is the primary cause of practically all the evils that curse society. It therefore follows that the first and most important thing to do, if we are to save our civilization from destruction, is to reform our system of taxation.

IN CIVILIZED SOCIETY PUBLIC REVENUE IS NECESSARY. Also, as civilized society develops, there arises and grows a value that this very progress of society creates and maintains. That socially-created value attaches to LAND and to nothing else.

Imagine a perfectly wild and empty tract of land around the head of navigation on the Mississippi River.

This should not be so difficult to imagine, for there are men now living who can remember when that was practically true.

The Falls of St. Anthony poured their waters over the precipice in an untenanted wildness.

At the time the land upon which now stand the cities of Minneapolis and St. Paul had no value.

It had no value because there were no people here.

No one wanted it.

No one would pay anything for it.

But the land around the Falls of St. Anthony is the natural site of a great industrial and commercial center.

People began to locate here and go to work.

Their work produced WEALTH. Houses, shops, stores, food, clothing, and all the other needs of life are products of their WORK of production and exchange.

All this wealth is the product of individual and associated labor and belongs naturally and morally to the individual men and women who produced it.

If you have plowed and planted and harvested, then the crop is yours—it belongs to no one else.

If you have built a house, then the house is yours. No one else has any moral right to it, nor to any part of its value, except as you may agree.

If you have brought into this little growing community a stock of goods of any kind, that stock of goods is yours and all the laws of God and man will protect you in its ownership, except as against the assessor.

BUT

All the while this little community has been settling here and going about its daily work, another kind of VALUE has been arising—this is the VALUE of the LAND on which the town is located.

This value is NOT directly the product of individual or cooperative effort.

This is an entirely different kind of value.

It is the result of community growth and development.

Every new family settling here increases this LAND value.

Every improvement made—every street opened—every sidewalk laid—every dwelling or public building erected—provided it is needed—all these things increase the value of the land on which this community is living and growing.

From all this it would seem to follow that this publicly-created value was intended in the very nature of things to meet public needs, that it morally belongs to all the people and should be taken and used to pay for the administration of the common affairs of the community.

If it is not so taken and used, it will, of course, remain in the possession of the fortunate lot owners.

They will become rich, and taxes will have to be levied on the food, clothing, houses and other buildings, and on the processes and products of industry.

Then will follow all the disastrous results of high priced lots and land and low wages—of vacant lots and unemployed labor.

This is what our wrong system of taxation has brought us to. Let me repeat and emphasize: Practically every social evil can be traced, directly or indirectly, to our crooked and dishonest system of taxation.[7]

Buell and Stockwell were not deterred by the cool reaction of farmers and Alliance members to their statement of the case for the single tax. On February 10, Stockwell presented to the house a petition, from Buell and others, relative to the submission to the people of the state at the next regular election of such amendments to the constitution as would permit the exemption of personal property and improvements on land from all taxation. The petition was read and submitted to the Committee on Judiciary; it, too, came to naught.

Thereafter Stockwell backed a measure exempting personal property and improvements on land from all taxation. This did not clear committee and, according to Chrislock:

> An attempted compromise on the single tax, which would have left each community free to adopt it for its own needs, failed miserably. A later generation may doubt the wisdom of such a measure, but a friendly disposition toward it by the Alliance would have contributed greatly to a unity within the combine's reform wing.[8]

The woman suffrage movement progressed in Minnesota as elsewhere in the country by the year 1891. Wyoming's territorial legislature in 1869 had acted first in granting voting rights to women. At its outset, suffrage was linked with the temperance movement. In the 1871 gubernatorial election in Minnesota, the Temperance party not only fielded a candidate for governor but also came out for woman suffrage. As a first step, Stockwell sought to gain the vote for women in municipal elections. On February 13, he presented to the house the petition of Mrs. D. A. Sherman and others of Sleepy Eye calling for municipal suffrage to women over the age of twenty-one. This petition, with others later introduced by Stockwell from citizens of Red Wing, Aitkin, and Pipestone, was read and referred to the Committee on Elections.

On February 16, Stockwell presented a petition of citizens of Hennepin County urging the passage of a measure then before the Judiciary Committee for the abolishment of capital punishment.

Another measure partly engineered through the house by Stockwell was HF129, the Australian secret ballot measure introduced by John A. Keyes.[9] Introduced early in the session, its passage was not attributable to Alliance-Democratic party cooperation. Chrislock has pointed out that final enactment occurred despite Democratic-Alliance joinder:

> Another important enactment of the 1891 legislature was the Australian ballot law. That it passed in spite of the combine was so obvious that Democratic-Alliance spokesmen could claim no

57

credit for it. When the Keyes bill, as the secret ballot was called, came up for consideration, a deep split developed between Democratic and Alliance legislators. The issue was not whether a secret ballot should be adopted; virtually everybody wanted that. But the Democrats objected strenuously to a provision in the Keyes bill which made it mandatory for the elector to place a check by the name of every candidate for whom he was voting. Instead, Democratic spokesmen wanted a ballot which would permit the voter, were he so minded, to indicate in a box at the top that he wished to vote for all the candidates of a given party. Democrats argued that the ballot prescribed by the Keyes bill discriminated against the foreign born and placed their right to vote under the control of Republican employers. This reasoning made no impression on either Republican or Alliance legislators, whose solid front was formidable enough to push the bill through both houses.[10]

The *St. Paul Globe*, the only major Democratic newspaper in the area, bemoaned the manner in which Keyes's bill had been modified. In its April 17, 1891, edition, the newspaper declared:

As passed by Republicans and recent reformers, the election bill, as amended, required that every candidate voted for must have a cross opposite his name. One could not vote a straight ticket. Many foreign born voters would be defranchised, because an employer can use a club over the votes of his foreign employees and those unable to read by having an agent with them when they go into the voting booth.

Stockwell sided with his Democratic colleagues. On February 5, he introduced HF267, declaring it a misdemeanor on the part of employers to require as a condition of employment the surrender of any right of citizenship. The bill, an attempt to prevent disfranchisement, saw progress but was not enacted. While the law as enacted was not perfect, Stockwell had nothing but praise for John A. Keyes and the overall progress made:

We accept the Australian ballot law today without any question, we think it has been here always and yet . . . it took years of strenuous work to secure the Australian ballot law for this state. I have not the time to go into all the struggles to secure it, but simply to say that the influence that started that movement was the old Single Tax League, and the mixed assembly #805 of the Knights of Labor, of which I was a member forty-five years ago.

Those of us who had occasion to work in politics before the adoption of the Australian Ballot Law will know something of the conditions that prevailed before it came to us. It came by the honest effort of the legislature of 1891, when the Farmers' Alliance and a few democrats controlled the situation, and the one major force in bringing it to a conclusion was John A. Keyes.[11]

The election of Democratic and Alliance candidates to both house and senate in sufficient numbers to establish a majority by combination theoretically should have resulted in a record of achievement for the 1891 legislature. The two parties' platforms meshed. Hopes ran high for legislation regulating the railroads, prohibiting usurious interest rates by lenders, bolstering the farmers' bargaining position with respect to use of grain elevators, protecting the health of workers, and tax reform.[12]

But these expectations were not reached. When and where cooperation was needed it was not forthcoming. One difficulty was the inexperience of the legislators making up the combination. When there was experience, as in the case of the veteran Ignatius Donnelly, who was president of the Alliance when elected to the state senate in 1890 and who gained the chairmanship of the Railroad Committee, there was more oratorical skill and personal ambition than capacity to gain compromise. Another difficulty confronting the combine was the stridence of the press. Virtually all the daily newspapers were Republican. The upshot of these difficulties was the failure of interest-usury bills because agreement could not be reached on the nature and degree of penalty for violation. While railroad legislation was finally adopted at the close of the session, essentially all it did was modify with corrective language an earlier law held unconstitutional. No significant labor legislation was adopted. The single tax was no closer to adoption, and Stockwell's proposal for free textbooks had died in committee.

The 1891 legislature was criticized not only for what it failed to do but also for what it did. Both Republican orators and the press widely assailed the level of spending. Taxes were increased along with total appropriations. While the Republicans were not without responsibility for these increases, in the eyes of the farmers the Democratic-Alliance majority was the culprit.

This disenchantment did not bode well for the success of Democratic and third-party candidates in 1892. The Populists replaced the Farmers' Alliance on the Minnesota ballot.

The Populist movement saw a complete breakdown of the old frontier tradition of individualism; the Populists demanded government intervention in more definite terms than their predecessors ever dreamed. Morison and Commager described the state of the nation at the time the Populist party shot to the fore:

Railroad regulation had proved all but futile, and the anti-trust law was to prove effective only against labor organizations. Discontent with the McKinley tariff was widespread, and the prospect of any effective tariff reduction was dim. Money was tight, credit inflexible, banking facilities woefully inadequate, and the Sherman Silver Purchase Act did little to satisfy the advocates of free and unlimited coinage of silver and less to settle the money question. The political machinery was not articulated to democracy; the Senate, chosen not by popular vote but by state legislatures, was the stronghold of special interests; the Supreme Court reflected the ideas of the privileged. Dissatisfaction was most acute on the farms of the South and West. . . . In the four years from 1889 to 1893 over eleven thousand farm mortgages were foreclosed in Kansas alone. . . . The stage was set for the entrance of a party of revolt, and with astonishing promptness the Populist party made its appearance. The rank and file of the new party was recruited from the silverites, disciples of Edward Bellamy, and the followers of Henry George; the leadership, drawn almost exclusively from the Alliances, furnished a refreshing contrast to the bankrupt and dismal leadership of the major parties during the eighties and nineties.[13]

George Leonard, a radical young immigrant who had just arrived in Minneapolis from czarist Russia and who was to become a close friend of Stockwell, described his surroundings:

Minneapolis was a seething hotbed of populism when I got here. Minneapolis was the last frontier of industrial development. Beyond it were the great plains, then forests and mountains. So it was here that the great battles between capital and labor were fought.[14]

The Populist party was not formally organized until 1891. In 1890, however, the Populists managed to gain control of the Democratic party in a number of southern states, and, in the West, they joined forces effectively with the Democrats. Four Populist senators and fifty congressmen were elected that year, and the Populists gained control of some twelve state legislatures. These victories were heady stuff for the party leaders who convened in Omaha on July 4, 1892, to prepare for the fall elections.

Excitement and enthusiasm charged the atmosphere at the national convention. The indefatigable Ignatius Donnelly of Minnesota was the man of the hour. Renowned for his eloquence, he did not disappoint with his ringing speech:

We meet in the midst of a nation brought to the verge of moral, political and material ruin. Corruption dominates the ballot-box, the legislatures, the Congress, and touches even the er-mine of the bench. The people are demoralized . . . The newspapers are largely subsidized or muzzled; public opinion silenced; business prostrated; our homes covered with mortgages; labor impoverished; and the land concentrating in the hands of the capitalists. The urban workmen are denied the right of organization for self-protection; imported pauperized labor beats down their wages; a hireling standing army, unrecognized by our laws, is established to shoot them down, and they are rapidly degenerating into European conditions. The fruits of the toil of millions are boldly stolen to build up colossal fortunes for a few, unprecedented in the history of mankind; and the possessors of these in turn despise the republic and endanger liberty.[15]

The Populist platform, also drafted by Donnelly, demanded the free and unlimited coinage of silver and the printing of paper money as legal tender in payment of debts; a flexible currency system, controlled by the government and not by the banks; a graduated income tax; a subtreasury plan allowing farmers to deposit their agricultural produce in government warehouses in exchange for legal tender certificates; postal savings banks; public ownership and operation of railroads, telegraphs, and telephones; prohibition of alien land ownership and reclamation of railroad lands illegally held; immigration restriction; the eight-hour day for labor; prohibition of the use of labor spies; the direct election of U.S. senators; the Australian ballot; and the initiative and referendum.[16]

The eastern press lambasted the Omaha convention, the Populist platform, and the party's nominee for president, James B. Weaver of Iowa. The New York *Evening Post* reported the dominant tone of the convention as one of discontent, the "vague dissatisfaction which is always felt by the incompetent and lazy and shiftless when they contemplate those who have got it better in the world."[17]

After violently attacking the platform, the *Evening Post* flailed Weaver:

Weaver is the proper candidate for president of such a party. He is a demagogue who came to the surface in the Greenback period. . . . No platform could be constructed so ridiculous that he would not gladly stand upon it. He is the fit product of a convention in which Ignatius Donnelly was one of the most popular orators.[18]

Grover Cleveland, Democratic candidate running again against Benjamin Harrison, who defeated him in 1888 though Cleveland received a larger popular vote, won the November election of 1892 decisively. But Democratic party fortunes for the most part declined. Populism had made no genuine impression nationally, though Weaver received twenty-two electoral votes and Populist candidates in Kansas and Nebraska achieved considerable success. This could not be said for Populist candidates in Minnesota. Ignatius Donnelly, running for governor of Minnesota as a Populist, polled twenty thousand fewer votes than Owen had two years before, and he met defeat along with other former members of the Alliance party now running for statewide office as Populists. Republican Knute Nelson was elected governor, outdistancing Democrat David Lawler and Donnelly by wide margins. Chrislock has attributed the poor showing of Populists in Minnesota to the meager record of the 1891 legislature:

> There can be no question . . . that the reputation of the legislature of 1891 lent plausibility to the thesis of Populist "radicalism" and Democratic "irresponsibility." With a zeal not entirely justified by the facts, Republican campaigners of the 1890s pointed to the 1891 session as proof that political "soundness" was a monopoly of the Grand Old Party. The alleged incompetence, extravagance, and general ineffectiveness of the only non-Republican legislature within immediate memory became a political myth, comparable in a limited way to the "Hoover depression," "Truman's war," or the "terrible Eightieth Congress." And a myth which commands belief is a more effective determinant of political behavior than a reality which is ambiguous.[19]

Stockwell ran for the legislature again in the election of November 8, 1892, this time as a fusion candidate. He had the endorsement of both the Democratic and Populist parties, as did A. M. Goodrich, the other representative from the Thirty-third District. Both were defeated:

W. S. Elliot, Rep.	2,935	
Geo. Wilson, Rep.	2,557	
S. A. Stockwell, Fus.	2,503	
A. M. Goodrich, Fus.	2,319	[20]

References

1. Material here and following is based largely on or taken directly from Carl H. Chrislock, "The Alliance Party and the Minnesota Legislature of 1891," in *Minnesota History*, 35: 297-312 (September 1957). Chrislock

points out that while joinder and cooperation between the Democratic and Farmer-Labor parties in Minnesota seemed logical and customary in the 1950s, such was not the case in 1890.

2. *Legislative Manual*, 1891, p. 566.

3. Chrislock, "The Alliance," p. 304.

4. Copies of some but not all house files (HF) or house bills as first submitted by legislators are available in the Minnesota Historical Society. Abstracts of proposals are to be found in the *House Journals*, which are well indexed.

5. Undated clipping from *Minneapolis Labor Review*, at the Minneapolis Public Library.

6. Stockwell traveled to and from the capitol by streetcar, on a twenty-four-mile round trip for which he was reimbursed by the legislature. His January 1891 excursions reaffirmed his belief that something must be done to protect the motormen from the wind and cold, and he later introduced a bill making vestibules compulsory on all streetcars. According to an undated clipping from the *Minneapolis Labor Review* at the Minneapolis Public Library:

> Prior to the passage of this law, motormen and conductors breasted the elements in way below zero weather without any protection whatever, the raw winds driving the snow and sleet into their faces and

Street car in winter. (A pen-and-ink drawing courtesy of Ben Campbell, 1984)

chilling them to the marrow. The pneumonia casualties ran high among streetcar employees in the days before the passage of the Stockwell law.

7. C. J. Buell, *Minnesota Legislature of 1923*, pp. 47-48. Though the single tax was never adopted in Minnesota, Buell became one of the state's most highly respected tax experts, and he was responsible for significant improvements in state tax laws.

8. Chrislock, "The Alliance," p. 309.

9. *House Journal*, 1891, p. 92.

10. Chrislock, "The Alliance," p. 309.

11. Remarks, Complimentary Birthday Dinner, June 8, 1927. Among conditions prevailing before adoption of the Australian ballot was that of employees being informed of candidates supported by their employers; an employee who declined to vote as directed was penalized with the loss of his job.

12. Chrislock, "The Alliance," here and below.

13. Morison and Commager, *Growth of the Republic*, 2:237-39.

14. *Minneapolis Tribune*, February 10, 1952.

15. Morison and Commager, *Growth of the Republic*, 2:240-41.

16. Morison and Commager, Growth of the Republic, 2:241.

17. Everts, "E. L. Godkin." Godkin was editor of the *Evening Post* in 1892.

18. Everts, "E. L. Godkin."

19. Chrislock, "The Alliance," 312.

20. *Legislative Manual*, 1893, p. 476. In 1893-1894 the country experienced the most severe depression of the nineteenth century. By the close of 1893 there were four million unemployed out of a population of about sixty-five million. Industrial production neared a standstill. While Stockwell held no public office at the time, he could not remain on the sidelines. In a letter on May 24, 1894, to his friend and client Albert Dollenmayer, he wrote of an emergency proposal befitting a single-taxer:
> I have been out among the unemployed all this week when business would permit and Dollenmayer it is hell. Strong men who have been out of work six eight ten mos and a year discouraged and ready for anything . . . I am going to introduce a resolution in the Board of Trade tomorrow morning requesting holders of unused land to allow the unemployed to use such land free. I hear the rumblings of the volcano it will open now.

Chapter 6

Hastening—1897

By the fall of 1894, the political situation in Minnesota had not materially changed. That Cleveland had named Democrats to a few federal offices had not seriously damaged the Republican machine. The Republican state convention in 1894 renominated the popular Nelson by acclamation. The Populists, unwilling to experiment further with Ignatius Donnelly, nominated Sidney M. Owen, who had been the Alliance candidate four years earlier. The state Democratic party in 1894 was satisfied to adopt resolutions endorsing the Cleveland administration and the national party platform of 1892. The Populists reaffirmed the platform of the national party adopted at Omaha on July 4, 1892.[1]

In the November elections, Republican nominees for state positions were chosen by large majorities. Nelson, who had gained widespread approval, received 147,943 votes, a plurality of 60,053 over Owen. George L. Becker, the Democratic candidate, limped in third with only 53,584 votes. Nationally, the Populist party's vote in 1894 was more than forty percent higher than it had been in 1892. The financial panic of 1893, which shook popular belief in the major parties' inclination or ability to assist the common people, helped the Populists, and, in Minnesota, the Populists temporarily became the state's second-ranking party.

Stockwell did not run in 1894. He was politically astute enough to recognize that reelection to the house in 1894 would be difficult for a Democratic-Populist party candidate and, indeed, the thirty-third district did send two Republicans to the house. They won easily. Yet Stockwell was never a man to back off in the face of defeat. He loved the fray. Perhaps the demands of his job at Provident Life and Trust Company—he was still something of a newcomer in the insurance field—lead to his decision. A third daughter, Elizabeth Conkey Stockwell, had been born on May 6,

1893.[2] While striving to balance responsibilities of work, home and political life, he would not have disagreed with Emerson, who wrote in his essay *Self-Reliance*:

> I shun father and mother and wife and brother when my genius calls me. I would write on the lintels of the doorpost Whim. I hope it is somewhat better than whim at least, but we cannot spend the day in explanation. Expect me not to show cause why I seek or why I exclude company.

Stockwell's genius was his commitment to work for the public betterment as he saw it. Passing up a chance to regain the seat he lost by fifty-four votes in 1892 cannot have been easy.

Following the 1894 elections, the Populists had reason to be optimistic. Nationally, their party's vote, after all, had been over forty percent higher than in 1892. The outlook for 1896 was bright, but they failed to take into consideration sentiment within the Democratic party for the free coinage of silver and the magnetism of William Jennings Bryan of Lincoln, Nebraska. At the Democratic convention in Chicago in the summer of 1896, the silver delegates were in control. The New York leaders, who for many years had controlled the party, were thrown aside. A new alignment, composed of western and southern delegates, formed.

It was in discussion of the Democratic platform that Bryan made his famed "Cross of Gold" speech. He told of the history of the silver movement, setting forth how silver Democrats had gone from victory to victory but were now assembled not to discuss, not to debate, but to enter upon the judgment already rendered by the plain people:

> Having behind us the producing masses of this nation and the world, supported by the commercial interests, the laboring interests, and the toilers everywhere, we will answer their demand for a gold standard by saying to them: You shall not press down upon the brow of labor this crown of thorns, you shall not crucify mankind upon a cross of gold.

The speech swept the silver ranks like fire, and it won him the presidential nomination on the fifth ballot.[3]

With William Jennings Bryan at age thirty-six leading the Democrats on the silver crusade of 1896, the fate of the Populists, and other third parties in the United States, was sealed: absorption of their platform by a major party and ultimate demise. The Populists in Minnesota accepted the inevitable and agreed, as did Populists in many other states, to a fusionist ticket composed of Populists, silver Democrats, and silver Republicans. John Lind, a silver Republican and the fusionist gubernatorial candidate, narrowly lost to the Republican nominee, David M. Clough.

Bryan lost, but only after a remarkable campaign that he viewed as a conflict between Wall Street and the great "toiling masses." His defeat, however, can be attributed more to silver than to class. Republican William McKinley's popular majority over Bryan was 600,000 in a total vote of 13,600,000. McKinley defeated Bryan in Minnesota by 193,503 to 130,735. The electoral vote came in at 271 to 176.[4]

Clearly these were exciting times—too much so for Stockwell to remain a bystander. His wife, three daughters, and Penn Mutual to the contrary notwithstanding, he ran for the house in 1896 from the thirty-third district as a Democrat-Populist, winning a seat. Darrell T. Davies, a Republican, received 4,098 votes. Stockwell finished second with 3,696.[5]

Also elected to the Minnesota house that year was Ignatius Donnelly, the Populist candidate. Born in Philadelphia in 1831, Donnelly had headed west in 1857 to seek his fortune, and he settled in Nininger, fancying himself the founder of a future metropolis. The panic of 1857 killed those dreams. Personal ambition and public speaking skill drew him to politics, and he decided to run for office. At the age of twenty-eight, he was elected lieutenant governor on the Republican ticket in 1860. In 1862, he was elected to Congress, and he served three terms in Washington. From 1875 to 1879 he served as state senator. He was elected to the Minnesota house in 1886 as a Farmers' Alliance leader, and he served again in the state senate from 1891 to 1895. Widely recognized as a rousing orator, Donnelly was criticized by some who regarded him as ambitious, unstable, and a hopeless visionary. Consistent with his reputation as a visionary were

Ignatius Donnelly. Detail from a group photo of the state officials and the clerks of Minnesota in 1860. (Courtesy of the Minnesota Historical Society)

his writings. He wrote several novels, of which *Caesar's Column: A Story of the Twentieth Century* (1891) demonstrated an eerie capacity to anticipate what America would be like in 1980, visualizing airships and future communications systems in Jules Verne-like fashion.

When Donnelly returned to the house in 1897, he was serving in the same legislative session with Stockwell for a second time. Each had served in 1891—Donnelly in the senate, Stockwell in the house. Now they were in the same chamber. The men worked closely during the session though at times they parried good-naturedly. In the election for speaker, Stockwell voted for Donnelly and Donnelly for Stockwell. But the Republicans controlled the house, and their candidate, J. D. Jones, was chosen speaker by a wide margin.

Stockwell was eager to go to work when the Thirtieth Legislature convened on January 4, 1897. He had missed the capitol. To his dismay, soon after the house had been organized, he found that a recess of three days was in store for Saturday, Sunday, and Monday, January 16, 17, and 18. With the session just getting under way! Theoretically, newly established committees would work during the three-day recess, but as Stockwell and his colleagues knew full well, the members all would go home and no work would be done. Stockwell, C. F. Staples, and Jacob F. Jacobson decided to keep school in session. As reported in the *Pioneer Press* for Saturday, January 16:

"The three bad boys wouldn't let them out." (*St. Paul Pioneer Press*, January 16, 1897)

The only feature about yesterday's session of the House was the adjournment. And when it was all over the House discovered that it was due to gather itself together again this morning at 10:00 o'clock, instead of having taken a three days vacation from its arduous labor, as it supposed it was doing when it voted to knock off work for the day. This blasting of hopes was due to Messrs. Staples, who was in the chair, and Jacobson and Stockwell, who worked the floor end of the deal. It is to be hoped that today's session will save at least a half an hour on the last night of the session, although there is nothing in experience to justify the hope.

Stockwell had been named to the committees on education, insurance, prison labor, crimes and punishments, and taxation. In his campaign, he had singled out as a major issue a provision in the General Statutes of 1878 that exempted mines from taxation when not in operation. Such favoritism he saw as totally unfair. He would seek its repeal if elected. The Republicans controlled the legislature. Many of them felt beholden to the steel industry and favored maintaining the status quo. Other Republicans were more evenhanded. Working with the latter, in particular with Republican Edward E. Smith of Minneapolis, chairman of the Committee on Taxation, Stockwell accomplished his purpose. Smith introduced HF30 on January 13. Stockwell kept to the background and succeeded in gaining repeal of the exemption.[6]

On January 12, Stockwell offered a resolution calling for endorsement by the house of a bill pending before the U.S. Senate that provided for the submission of a constitutional amendment to permit the election of United States senators by popular vote, and calling upon Minnesota's senators to work and vote for its passage. His resolution was adopted.

On January 14, Stockwell introduced a bill, just as he had six years earlier, providing for weekly payment of wages by certain corporations. Again the measure was referred to committee and indefinitely postponed.

On January 15, Stockwell introduced HF63, a bill to amend Section 156 of the penal code providing that "murder in the first degree is punishable by death." Stockwell's proposal called for doing away with capital punishment and making life imprisonment the punishment for murder in the first degree. Stockwell's bill was referred to the Committee on Crimes and Punishment; action of the house on a separate measure foreshadowed the fate of this proposal.

In 1897 in Minnesota, the death penalty was imposed by hanging. Every county "cared for" its own criminals. A. F. Ferris, representative of Brainerd, had introduced HF1, the first bill before the house, to change the system. There would be no more hangings in the county seats. Stillwater, site of the state penitentiary, would become the sole situs for executions.

The *St. Paul Pioneer Press* for February 6, 1897, covered the debate in the house:

Mr. Ferris said that the bill had the endorsement of the board of prison managers. "We had a hanging at Brainerd last summer and I think that any member who lives in a town where they have had this experience will favor this bill," said Mr. Ferris. Mr. [Henry] Johns substantiated this statement by a reference to the experience of St. Paul when Ermisch and Wonigkeit were hanged, and 10,000 or 15,000 people gathered about the court house when the last penalty of the law was being executed.

Mr. Stockwell opposed the bill. He said it was a silent yet eloquent argument in favor of his bill to abolish capital punishment. "The gentleman from Brainerd says that that city wants no more judicial murders," he continued. "What has Stillwater done that this disgrace should be put upon her? I would no more take a child of mine to live in Stillwater if this bill passes than I would lead him into the jaws of Hades. Why should the warden of the penitentiary be made the State's hangman? The warden is opposed to the passage of the bill because it would destroy his influence among the convicts. If capital punishment is a deterrent from crime, why should it not be executed in the place where crime occurs? It will be a dangerous policy to introduce this punishment into the penitentiary among men susceptible to influences of this character. The infliction of the death penalty ought to be removed from the cities but it should not be taken to Stillwater."

HF1 passed with sixty-five yeas and eighteen nays. Donnelly was among those who voted in the affirmative.

On February 9, Stockwell's proposal calling for the elimination of capital punishment, favored by a majority of his committee, came before the full house on special order. The *Pioneer Press* on February 10, 1897, reported:

The debate was marked by one of the best speeches that have been made in support of any measure during the present session. Indeed old members say that Mr. Stockwell's defense of his bill was the best argument in favor of the abolishment of capital punishment that has been made for a great many sessions, and the proposition has been up for discussion biennial-ly. Mr. Stockwell opened the debate, regretting the lack of elo-quence to plead for a larger civilization, for the breaking of one link in the chain that binds us to our savage ancestry. In answer to the argument that capital punishment is in the inter-est of the preservation of society, he claimed that instead of being a protection it was a positive destroyer. Society has the right to protect itself but it should see to it that the means employed do not defeat the very end. In answer to the argument that capital punishment is a deterrent of crime, Mr. Stockwell insisted that it is a developer of crime. He referred to the indig-nation meeting held at Stillwater on Monday evening when a committee was appointed to urge the defeat of the bill which recently passed the house providing for executions at the peni-tentiary.

"We must look at this question from the viewpoint of the criminal," said he, "if that is possible, and not from the view-point of honorable, reputable members of society. We should look at it through the eyes of the man capable of committing murder. The coin of their character has been greatly debased. How is it to be raised? By further debasing it?"

Mr. Stockwell quoted at some length from specialists in crim-inology, and read a number of newspaper extracts detailing crimes committed in the very shadow of the gallows, in support of his position on both phases of the argument. He drew a fur-ther lesson from the crime of Harry Hayward, claiming that the life imprisonment of Blixt had had much more of an influence for good than the execution of Harry Hayward, whose fiendish, abominable influence is going on and on corrupting the world. "If it had not been a capital punishment that man would have been convicted and behind the prison bars in four weeks," insisted Mr. Stockwell. He cited the five states, Maine, Michigan, Iowa, Wisconsin and Rhode Island, that have abol ished capital punishment and named many European coun-tries which have done the same thing. In answer to the argu-ment sometimes drawn from the Bible to support the adherents of the continuation of the practice, Mr. Stockwell said that there was nothing in the new dispensation to support them. He said that future generations would call this legislature blessed if they could rise above the influences and traditions that sur-rounded them and do away with the "infamous practice." He concluded by promising a continuation of the agitation until the question was finally settled in accordance with his position.

Judge Littleton opposed the bill as one of the minority of the committee which had reported it. He contended that it was not the duty of the legislature to legislate from sympathy. "This is called a barbaric relic," said he, "but if it is, it is the only barbaric relic that has found its way onto the statute books of every civilized nation . . . The gentleman who supports this bill as in the interests of a Christian civilization does so by quoting Tom Paine, the greatest infidel the world has ever known.

"He has referred to Blixt. I saw him the other day with his mouth full of tobacco running his engine in the penitentiary. A modern penitentiary is not regarded as much of a menace by the criminal. It is almost a palace. It is a credit to the warden who keeps it in the condition it is in, but it struck me as a very nice place for a summer resort where one might take his family and spend a few days . . . "

Mr. Stockwell closed the debate. He said that he was not actuated by sympathy or sentimentality but in his opinion capital punishment brutalizes and debases and from that springs murder. He answered Mr. Littleton's fling at Tom Paine very effectively by a reference to his firing the hearts of the patriots at Lexington, and steadying and staying the fainting courage at Valley Forge. He said it ill became an American to cast a slur upon Tom Paine. "If capital punishment deters from crime, why not enlarge its scope?" queried Mr. Stockwell. "We enjoy our present civilization in spite of it and not because of it." He quoted Warden Wolfer as saying that capital punishment did not amount to a snap of the fingers as deterrent from crime. The warden was a believer in the theory that the way to deal with capital offenders was to remove them from society and uproot the tares of sin and plant the flowers of love and peace within them.

The house rejected Stockwell's proposal with twenty-three ayes and seventy-three nays. Capital punishment was abolished in Minnesota fourteen years later in 1911.

On January 20, Stockwell reintroduced his bill to provide free textbooks and school supplies in the state's public schools. On March 17, it passed in the house and was sent to the senate.

On January 21, Stockwell made another push for the single tax. HF153 called for an amendment to Section 3 of Article 9 of the constitution by adding a provision permitting the people of the state or any county or city by majority vote to remove the tax levied on personal property or improvements or both. In support of the measure, Stockwell explained that the vote of the people would be taken upon petition of one percent of the voters. He pointed out that his bill was a copy of one recently passed by the New York Assembly and noted that Washington and Colorado would probably vote for such exemptions at the next elections in those states. Further, Ohio's governor had recommended the proposition in his last annual message. Adoption of the amendment would permit experiments in taxation, which Stockwell thought could hardly fail to achieve improvement over the present system. The system would remain in force for a term of years determined in the petition for a vote.[7] Stockwell's proposal was indefinitely postponed on February 9.

On January 28, Stockwell introduced HF242 relating to the taxation of railroad lands. The measure was, essentially, a reenactment of the so-called Anderson law passed by the 1895 legislature. But Stockwell feared the earlier law was fatally flawed because of a defect in the taking of the senate vote. Stockwell's measure was precautionary, aimed at preventing the possibility of the railroad's escaping taxes entirely if the courts agreed the Anderson law should be nullified. The opposition, admitting Stockwell's bill was introduced in good faith, did not wish to stir things up. The *St. Paul Pioneer Press* on February 10, 1897, reported on the previous day's debate. (Having left American Express Company, Stockwell faced no possible conflict of interest.):

> Mr. Stockwell asked that the bill be sent to the committee of the whole . . . In coming to the defense of his motion and measure, he said, "The gentleman is right when he says this bill was introduced in good faith. For ten years I have been supporting the taxation of railroad lands. The passage of this bill will not delay taxation a day. It may make it possible to tax these lands four years earlier than if the bill is rejected. We should serve notice on the railroads that we propose to enforce the Anderson law. This bill does not repeal that law. I have not consulted a single attorney who does not say that there is a cloud on the Anderson law. I am not sure that it will not be criminal negligence on our part not to pass this bill . . ."
>
> Mr. Stockwell went on to say that he had consulted one of the most eminent lawyers in the state and he had said that the cloud was there. "It makes no difference what the members of the house may say now," continued Mr. Stockwell, "and it is simply blind folly to attempt to maintain that there is no cloud on the Anderson law. It has already been detected. My only purpose is to say to the railroads that we propose to have the law enforced. The unseating of Mr. Day was brought about by the corporations to invalidate the Anderson bill, and it has cast the cloud upon it."
>
> Donnelly agreed with Stockwell, saying, "If the Anderson law is set aside and we fail to pass this bill, it will delay the question of taxing these lands at least five years, until another legislature can meet and another law be passed."
>
> But when the roll was called on Mr. Stockwell's motion to send his bill to the committee of the whole, the motion was lost 15 to 82.

On February 11, Stockwell offered HF416, calling for provision that public notice of application and opportunity for hearing must be given before a county auditor could recommend to the state auditor a reduction of taxes. The bill was referred to the Committee on Taxes and Tax Laws, which returned it with an unfavorable report. Stockwell opposed adoption of the report. He said his bill "was designed to correct an abuse that was growing to large proportions." Persons with "pull" were in the habit of getting an abatement through the exercise of political or other influence without any consideration of the merits of the case. He cited the case of a prominent politician who owned an extensive farm in Hennepin County. His farm was assessed at $65.00 an acre, and he worked through an abatement to $39.00. A man of color owning a truck farm adjoining the stock farm was assessed $112.00 an acre. HF416 was ultimately defeated, fifty-four to twenty-five, by vote of the house sitting as a committee of the whole.[8]

On March 29, Stockwell introduced HF967, a bill governing the disposition of unclaimed bank deposits. Under the proposal, on February 2 of each year, a treasurer or cashier of every bank would be required to deliver to the state treasurer a statement of the deposits whose owners had not deposited or withdrawn for twenty years. This would not apply to deposits made by persons known to the cashier to be living. The deposits would be turned over to the permanent school fund of the state. Stockwell's proposal was referred to the Banks and Banking Committee and there indefinitely postponed.[9]

Stockwell also took great interest in a proposal to expunge from the records of the hospital for the insane in Fergus Falls certain statements about Frank Hoskins said to be false and damaging. HF954 sought to correct the record to show that Hoskins had been committed illegally and was thereafter released on writ of habeas corpus.

Hoskins, whose bizarre behavior led to his commitment, had been the radical editor of a newspaper in Grant County. The court committing him based its decision on the report of examining physicians selected by Hoskins himself. The physicians determined he was sufficiently insane to need medical treatment. Hoskins subsequently gained his release in habeas corpus proceedings on the grounds that the 1893 act under which he had been committed was unconstitutional.

HF954 had been referred to the Committee on Hospitals for the Insane, of which Stockwell was a member. Joseph B. Kendall of the committee recommended to the house on April 8 that the bill be postponed indefinitely on the basis of the majority report. Stockwell moved as a substitute motion that the minority report be adopted. The *Pioneer Press* covered the proceedings:

> In support of the minority report, Mr. Stockwell said that the record at Fergus Falls hampered Mr. Hoskins in his literary work, preventing him from obtaining life insurance, and gave rise to some embarrassment in social intercourse. He had known Mr. Hoskins for seven years and did not deem him any more insane than any man on the floor. He was a radical whose habits of thought and expression were distinctly unfashionable . . . Henry Feig, who testified to a longer acquaintance with Hoskins than any of the other speakers, agreed. The principal allegation upon which Hoskins was adjudged insane was that he had brought the Bible into court to prove that certain men were usurers.
>
> Chairman Kendall of the committee said that even if the hospital record was wiped out, there would still remain the record in the probate and district courts. Mr. Kendall could not see that the record cast any stigma upon Mr. Hoskins, and if any wrong had been done, the attempt to right it should begin in the probate court. Mr. [Louis O.] Foss said that he had been abused by Mr. Hoskins when the latter ran a paper in Grant County, yet for this Mr. Foss was broad enough to take his side on the case on the floor.
>
> The house was evenly divided. On the question of adoption of the minority report the vote was 45 to 45, and on the adoption of the majority report, 45 to 46, so the house declined to adopt either and the matter was laid on the table.[10]

One issue stirring debate in the session of 1897 was where to locate a proposed new hospital for the insane. Minnesota already had three such hospitals; the legislature had determined that a fourth was needed. Stockwell, ever mindful of the need to be economical with the state's money, had not necessarily favored incurring the expense of constructing a fourth hospital, but the decision to build had been made. Now, the only question was whether the hospital should go to Anoka or Hastings, a city in Dakota County just five miles from Donnelly's home.

The legislature had established a commission to select the location of the hospital and implement the project. Initially, the commission chose Hastings; it reversed itself when a Mr. Hoper, one of the commissioners, changed his mind. A special joint committee of the legislature was established to conduct an inquiry into the reversal. The ensuing majority report of the committee favored Hastings, the commission's original selection, with the minority holding out for Anoka.

Feelings ran high during debate in the house on March 5. City pride and a boost for the economy of the winner were at stake. Stockwell, pitted against a famed orator, knew that, in this setting, Donnelly would pull out all the stops. So Stockwell elected to rely on economics in presenting the case for Anoka. He moved to have the minority report of the joint committee adopted and prefaced his argument in support of Anoka by saying that he was born at that place and his father was still an honored citizen of that community in which he had settled forty-one years earlier.

Taking up the question of geography, he said that with the hospital designed to accommodate the insane of the Twin Cities and the northeastern portion of the state, there could be no question of the advantages of Anoka. He said the majority of the commission gave its case away when it conceded the advantages of Anoka's geography, train facilities, and bricks. There was nothing in the stone proposition [Hastings supporters had offered to throw in a stone quarry], for the hospital would be built of brick on the cottage plan. Stockwell defended the character of the Anoka County soil and denied absolutely any low land on the Anoka site other than a twenty-acre meadow available for hay. He said that Hoper's initial vote for Hastings was brought about by the influence of an army comrade who lived at Hastings, but that no corruption in this change of vote had been found by a committee after a month's investigation.

On the question of sewage, Stockwell gave figures to show that the Anoka site could be drained easily and cheaply. The water supply at Anoka was adequate in quantity and quality. It cost sixty-five cents more per ton to take coal from Duluth to Hastings than to Anoka. The Fergus Falls hospital had, during the previous year, burned ten thousand tons of coal. With similar consumption at the new hospital, the location at Anoka would save in coal alone six thousand dollars a year, the interest on a hundred thousand.

In conclusion, Stockwell contended that in every essential respect the Anoka site was fully equal to the Hastings offering, while the geographical advantages and those of transportation facilities, passengers, and freight, made it on the whole far superior.[11]

Then it was Donnelly's turn:

> He sketched the history of Dakota County, one of the first three counties organized in the state, which had never received a gift of any character from the state.

He attacked the geographical argument as false in fact and false in logic, because the act of 1895 confined the selection to a point convenient to the Twin Cities.

"I want to wipe away one thing that has been said here," continued Mr. Donnelly. "It has been intimated that this Mr. Hoper who has sprung suddenly into ignominious fame is a Populist. I am sort of grandfather to all the Populists of this state, and I deny all responsibility for this man. If he is a Populist, he is a Populist as Judas Iscariot was a Christian."

Mr. Donnelly contended that the whole matter was one of the most infamous nefarious pieces of business that had ever disgraced the record of this state, and drew a pathetic picture of the disappointment of the people of Hastings when deprived of their prize after nine days' pride and happiness by a trickster, a knave as he characterized Mr. Hoper. Mr. Donnelly used all the colors of his oratorical palette in painting a wonderful word picture of the scenic beauty of the Hastings site and the view it commands . . . "a picture on which the eyes of God and his angels rest lovingly." One of the causes of insanity was monotony, and it would be effectually banished by placing the hospital at Hastings. "Now what have we at Anoka?" said the sage with a sardonic smile. "A sand bank with nothing to illumine it but Alvah Eastman [editor of the *Anoka Herald*]. Why, even white beans won't grow there. They will have to have a cemetery for the unfortunate who die, and unless there is a rich top dressing, they will refuse to rise even when Gabriel blows his horn. It would be absolute cruelty to minds diseased to send them to this place."[12]

After almost eight hours of debate, the house sustained the majority. Hastings had won and Anoka had lost. But the battle was not over. Governor David M. Clough vetoed the entire measure. The cities were right back where they started. Debate between losers continued in the house on March 30. As reported in the *St. Paul Pioneer Press* on March 31, Donnelly delved into English history:

"I have no hostility for Gov. Clough," he began, "and those who have expected me to attack him will be disappointed. We have been friends for years, although we have differed upon public matters. Neither have I any hostility for the good people of Anoka. I honor any community which stands up for its rights and strives to improve its condition. I honor the people of Anoka for the spirited and lively battle they have carried on for the fourth hospital for the insane. I have no ill feeling for any man on this floor and if the question was the same as that formerly presented to us, I would not blame any member for expressing by his vote his preference for Anoka on geographical or other grounds.

"But that is all past. If this veto is sustained it does not give the hospital to Anoka. That is manifestly impossible at this session. On the contrary, the question will enter the politics of the future to distract us. There is nothing to be gained by Anoka in defeating Hastings. It will only result in animosity and bad blood.

"The veto power in our constitution was a great mistake on the part of those who founded this state and made its constitution. It is a power that comes down from William the Norman and his despotism, when it was held that all power was lodged in the king. As parliament grew everything had to be submitted to the king, and unless he approved, no act of parliament could stand. This idea has become so modified that for 190 years no king or queen of England has ventured to exercise the veto power against parliament. The last instance was in 1717 when Queen Anne vetoed a scheme for the colonization of soldiers in Scotland. If the Queen of England should now venture to veto an act of parliament her dynasty would not last forty-eight hours.

"As our colonies grew into states they put into their constitutions the veto power, that relic of monarchial despotism, and yet eight of our states do not have it. They are Rhode Island, Delaware, Maryland, Virginia, North Carolina, South Carolina, Tennessee and Ohio. It is a relic of king-craft. In England it has become a mere form. Yet here we are met by the reality, where one gentleman, himself formerly a member of this legislature, but in no respect possessed of any great mental superiority over the members of this house, says in effect, 'I know more than all the rest of you. When the anointing oil was rubbed on my forehead I became possessed of divine guidance . . . '"

Mr. Donnelly then had read a communication from Anoka to a Minneapolis paper in which Gov. Clough was lauded to the skies for his veto message and was urged in the most incendiary language to club the legislature into line. Mr. Donnelly said that the language was the strongest argument he had yet heard for placing the hospital in Anoka.

In conclusion Mr. Donnelly argued that there was involved a question greater than the interest of Anoka or Hastings. If this bill was defeated, it meant that the insane wards of the state would be crowded into the present hospitals, already overcrowded, for two, three or four years longer. The rights of unfortunate humanity were involved, and he besought the legislature to deal justly with the unfortunate and helpless whom God had deprived of the thread of consecutive thought. "Those whom God has afflicted," he solemnly concluded, "let not man punish."

78

Then it was Stockwell's turn, and he rose as to close the argument. But it seemed best only to gently chide his friend:

He said that Mr. Donnelly on a previous occasion had found nothing good in England, but now he praised their institutions and abused our own. Referring to the letter from Anoka which Mr. Donnelly had read, he said that it was like a chapter from *Caesar's Column* and had certainly not originated at Anoka.

He said that he differed with many of his Anoka friends and did not believe in the necessity for another hospital. It was time for the state to stop building the large custodial hospitals and take up the detention hospital or county system in dealing with the insane. Nevertheless Anoka had some rights that the legislature was bound to respect. The legislative investigation suggested by the courts had been had and no corruption found.[13]

Two years later, Anoka prevailed. In the last week of the legislative session, Governor John Lind signed a bill providing for the erection of an insane asylum in Anoka while calling also for the purchase of a site in Hastings. Hastings had gained solace. Bitterness vanished, and there was no talk of bribery or corruption as had been the case earlier.[14]

Donnelly died on January 1, 1901, the first day of the twentieth century. Stockwell's admiration for him continued. In 1934 Stockwell headed a movement to preserve the Donnelly mansion as a historical shrine. But the dilapidated condition of the house placed it beyond repair.[15] On another occasion late in his own career, Stockwell paid special tribute to Donnelly as a debater:

I had the pleasure of serving in the legislature with Ignatius Donnelly, the most brilliant citizen of Minnesota. No one who worked with Donnelly in the legislative body could help recognizing his brilliance—the most formidable foe I ever saw in a public body, absolutely resourceful, a most remarkable debater, and it may not be amiss to tell you something of his ability as a contender.

The legislature of 1889 made an appropriation of $50,000 for a Minnesota exhibit at the Pan American Exposition at Buffalo. This appropriation had been made over the protest of Mr. Donnelly. At the end of two years they came back for another appropriation of $50,000. I would give a great deal if I could have a reproduction of Mr. Donnelly's criticism of the commissioner's expenditures. It was a marvelous piece of wit and sarcasm.

To show you something of his quality—he was opposing strenuously the additional appropriation whereupon Senator H. Kellogg of Stearns County made the statement that he believed that he could offer an amendment to the appropriation bill that would secure the support of the gentleman from Dakota County. "I move you, Sir, that a picture of the senator be painted and hung at the Minnesota Exposition Building of the Pan American centennial. If that is done, I believe the Senator will withdraw his opposition." Mr. Donnelly arose: "I wish to second the amendment of the gentleman from Stearns. I believe this should be done. But I would like to offer a further amendment. I think that the picture of the gentleman from Stearns should also be painted, and I would suggest, Mr. President, that it be painted with ears extended and further, Mr. President, I would suggest that it be hung in the stock department." That was the quality of his ability as a debater.[16]

References

1. Material here and following is based in part on Morison and Commager, *Growth of the Republic*, pp. 237-265; Blegen, *Minnesota*, pp. 389-390; and Carl H. Chrislock, *The Progressive Era in Minnesota* (St. Paul: Minnesota Historical Society, 1971), pp. 1-21.

2. Stockwell had been hoping for a son. He wrote his friend and client Albert Dollenmayer on the day before Beth's birth: "We expect 'Henry George' any day now and Mrs. Stockwell seems in excellent shape for the mal but of course I am more or less anxious." On May 10, he wrote again: "'Henry George' is another girl. Three times and out! Mrs. Stockwell and the little one are OK."

3. *Dictionary of American Biography*, 2:192.

4. *Legislative Manual*, 1897, pp. 416-17.

5. *Legislative Manual*, 1897, p. 496.

6. *History of Minneapolis and Hennepin County*, p. 495; *House Journal*, 1891, p. 44.

7. *St. Paul Pioneer Press*, January 22, 1897.

8. *St. Paul Pioneer Press*, March 14, 1897; *House Journal*, 1897, p. 901.

9. *St. Paul Pioneer Press*, March 30, 1897. Some fifty-five years later, the legislature of Massachusetts enacted an abandoned property law similar to Stockwell's proposal. His grandchildren received a small amount of money through the Massachusetts law.

10. *St. Paul Pioneer Press*, April 9, 1897. Attorney Benjamin Drake said of Stockwell years later: "All his life he has been fighting for minorities, fighting for the weak, for the underdog, and naturally if you wanted to find Mr. Stockwell at any given time, you had to look at the bottom of the heap for him."

11. *St. Paul Pioneer Press*, March 6, 1897.

12. *St. Paul Pioneer Press*, March 6, 1897.

13. *St. Paul Pioneer Press*, March 31, 1897.

14. *Minneapolis Journal*, April 18, 1899.

15. *Minneapolis Star*, October 19, 1934; *Minnesota History*, 16 (1935): 127.

16. Remarks, Complimentary Birthday Dinner, June 8, 1927.

Chapter 7

Anti-Imperialist

Like Walt Whitman, this man knows no boundary lines or distinctions of race . . .
In him all peoples have fused to one humanity.—E. Dudley Parsons

S tockwell dealt primarily with state and local issues in the 1891 and 1897 legislative sessions—a domestic agenda. But, by the end of the 1800s, the spirit of manifest destiny— belief that the United States, because of its economic and political superiority and rapidly growing population, should dominate the entire Western Hemisphere—was revived and expanded. For Stockwell, the importance of state and local issues paled to the implications of such a policy. Thus he would have deplored the stance of U.S. Senator Henry Cabot Lodge, who contended:

> From the Rio Grande to the Arctic Ocean there should be but one flag and one country . . . In the interests of our commerce . . . we should build the Nicaragua Canal, and for the protection of that canal and for the sake of our commercial supremacy in the Pacific, we should control the Hawaiian Islands and maintain our influence in Samoa. England has studded the West Indies with strong places which are standing menace to our Atlantic seaboard. We should have among those islands at least one strong naval station, and when the Nicaragua Canal is built, the island of Cuba . . . will become a necessity.[1]

These views were wholly repugnant to Stockwell. Yet more and more Republicans, including William McKinley and Theodore Roosevelt, were fully in accord, as were growing numbers of Democrats and Populists.

The Spanish-American War, declared, fought, and won in 1898, had its beginnings in 1895 when Cuban nationalists rose against Spain. Sympathy for the rebels' cause mounted in the United States with newspaper accounts of alleged Spanish atrocities. Relations between the United States and Spain grew tense, and on February 15, 1898, the battleship *Maine* was sunk in the

Havana harbor. The press fanned a public fervor. Spain and the United States were at war by April 25.

The war spread to the Pacific as Admiral George Dewey led his fleet to the Spanish Philippines. On May 1, he was victorious in the naval battle of Manila Bay, losing not a man. Manila capitulated, and the war ended with the signing of the Treaty of Paris on December 10, 1898. Spain withdrew from Cuba and ceded Guam, Puerto Rico, and the Philippines to the United States. The United States paid Spain an indemnity of twenty million dollars.

"The way we get the war news. The Manilla [sic] correspondent and the McKinley censorship." This cartoon appeared in *The Verdict*, August 21, 1899. (Courtesy of the Theodore Roosevelt Collection, Houghton Library, Harvard University)

The U.S. Senate ratified the treaty on February 6, 1899, but with only one vote more than the required two-thirds. A strong anti-imperialist sentiment remained in the Senate.

Emilio Aguinaldo, who had headed a revolt in the Philippines against Spain in 1896 and 1897, was in exile in Hong Kong when Dewey ousted the Spanish fleet at Manila Bay. With Dewey's help, Aguinaldo returned to the Philippines, reorganized

"Merely a Financial Investment: Don't blame the soldier—He is getting $15.60 per month and his canned beef for this." This cartoon appeared in *The Verdict*, September 17, 1900. (Theodore Roosevelt Collection, Houghton Library, Harvard University)

his forces, and liberated several towns south of Manila, in furtherance of Philippine independence, or so he thought. On behalf of his
country, Aguinaldo declared independence, but American troops in
Manila would not permit Filipino forces to enter the city. This was
betrayal in the eyes of Aguinaldo; earlier assurances from Dewey
and others of United States' support for Philippine independence
proved worthless. Filipino leaders refused to recognize U. S. sover-
eignty over the islands; the United States gave no weight to Filipino
claims of independence. Morison and Commager wrote of the
dilemma:

> The United States now found that it had purchased, for twenty
> million dollars, a first-class Filipino insurrection. For the
> Filipinos, who had been good Catholics for over three centuries,
> did not wish to be "uplifted and Christianized" by the Amer-
> icans; but when on February 4, 1899, Aguinaldo's troops disre-
> garded the command of an American sentry to halt, the United
> States Army undertook to "civilize them with a Krag." Before the
> Philippine insurrection was stamped out it had cost the United
> States almost as many lives as the Spanish War and more scan-
> dals; for a war between the white soldiers and semi-civilized
> men of color is something worse than what Sherman said it
> was. Within a short time the United States found itself doing in
> the Philippines precisely what it had condemned Spain for
> doing in Cuba. Soon stories of reconcentration camps and
> "water cures" began to trickle back to the United States, and
> public opinion, already highly skeptical of a venture dubious
> alike in origin, method and purpose, became inflamed. The re-
> sult was a vigorous anti-imperialism crusade which command-
> ed the support of men from all parties and all walks of life.[2]

Such was the climate when Stockwell decided to run for the
Minnesota Legislature again in 1898. This time he set his sights on
the senate.

Also on the stump again was John Lind. Born in
Sweden in 1854, Lind started out as a teacher and then became a
lawyer. He served three successive terms in Congress (1887-1893)
as a Republican, but as a believer in the free coinage of silver, he
was out of step with the party. In 1896 he ran for governor as a
fusion candidate, endorsed by Democrats, silver Republicans, and
Populists, but he was defeated by a mere 3,552 votes.[3]

In 1898, Lind was again the odds-on choice of Democrats,
Populists, and silver Republicans. Early that year, he had served
briefly with the Quartermaster Corps in the Spanish-American

War. He was nominated while still in uniform. As a candidate for governor, he maintained that the national issues, including free silver, had nothing to do with his campaign. But he spoke out against McKinley imperialism on the question of retention of the Philippines. On his second try for the governorship, Lind decisively defeated the Republican candidate, William Henry Eustis, former mayor of Minneapolis. The margin was 20,000 votes.[4]

Stockwell's district, the Forty-second, consisted of the Seventh, Eleventh, and Twelfth Wards in Minneapolis, the village of Edina, and the towns of Richfield, Bloomington, Eden Prairie, and Excelsior, all in Hennepin County. The Democratic-Populist candidate, Stockwell defeated Gustaf Theden, Republican incumbent, with 2,932 votes to Theden's 2,722. There were strong Republican majorities in both houses of the legislature, making his victory a personal triumph. The *Minneapolis Journal* gave this account of the election:

> Hennepin County elects two fusion and five Republican senators . . . Senator Gustaf Theden of Minneapolis, connected with the anti-department store agitation in the session of 1897, and known all over the state because of his connection with Henry Keller of Stearns County in the beet sugar matter, like Keller, is defeated for reelection. S. A. Stockwell, Democratic member of the House of 1897, will take his place in the senate. The district is heavily Scandinavian and it is not easy to account for Theden's defeat. Perhaps the explanation lies in the fact that, owing to the starting this fall of the beet sugar factory, he had little time to devote to his political canvass. Stockwell is perhaps the strongest Democrat in the district and has confidence there of men in all parties. The returns indicate that he will be elected by perhaps not more than 150 majority.[5]

Stockwell's joy in scoring an upset victory was short-lived. On December 26, 1898, Albert and Maud's oldest daughter, Ruth, died of peritonitis at the age of nine years, nine months. She had been stricken with appendicitis ten days earlier. Albert never fully recovered from the loss, and much later in life he told daughter Charlotte that he mourned for Ruth every day of his life. Christmas became a day he could hardly bear. Characteristically, he offered the following resolution in an attempt to give solace to a colleague whose child died not long after Ruth: "Resolved, That the Senate extends its sincere sympathy to Senator Batz in the loss of his little son."[6]

The senate convened on January 3, 1899. Stockwell was named to the Committee on Education, Taxes and Tax Laws,

Insurance, and Normal Schools, among other committees. He quickly assumed a leadership role, making nominations for officers and clerks, proposing resolutions and motions to expedite organization, and meeting with the governor and governor-elect in liaison sessions. Early indications that his role would be that of a leader proved to be the case. Governor Lind's biographer, George M. Stephenson, observed that

> while Republicans were in the firm majority, their leadership in the senate was generally lacking . . . Among the minority members was S. A. Stockwell of Minneapolis, a Democratic-Populist, who in a sense was the minority leader. He usually supported the governor's nominations and policies.[7]

John Lind had outlined his anti-imperialist view in his successful campaign. He saw the heightening of national fervor for expansion as a Wall Street means to divert public attention from internal problems crying out for remedy. In his message to the legislature on January 5, however, Governor Lind did not raise the subject. Stockwell from the beginning felt the Philippines question must be addressed. On January 19, a few days after the legislature had reelected Republican Cushman K. Davis to the U.S. Senate (Stockwell cast his vote for Democrat Towne), Stockwell proposed a resolution to be sent to Congress:

> WHEREAS, Governments derive "their just powers from the consent of the governed," and
> WHEREAS, The lands of a country belong of right to the people of that country, and
> WHEREAS, Any attempt on the part of this country to obtain possession of the Philippines by purchase or otherwise would be Un-American, dangerous to our institutions (in numerous ways, but especially to the menace of a large standing army) and worse than "criminal aggression;" therefore, be it
> RESOLVED by the Senate, the House concurring, that we call upon our United States Senators and respectfully request our Representatives in Congress to oppose vigorously any attempt on the part of this Government to govern the people of any other country on earth without the consent of the people of that country, or to subject them to our control in any way against their will; and be it further
> RESOLVED, That we believe it the province of this Government to assist in all proper ways the people of Cuba, Puerto Rico and the Philippines to at once establish self governing [sic] Republics.

The *St. Paul Pioneer Press*, on January 21, 1899, covered the senate proceedings:

In moving the adoption of his resolution, Senator Stockwell said that he felt that any appeal he could make would fall on deaf ears, although he believed that if senators stopped for sober second thought, they would favor the resolution. "I understand however," said Senator Stockwell, "that if Republican senators vote for the measure it would show a lack of confidence in the distinguished man they recently elected to the United States Senate.

"I believe, however, that the ear of the President of the United States is again close to the ground and that he has already heard the rumble of the consciences of the people protesting against the larceny of the lands of another people. I believe that the doctrine of expansion is the most dangerous proposition that has confronted this country during the past decade, and I want the privilege of recording my vote against it."

Democrats joined with Republicans to defeat Stockwell's resolution. The vote in the Senate was forty-eight to three, against. The *Minneapolis Journal* scoffed at Stockwell's efforts. The January 19 edition reported:

Senator Stockwell gave three cheers for Bryanism, populism and anti-expansionism and while he failed of applause he received much flattering attention from Republicans as no fewer than three strove for the honor of sending his resolution over on notice of debate.

The next day's paper reported:

Contrary to the expectations of most senators and much to the disgust of some of them, the Senate this morning discussed just what the disposition of acquired territory should be made by the Congress. Up to this time, the Senate has carried on its business with Senate-like decorum and without a family rumpus, but Senator Stockwell touched the Senate fireworks off today, and they flew for two hours while the rights and liberties of the distant Filipinos trembled in the balance.

This disposition of Senator Stockwell's resolution, lost 48 to 3, is understood to be a minority protest against the assumption of leadership on the part of the Hennepin senator and this opposition was made especially prominent as it was led by Senator Johnson (Nicollet), who is also a Populist, and was backed up by Senator Schaller and other Democrats.

Governor Lind had favored the Stockwell resolution, and the country at large was becoming increasingly uneasy about the war. With newspapers publishing casualties among Americans engaged in fighting against the Filipinos, protest mounted. In Minnesota the opposition took concrete form in the demand for the speedy return from the Philippines of the Thirteenth Minnesota Volunteer Infantry. The longing for home by soldiers having served more than the full year of their enlistment and the desire of friends to see them took the form of demands on the governor, congressmen, and senators to make every effort for the issue of return orders. In a communication to the legislature on April 17, 1899, Governor Lind expressed disappointment that he was unable to report a definite time for the return of the regiment. He had telegraphed President William McKinley but received no reply. He left it to the legislature to determine what action should be taken.[8]

In furtherance of Governor Lind's request, Senator Peter McGovern offered a resolution whereby the president would be requested "if compatible with the public interest," to communicate to the legislature, if in session, otherwise to the governor of the state, the purpose of the general government with reference to the retention of the Thirteenth Minnesota Regiment at Manila.[9]

Heated debate on the resolution followed the next day, with senators Stockwell and P. Fitzpatrick "fiercely attacking" the McKinley administration:

> The two democrats recited with vigor the anti-expansion, freedom-for-all arguments at present so often used by the minority party. Senator Stockwell then moved the adoption of the McGovern resolution in lieu of the Military Affairs Committee report which opposed any further communication with Washington. On an aye and nay vote the McGovern resolution was killed, the minority voting for it with the exception of one senator and the majority against it.[10]

The regiment finally returned to the United States in August 1899. On October 12, President McKinley was on hand for a huge welcoming celebration in Minneapolis. In his speech, he sought to justify his policy of acquiring territory. Governor Lind, the second principal speaker, made no direct reference to the presence of the president of the United States. But he touched the hearts of a volunteer regiment reluctantly engaged in a war of conquest:

> By our growth and development the mission of the American volunteer soldier has come to an end. For purposes of conquest and subjugation he is unfit, for he carries a conscience as well as a gun. The volunteer soldier has always stood for self-government, liberty and justice. With your generation he will pass the stage of our national life. His fame and his example will continue the heritage of our people—the theme of story and song. May the spirit which has actuated him ever guide our people, and temper the strength of the nation which has outgrown him, with the eternal principles for which he has fought and died.[11]

Filipino troops controlled the entire archipelago except for Manila in early 1899, and the conflict, marked by fighting in the Central Luzon Plain, continued until the summer. Later, Aguinaldo retreated into the northern mountains, leading the fighting from there much as César Augusto Sandino would in Nicaragua against the same adversary some twenty-five years later. Bitter guerrilla warfare continued until 1902. The United States declared an end to the "insurrection" in that year, but outbreaks of fighting persisted.

Stockwell's commitment to the Filipino cause was overriding. He was determined to proceed no matter what. Voted down in the senate, he moved laterally to the grass roots. He moved in good company, as Morison and Commager have described:

> Never in our history had any reform movement attracted a more distinguished group of supporters than that which rallied to the banner of anti-imperialism. Party lines were disregarded: Republicans like Senators [G. F.] Hoar and [George F.] Edmunds and speaker [T. B.] Reed joined hands with Democrats like Cleveland and Bryan, Ben Tillman, and John G. Carlisle. Samuel Gompers spoke for labor, and Andrew Carnegie paid the bills. The press was represented by E. L. Godkin of *The Nation* and [Samuel] Bowles of the Springfield *Republican*. President [Charles W. of Harvard] Eliot spoke for the intellectuals of New England . . . Philosophers like William James . . . social workers like Jane Addams, all worked together for a common cause. Effective aid came from the men of letters. Mark Twain was deeply embittered by our conquest of the Philippines, and in his letter "To the Person Sitting in Darkness," he charged McKinley with "playing the European game" of imperialism and suggested that Old Glory should now have "the white stripes painted black and the stars replaced by the skull and crossbones."[12]

Boston was the center of anti-imperialist activity. The Anti-Imperialist League had been founded there in November 1898, and Senator Hoar of Massachusetts was the national leader. Although a Republican, he strenuously opposed the administration's Philippine policy. His speeches and those of former Secretary of the Interior Carl Schurz were widely circulated by state and local organizations seeking to tell the side of the story disdained by the press.

Stockwell was one of the organizers and became the first president of the Anti-Imperialist League of Minnesota.[13] He had organized mass meetings protesting the Spanish-American War, and, thereafter, the massacre of Filipinos. When the thirty-first legislative session adjourned on April 18, 1899, Stockwell turned all his energies to the anti-imperialist cause.

On October 17 and 18, 1899, Stockwell attended a national anti-imperialist conference in Chicago, called to consolidate many United States organizations against the administration's policy in the Philippines. Carl Schurz was the principal speaker. Industrialist Edward Atkinson of Boston, a consistent advocate of sound money who was pacifist and anti-imperialist, was among those present. The *Minneapolis Journal* for October 23, 1899, described Stockwell's plans for a follow-up:

> "Antis" of Minneapolis have not abandonded their intention of holding a big public mass meeting to protest against the administration's Philippine policy . . . It is proposed to import [as speaker] some one anti of national fame . . . S. A. Stockwell says that a Minneapolis branch of the Anti-Imperialist League of America will soon be organized and that it is hoped to have one in every ward. Owing to the fact that the bulk of the influential newspapers of the country are upholding the administration's policy, the antis have difficulty gettng their side of the case before the people. So they intend to hold numerous public meetings and distribute a vast amount of literature of their color, including 1,000,000 copies of the speech Carl Schurz delivered in Chicago.
>
> As an illustration of the way this expansionist question is creating a new line, Mr. Stockwell says that forty percent of the delegates to the Chicago conference were McKinley men in 1896. Thirty percent were gold Democrats and the rest were Bryan men. Edward Atkinson, who had serious doubts in 1896 as to the mental soundness of any man who would for a moment consider an argument in favor of free silver, now considers the standard question of the utmost insignificance compared with that of imperialism. Mr. Stockwell and other ardent silvermen went to Atkinson and asked him what he would do if Bryan were nominated on an anti-expansion and silver platform. He replied that a little question like that of the monetary standard could be settled afterwards, that the first duty was to put out the fire in the house, and that he would be for Bryan on the anti-imperialism issue, silver or no silver.

Immediately after Stockwell's announcement appeared in the press, an opposition imperialist group announced plans to "copper" all meetings of the antis.[14]

Stockwell forged ahead to implement the plans mapped out in Chicago. He sought John P. Altgeld, as speaker at a mass meeting in late January 1900. Altgeld was unable to attend, but the Anti-Imperialist League of Minnesota did hold its first public meeting at the Odd Fellows Hall on February 17. Sidney M. Owen and Colonel George C. Ripley discussed "What Should Be Done with the Philippines?"[15]

The Minneapolis branch of Minnesota's Anti-Imperialist League met on March 29. Stockwell's hand is clearly visible in the resolution adopted at this meeting. The *Minneapolis Journal* displayed scorn in the heading of its March 30, 1900, story:

PRESIDENT WILL FEEL BADLY

Minneapolis antis don't approve of the presidential policy of treating bushwhackers in the Philippines. At the last meeting of the local Anti-Imperialist League the following resolutions were adopted and a copy sent to President McKinley and to each senator and representative from the states.

WHEREAS the peoples of the Philippine Islands are engaged in a just war of defense against the "criminal aggression" of a foreign power;

WHEREAS the said people who are defenders of their honor against such aggression are belligerent in the full meaning of the term; and,

WHEREAS recent news from the said islands . . . indicates that resistance by the Filipino people is not confined to one small part of one small tribe or one island, but is coextensive with the advance of the American forces; although such resistance is by smaller bodies of Filipino soldiers than formerly; and

WHEREAS it has been seriously stated from credible sources near the president that he intends to treat such small bodies of Filipino troops as bandits, and when any of them are taken prisoner, to cause them to be tried before a military tribunal on the charge of murder;

THEREFORE, be it

RESOLVED, by the Anti-Imperialist League of Minneapolis that we protest against this proposed added adoption of Spanish methods by our present chief executive, and demand in the sacred memories of Sumter, Marion and other revolutionary guerilla heroes, humane and civilized treatment of Filipino captives.

RESOLVED further, that a copy of these resolutions be sent to our representatives in both branches of Congress, with the request that they present them to their respective bodies and that a copy be sent likewise to the President.

Stockwell and his fellow members worked closely with their Massachusetts counterparts throughout the spring of 1900. An editorial in the *Minneapolis Journal* for May 23, 1900, described the activity:

The secretary of the Anti-Imperialist League in Boston announces the receipt of a letter from the Minneapolis League detailing the hard work the antis are doing here. They have distributed about a hundred thousand copies of anti-imperialist literature, including Senator Hoar's speech and "many conversions" are reported. The secretary announces that Boston will circulate hundreds of thousands of Hoar's speeches all through the campaign.

These anti-imperialist league people have set forth their creed as opposition to the retention of the Philippines and favoring the setting up of Aguinaldo as president of the mystical Filipino republic which never existed and cannot exist, and of opposition to militarism meaning opposition to maintaining the army up to 100,000 men, on the ground that a considerable number of them are used to defeat the treasonable efforts of their precious Aguinaldo to expel the United States from Luzon and the archipelago.

They declared also that there is terrible danger that the increase by Congress of the army . . . will fasten us all very tightly and hopelessly in the fetters of "Caesarism" . . .

How effectively the federal despotism has suppressed free speech is indicated by the mass meetings of the antis in Minneapolis at which they avow their sympathy with the enemies of our country and denounce the national government in abusive terms. So stifled is popular freedom that these oppressed ones on every public occasion demand the substitution of the Tagal flag for the Stars and Stripes in the Philippines. These oppressed citizens, who have been doing all along their best to keep Aguinaldo in the field against our forces, complain loudly of the cost of the Tagal revolt, ignoring the fact that the continued expense is due largely to their encouragement and aid and comfort to the rebels.

But it was up to Mark Twain, as so often with comment on a delicate issue, to illuminate the question of right to dissent during an unpopular war. Speaking at the Lotus Club in New York on March 23 1901, he told how a clergyman had publicly attacked him:

"He said that if I had my just deserts I should be dangling from a lamp post somewhere . . . He hadn't anything personal against me, except that I was opposed to a political war, and he said I was a traitor." Then Twain added, "It would be an entirely different question if the country's life was in danger, its existence at stake; then we would all come forward and stand by the flag, and stop thinking about whether the nation was right or wrong; but when there is no question that the nation is any way in danger, but only some little war away off, then it may be that on the question of politics the nation is divided, half patriot and half traitors, and no man can tell which from which."[16]

In the November 1900 elections, John Lind was narrowly defeated in his run for reelection. Stockwell's term was four years, and he returned to the senate as a holdover for the 1901 session, picking up where he left off. He offered the following resolution on February 16:

WHEREAS, the words of the Declaration of Independence, "We hold these truths to be self-evident, that all men are created equal, that they are endowed by their Creator with certain inalienable rights, that among these are life, liberty, and the pursuit of happiness. That to secure these rights governments are instituted among men, deriving their just powers from the consent of the governed. That whenever any form of government becomes destructive of these ends, it is the right of the people to alter or abolish it, and to institute new government, laying its foundations upon such principles and organizing its powers in such form as to them shall seem most likely to effect their safety and happiness," are as true today as when given to the world by our forefathers, and

WHEREAS, Under the Constitution of the United States the Federal government has no power to rule over colonial dependencies, but is restricted in its operations to states as integral parts of the Union and to territories intended for future states, and

WHEREAS, the expansion of our commerce has not been and cannot be dependent upon the adoption of a policy of imperialism involving the subjugation and annexation of Asiatic colonies, but would in the end be hindered by such policy.

THEREFORE, Be it resolved by the Senate, the House concurring, that we are opposed to the retention of the Philippine Islands by the United States and call upon our Senators and Representatives in Congress to support a resolution assuring the Filipinos of our purpose to consent to their independence as soon as a stable government shall be established by them, and toward the prompt establishment of such government we pledge our friendly assistance.

Senator E. T. Young moved that the resolution be laid upon the table. His motion was upheld, yeas thirty-six and nays four.

On March 10, 1902, Stockwell tried again:

WHEREAS, There appeared in the *Minneapolis Sunday Tribune* of March 9, 1902, a Republican newspaper, an interview with a Republican congressman in which he says among other things, the following: "But the Filipino is at heart in a state of rebellion against the United States authority, and he always will be. You never hear of any disturbances in northern Luzon, and the secret of its pacification is, in my opinion, the secret of the pacification of the archipelago. They never rebel in northern Luzon because there isn't anybody there to rebel. That country was marched over and cleaned out in a most resolute manner. The good Lord in heaven only knows the number of Filipinos that were put under the ground, for our soldiers took no prisoners; they kept no records; they simply swept the country, and wherever or however they came upon a Filipino they killed him. The women and children were spared, and may now be noticed in disproportionate numbers in that part of the island. The Spaniards, differently constituted, would go out after a band of insurgents for a day's journey, and then get back to barracks, while our soldiers have pursued them persistently, and for that reason our conquest of the archipelago is very much more effective than that of Spain ever was. I look for no real peace short of such measures as those pursued in northern Luzon."

"But will the moral sense of the American people stand a policy of extermination?"

"I dare say. The American people have stood it with the Indian, although today we are treating him pretty well; he is a 'star boarder,' and we are supplying him with schools and all sorts of things he has no use for. We are planting him, as far as possible, in the lands that we do not wish for ourselves. If American investors find property they want in the Philippines, I do not think they would be embarrassed by any sentiment at home against sweeping off the Filipinos. Our vigorous policy of maintaining law and order would never be designated extermination; party platforms and party organs would choose some gentle term; but as I gauge the American sentiment, there was no real opposition to the course pursued by Funston and others in northern Luzon, and there would not be to a similar course in the rest of archipelago."

AND WHEREAS, The above statement is corroborated by undoubted evidence and is a true statement of the facts, and

WHEREAS, This damnable war of conquest and extermination is costing this government hundreds of lives and more than $90,000,000 annually (enough to almost build a trans-continental railroad) which is taken almost wholly from the toiling of masses of this country, and,

WHEREAS, But one result can follow the continuance of this war, namely, the destruction of liberty at home and abroad;

THEREFORE, Be It Resolved, That we call upon the President of this Republic as Commander-in-Chief of the Army and Navy to end this cruel war, assuring the Filipino patriots that it is our purpose to grant them independence.

A vote was taken on March 11. Again Stockwell lost, but this time there were twelve yeas and twenty-two nays.

The Filipinos risking their lives for the right to govern themselves were finally repulsed. The United States held possession of the Philippines until 1946.

Aftermath

The struggle of Stockwell and other anti-imperialists was not in vain. Their striving imbued Minnesotans with a sense of fairness and decency—a sense of "justice-injustice"—that is stronger than ever today. A noteworthy example can be seen in their reaction to overkill on the part of the Reagan administration in 1988. In March of that year the Sandinistas in Nicaragua under Daniel Ortega were engaged in bitter fighting with contra forces near the border of Honduras. Honduras had long served as a contra sanctuary. Reportedly, several Sandinistas crossed into Honduras in hot pursuit. President Reagan responded by rushing U.S. troops to the Honduran-Nicaraguan border. Many believed that Reagan sought any excuse to invade Nicaragua.

Within a matter of hours, Minnesota peace groups rose in outrage as one. Their concerted action was made possible by the formation five years before of the Twin Cities Peace and Justice Coalition. More than one hundred organizations belonged to the coalition, which in turn belonged to a national coalition called Mobilization for Survival. In Minnesota the coalition has become the clearinghouse for information on demonstrations and boycotts, twice a month sending a calendar of events to its members.

On Thursday, March 17, 1988, when two coalition members—Women Against Military Madness and the Pledge of Resistance—wanted to organize a demonstration against U.S. troop movements, they were able to call key organizers, who could activate prearranged telephone networks. The cry was on.

Hyman Berman, professor of history at the University of Minnesota, has affirmed that quick reaction by Minnesota peace groups to news of U.S. troops maneuvers in Honduras reflected a social justice tradition traceable to the state's reaction to the Spanish-American War. This tradition, coupled with the increasing sophistication of the coalition and ability to mobilize members on short notice, made the state one of just a few in the country where demonstrations could be held almost instantaneously.

Berman called the response part and parcel of the deep, ingrained, progressive, populist tradition that is an integral part of the political culture of the state. All that is needed to mobilize it is some external event. In his view, even when crises do not prompt widespread participation, the groups seem to survive. Thus, the Women's International League for Peace and Freedom, the Fellowship of Reconciliation, Unitarian-Universalist groups, and Catholic peace groups have been active in Minnesota for decades. The emergence of the populist movement and the anti-imperialists around the time of the Spanish-American War was the first major expression of Minnesota's desires to restrain national aggression. In Minnesota, Berman affirms, there has long been a sense of justice-injustice that transcends national boundaries.[17]

References

1. Morison and Commager, *Growth of the Republic*, 2:323.

2. Morison and Commager, *Growth of the Republic*, 2:338.

3. Here and below, George M. Stephenson, *John Lind of Minnesota* (Minneapolis: University of Minnesota Press, 1935), pp. 105-158.

4. *Legislative Manual*, 1899.

5. *Minneapolis Journal,* November 10, 1898. The newspaper also reported that Frank Wheaton, a black man elected to the house from the Forty-second District, was "the first man of his race to be so honored in the history of the state."

6. *Senate Journal,* 1899, p. 424.

7. Stephenson, *John Lind,* p. 163.

8. Stephenson, *John Lind,* pp. 172-74.

9. *Minneapolis Journal,* April 17, 1899.

10. *Minneapolis Journal,* April 18, 1899.

11. *Minneapolis Journal,* October 12, 1899; Stephenson, *John Lind.* p 175.

12. Morison and Commager, *Growth of the Republic,* 2:339.

13. Dorothy Walton Binder, "The Stockwells of Minneapolis," *New Republic,* December 22, 1937.

14. *Minneapolis Journal,* October 31, 1899.

15. *Minneapolis Journal,* February 16, 1900.

16. Samuel Eliot Morison, Frederick Merck, and Frank Freidel, *Dissent in Three American Wars* (Cambridge: Harvard University Press, 1970), p. 95. The quotation from Mark Twain appears in John Elderkin, et al., eds., *Dinner Speeches at the Lotus Club* (New York: Printed for the Lotus Club, 1911), pp. 14-15.

17. *Star Tribune,* March 19, 1988.

Chapter 8

A Forecast of Progressivism

T he progressive movement has been called a "diffuse reform effort of the first two decades of the twentieth century." Diffuse because it had supporters in both major political parties. Concerned Republicans and Democrats alike could see the effects of a distressing, unsavory shift in the country's direction; they read in the newspapers, particularly in the columns of the muckraking journalists, of deplorable conditions; on Sundays they listened to sermons about the country's woes, about the slums of the cities, the hazards of dangerous machinery for factory workers, child labor, corruption of the political process at all levels, the waste of natural resources, and about the displacement of idealistic values by a selfish materialism.[1]

The movement's goals were also diffuse, ranging from prohibition, woman suffrage, and abolition of child labor to antitrust legislation, regulation of industry, workmen's compensation, and tax reform. So disparate were the movement's objectives that the very designation movement, typically linked with a single cause such as antislavery, seems a misnomer. In any event, in broad terms, the movement sought departure from the laissez-faire politics of the nineteenth century. The government must be made more democratic; honesty must be restored to government. And government must be made more effective in correcting the imbalances of power that large-scale industrialism produced.[2]

Historian Carl Chrislock has linked the beginning of the progressive movement in Minnesota to John Lind's governorship:

> The inauguration of Governor Lind on January 2, 1899, heralded the progressive era in Minnesota. Lind's opening message to the legislature and people has been called "an inventory of Minnesota life and problems at the turn of the century." It also served as a blueprint for reform that influenced the policies of

both Lind's immediate successors in the governorship, Republican Samuel R. Van Sant and Democrat John A. Johnson.

The most urgent recommendations in Lind's message dealt with taxation. The new governor called for an immediate increase in the railroad gross earnings tax, a proposal that several previous legislative sessions had debated without adopting. He also requested that the legislature create a special commission to formulate a comprehensive reform of the existing tax structure. His other proposals included a reappraisal of Minnesota's antitrust statutes; the future retention by the state of title to mineral rights in state lands transferred to private ownership; the establishment of a board of control to supervise state institutions; and an investigation of the merits of the direct primary, the initiative, the referendum, and the recall.[3]

John Lind, governor from 1899 to 1901. (Courtesy of the Minnesota Historical Society)

Also called for was legislation for a different method of caring for the insane, the prohibition of free passes on railroad trains, and the free printing by the state of school textbooks.

Democrats, Republicans, and Populists praised Governor Lind's message—in the view of many the best statement ever delivered by an incoming governor. Stockwell, beaming approval, loudly applauded at every pause. With uniform acceptance, hopes were high that the 1899 legislative session would be one of solid achievement. This did not prove to be the case. The Republicans held clear majorities in both houses and were simply unwilling to cooperate in the passage of remedial legislation that would inure to the benefit of a highly popular fusionist governor. The minority was rendered nearly powerless in the terms of furthering Lind's program. For the most part, the legislature ignored his demands. In a comprehensive review of the 1899 session, W. W. "Jerry J." Jermane of the *Minneapolis Journal*, perhaps the ablest political reporter of his day, calculated that of twenty-one proposals advanced by Lind, only four were approved by the legislature. The session was deemed more remarkable for the important bills killed than for those passed:

The greatest political mistake of the session was the wholesale slaughter of all bills looking to increase revenue for the state. At the head of the list of bills stands the gross earnings bill and after it came the bills increasing the revenues from sleeping car, telegraph, telephone and other companies.[4]

Jacob F. Jacobson, tireless Republican ally of Lind in the house, introduced a bill to increase the railroad gross earnings tax from three to four percent. Passed in the house on February 7 with but five votes against, it was killed in the senate in a close vote. With defeat of the measure so clearly in the interest of the railroads, talk of bribery was widespread. Fair-minded members of both parties and informed citizens throughout the state were outraged. Lind stated publicly that he believed the corrupt use of money brought about the bill's defeat in the senate. The *Luverne Herald* attributed defeat to a "damnably rotten railroad lobby and the men who served its purpose for their own private gain."[5]

Jacob F. Jacobson. (Photo by Zimmerman. Courtesy of the Minnesota Historical Society)

The *Minneapolis Journal*, the only major daily to support the bill, was suspicious. Its review of the session took note of a poker game at St. Paul's Hotel Ryan, reportedly financed by the railroad lobby. Players "from one of the houses," who had never seen three thousand dollars in their lives and whose stakes were typically penny-ante, watched one player win that amount in a single jackpot. The *Journal* asked why Senator J. T. McGowan, a Democrat from Hennepin County who had come out strongly in favor of the bill, absented himself from the senate chamber the day of the vote.

The *Journal* did not cite hard evidence of wrongdoing in connection with the senate vote on the railroad tax but, relying on unnamed sources, described the defeat of a bill that would have increased taxes for the lumber industry:

> After the bill had been safely lodged in committee, a messenger from the legislature combine was sent post haste to Minneapolis with word that for a petty $2,000 the matter would be dropped. A meeting of certain leading lumbermen was called and the proposition submitted. There was great difference of opinion, some thinking the sum should be paid, others objecting to the proposed "hold up." Finally, one of the veteran lumbermen got up and said:

"If I were driving through a forest in the winter, with a carcass of beef on my sled, and were pursued by wolves, I am certain that I would throw off one or two quarters if by so doing I could save the rest and myself. I favor paying the money."

This statement struck the assembly in the end as being about the right view to take, and so it was arranged that the money should be paid . . . The bill never saw the light of day.[6]

Such obstacles confronted honorable senate members. Jermane gave Stockwell high marks for his performance in session, seeing him a leader and one of the ablest speakers. He noted Stockwell's concern for his constituents, for example, that he was instrumental in getting legislation passed whereby the Hennepin County commissioners reimbursed Excelsior for $2,500 incurred in the construction of a bridge across St. Alban's Bay on Lake Minnetonka. While not referred to in Jermane's analysis, Stockwell served as liaison between the community and the senate. He offered this resolution to be printed in the *Senate Journal*, from a citizens group favoring an increase in the railroad gross earnings tax:

WHEREAS, Since taxes are "the legally enforced contributions of individuals and corporations for meeting the necessary and general expenses of the state," it becomes the first duty of every just government to so adjust such contributions that each individual and corporation shall pay in proportion to the amount of property owned; and

WHEREAS, In the State of Minnesota, the owners of railway property are not taxed to the extent or in the manner that other property holders are taxed; and to mitigate this wrong, in part, and to the end that taxation may be more nearly apportioned and equalized upon all property and among all persons, according to their ability to pay, we, businessmen and taxpayers of Hennepin County, Minnesota, do hereby

Resolved, That the railroad gross earnings tax as now provided by law, should be increased from the present rate of three (3) percent to at least four (4) percent; such increase will not then be sufficient to equalize the discrepancy that now prevails in the tax laws between the owners of railway and the owners of other property.

Resolved, Further, that the bill pending in the Minnesota Legislature, having for its principal purpose and aim the increase of the gross earnings tax as herein suggested, has our hearty support and approval, and we request that it be enacted into law.

Revolved, Further, that we especially request the Honorable Senators and Representatives from Hennepin County to aid in every legitimate way the passage thereof.

Resolved, Further, that these expressions of the unanimous sentiment of this meeting be transmitted to the Honorable the

Senate and House of Representatives of the State of Minnesota. Dated at Minneapolis, Minnesota, March 15, 1889.

Wm. Baldwin, Chairman; Sydney M. Owen; F. B. Long; James C. Haynes; John H. Wingate; John H. Nickell, Vice-Chairman; and, Harry Lind, Secretary.[7]

In like fashion, Stockwell read a communication from labor's camp. The prose has Stockwell's fiery ring and, though signed by others, may have been his work at least in part:

American Federation of Labor
Cooper's Machine Workers Union No. 7124
Minneapolis, March 20, 1899.
To the Honorable Senate of the State of Minnesota:

WHEREAS, A bill known as the "O'Neill Anti-Boycott Measure" has passed the lower house of the state legislature and now awaits action in the Senate, and

WHEREAS, Said measure is a blow aimed at the rights, privileges and liberties of a class of people whose labor is their capital, and thereby becomes the most pernicious class legislation, and is evidently only intended to lower and degrade the laboring classes to a condition now worse than African slavery; therefore, be it

Resolved, By the Coopers' Machine Workers Union in Minneapolis, that said bill is pernicious in its effect, unconstitutional in its action, and if adopted will place the laboring classes of this state in a position of direct antagonism to those who represent capital, and thereby widen the breach between the two classes, who should by all means work in unison together;

Resolved, That said bill permits the formation of organizations who represent capital, such as the grocers, bankers, railroads, coal dealers, and all others representing commercial enterprises, granting them the utmost liberty in boycotting in its worst form by depriving others of the privilege of buying goods if they sell under schedule price, while labor alone is debased, thus protecting and encouraging trusts and commercial organizations while enslaving and debasing the great majority of the people who are compelled to labor for their daily bread, and is decidedly not a law for the "greatest good to the greatest number."

Resolved, That we earnestly ask the Honorable Senate of the State of Minnesota to vote against this bill when it comes before them for action, and thereby help elevate labor instead of degrade it.

Yours respectfully,
V. E. Hoskner, President
J. A. Kaltenback, Secretary[8]

In a very real sense Stockwell opened the legislature to the people, personalizing it and making it their own instrument—a forum where they could state their case not only in writing but also in person. Through his invitation and auspices some years later, A. Philip Randolph, black union leader who, with St. Paul's Frank G. Boyd, organized the Brotherhood of Sleeping Car Porters, spoke to house members about his union's objectives. When the University of Minnesota refused to admit a young black woman for nurse's training, Stockwell rallied to her side, inviting the director of Phyllis Wheatley Settlement House (established in the North Minneapolis black district in 1924) to speak to the legislature.

Settlement houses such as Phyllis Wheatley traced their origins to the beginnings of the progressive movement. Their creation was a consummation of the desire held by young people to enter fields that would improve society. Social work generally offered opportunities to lend immediate, tangible help with the results of one's labors often clearly visible. The profession grew rapidly. Women were particularly well suited for work in child welfare. Young reformers entered the field with buoyant enthusiasm. Every evil had a remedy, and men and women worked in countless charitable, rescue and humane societies to ameliorate social injustice.[9]

Reformers recognized the relationship between poverty and crime, and much intelligent thought was given to the systematics of charity. Two types of charitable organizations emerged. On the one hand were public charities such as orphan asylums. Some states, with Massachusetts taking the lead, formed boards of charity to coordinate charitable institutions and state agencies. On the other were the private charities. Before the turn of the century, the citizens of Buffalo, New York, had set up a charity organization society that amounted to a confederation of charities. By 1900, citizens in many other cities had followed Buffalo's example.[10]

A third agency in the field was the social settlement or settlement house. It provided educational, recreational, and moral opportunities, particularly for the younger generation, in crowded, impoverished neighborhoods. The settlement house, like preventive medicine, sought to eliminate damage before it occurred; criminality was to be staved off before sinking its roots. Hull House, founded in Chicago in 1889 by Jane Addams following visits to the Toynbee Hall settlement house in the Whitechapel industrial district of London, set the standard. Of its beginnings, Addams wrote:

> We early found ourselves spending many hours in efforts to secure support for deserted women, insurance for bewildered widows, damages for injured operators, furniture from the clutches of the installment store. The settlement is valuable as an information and interpretation bureau. It constantly acts between the various insti-

tutions of the city and the people for whom these were erected. The hospitals, county agencies, and state asylums are often but vague rumors to the people who need them most. Another function of the settlement to its neighborhood resembles that of the big brother whose mere presence on the playground protects the little one from the bullies.[11]

Stockwell favored public over private charities. Both sought to put the recipients back on their feet, but, in his view, private charity smacked of miscellaneous almsgiving. His daughter Charlotte's friend Althea Heitsmith Atwater recalled his reaction to her switch from a job at the Howe School for Delinquent Girls to Associated Charities in Minneapolis: "OM [for Old Man, which she called him at his request] was angry that I had left a state agency to come down to work for a private agency. Associated Charities just sustained the status quo in his view." When Althea later became a social worker in the public school system, he applauded her move.

Settlement houses, too, met with his approval. Jane Addams was to become a friend of the Stockwells, and Albert himself became active at Phyllis Wheatley Settlement House.

Much of that was still to come, however, when Jermane noted the broad reach of Stockwell's agenda in 1899:

The Hennepin delegation did not confine itself wholly to legislation for the city and county. Senator Stockwell attempted to give the people a chance to vote on the initiative and referendum at the next election (S.F. No. 14), but the bill was killed in the judiciary committee. He also introduced a bill (S.F. No. 127) designed to extend local self-government so as to include taxation giving the various sections of the state local option on taxation. One possible result of the enactment of such a law would be the adoption of the single tax system.[12]

The judiciary committee killed SF127.

But it should not necessarily be inferred that the 1899 session was a failure. Governor Lind did not so regard it. And the fusionists, though in the minority, were able to kill numerous reactionary proposals advanced by the majority. Indeed, it was here that Stockwell made his greatest contribution.[13] Through committee he successfully fought a resolution calling for unequal pay of white and black janitors and caretakers doing the same work. Another measure he successfully blocked was a teachers' retirement bill he deemed inequitable. Unable to block it in the senate, he did not give up the fight but worked with members of the house to have it killed in that body. And in the senate, he successfully led the fight against the O'Neill Anti-Boycott bill, which had already passed in the house, prompting a letter from the Trades and Labor Assembly to the members of the senate thanking them for the defeat of the "obnoxious Anti-Boycott Bill."[14]

If the progressive movement made a faltering start in Minnesota, the blueprint was there for others to follow.

On the last day of the session, Stockwell offered the following resolution, which was adopted:

> Resolved, That the members of the minority of the Senate hereby express to Lieutenant Governor Lyndon A. Smith [Republican leader of the opposition] their high appreciation of his uniform courtesy and high impartiality toward them during the thirty-first session of the Senate.[15]

Charlotte Stockwell Baker told this author years later that her father's "uniform courtesy" was a quality that always stood out in her mind.

References

1. *Dictionary of American History* (New York: Charles Scribner's Sons, 1976) 5:427-428; Chrislock, *Progressive Era*, pp. 1-21.

2. *Dictionary of American History*, 5:427.

3. Chrislock, *Progressive Era*, p. 9.

4. *Minneapolis Journal*, April 11, 18, 1899; Chrislock, *Progressive Era*, pp. 13-14.

5. Stephenson, *Lind of Minnesota*, pp. 162-65.

6. *Minneapolis Journal*, April 18, 1899.

7. *Senate Journal*, 1899, pp. 602-603.

8. *Senate Journal*, 1899, pp. 603-604.

9. Morison and Commager, *Growth of the American Republic*, 2:371; Schlesinger, *Rise of Modern America*, p. 231.

10. Schlesinger, *Rise of Modern America*, p. 108.

11. Morison and Commager, *Growth of the American Republic*, 2:372.

12. *Minneapolis Journal*, April 18, 1899.

13. *History and Biography of Minneapolis and Hennepin County*, p. 495.

14. Binder, "The Stockwells of Minneapolis"; *St. Paul Dispatch*, February 27, 1899; *Senate Journal*, 1899, p. 1239.

15. *Senate Journal*, 1899, pp. 1230-31.

Chapter 9

Combating the Trusts

The legislature was not in session in 1900, but that did not necessarily mean that Stockwell took the streetcar to his office every day, his mind occupied solely with matters of life insurance. The plague of industrywide monopoly incensed him, and he took the train to Chicago in February to attend a three-day convention of the National Antitrust League. He also gave thought to running for Congress in November. But first off there was to be the Jackson Day dinner, on January 10, at the West Hotel in Minneapolis. This promised to be an auspicious beginning for the 1900s for Democrats and Fusionists.

William Jennings Bryan, running again for the presidency, Senator Charles Towne of Duluth, appointed but days earlier by the governor to fill a vacancy in the U.S. Senate, and Governor Lind were the principal speakers at the gathering, which the *Minneapolis Journal* called "the most successful festal day in the history of the Democratic Party in Minnesota.[1] Lind, who in 1898 described himself as a "political orphan," meaning that he acknowledged no partisan identification,[2] took dead aim at the Republicans in his address. He said that events since 1896 had justified the position of the Bryanites on money, that better times had come despite McKinley's monetary policy. He castigated the trusts, and he proposed as remedy a revision of the antitrust laws, judicious taxation, and a prohibition against stock watering. He deplored the war against the Filipinos, the increased appropriations for the army and navy, and "an imperialism imposed solely by the corporate interests, by commercialism, by the commercial spirit for gain."[3]

Bryan, too, lambasted the imperialists:

The man who says that God created any people and did not give to them the capacity to govern themselves libels the Almighty

106

West Hotel, ca. 1900. (Courtesy of the Minnesota Historical Society)

and makes his work mockery. And now men go into the pulpit and you will hear ministers bellowing about as if they had a scent of blood, advocating a war of conquest and appealing to the Almighty to help carry it on.[4]

Governor Lind declared himself an out-and-out Democrat. The seven hundred Democrats gathered at the hotel thundered their approval. In the view of the *Minneapolis Journal*, his speech made such an impression that any suggestion of someone else being the next Democratic candidate for governor was hopeless.[5]

In all probability, Stockwell was present and among those who applauded loudest. Jackson Day was a triumph. The Democratic Party was on high, moral ground. The company, the leadership, the priorities—these were all to his liking. He knew that he worked well with John Lind. What if he, Stockwell, were to go to Washington? Wouldn't the same cordial relationship continue if he were there and Lind remained at the state capitol? Might he not be able to do more for the people of Minnesota and, yea, the country if he were in Congress? Friends and colleagues had talked in the past of his running for the House of Representatives. And hadn't Jerry J. Jermane written, back in April 1899, that

> The fifth district democrats are thinking about Stockwell for Congress . . . He had been talked of by a number of Hennepin County fusionists as the proper man to make the campaign for Congress next year, and it is not impossible that the allies will turn in his direction, unless Mayor James Gray should take the nomination himself, of which there has been some talk. Stockwell is one of the good members of the senate and to his credit be it said that he has never supported any measure save for reasons which were generally admitted to be sincere.[6]

If Stockwell did not reach a decision about the election before the Jackson Day dinner, it seems likely he did so on that "most festal day." He would run for Congress. Before anything else, though, he turned his attention to the worsening problems of business monopolies.

National monopolies first arose when railroad networks made it possible for manufacturers to widen their markets. Maximum output was urgent if they were to reduce the costs of manufacturing their products and make a profit. In a depressed economy, temporary shutdowns were costly, but continuity of production led to overproduction and cutthroat competition. The dilemma of overproduction could be solved by increasing the demand through salesmanship and advertising or by decreasing the supply and raising the price. The latter course, if it were to work, required the formation of a monopoly. Many manufacturers chose that course. The victimized consumer had to pay a higher price for needed goods when the economy was depressed than in time of prosperity? Why? Wasn't this an anomaly?

Initially monopolies took the form of pooling agreements whereby "competitors" agreed to limit production, fix prices, and set quotas. Such agreements were not enforceable at common law, however, and if a renegade decided to charge less, the dam burst.

The Standard Oil Company in 1882 came up with an ingenious solution in the industrywide monopoly or trust. Systematics of the trust called for stockholders in several refining companies, pipeline companies, and related companies to assign their stock to a board of trustees for a stated price. In return, the stockholders received trust certificates. The trustees had legal title to the stock along with voting rights, while the stockholders as equitable or beneficial owners received the profits. The trustees were positioned to set prices.

"His Hands Full: The Octopus—Guess I'll have to grow some more arms." A cartoon depicting the tentacles of J. Pierpont Morgan clutching holdings that comprised United States Steel Corporation, which he had successfully organized and incorporated on February 25, 1901, under the laws of New Jersey. Oliver (Iron) Mining Complany on the western Mesabi was among his acquisitions. (*Minneapolis Journal,* February 21, 1901)

Other industries soon copied the trust device. Public outcry, loudest within the Populist movement, led to passage of the Sherman Antitrust Act in 1890. The act declared illegal every combination in restraint of interstate or foreign commerce and prohibited monopolization of any part of such trade. For ten or fifteen years following enactment, enforcement of the Sherman Antitrust Act against business combinations was for the most part feeble, and by 1904 there were 318 trusts controlling twenty percent of the manufacturing capital of the country. The attitude of the executive branch of the government remained passive until the administration of Theodore Roosevelt.[7]

Public agitation over the size and power of the trusts, which appeared to be ruling the country, led to the formation of the National Antitrust League. On February 12, the league held a key meeting in Chicago. Delegates came from most of the states. Former Governor Altgeld of Illinois attended, and from Minnesota came the Reverend S. W. Sample, Ignatius Donnelly, S. A. Stockwell, and C. J. Buell.[8] (Donnelly had supported Bryan in 1896 despite grave misgivings about fusion. Thereafter, he came to regard fusion as a betrayal of reform. At the time of the National Antitrust League Convention he was a leader of the middle-of-the-road Populists; he would become their vice-presidential candidate in November).

That the most important work of the convention would fall to the Resolutions Committee, of which Stockwell was a member, was clear at the outset. Buell and Sample were among the speakers.[9] The question speakers were asked to address on the first day was: What is the remedy? Their answers were wide-ranging.

Fred Lockwood, a member of the executive committee of the Antitrust League and the convention chairman, looked to government ownership of the railroads for relief because "there is hardly a monopoly in America today that has not been created and maintained by the railroads. But how can this reform be brought about." Only by the ballot, he concluded.

Chicago's Mayor Carter Henry Harrison, after welcoming the delegates on behalf of the city, denounced trusts in general as dangerous to the integrity of the nation. Already, he said, the U. S. Senate had been reduced to a small convention of the owners and representatives of the trusts.[10]

A Captain Black of Illinois favored making every stockholder in any corporate enterprise civilly liable for the criminal practices of agents or employees committed under such circumstances as to impart guilty knowledge.

Governor Andrew Lee of South Dakota said that regulations wouldn't work; they never had. He called for revolutionizing the control of production and distribution. Substitute public for private ownership, he urged, throwing off private for public monopoly. He freely granted that these propositions would be met with accusations of socialism but said they only confirmed the truth. The trust is socialistic, he said: "It is unregulated socialism run for the few at the expense of the many."

A Dr. Stevens of Detroit called for direct legislation under the initiative process. He saw such a course as a return to first principles and an educative force.

The Reverend S. W. Sample of Minneapolis saw the abolition of private monopoly as a remedy. The land monopoly, he said, could be removed by the single tax. The transportation monopoly should be removed by public ownership of railroads. The resolutions committee in due course reported in favor of government ownership of railroads.

John Altgeld, revered by the gathering and the one many believed would have been the Democratic candidate for president in 1896 but for ineligibility due to alien birth, spoke on the last day:

> The great industrial establishments of today were not built up by the railroad trusts. The trust simply gobbled them. The men who run our country today are not captains of industry. They are simply manipulators.
>
> Today the trust stands in every public place of America and not only sucks the blood of toil but insolently lays its polluted hands on everything in church or state that is either vital or sacred to our people. But ere long the men and women who are doing the work of the land will rise up and say "Nay, sire, we are still the state."[11]

A major dispute broke out on the second day. The membership had adopted as a first order of business a resolution condemning as infamous a "currency" bill already passed by the House of Representatives and then before the Senate. The bill would have relegated to the national banks the government's right to issue currency "and extend further special and exclusive privileges to favored classes." Immediately after the adoption of this resolution, Amasa Thornton of New York notified the presiding officer that he was refusing to deliver his scheduled speech. Later, in an interview, he explained that he had been assured the gathering would be nonpartisan. The resolution against the currency bill he did not regard as nonpartisan.

The *Minneapolis Journal* for February 14 declared that the "Chicago antitrust conference proved after all to be a popocratic convention in disguise" and generally downplayed the success of the meeting. But two days later, the paper reported another side of the story:

> Minneapolis members of the antitrust convention are getting home one by one, and they seem well satisfied with the results of the Chicago meeting. At least that element in the convention

which S. A. Stockwell represented is pleased. It is not to be supposed that Ignatius Donnelly and his associates are as well satisfied. Mr. Donnelly had not returned today, but he is not particularly enthusiastic. Stockwell declares that Donnelly and his crowd went down there for the express purpose of trying to make a splurge for the mid-road populist party and to bring politics into the convention, and thus they were handled as they deserved. He regards the address or platform as a compromise necessary on account of the many phases of thought represented in the convention. That this was partisan in any sense he denies emphatically. When asked if, as a matter of fact, the convention was not made up pretty largely of members of one party, he said:

"I should say that a majority of the people in the convention were not members of any party. I mean by that that they are in an independent frame of mind and will not follow any party, however closely they may have been associated with it, if it does not conform to their present views.

"The convention was made up of a very fine body of men. They represented thirty-one states and several territories and all the old parties. The president was an Ohio republican, and the gold democrats were there in force. I believe the effects of the convention will be distinctly educational. The proceedings will be published and widely circulated."

Mr. Stockwell gives an entirely new version of the withdrawal of Amasa Thornton of New York and his announced refusal to deliver his speech on account of the partisan attitude of the convention. "He was a paid spy and employee of the trusts," said Mr. Stockwell, "and if he had not gotten out he would have been ridden out of the hall on a rail. He tried to get onto the program, and, until the program committee learned who he was, he was given a place, but when those eastern men got there, they explained the situation and the program committee promptly refused to allow his address to have a place."[12]

Then came the November elections. Bryan was the unchallenged leader of the Democratic party in 1900. The money question had become secondary with the return of prosperity, and he determined to make imperialism the main issue of the campaign. On this point the Democratic platform closely paralleled Bryan's address to fellow Democrats at the Jackson Day dinner in Minneapolis.

The Republicans, beneficiaries of muscle-flexing and flag-waving across the land, welcomed the challenge. Their plea was, "Don't haul down the flag." Prosperity, coupled with victory in the Spanish-American War, made victory for McKinley in November a

"A Gait Like a Pair O' Bars: Bryan says Democracy ought to set the gait for the Republican Party in the coming campaign." (*Minneapolis Journal*, February 14, 1900)

near certainty. He won far more decisively than in 1896, receiving 292 electoral votes to 155 for Bryan. His popular plurality neared 900,000.

In Minnesota's race for governor, John Lind ran far ahead of his ticket but lost to Republican Samuel R. Van Sant by a mere 2,300 votes. Except for the invalidation of some 20,000 ballots intended for Lind but unintentionally mismarked, he would have been elected.

A new primary law for local elections in Minneapolis and Hennepin County was tested for the first time on September 18, 1900. Stockwell was nominated as Democratic candidate for Congress from the Fifth Congressional District embracing Hennepin County. In the primary he received 3,338 votes, R. R. Odell received 2,789, and Wilt Vanderburger 1,793. The relatively small number of votes cast in the Democratic primary did not bode well for November; far more voters were making their choices in the Republican primary.

Stockwell ran his race on a platform of anti-imperialism, and he fell in the Republican sweep. Loren Fletcher, a sixty-two-year-old Republican who had been elected to Congress in 1881, defeated Stockwell with 24,724 votes to Stockwell's 14,269.[13]

As a holdover in the Minnesota senate with two years remaining in his term, Stockwell retained a forum for his beliefs. Never one who seemed to need consoling, he simply geared up for the next session of the legislature with renewed determination. Nevertheless, he was probably pleased to note that he received two thousand more votes in his district than did William Jennings Bryan.

References

1. *Minneapolis Journal*, January 11, 1900. See also Stephenson, *Lind of Minnesota*, p. 178.

2. Chrislock, *Progressive Era*, p. 14.

3. Stephenson, *Lind of Minnesota*, pp. 179-80.

4. *Minneapolis Journal*, January 11, 1900.

5. Stephenson, *Lind of Minnesota*, p. 179; *Minneapolis Journal*, January 11, 1900.

6. *Minneapolis Journal*, April 18, 1899.

7. *Dictionary of American History*, 7:121-24.

8. Maud Stockwell had been a delegate to the woman's suffrage convention in Washington, D.C., the previous week. The Stockwells never traveled just for pleasure.

9. *Minneapolis Journal*, February 12, 1900. The account of speeches and proceedings herein is based almost entirely upon articles appearing in the *Minneapolis Journal* of February 12, 13, and 14, 1900.

10. Outrage against trust-controlled government reached its climax in David Graham Phillips's series, "The Treason of the Senate" in *Cosmopolitan* (1906-1907). The senators were considered one by one, with the startling conclusion that seventy-five of the ninety served the railroads, the beef and sugar trusts, Standard Oil, and the steel interests. See also Schlesinger, *Rise of Modern America*, p. 202.

11. *Minneapolis Journal*, February 14, 1900.

12. *Minneapolis Journal*, February 14, 16, 1900.

13. *Legislative Manual*, 1901, p. 537.

State Senator—1901

The holdover Minnesota senate of forty-six Republicans and seventeen Democrats met on January 8, 1901, to begin the Thirty-second Session. Stockwell returned to his seat for the second half of his term, demonstrating frugality, parliamentary skills, and courtesy, though he could not later point to a particular substantive achievement. Samuel R. Van Sant, a veteran of the Civil War, in which he had served with the Ninth Illinois Calvary as a teenager, was now governor. He was a politician of the old school—personable, loyal to his party, popular with and active in the Grand Army of the Republic.[1]

Ignatius Donnelly had died on January 1, 1901. Somehow his death signified change in the political landscape: Republicans were back in power in all branches of the government. Things were different from two years earlier, when Governor Lind outlined his plans for Minnesota in a memorable opening address.

The legislature had been in session just two days when Stockwell offered two resolutions directed at Washington. The first resolution urged Congress to call a convention for the purpose of proposing an amendment to the Constitution providing for the election of U.S. senators by direct vote of the people:

> Whereas, a large number of state legislatures have at various times adopted memorials and resolutions in favor of election of United States Senators by popular vote;
>
> And Whereas, The National House of Representatives has on four separate occasions, within recent years, adopted resolutions in favor of this proposed change in the method of electing United States Senators, which were not adopted by the Senate;
>
> And Whereas, Article V of the Constitution of the United States provides that Congress, on the application of the legislatures of two-thirds of the several states, shall call a convention for proposing amendments;

116

And Believing that there is a general desire upon the part of the citizens of the State of Minnesota that the United States Senators should be elected by a direct vote of the people;

Therefore, be it Resolved (if the House concur), that the Legislature of the State of Minnesota favors the adoption of an amendment to the Constitution which shall provide for the election of United States Senators by popular vote, and joins with other states of the Union in respectfully requesting that a convention be called for the purpose of proposing an amendment to the Constitution of the United States, as provided for in Article V of the said Constitution, which amendment shall provide for a change in the present method of electing United States Senators, so that they can be chosen in each state by a direct vote of the people.

Resolved, that a copy of this joint resolution and application to Congress for the calling of a Convention be sent to the Secretary of State of each of the United States, and that a similar copy be sent to the President of the United States Senate and the Speaker of the House of Representatives.[2]

The resolution was the same as that being introduced in the legislatures of thirty-one states. Calling for a constitutional convention was a way to get around the continued opposition to the amendment of the upper house. Two-thirds of the states passing this resolution would mandate that Congress call a convention for drafting and submitting a proposed amendment to the states for ratification.[3]

Stockwell's resolution died in the judiciary committee. It was not until 1913 that the Seventeenth Amendment providing for direct election of senators was adopted.

The target of Stockwell's second resolution was the Hanna-Payne ship subsidy bill. Mark Hanna of Ohio, an enormously wealthy Republican mastermind deemed by Morison and Commager as the nearest thing to a national "boss" ever to emerge in this country, had gained a seat in the Senate in 1897.[4] Previously he controlled the party from without. In the Senate he became leading champion of a ship subsidy scheme designed to restore the American flag to its former place on the high seas. With Congressman Sereno Elisha Payne, he coauthored the highly controversial Hanna-Payne ship subsidy bill.[5]

Stockwell's resolution deplored it:

Whereas, There is now pending before Congress a bill commonly known as the Hanna-Payne ship subsidy bill, and

Whereas, This bill proposes to tax the great mass of the American people for the benefit of a few already over-rich ship owners, and

117

Whereas, There can be but one result from the passage of such legislation, namely to build up another monopoly out of the sweat and toil of the already overtaxed and impoverished masses; therefore, be it

Resolved, That we emphatically protest against the passage of this bill and call upon our senators and representatives in Congress to use all honorable means to defeat the bill and all subsidy bills.

Brought to a vote, Stockwell's resolution was defeated by a three-to-one margin.[6] In Washington Hanna was able to engineer the bill through the Senate only to see it lose in the House.

Two weeks later Stockwell and his colleagues were called upon to perform the very duty he sought to shift to the people at large. The legislature met to elect two U.S. Senators. Senator Cushman K. Davis had died on November 27, 1900. Governor Lind appointed Towne, a silver Republican, to fill the vacancy until the legislature could elect a successor. Senator Knute Nelson, Republican incumbent, was up for reelection. On January 27, 1901, Nelson was reelected, and Republican Moses E. Clapp was elected to fill the vacancy. Voting in the Minnesota senate followed party lines. Towne's tenure had been brief, less than two months. But there was time enough for him to make a ringing address attacking the president's policy in the Philippines.[7]

Stockwell's committees were Education, Enrollment, Insurance, Legislative Expense, Retrenchment and Reform, and Taxes and Tax Laws. He had served on all but Legislative Expenses in the previous session. But he was a natural for it—his lifetime creed was that the legislature holds public monies in a sacred trust—spend not a penny unless it be for the public good. He had demonstrated this conviction in 1891 when newspapers cost only a penny. Another house member had proposed a resolution whereby a thousand copies of the *House Journal* would be ordered, of which four hundred should be for the daily use of members and six hundred as a weekly edition for constituent use; in addition, copies of two daily newspapers would be ordered for the use of members. Stockwell, a freshman with ten days' experience, saw no good reason for the charity. He moved to amend the resolution "by striking out that portion of the same relating to the daily newspapers."

In 1901 he stepped forward again. A custom had arisen whereby the legislature, typically at the end of a session, appropriated $150.00 for reporters who covered their proceedings. (The *Minneapolis Times* and *Minneapolis Journal* had declined to participate in the gift-giving). Stockwell vehemently opposed the practice and led the fight against it: the legislature had no legal or constitutional right to vote away the people's money. A joint house and senate committee decided to drop the practice.[8]

Stockwell strove to save money for the public at large as well as protect the public treasury. His support for the Torrens system of land registration saw him siding with home buyers against the legal fraternity. The system was developed by Sir Richard Torrens (1814-1884), a reformer of Australian land laws under which, upon the landowner's application, a court might, after appropriate proceedings, direct the issuance of a certificate of title. With certain exceptions, the certificate was conclusive as to the applicant's estate in the land. The Torrens system differed from the age-old system of recording evidence of title at the registry of deeds in that it eliminated the abstracting of titles, an expensive and unsatisfactory feature of land transfers, with which costs invariably fell to the buyer. Lawyers, particularly those representing banks holding mortgages on real estate where certainty of title was crucial, generally opposed the Torrens system. Title search was their stock in trade. The lawyer who had previously searched a title would, when it changed hands, often charge full fare for little or no work.

In 1901 the Torrens system had been adopted in Illinois, Massachusetts, and Manitoba. Many legislators in the Thirty-second Session were supportive. Among them was Senator F. B. Snyder, Republican attorney from Minneapolis, who was expected to take the lead. On March 1, he introduced a bill for adoption of the new system. The bill was referred to the Committee on Judiciary, which included many lawyers. Four days later the committee referred the bill back to the senate without recommendation. When Snyder saw opposition gathering and realized that chaperoning the bill through strong opposition would be time-consuming and unlikely to succeed, he had second thoughts about his role. Stockwell assumed responsibility. On April 15, the bill had all but lost (senators from rural districts feared it because the bill made it optional for counties to adopt the new system or stay with the old) when Stockwell changed his vote for the sole purpose of moving for reconsideration. His motion was granted. Working through Snyder, Stockwell then amended the bill so as to apply only to Minnesota's three largest counties—Hennepin, Ramsey, and St. Louis. The bill then passed with just one negative vote. The constitutionality of the measure was afterwards savagely attacked, but it was upheld by the state supreme court.[9]

The *Minneapolis Journal* had previously taken note of Stockwell's parliamentary surefootedness when disposition of a badly drafted teachers' tenure bill puzzled the senate:

Senator Stockwell scored a home run this morning when he went to the plate to take the kinks out of Senator [Allen J.] Greer's delivery. The Lake City statesman was pitching a bill known as SF10, the same being a bill to make more certain and secure the tenure of office of teachers. This bill would give school teachers a life tenure after having served continuously in one district or school for two years and after being appointed for a third.

Senator [F. B.] Snyder poked a little "bunt" down to the pitcher which exempted the state university from the effects of the bill.

Senator [R. F.] Thompson knocked a "delay cutter" which Senator [P.] Fitzpatrick tried to field but fumbled. Mr. Thompson said that the bill was entirely too indefinite; that while it provided that teachers could be removed for cause and after due notice and a full hearing, it did not state what constituted "cause" nor what constituted "due notice" or "a full hearing."

Senator [E. K.] Roverrud and others pasted the ball good and hard until the shortstop from Hennepin came up and duplicated Perry Warden's famous stunt of sending the ball over the fence with a motion to "indefinitely postpone" the bill. Nobody could find the ball and the senate proceeded to other business.[10]

Benjamin Harrison, twenty-third president of the United States, a Republican whose four-year term (1889-1893) was sandwiched between the terms of Grover Cleveland, died in Indiana on March 13, 1901, at sixty-seven years of age. When the Republicans in the legislature overlooked his death the next day, Stockwell introduced a resolution to honor his memory.[11]

President Benjamin Harrison. (Courtesy of the Minnesota Historical Society)

The senate also addressed the problem of the trusts during the second half of Stockwell's term. Many state legislatures, frustrated with the failure of the Sherman Antitrust Act to achieve stated goals, tried to eliminate the evils of monopoly with measures of their own. These efforts met with limited success usually because the trusts were interstate conglomerates beyond the state's control. Nonetheless the Minnesota legislature was determined to do what it could. In the senate, the trust question came up for debate with the introduction of SF113, a bill seeking to prevent and restrain the operations of pools, trusts, and conspiracies. A typical angry denunciation one senator leveled against the lumber industry: he found that no matter how many lumber dealers were asked for prices, the same figure was quoted, indicating a combination to keep prices up and competition down.

Stockwell was pessimistic about SF113: "In my opinion the bill is not worth the paper on which it is written," he declared, "as it will not reach the combinations injurious to the people; but in order to be consistent, I will vote in favor of the bill."[12] Nevertheless, SF113 was passed overwhelmingly: yeas forty-four, nays two.[13]

In 1889 reform legislation had been enacted to apply the direct primary to Hennepin County. The law was extended by the legislature in the Thirty-second Session to cover all county offices, state legislative races, and congressional contests. Statewide offices remained under the convention system.[14] In the course of discussion of the primary bill, senators probed the pros and cons of primary elections generally, the place for party caucuses, and the need for party organization. The *Minneapolis Journal* took note of the views of Stockwell and E. T. Young:

> Senator Young made a strong plea for the strict maintenance of party organization. He declared that the personal qualities of McKinley were not responsible for his triumph over Bryan but that his election was due simply to the principles he represented as enunciated by his party. The election should not be made to apply to state and congressional office but solely to offices of the city and county. He saw the primary as obliterating party lines and doing away with party organization.
>
> The awful danger of wiping out political parties did not affect Senator Stockwell in the least. "Why the curse of America today is party and politics," said he. "If this country ever goes down it will be because of her parties and her politics. Everybody in this chamber knows that a party platform is only a scheme to get into office."[15]

Stockwell persevered for legislation allowing voters, if they wished, to adopt the single tax. At the close of the 1899 session, he had moved for the indefinite postponement of his bill to enable voters by majority vote to reduce taxes on lands that were improved but held idle. He knew it was too late for any action toward the adoption of the single tax system, but he served notice that he would bring it up at the next session.[16] He did so on March 29, 1901, with SF492, a bill proposing an amendment to the Minnesota constitution authorizing the legislature to collect sufficient revenue for all state and local purposes in accordance with a land value tax system as seen by Henry George while also authorizing adoption of the system of home rule or local self-government in taxation. Stockwell stoutly denied that it was a "single tax" measure; its primary object was to allow the voters in each county a modicum of home rule, that is, to determine themselves how they would be taxed.

SF492 was sent back to its author and the subject matter referred to the tax commission.[17]

Senator S. A. Stockwell expresses frustration while arranging for a senatorial caucus meeting with the House. (*Minneapolis Journal*, January 10, 1901)

Late in the session the general question arose as to whether the state should reimburse a county for costs incurred in the criminal trial of a nonresident defendant. Stockwell had sought reimbursement for cost incurred by Hennepin County in the arrest, trial, prosecution, and execution of John Moshik for the murder of John Lemke. It was not an easy question for Stockwell because he was opposed to execution as a matter of principle as well as opposed to the submission of such claims generally. Still, there was some obligation to Hennepin County. Inasmuch as other counties were filing isolated claims, he decided, in the words of the *Minneapolis Journal*, that he might as well come in for his share of the spoil. The matter was resolved when all such claims, with one exception, were rejected by the house.[18]

The Thirty-second Session, seen generally as one of solid accomplishment, ended on April 12, 1901. Passage of the railroad gross earnings tax bill raising the tax from three to four percent, was the crowning achievement. Enactment was due mainly to the efforts of Republican Jacob F. Jacobson in the house, where the bill originated. The vote in the senate was fifty-three to eight. Stockwell was unavoidably absent at the time of the voting, but later he appeared and requested that the Senate Journal indicate that he would have voted in favor of HF291.[19]

More needed to be done in the matter of state and local taxation, and the legislature passed a bill establishing a three-man tax commission whose assignment was to survey the tax laws of Minnesota and prepare a code to make them more equitable. The governor called a special session of the legislature to meet in 1902 to take action on the commission's report.

References

1. Stephenson, *Lind of Minnesota*, p. 177. The Grand Army of the Republic (GAR) was an association for Union veterans of the Civil War founded in 1866.

2. *Senate Journal*, 1901, p. 40.

3. *Minneapolis Journal*, January 10, 1901.

4. Morison and Commager, *Growth of the Republic*, 2:257.

5. *Dictionary of American Biography*, 4:227.

6. *Senate Journal*, 1901, pp. 146, 209.

7. *Minneapolis Journal*, January 28, 1901.

8. *Minneapolis Journal*, April 12, 1901; *History and Biography of Minneapolis and Hennepin County*, p. 495. In the extra session called the following year, Stockwell proposed what he would have contended a far better way to spend public monies—a modest increase in pay for Walter McCoy, janitor and watchman of the senate chamber, and for James Woodfork, keeper of the lieutenant governor's room and toilet room, to five dollars per day, retroactive to the beginning of the session. See *Senate Journal*, 1902 Extra Session, p. 133.

9. *Minneapolis Journal*, March 1, March 5, and April 6, 1901; *History of Minneapolis and Hennepin County*, p. 495.

10. *Minneapolis Journal*, February 18, 1901.

11. *Senate Journal*, 1901, p. 484.

12. *Minneapolis Journal*, March 21, 1901.

13. *Senate Journal, 1901*, p. 580.

14. Chrislock, *Progressive Era*, p. 17.

15. *Minneapolis Journal*, March 29, 1901.

16. *Minneapolis Journal*, April 15, 1899.

17. *Senate Journal*, 1901, pp. 716, 795; *Minneapolis Journal*, March 29, 1901.

18. *Minneapolis Journal*, March 30 and April 8, 1901.

19. *Senate Journal*, 1901, p. 821.

Chapter 11

The Boer War Reaches Minnesota

When the tax commission had duly completed its work in the summer and fall of 1902, the responsibility for implementing the commission's report fell to Jacob F. Jacobson, hardworking, Norwegian-born chairman of the House Committee on Appropriations. He performed yeoman service. The legislature met on February 4, and his bill, HF56, passed in the house overwhelmingly: yeas eighty-four, nays twenty-five. Then it stalled. Lobbyists in the senate gouged HF56 almost beyond recognition. The mining interests objected to the proposed tonnage tax on iron ore; the merchants of major cities objected to the establishment of a permanent tax commission; public service corporations such as the street railway companies objected to the franchise tax. A skeleton bill could probably have passed with decimating amendments, but nonaction seemed preferable. On March 5, with thirty-seven yeas and twenty-six nays, the senate voted to adopt the report of the tax committee majority, of which Stockwell was a member, calling for indefinite postponement. Stockwell said he would have voted for the franchise tax alone but disliked the rest of the bill.[1]

Inasmuch as the measure had originated in the house and was primarily its responsibility, the workload in the senate was lighter than during a regular session. Bills outside the tax field were considered, and Stockwell took advantage of the chance to try to correct an environmental problem. Residents of the Lake Calhoun area claimed the Minneapolis Ice Company was polluting their lake. The company's cutting of ice for home use was causing contamination, as oil and debris from its operations spilled onto the ice into the water. Stockwell introduced SF22, a bill to prohibit the cutting and sale of ice from lakes and ponds in cities of more than two hundred thousand inhabitants, with violation a misdemeanor. The bill was to become effective the following October.

At a meeting of the Hennepin County legislative delegation in the Minneapolis Commercial Club, Representative W. O. Washburn reported that officials of the ice company using Lake Calhoun had told him they would move out within two years should Stockwell's bill be turned down. It was suggested the matter be referred to Stockwell with instructions to get signatures of the company officers affirming such an agreement. Compromise was not attained, and the bill, while adopted by the senate, never reached final passage in the house.[2]

Stockwell also introduced early in the session a bill, SF41, that would authorize the Social Democratic party of Minnesota to change its name to Socialist party and to have candidates' names printed on official ballots with that designation. Impetus for the bill came from the Socialist party itself. Stockwell advised the senate that a national convention of the Socialist party had fixed upon the name. New York and Massachusetts already had passed similar laws.[3]

Stockwell had a personal reason to seek the name change. If he could not right a past wrong to a friend at least he could try to prevent another. John Lind had been the heavy favorite when he ran for reelection in 1900. Victory seemed certain even though Van Sant was a much stronger Republican opponent than William H. Eustis had been in 1898. The day after the election, the *St. Paul Globe* announced Lind's reelection, predicting his plurality would reach eighteen thousand. But the newspaper failed to take into account a stratagem of Tams Bixby, Republican mastermind and Lind's childhood schoolmate.[4] Lind's biographer has explained:

> When the returns were in, Van Sant had 152,902 votes to 150,651 for Lind, with the latter running about seventy thousand votes ahead of his ticket. While Van Sant was perhaps legally elected, Lind was undoubtedly the choice of the people. Lind himself said he was counted out by a trick, but Frank A. Day was more specific in his language. He said that Tams Bixby's "rascally trick" of placing Tom Lucas on the official ballot as the Social Democrat candidate for governor cheated Lind out of twenty thousand votes. It is a fact that from fifteen to twenty thousand ballots obviously intended for Lind were invalidated because they were marked for both Lind, designated as "Peoples-Democrat" and Thomas H. Lucas, designated as "Social-Democrat." It appears that this number of voters, in glancing down the list of candidates, placed a mark opposite every candidate designated as a "Democrat," as Bixby intended they should, thus invalidating the portion of the ballot pertaining to the governorship. In the official returns Lucas received only

about three thousand votes—proving that the ballots marked for both Lind and Lucas were intended for Lind.[5]

Stockwell's proposal was viewed with a cool eye by the Republican-controlled steering and judiciary committees. The latter voted indefinite postponement, and on February 25 the senate tabled the measure.[6]

The senate remained in session only thirty-five minutes on February 25, but that was time enough to deal Stockwell a second blow. The house had adopted a resolution asking Congress to establish an army post at Crookston, Minnesota. Stockwell objected to a motion for senate concurrence, declaring that the only use for soldiers in Minnesota was to "subjugate working men at the behest of corporate influence." He demanded a count; there were twenty-eight yeas and three nays. Two days later on a motion to reconsider, Stockwell said he understood many people in Crookston were opposed to the installation, comparing an army post to a pesthouse. But he lost again.[7]

The Boer War, raging in South Africa in 1902, was also of concern to Stockwell. The conflict, the largest in which the British were engaged between the Napoleonic Wars and World War I, was extremely one-sided in numbers. British military strength neared 500,000 men against the 88,000 Boers seeking to defend the South African Republic and the Orange Free State. The uneven numerical strengths coupled with the shocking British mistreatment of women and children in concentration camps, where over 20,000 died, brought the Boers wide public sympathy.

Among the sympathizers was Stockwell. He called for non-interference in the war with this resolution:

> Whereas the treaty of Washington concluded between Great Britain and the United States, May 8th, 1871, remains in full force, and
>
> Whereas, Under the terms of this treaty either party thereto is not to permit or suffer either belligerent to make use of one of its ports or waters . . . for the purpose of the . . . augmentation of military supplies or arms or the recruitment of men, and
>
> Whereas, This treaty is being constantly violated by the United States in permitting horses and mules to be shipped from its ports by agents of the English army to be used against the South African Republic, thus aiding and abetting England in her unholy war of conquest of the Boer republic.
>
> Therefore, Be It Resolved, by the Senate, the House concurring, that we call upon the Chief Executive of this nation to enforce the treaty of Washington in letter and spirit.[8]

Extended debate followed Stockwell's resolution. The *Minneapolis Journal* reported:

> The senator from Hennepin disclaimed any intention to twist the lion's tail, but thought nine out of every ten Americans were in sympathy with the Boers.
>
> Senator [E. T.] Young thought the adoption of the resolution would be a direct slap at President Roosevelt.
>
> The resolution was finally passed [after an unsuccessful attempt to have the word "unholy" stricken] 36 to 5, but not before Senator Stockwell had disclaimed all intent of partisanship. He said he was not much of a party man and then drew applause from the Republican members by saying: "If in the next election I must choose between voting for David B. Hill and Theodore Roosevelt, then I'll vote and work my d - - - dest for Roosevelt."[9]

Stockwell's resolution lost in the house by one vote, with many absentees. In a roundabout way his plain talk during debate in the senate had tripped him up. It so happened that debate on the Boer War resolution coincided with a goodwill visit to the United States by Prince Henry of Prussia, brother of William II, Emperor of Germany. The people of the Twin Cities were agog. The royal visitor was wined and dined in Minneapolis and St. Paul—dinners and receptions, bowing and scraping, "your highness" this, "your highness" that. Overalls and everyday clothes were cast off for finery. The *Minneapolis Journal* breathed a sigh of relief when Governor Van Sant hobnobbed with Prince Henry at a down-home gathering:

> Not till Prince Henry met Governor Van Sant of Minnesota did he make the acquaintance of American Democracy. So successfully had we imitated the manners of Europe and worn the outward air of obsequiousness that we supposed the occasion demanded, the prince would never have known how we act in this country when we are at home.[10]

There was no "your highness" from Governor Van Sant and none from Stockwell. The *Minneapolis Journal* reported:

> When Senator Stockwell's pro-Boer resolution was read in the House this morning, Mr. Umland of Ramsey gave notice of debate and the resolution went over for one day. As Mr. Umland is a Democrat and a German, his action caused surprise. The reason for it came out a little later. It seems that Senator Stockwell in his speech to the Senate referred to the country's royal guest as "Mr. Henry." Mr. Umland took his revenge for this incident this morning.[11]

127

But Stockwell had the last word. The *Minneapolis Journal* provided this sequel:

> In view of the last two British defeats in South Africa, Senator Stockwell should pause and consider whether he was befriending the Boers in urging the adoption of a resolution forbidding the exportation of American mules to South Africa. On both occasions, Lord Kitchener "regrets to report" that the mules, at the critical moment of the fight, rendered very effective service to the Boers by stampeding, wagons and all. After they got through with their promiscuous charges, the Boers, who had been smoking their pipes and enjoying the fun in the meantime, came up and gave the remnant of the British forces the coup de grace. The American mule had done his large part toward inflicting two humiliating defeats on the British. We expect to see the anti-Boer party in this country come forward soon with a plan to keep our mules at home.[12]

The special session adjourned on March 11. Though the legislature had failed to come up with an overhaul of the tax system as directed, Van Sant's popularity remained high. Consolidation of the Great Northern, the Northern Pacific, and the Burlington railroads into a single system gave him an unexpected political boost. Two powerful groups had been vying for control of the Northern Pacific. James J. Hill, president of the Great Northern, and J. Pierpont Morgan headed one group, while Edward H. Harriman, president of Union Pacific, and Kuhn, Loeb and Company, headed the other. In November 1901, they reached a compromise and announced the merger of the three railroads into the Northern Securities Company. Pent-up distrust and anger erupted against trusts generally and against the railroad monopoly in particular. Carl Chrislock has described the backlash:

> Van Sant responded to the Northern Securities announcement with a speed and vigor that won him an enviable reputation as a champion in the battle against mergers . . . Court proceedings undertaken at the governor's behest ended in a blind alley. Federal action was required to down a giant like Northern Securities. This was instituted by President Roosevelt in February 1902, and culminated two years later in a United States Supreme Court decision invalidating the projected merger on the grounds it violated the Sherman Antitrust Act.
>
> Nevertheless, the governor's apparently courageous stand against railroad monopoly paid rich political dividends; he won reelection in 1902 by an overwhelming majority. For the next few years Minnesota politicians found "anti-mergerism" as useful politically as a later generation of office seekers would find anti-Communism.[13]

"Good Riddance. the Boer—'Anything to swap?' Johnny Bull—'Nope, keep 'im! Hi got a lot more like 'im you'd be welcome to.'" Paul Sanford Methuen, British Military commander, was captured by the Boers in the fighting of March 1902. (*Minneapolis Journal*, March 12, 1902)

Stockwell ran for the Senate again in 1902, the underdog; Republicans were cresting locally and nationally—these were glory days for Republican candidates. Roosevelt, who had taken his oath of office in Buffalo, New York, on September 14, 1901, brought excitement and color to his party and to Washington. His attack on the Northern Securities Company, whose dissolution earned him the trust-buster title, gained national approval from both parties in Minnesota. The ideas of populism were now becoming respectable—the more so since there was no longer any danger that the Populist party would be establishing them.[14]

In the Hennepin County primary, Stockwell again won the Democratic nomination for senator from the Forty-second District. Henry J. Gjersten won the Republican nomination. Gjersten, a forty-one-year-old lawyer born in Norway, had the built-in advantage of all Scandinavians who run for office in Minnesota. Stock-

"Ain't That a Fine Paddle!" (*St. Paul Daily Pioneer Press*, November 6, 1902)

well was vulnerable; he dared back the untried and the unpopular, opening himself to attack. Benjamin F. Ward, Republican chairman of the Forty-second District Senatorial Committee, assailed Stockwell for a pamphlet Stockwell circulated, setting forth his own record in the senate.

Ward asserted that Stockwell failed to state that at the extra session of 1902, Stockwell voted against the Jacobson Bill to tax the franchises of public service corporations and the iron mines of the Rockefellers in the state; he was scornful of Stockwell's inability to gain passage for some fifteen bills introduced, succeeding only with "a local measure introduced in 1899 by unanimous consent and passed without opposition." Ward further faulted Stockwell for neglecting to record his vote on the gross earnings tax law of 1901, a measure he had claimed credit for helping to pass. And he criticized Stockwell for neglecting:

> to tell the voters that at each session of the legislature he has introduced resolutions the object of which was to discredit the Republican party, and he has supported his resolutions by bitter denunciations of President McKinley. One of the last things that he did as state senator was to introduce a resolution for the purpose of discrediting and denouncing the administration of President Roosevelt, and still Mr. Stockwell expects to be elected to the state senate by Republican votes in the forty-second district. A man with such a record, who solicits Republican votes, must have an unusual amount of "nerve."[15]

The election was a Republican landslide. Theodore Roosevelt's popularity, which reached new heights early in his presidency with one brilliant stroke—his successful institution of an antitrust suit against Northern Securities Companies, helped Republican candidates all across the land. John Lind returned to Congress as a Democrat, but he was an exception. Van Sant was reelected by a margin of more than 55,000 votes over his Democratic opponent, Leonard A. Rosing. And so it went, on down the line. Gjertsen defeated Stockwell for the Forty-second District senate seat, 3,513 to 2,870. Stockwell did reduce the Republican majority by more than 1,800 votes.[16]

Stockwell dropped out of state politics as a legislator following his defeat. In his words, he moved on "to take up the fight for the acquisition of the Minneapolis Gas Light Company's plant."[17] He became a candidate for alderman on that issue and did not return to the legislature until 1923.

References

1. *House Journal*, Extra Session 1902, p. 148; *Senate Journal*, Extra Session 1902, p. 192; *Minneapolis Journal*, March 4, 5, 6, 1902.

2. *Minneapolis Journal*, February 24, March 8, 1902; *Senate Journal, Extra Session 1902*, p. 240.

3. *Minneapolis Journal*, February 18, 1902.

4. *St. Paul Globe*, November 7, 1900; Stephenson, *John Lind*, p. 182.

5. Stephenson, *John Lind*, p. 183.

6. *Senate Journal, Extra Session 1902*, pp. 69, 112.

7. *Minneapolis Journal*, February 25, 27, 1902.

8. *Senate Journal, Extra Session 1902*, p. 133.

9. *Minneapolis Journal*, March 1, 1902. David Bennett Hill, who at one time had been on friendliest terms with Boss Tweed, was the bright but ambitious and unprincipled governor, later senator, of New York.

10. *Minneapolis Journal*, March 6, 1902.

11. *Minneapolis Journal*, March 4, 1902.

12. *Minneapolis Journal*, March 11, 1902.

13. Chrislock, *Progressive Era*, p. 17.

14. *Dictionary of American Biography*, 7:137.

15. *Minneapolis Journal*, October 31, 1902.

16. *Legislative Manual*, 1903, p. 525; *History of Minneapolis and Hennepin County*, p. 495.

17. Deposition, *J. E. Foster v. Al P. Erickson*, County Auditor, Supreme Court File No. 32676-1940, Archives, Minnesota Historical Society.

Chapter 12

Women's Rights

After the Civil War, the passage of the Fourteenth and Fifteenth Amendments gave blacks the right to vote, at least on paper, and women the hope for suffrage. Many women had already entered the temperance movement as a means of protecting their families; scores now became leaders in calling for the right to vote. Congress, however, was deaf to their plea for enfranchisement. Disappointed suffragists, seeing a long struggle ahead, followed two courses of action. The National Women Suffrage Association, headed by Elizabeth Cady Stanton and Susan B. Anthony, organized in 1869 to amend the Constitution. The American Woman Suffrage Association, led by Lucy Stone and Julia Ward Howe, sought to induce states to grant women the vote by amending state constitutions. In 1890 the societies merged into the National American Woman Suffrage Association.[1]

These organizations were important in gaining women the vote, but continuing activities in other areas of national life were probably more significant in advancing the cause of women generally. The economic revolution placed women in stores and factories. New jobs such as that of telephone operator came into being. More women entered the fields of nursing, teaching, and social work; slowly they made inroads in law, medicine, and theology.

Another factor making for the emancipation of women was the increase in women's clubs. They had an important effect on the middle class, almost none on those with few economic means. Initially, the subjects of art, literature, and religion made up the agenda of the clubs. As time went on, more and more attention was given to civic and social problems. Maud Stockwell, a dauntless clubwoman, was a charter member of the Minneapolis Women's Club in 1895 and the founder of the Woman's Economic Study Club.

Maud Stockwell (third in line), president of the Minnesota Woman Suffage Association, and other women suffragists in Minneapolis. (*Minneapolis Tribune*, November 11, 1908)

Realities refuted the contention that a woman's place was in the home. But changes in the voting exclusion were difficult to bring about because of hostility from men and, indeed, some women. Opponents of suffrage feared that woman would lose her charm, be dragged down to man's level, and that the family would be broken up. Some asserted that women were intellectually unfit to vote. Many men just did not want to share the power.

There was some slight progress politically. In 1871, the Temperance party candidate for governor in Minnesota came out for woman suffrage, but he received few votes. In 1876, Minnesota gave women the right to vote but only in the most restricted sense; they were allowed to vote for school officers. Twenty years later they were also permitted to vote for library board members. For the most part, headway in the legislature was minimal.

(Found in the *Twin Cities, A Pictorial History of St. Paul and Minneapolis* by L.M. Kane and A. Ominsky. Courtesy of the Minnesota Historical Society)

Stockwell did everything he could. As a legislative freshman in 1891, he introduced a bill designed to confer municipal suffrage on women. A hearing was granted by the elections committee, but his bill was indefinitely postponed by the house acting as a committee of the whole—yeas fifty-two, nays forty. In the same

session he submitted several citizens' petitions calling
for women's enfranchise-
ment, but his action was in
vain.[2]

The Minnesota Woman
Suffrage Association was
organized in 1881. Its annual conventions initially
met in Minneapolis and St.
Paul, but later they con-
vened throughout the state,
typically in cities and towns
where local suffrage clubs
had been formed. Noted lecturers such as Susan B.
Anthony, Julia Ward Howe,
and Jane Addams came to
Minnesota to address the
state conventions. To raise
funds for its work, the association conducted oratorical
contests, sponsored plays
spreading the message of
women's rights, and pro-
moted suffrage with lun-
cheons, teas, lawn parties,
rummage sales, and picnics.
Having met with but

Maud Conkey Stockwell, 1914. (Family photo)

limited success in the 1880s and 1890s in gaining the enactment
of legislation to broaden the right to vote, the association for a time
pressed the legislature to pass bills that would improve the living
and working conditions of women and children. In 1902, Stockwell
introduced a bill in the senate to grant women co-guardianship of
their minor children. The bill failed to pass that year but was
adopted in 1904. In 1905, the association, together with other
organizations, successfully pushed for the enactment of a juvenile
court bill.[3]

Albert and Maud Stockwell worked side by side for the
cause. He was the initial advocate. Years later she recalled that
only after her marriage was she converted to being a fighter for
women's suffrage. Thereafter, for as long as he lived, she supported his causes and he supported hers.[4]

In 1900, Maud Stockwell was elected president of the Minnesota Woman Suffrage Association, a position she held for ten years. Albert served with her much of the time as chairman of the association's legislation committee and as a member of the advisory committee. When Maud Stockwell resigned as president in 1910, she stayed on as a member of the board of directors for ten more years, serving also as corresponding secretary from 1914 to 1918. As state president, she traveled more widely than ever before in her life, representing Minnesota at national conventions of the National American Woman Suffrage Association The thirty-third annual convention held in the spring of 1901 in Minneapolis was only a streetcar ride away, but she probably took the Illinois Central to the thirty-fifth annual convention held in March 1903 at the Athenaeum in New Orleans, and the Northern Pacific to the thirty-seventh convention in Portland two years later.[5]

As state association president, Maud Stockwell spoke out on a wide range of equal rights issues. Typical was her support of Gracia Countryman, assistant librarian of the Minneapolis Public Library, who in 1903 decided to run for chief librarian. The board, overcoming its reluctance to appoint a woman, voted six to three to select her, but the members decided to pay her an annual salary of only two thousand dollars (her predecessor, James Hosmer, had received three thousand dollars) and to abolish the position of assistant librarian. As reported in the *Minneapolis Journal*, Maud Stockwell immediately charged discrimination:

> The Equal Suffrage Association has as one of the strongest planks of its creed equal pay for equal work. Its protest made through the state president, Maud C. Stockwell, is prompt and decisive. Mrs. Stockwell said this morning: "I am much gratified to learn that the library board has recognized Miss Countryman's real worth and the valuable service she has rendered to the library by appointing her librarian. The action in cutting her salary and giving the new librarian the work of two persons shows a most unjust discrimination against women and every high-minded citizen should protest against such injustice."[6]

Early in January 1905, she led a delegation of twenty-five women in calling upon John A. Johnson, newly elected governor of Minnesota, to ask him to recommend woman suffrage in his message to the legislature. He had previously expressed a desire to see the women of Minnesota enfranchised, but he failed to make the recommendation. Other disappointments followed as one suffrage bill after another, as well as proposed amendments to the state constitution, met with defeat.

OFFICIAL SUFFRAGE CAP TO BE WORN BY YOUNG WOMEN IN PARADE SATURDAY

* * * *

Miss Elizabeth Stockwell is to be one of a group of young girls who will wear the official suffrage parade cap at the suffrage parade Saturday afternoon. Dr. Ethel E. Hurd at a meeting late yesterday said: "Nobody needs to wear the cap, but I believe they all will, because it is extremely becoming."

The cap is white and the stars are in blue. It has eleven stars, ten for the states which have woman's suffrage and one for Alaska territory, which recently was granted suffrage. "Minnesota" is in blue in the back. It is expected that caps will be worn by at least 500 young women.

—Photo by Brush.

MISS ELIZABETH STOCKWELL.

* * * *

Elizabeth (Beth) Stockwell. (*Minneapolis Journal,* April 26, 1914.)

But a highly successful suffrage parade sponsored by the Minnesota Woman Suffrage Association as part of a nationwide celebration on May 2, 1914, sent spirits soaring. One thousand persons had pledged to march in the parade, but two thousand actually took part. According to the *Minneapolis Tribune,* the suffragists, silent and dignified in their procession, placed equal suffrage on an entirely new plane:

S. A. Stockwell, 1914. (Family photo)

The parade was a revelation and a bump for those who have formed their ideas of suffrage from the cartoonists, the humorist . . . It was not what the majority of people had expected. They saw women of every walk of life, young women, old women, middle-aged women, working women, rich women, women beautiful, women otherwise. But always patiently dignified . . . Minneapolis learned by practical demonstration that those who ask the ballot for women are distinctly not a bevy of hopeless spinsters, unhappily married women, and persons who have nothing else to do.[7]

Maud, Charlotte, and Beth Stockwell marched with banners aloft. In the men's division, along with some two hundred others, marched Albert Stockwell.

Stockwell's participation was typical. Throughout his life he attended meetings and rallies just to fill a seat, to boost morale, to lend support. He appeared at community meetings in black neighborhoods when he knew the home, the hall, or the church would be almost empty. Sitting in the fourth or fifth row, he wanted the speaker and others to know that someone else cared.

And so it was with the suffrage movement. Although male speakers tended to be rare, Stockwell spoke frequently. When the Minnesota Woman Suffrage Association met in Minneapolis for the twenty-seventh annual convention in 1908, Stockwell, whose topic was legislation, "was the only man to grace the program."[8]

At the state convention on October 31, 1913, when matters got out of hand on a procedural question, "the one man delegate at the convention, S. A. Stockwell of Minneapolis representing the Minneapolis Political Equality Club, was obliged to call for order several times during the morning meeting. (A newspaper's caption: "Mere Man Calls for Order.")[9]

On May 15, 1916, the Hennepin County Suffrage Association held a free meeting at noon at the Shubert Theatre with Frances Nielson, M.P., as speaker:

> Mr. Stockwell paid the rent of the theatre for the meeting but the collection was not nearly enough to meet that expense. It was a rainy day and also came directly on top of the Mississippi Valley Suffrage Conference, which had much to do with the small sized audience.

At another meeting that year, "S. A. Stockwell was the only man in attendance . . . He presented the Association with a large bouquet of marigolds raised in his own garden." And on September 8, 1916, he spoke at the state fair "outside the suffrage tent."[10]

Stockwell never seemed to need plaudits or approval, but he must have been gratified to read Jane Addams's tribute in a letter to Maud Stockwell years later: "It is easy for women who have the suffrage to forget the men who stood for their interests through the years when such opposition was sure to invite opprobrium and ridicule."[11]

The period of nationwide dissemination of information advancing the cause of woman suffrage ended by 1916. That was the year the Democratic and Republican parties made the leap, and each placed a suffrage plank in their national platforms, as the Socialist party had done in 1912. From then on the suffragists concentrated on making the parties fulfill their pledge. By act of Congress in June 1919, the nineteenth amendment forbidding denial of the vote on account of sex was submitted to the states for ratification. On the first day of a special session of the Minnesota legislature, September 8, 1919, the house and the senate by near unanimous vote ratified the amendment. Folwell described the excitement:

In expectation that the matter would come up, the galleries were filled with women, among them many of the most prominent leaders of the woman suffrage movement in Minnesota. After the voting the ordinary decorum of the houses was abandoned for long-continued demonstrations of flag-waving, cheering, and the singing of the "Battle Hymn of the Republic." The proceedings culminated in "an old fashioned chicken dinner" served during a recess, in the Capitol restaurant by ladies of the Twin Cities to the members who had so gallantly helped to grant suffrage to women.[12]

Thirty years later Maud Stockwell looked back at the long fight:

> We fought for the right to vote for school boards and library boards . . . We fought to repeal laws giving a wife's earnings to her husband. We fought for the right to go to college.
>
> In the beginning, only one state—Wyoming—gave women the right to vote [1869]. It was one state, and then one more, with the best luck in the west, where states dared to do things. There were Colorado and Utah, Idaho, Oregon and Washington. Finally in 1910 there was California.
>
> Women all over the country then turned their attention to winning New York—sending speakers and money east. In 1915 they lost. In 1917 they tried again, won, and the end was in sight. Congress soon passed an amendment to the constitution, and the states quickly ratified it . . . After we won the right to vote, I was entertaining some friends—society people. The postman left a notice for jury duty and they began to sympathize with me—telling me I could probably get out of it. "Get out of it?" I replied, "I've been fighting for this opportunity for 25 years."[13]

References

1. Much of the discussion here and in the following paragraphs is based on the author's studies under Professor Arthur Schlesinger of Harvard University.

2. Susan B. Anthony and Ida Husted Harper, *History of Woman Suffrage* (Indianapolis: The Hollenbeck Press, 1902), pp. 4: 775; *House Journal,* 1891, pp. 224-225.

3. Minnesota Woman Suffrage Papers, Hennepin County Suffrage Minutes, Minnesota Historical Society.

4. Albert Stockwell took credit for changing Maud's mind. While outlining his career in the course of a legal proceeding, Stockwell testified that he

spoke for women's suffrage repeatedly, even went to Iowa during a campaign, and worked all his life for the right of women to vote. The adroitness of his attorney, Benjamin Drake, who conducted direct examination, was noteworthy:

> Drake: Did you take part in the campaign for women's suffrage leading up to the passage of the national amendment in 1920?
>
> Stockwell: Yes, I converted my wife to that position.
>
> Opposing attorney Granbeck: May my objections stand, Mr. Drake?
>
> Drake: I will allow you to strike that out, if you want to so move.
>
> Granbeck: I suppose you would like that stricken out for fear someone might believe he had to convert his wife to that.
>
> Drake: That shows, at least, I am not leading the witness.

See *J. E. Foster v. Al P. Erickson, County Auditor*, Supreme Court File No. 32676, 1940, Minnesota Historical Society; *Minneapolis Tribune*, May 16, 1949.

5. Programs for the thirty-fifth (New Orleans, 1903) and thirty-seventh (Portland, Oregon, 1905) conventions of the National American Woman Suffrage Association were found in the attic at 3204 E. Fifty-First Street by the present owners of the house. A list of the organizations extending personal greetings to the Portland assemblage demonstrated broad, liberal support: Oregon Equal Suffrage Association, National Council of Women, National W.C.T.U., National Grange, National Federation of Labor, Ladies of the Maccabees, Federation of Women's Clubs, Forestry Association, Woman's Henry George League.

6. *Minneapolis Tribune*, November 7, 1903. See also, Barbara Stuhler and Gretchen Kreuter, *Women of Minnesota* (St. Paul: Minnesota Historical Society Press, 1977), p. 178.

7. *Minneapolis Journal*, May 3, 1914.

8. Unidentified newspaper clipping in the possession of the author.

9. *St. Paul Post Dispatch*, October 31, 1913.

10. Minnesota Woman Suffrage Papers, Hennepin County Suffrage Minutes, Minnesota Historical Society.

11. Jane Addams to Maud Stockwell, June 2, 1927.

12. Folwell, *History of Minnesota*, 4:336.

13. *Minneapolis Tribune*, May 16, 1949. A history of suffrage in Minnesota by Maud Stockwell is among the papers of the Political Equality Club of Minneapolis, 1892-1920, Minnesota Historical Society.

Chapter 13

Minneapolis Rampage

When Stockwell turned from state to city politics to take up the fight for acquisition of the Minneapolis Gas Light Company by the City of Minneapolis, much of city government in America was a disgrace. James Bryce of England in his *American Commonwealth*, a classic study generally admiring of the American people and government, saw municipal government as the one conspicuous failure of the democracy.[1] There were several reasons for the dire state of American cities. One major difficulty was their structure. The city manager plan was then unknown; government by mayor and city council was the norm, and this system, patterned after the federal system, did not work well for municipalities. The city council, the real center of authority, held a key role in legislative and administrative matters, but party bosses typically gained control of city councils and used them for purposes of party advantage and private gain. Inroads for the unscrupulous were wide open, and corruption was difficult to police.[2]

Another problem was inexperience—on the part of voters and those they elected. Americans had developed their political institutions under simple, rural conditions and had not yet learned to govern densely populated communities. City governments were seeking to cope with urban questions seldom or never before faced: street lighting, extensive bridge-building, sanitation, fire prevention, police protection, and education. These functions were costly and complex, but the populace demanded solutions.[3]

Political corruption was the most dismaying problem. A principal source of corruption in the cities was the public utility. Minnesota did not have a state public utilities commission. Utilities had grown rapidly, and regulation by any governmental agency was minimal or nonexistent. Collusion between favor-seeking utilities and dishonest politicians was flagrant. A corps of eastern men—C. T. Yerkes, P. A. B. Widener, W. L. Elkins, W. C. Whitney, and Thomas Ryan—controlled most of the country's utilities. They maintained control by running the politics of the cities.[4]

Central to the corruption was the political boss. Stockwell had witnessed from the capitol the depredation of Minneapolis by Albert Alonzo "Doc" Ames. A "genial reprobate," skilled as a surgeon and generous with his professional services—especially to the poor—Ames was both boss and mayor of the city. The people "gave him votes for his smiles." Elected mayor first as a Republican (1876) and then twice as a Democrat (1882 and 1886), his loose life and barroom residency brought disapproval from the "good people" of Minneapolis but did not phase his wide, devoted following. Despite a disgraceful reputation, he decided to make one more try as a Republican candidate for mayor in 1900. He won the nomination in the primary. Republicans, voting to a man for McKinley and unwilling to split the ticket, elected him mayor again.[5]

The rampage began January 7, 1901. Ames's first appointment was that of his brother, Fred W. Ames, as police chief. A massive purge of the police department, ostensibly to create a Republican force, followed. His brother then fired 107 honest men on the force of 225. Lincoln Steffens described the mechanics of Ames' operations in his autobiography:

> The mayor was the head of the graft organization . . . The police graft . . . was a deliberate, detailed management of the police force, not to prevent, detect, or arrest crime, but to protect, share with, and direct criminals. The so-called moral element of the people played into the hands of the police criminals . . . by requiring strict laws against vice and crime. The liquor business was to be regu-

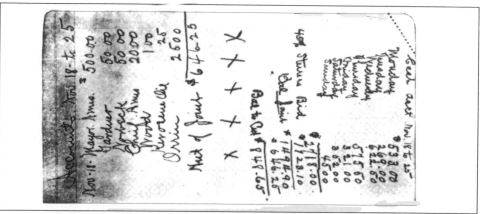

First page of the "Big Mitt Ledger," showing payments to Mayor Ames and others. (From *Twin Cities: A Pictorial History of St. Paul and Minneapolis* by L.M. Kane and A. Ominsky. Courtesy of the Minnesota Historical Society)

lated, prostitution and gambling were forbidden . . . But Mayor Ames and the police force, with professional criminals to advise them, made a schedule of prices for the privilege of breaking the laws. Saloons paid so much a month to ignore the closing-hours, the laws against slot machines and gambling . . . Houses of prostitution, which were a necessity in this center for lumberjacks, had been regulated by a system of formal, regular arrests and small fines once a month. Ames cut the fines and, for the regular payment of bribes, let these houses run, increased the number of them, and encouraged panel games and other forms of robbery. Gambling on a large scale was allowed, with the mayor and police as partners in the profits, and the profits were increased by making the games "crooked" . . . Word was also passed out into the underworld outside that clever crooks would be welcomed in Minneapolis if they would play fair with the police.[6]

The spree could not last forever. A grand jury, headed by Hovey C. Clark, its courageous foreman, bared the corruption of Ames's machine and broke its power. In August 1902, Ames was indicted. David P. Jones, the president of the city council, took over as acting mayor. Stiles P. Jones, a journalist, served as his secretary. Stiles Jones, one of Stockwell's close friends, and principal founder of the Saturday Lunch Club some years later, had investigated Chicago's form of municipal government and was regarded as an expert in the area of municipal reform.[7] Steffens took note of the city's change in leadership predicting that "Minneapolis should be clean and sweet for a little while at least, and the new administration should begin with a clear deck."[8]

Stockwell and others at a meeting of the Municipal Ownership League of Minneapolis. (*Minneapolis Journal*, September 11, 1906)

Revelation of the political corruption of Minneapolis, as bared in the criminal trials of Ames and his cohorts and given national notoriety in Steffens's "The Shame of Minneapolis" appearing in *McClure's Magazine*, sounded the alarm for decent citizens. They demanded reforms. One response was the establishment in 1904 of the Minneapolis Voters' League, a blue-ribbon group that included Stiles Jones. Modeled on the Chicago Municipal League, it planned to concentrate its efforts on improving the city council. In advance of primary and general elections and with the assistance of a paid staff, the league proposed to disseminate information relating to the qualifications and shortcomings of alderman candidates. While the organization occasionally made recommendations, its founding statement professed confidence in the ability of voters to decide wisely on the basis of the information supplied by the league.[9]

Stockwell ran for city council at the first opportunity. In 1904 he filed for Twelfth Ward alderman (councilman) in the Democratic primary. On September 14, the Voters' League issued a preprimary report dealing with the qualifications of candidates for alderman. It recommended a vote for Stockwell:

> General agent, Pennsylvania Mutual Life Insurance Company . . . Born in Anoka 47 years ago. Lived in the city twenty-six years and in the ward sixteen years. Republican previous to 1888. Representative in the legislature two terms, 1891 and 1897. State senator 1899 to 1901. Legislative record first class . . . Personal and business reputation good. Active, alert and takes a keen interest in municipal affairs. Quite radical in his makeup. Would be an aggressive official and a stirring factor in the city council.[10]

Stockwell was nominated, easily defeating Nels C. Nelson 116 to 41. Six Republican candidates divided 1,163 votes. W. H. Ehle with 468 votes was nominated, decisively defeating the league choice. The large Republican turnout was a bad omen for Stockwell and Ehle defeated him in the election, 779 to 633.[11]

Denied a seat on the city council from which to lead the fight on behalf of Minneapolis to acquire the Minneapolis Gas Company, Stockwell chose other means. He would work instead to educate the public about the advantages of municipal ownership. Typical was this letter to the editor of the *Minneapolis Journal*, written after the gas company announced a reduction in rates early in 1906:

> In regard to the "dollar gas in Minneapolis," is it not just possible that this liberal(?) concession on the part of the Minneapolis Gas Light Company is due to the fact that their franchise (the

only one they have on the west side of the river) expires in 1910 and they want to keep the people quiet while they do things for its renewal? Everyone should know that "dollar gas" is at least 25 percent higher than it would be under municipal ownership and operation, to say nothing of having better service and a much better lighted city.

We have not tried to analyze the motives of the company, but it would be quite natural for it to wish to have the good will of the public, and it seems to us to have done something in this reduction to one dollar well calculated to engender it. As for the advantages of municipal ownership, that is a matter which this and every other community should study carefully. The question is not settled yet.[12]

At the same time Stockwell rallied and brought together those favoring public ownership by organizing the Municipal Ownership League of Minneapolis. The *Minneapolis Journal* reported:

At a meeting of municipal ownership propagandists in the rooms of the state free employment bureau in the city hall last night, an organization was effected with the following officers: President, S. A. Stockwell; secretary, H. H. Austin; treasurer, H. S. Mead. Next Monday night a vice president will be elected from each ward in the city and an executive board will be formed. The organization will then organize its campaign, beginning with a movement to issue bonds for the purchase of the plant of the gas company on the expiration of its license in 1910. The fight will be opened with a public meeting. Mayor Dunne of Chicago will be secured as the principal speaker. Another speaker will be secured from Milwaukee, where the city has just completed a municipal gas plant at a cost of $2,000,000.

At present there is a resolution before the council calling for the issuance of $1,500,000 in bonds for the purchase of the gas property in 1910. This ordinance by Alderman Westphal, or a similar measure, will be pushed that it may be placed on the city ticket at the November election and as an expression of the people secured.

A general campaign for the measure will be undertaken in behalf of the bond issue plan.

Not all the attention of the league is to be lavished on the gas plan. A plan to regulate street car fares is in mind, and a test measure will be brought before the council to find where the members of that body stand. The franchises of the street railway companies have some time to run but it is maintained by the municipal ownership and control believers that this does not prevent regulation of rates.[13]

John A. Johnson, governor of Minnesota from 1905 to 1909. (Courtesy of Minnesota Historical Society)

Four months later Mayor Edward F. Dunne of Chicago appeared as principal speaker at the Minneapolis Auditorium. Also on the platform was Governor John A. Johnson, who had succeeded Van Sant as governor in 1905. Stockwell was the first speaker. He described the aims of the Municipal Ownership League, asserting that it was nonpartisan and simply working in the interests of the city as a whole. He said he also favored municipal ownership of the street railway, the telephone system, and the lighting plants.

Governor Johnson, "proud to sit on the platform with the man who was becoming one of the greatest champions of human liberty and the rights of the common people—Mayor Dunne of Chicago," was given an ovation when he came out for the public ownership of public utilities.

Mayor Dunne gave six reasons, based on his reading and experience, for municipal ownership. First and invariably, he said, under municipal ownership, costs of the utility to the public go down. Railway fares, streetcar fares, tax bills, gas bills, and electric light bills are reduced. Second, the efficiency of the service to the public increases. Third, the wages of employees operating these public utilities increases. Fourth, the hours of labor of men employed in working these utilities decreases. Fifth, strikes and labor difficulties are eliminated or reduced. Then he singled out the sixth and greatest blessing of all:

> The last and probably the most important result which follows from municipalization or nationalization of public utilities is the abolition of graft, corruption, and boodle. When a municipality or nation takes over and operates a utility, the incentive for bribery and public debauchery ceases to exist. There is no one to furnish a corruption fund to persuade weak or corrupt public officials not to do their duty by the public. At the bottom of every shameful and scandalous example of public bribery in America, from the days of the credit mobilier down to the day of Yerkes and the boodle alderman of St. Louis, will be found a private utility corporation and its yellow dog fund. The money for every scandalous piece of legislation that has been jammed down through our legislatures has been furnished by privately owned public utility corporations, or the financial agents of

these companies, in the endeavor to obtain from the public extensions of their grants and special privileges upon the public property of the community.[14]

Stockwell continued to further the aims of municipal ownership through the league and as a spokesman at large. Unfortunately for Minneapolis, the clear deck that Steffens had noted was muddied again. The Minneapolis Voters' League berated the city council and the city clerk's office in its report issued September 11, 1906:

> The city council is still unsatisfactory in the intelligence, efficiency and disinterestedness of many of its members. The drones, deadweights, and gangsters are too many. Men of positive convictions and the courage to fight for them are too few.
>
> No one not in touch with the situation can appreciate the influences, direct and indirect, proper and improper, social, business and political, that are brought to bear on aldermen by those selfishly interested in the action of the council . . . The city clerk's office has become a social center for contractors and lobbyists. The city clerk has shown a disposition to favor the granting of certain contracts, where he should be absolutely neutral. This office should be made elective.
>
> The Minneapolis Street Railway Company is the original corrupting influence in our city council and still continues its persuasive attentions to aldermen . . .
>
> The Northwestern Telephone Company also does far too many favors for aldermen.[15]

Stockwell ran for city council again in 1908. The voters' league in its September report once more endorsed him, one of four Twelfth Ward Democrats entered in the primary:

> Honest, independent and fearless, and [in the legislature] fought ably and steadfastly on the side of the people. Has a good knowledge of municipal affairs and is finely equipped for council service. Twelfth ward citizens could do their ward no higher service than to nominate and elect him. His election would go far to redeem the city from ring rule and bad administration.[16]

Stockwell was nominated in the Democratic primary. D. C. Bow was the Republican nominee. Bow, a coal salesman whose alderman term ended in 1906, had been ripped by the voters' league:

> Performed no useful service there except for the public service companies, the brewers, and other special interests. The general public interest consistently disregarded. A member of the city hall ring, and is backed vigorously by them in this present contest.[17]

William Jennings Bryan (center) and Governor Johnson (left) with Frank Day in Minnesota in 1908. (Photo by George E. Luxton. Courtesy of the Minnesota Historical Society)

Bow defeated Stockwell in November, 923 to 782. It was rumored that Stockwell might contest the election but he did not.[18]

Absorbed as he was with local matters, Stockwell nonetheless spoke out on state and national issues. A steadfast supporter of William Jennings Bryan, he took special interest in Bryan's renomination as the Democratic presidential candidate in 1908. Bryan had lost to McKinley in 1896 by 600,000 votes when the total cast were 13,600,000. The electoral vote margin was 271 to 176. Running against McKinley in 1900, Bryan received only 155 of the 447 electoral votes. In 1904 the Democrats turned to Judge Alton Parker of New York, a conservative, to oppose the progressive, aggressive, Theodore Roosevelt. Parker was defeated more decisively than Bryan had been in 1900, and Bryan regained control of the Democratic party organization to become the leading candidate for nomination at the convention in Denver four years later. Governor Johnson loomed as an attractive, favorite-son contender from Minnesota.

Johnson, editor and half owner of the *St. Peter Herald*, gained recognition in Minnesota through his leadership and high standing in newspaper circles. From a Republican district, he was elected to the state senate in 1898 as a fusionist. Although defeated for reelection in 1902, he had won wide respect and strong support in his party, and the Democrats nominated him for governor in 1904. A split in Republican ranks opened the gates, and after a vigorous campaign, Johnson was elected, though narrowly, notwithstanding Roosevelt's four-to-one sweep of the state.[19]

In 1906 Johnson was reelected by a majority of more than 72,000 votes. A popular governor, he gave Minnesota an intelligent and progressive administration. Among the laws signed by Johnson was one enabling municipalities to own and operate gasworks, street railways, telephone and electric light plants.[20]

Johnson was first mentioned as a serious presidential possibility after his stunning speech at the annual Gridiron Club banquet in December 1907. A guest of W. W. "Jerry J." Jermane, elevated to Washington correspondent for the *Minneapolis Journal*, he had been called upon to speak unexpectedly. He captivated perhaps the most critical audience in the country. Newspapers across the land acclaimed the Democratic newcomer from Minnesota.[21]

The conservative *New York World* on January 3, 1908, carried an interview with Johnson, presenting him as a candidate for the Democratic presidential nomination. From the interview and other statements in the paper, progressive Democrats took this to mean Johnson was shifting from the party's progressive principles and modifying his stance against railroads to gain the support of James J. Hill and corporate Democrats of Minnesota.[22] Stockwell spoke up in a letter to the editor of the *Minneapolis Journal*:

> My attention has been called to a "story" that appeared in the political news of the twin city dailies to the effect that I had been invited over to St. Paul and had dined with Governor Johnson and Mr. Day, and that as a result I was in line for Governor Johnson for the democratic presidential nomination. The boys on the capitol run must be hard up for "copy." I did dine as stated, but the occasion was as foreign to politics as a thing could well be. At the time of this visit I stated to Governor Johnson and Mr. Day what they already well knew: that I had no second choice for the democratic presidential nomination. I am for Bryan first, last and all the time, as are, I believe, 90 percent of the democrats in Minnesota and the country. While I entertain for Governor Johnson most cordial personal regards and good will, I do not think well of the servitors who are at the bellows of his boomlet. Rev. Joseph Cooke is reported to have said on one occasion: "Show me what a saloonkeeper and a gambler want, and I will show you what I do not want." By this same logic, show me what the *New York World* wants, what Jim Hill, Colonel Guffy [sic], Roger Sullivan, Dick O'Connor and the "bunch" want, and I will show you what I do not want politically.
>
> While I am for Bryan for the democratic nomination, I do not forget Tom Johnson who, however, has more important work to do than being president.
>
> Can Bryan win? Yes, if any democrat can; but whether he can or cannot is of slight moment compared with the all-important

matter of keeping the democratic party true to fundamental democratic ideals.

As to the issues: How very familiar this old weather-beaten hag of "tariff reform" looks after four years in the back yard of Sullivan, Guffy [sic], O'Connor & Co. Tariff reform! Certainly by its enemies with an ax. The issue in this campaign, as it has been in the last two, tho involved with some side matters, is privilege, and altho Mr. Bryan does not always think clearly, his heart is in the right place, and I predict his nomination at Denver by acclamation.[23]

With the Democratic convention fast approaching, Reverend William Wilkinson registered surprise in a letter to the editor of the *Minneapolis Journal* that any red-blooded Democrat from Minnesota could cast his vote at the convention for Bryan:

It is an amazing thing and a deplorable one that in this state any democrat can be found who for one instant will hesitate to give our governor his first and entire vote in the national convention. And the fact that Bryan would let this be done shows that with all his many gifts he lacks one which would make all others useless in the highest office in the gift of the people. No ungenerous man is fit to be president, and it was an ungenerous thing, to say the least, to oppose Governor Johnson for nomination in his own state . . .

I am a republican, but this does not prevent me from being just to the governor of Minnesota. His success in this great republican state is astounding; it is phenomenal . . . Mr. Bryan's attitude in Minnesota, as shown by his friends and not repudiated by him, is a signal success as a warning . . . and tells us the appalling blunders we might expect if he were president . . . I have been told by an eminent democrat that in the White House recently President Roosevelt said: "I believe Mr. Taft and Mr. Bryan will be the two candidates for the presidency. But if the democrats should name Governor Johnson of Minnesota, we should know we had a fight on our hands."[24]

Stockwell rebutted in a letter published under the heading "Fiery Mr. Stockwell":

I read Rev. William Wilkinson's letter in yesterday's *Journal*. It was interesting. So suggestive of the moral and political standards of some people. I suppose he would not be willing to dignify the processes by which a follower of Mr. Bryan reaches his conclusions as thought, but whatever the force is that directs his actions, he labors under what is probably a delusion that it emanates from himself—that he is able to decide what his duty is without a chart from Mr. Bryan. This will no doubt seem strange to Mr. Wilkinson, but it is nevertheless a fact. Coincidentally, if Mr. Bryan had offered advice on the Minnesota situation, he would have been invited to give his attention to Nebraska—or possibly a warmer place.[25]

Bryan was nominated on the first ballot at the Democratic convention. The Minnesota delegation presented Johnson's name, but support for his candidacy elsewhere was scattered. Bryan lost to William Howard Taft in the November election, receiving 162 of the 483 electoral votes. Wilson appointed Bryan secretary of state in 1913, but he never ran for elective office again. Johnson was reelected governor in 1908. Death overtook him the following year, plunging all of Minnesota into mourning.

References

1. Schlesinger, *Rise of Modern America*, p. 49.

2. Schlesinger, studies.

3. Schlesinger, *Rise of Modern America*, p. 49; Morison and Commager, *Growth of the Republic*, 2:382-83.

4. Schlesinger, studies; Charles B. Cheney, *Minnesota Politics* (Minneapolis: Reprinted from the *Minneapolis Morning Tribune*, 1947), p. 42; Morison and Commager, *Growth of the Republic*, 2:382-83.

5. Lincoln Steffens, *The Shame of the Cities* (New York: McClure, Phillips & Co., 1904), pp. 63-97. "The Shame of Minneapolis," which is now one of the chapters in *The Shame of the Cities*, first appeared in *McClure's Magazine* in 1903. Much written here and below is based on that chapter.

6. Lincoln Steffens, *The Autobiography of Lincoln Steffens* (New York: Harcourt, Brace and Company, 1931) 1:376-77.

7. Carl H. Chrislock, "Profile of a Ward Boss: The Political Career of Lars M. Rand," *Norwegian American Studies*, 31 (1986): p. 62.

8. Steffens, *Shame of the Cities*, p. 97.

9. Chrislock, "Profile of a Ward Boss," p. 63.

10. *Minneapolis Journal*, September 14, 1904.

11. *Minneapolis Journal*, September 26, November 15, 1904.

12. *Minneapolis Journal*, April 28, 1906.

13. *Minneapolis Journal*, May 23, 1906.

14. *Minneapolis Journal*, September 11, 1906.

15. *Minneapolis Journal*, September 11, 1906; Chrislock, "Profile of a Ward Boss," p. 64. Chrislock notes that Lars M. Rand, Norwegian-born alderman from the Sixth Ward, was singled out for a particularly harsh attack in the league's report on candidates published in the *Minneapolis Journal* on September 20, 1906. He was seen as an "oily . . . unscrupulous ward boss who had been a dangerous influence in city affairs during all his sixteen years . . . in the council." The report further denounced him for energetically backing "the interests of the saloon, the brewery, and every other influence contributing to wide open municipal conditions." While posing "as a champion of the people," the report charged, he was "in reality a most useful agent of the railroads and public service corporations." In his article, Chrislock has expressed the view that parts of the league's report were unfair to Rand. Chrislock surmises, and this author agrees, that Rand epitomized everything Stockwell deplored in public life. Rand was a skilled parliamentarian. The sparring between Rand and Stockwell, had they served on the same council, would have been memorable.

16. *Minneapolis Journal*, September 9, 1908.

17. *Minneapolis Journal*, September 9, 1908.

18. *Minneapolis Journal*, November 5, 1908.

19. Chrislock, *Progressive Era*, p. 18.

20. Chrislock, *Progressive Era*, p. 19.

21. *Dictionary of American Biography*, 5:104-05.

22. Winifred G. Helmes, *John A. Johnson: The People's Governor* (Minneapolis: University of Minnesota Press, 1949), pp. 251-252.

23. *Minneapolis Journal*, January 10, 1908. Frank Day was Johnson's private secretary. Roger Sullivan was a member of the Democratic National Committee and political boss of Chicago. James M. Guffey, also a member of the Democratic National Committee and perhaps the country's largest oil producer, was a longtime foe of Bryan. Richard T. O'Connor was the boss of the Democratic machine in St. Paul.

24. *Minneapolis Journal*, March 11, 1908.

25. *Minneapolis Journal*, March 16, 1908.

Chapter 14

Teacher

Although Stockwell gave up teaching as a career, in a broad sense he never left the field. He simply changed forums, going from the classroom to the halls of the legislature, to the First Unitarian Society, the Saturday Lunch Club, his own dining room. Through it all, he remained a friend of the young—a listener, a counselor, a giver of support—"inspiring them to go on acting in behalf of their dreams," said neighbor Violet Johnson Sollie.[1]

The Stockwells believed in the right to self-determination and would not have forsaken the principle to tell Charlotte and Beth where to devote their energies. Nevertheless, the two must have been inspired by their parents' progressive views (see Chapter 8). Almost destined to social work, the two sisters responded to the call of the times, at the same time following the example of a grandmother they never knew—Charlotte Bowdish Stockwell.

Young Charlotte attended Minnehaha and Hiawatha elementary schools in her neighborhood. She graduated from South High School in 1909 and entered the University of Minnesota—a long streetcar ride away—in the fall. There she majored in German, was a member of Kappa Alpha Theta sorority and of the Minerva Literary Society. (She was always a great reader with a broad vocabulary and a special love for well-turned phrases, which she copied upon finding or hearing, just to keep them on file.) True to family form, Charlotte belonged at the university to the Liberal Association, an organization addressing social problems of the day. She was chosen junior class secretary, and, according to the *Gopher* (senior class yearbook), she had "recently come into her own."

Charlotte's closest friend at college was Althea Heitsmith (later Atwater), who was two classes behind her. Because her parents were living in Oregon during her college years, Althea spent many weekends at Charlotte's house, where she became a close

154

friend of the entire Stockwell family. Following graduation in 1913, Charlotte became a probation officer for the juvenile court system, founded in Minnesota in 1905. She had charge of children on probation in northeast and southeast Minneapolis. Her mentor was the compassionate, widely respected Judge Edward Waite.

Beth Stockwell attended the same grade schools as Charlotte but did not graduate from South High. Instead she transferred to Graham Taylor's School of Philanthropy in Chicago. She did not go to college but directly to work, joining the staff at Hull House, an exciting, widely sought experience for any young social

MORE THAN 200 WOMEN TAKE PART IN NOVEL "TAG DAY" DISTRIBUTION OF CHARTER CAUSE LITERATURE

One of Charlotte Stockwell's activities (right) was distributing literature for the passage of a new charter giving Minneapolis complete home rule. (*Minneapolis Journal*, September 28, 1913)

Hull House, Chicago, Illinois. (The picture is taken from a postcard dated April 25, 1908, produced by the New York Postal Card Co., Chicago.)

Jane Addams, founder of Hull House. (Courtesy of the Jane Addams Memorial Collection, University Library, University of Illinois at Chicago)

Beth Stockwell. (Family photo)

worker.[2] Like Charlotte, Beth also served as a probation officer under Judge Waite, and they remained lifelong friends. Both young women would pass on what they learned to the next generation.

David H. Holbrook, a Minnesota teacher who later became secretary of the National Social Work Council in New York, remembered Stockwell as a teacher outside the classroom as well. Recalling early days when they were Saturday Lunch Club members, Holbrook wrote:

> I can never express to you the deep sense of indebtedness I feel for the lessons you taught me during those years and the ideas you illumined by your example, both then and since. For me, a young man, it was a rare privilege to share with you, Jones, Child and others, the thrill of disinterested effort for the common good. I have always regarded it as a post graduate course in citizenship . . . I am thinking especially of the part you have played in the education of many a young man and woman. Your patient listening to immature thinking, your quick recognition of honest search for truth, your understanding sympathy for those attempting ill-advised schemes and your critically Socratic analysis of projected plans, all these made you a real teacher. As one of those pupils, I am most grateful . . . Perhaps the most helpful lesson you taught me was the distinction between intolerance and difference of opinion.[3]

Louella B. Cook, family friend and teacher, recalled that in her own student days she was a frequent visitor to the Stockwell house. At supper time, Albert Stockwell would

> take in a lusty argument three women who were just beginning to think for themselves. I shall always remember with what scorn he regarded all book learning that had not been digested. And, although he would not have called it that, I took my first course in dialectics from Mr. Stockwell and shall always be grateful for having had the privilege of whetting my own thoughts against the cool, clean logic of his.[4]

Stockwell's interest in formal education and the role it must play in life continued. He believed education to be the indispensable ingredient in a democratic society and felt the educational process itself must exemplify democracy. Students in the public schools should have a right to intellectual freedom and the right to be instructed by teachers to whom the full privileges of citizenship were guaranteed. Inside and outside the classroom the teachers must be free to express themselves; only then would they be able to raise a free citizenry. Thus, Stockwell defended the right of university students to hear all sides of a question and to resist any restriction of discussion of any shade of belief. He defended the right of students at the University of Minnesota to resist compulsory military training. As Dorothy Walton Binder, writer and family friend known as Tommy, recounted, "When free speech was in danger at the University of Minnesota or in less intellectual circles, it was to S. A. Stockwell that people in the Twin Cities turned."[5]

Stockwell was outraged to see the educational process corrupted by unseemly outside pressure. In an address before the American Federation of Teachers in Minneapolis in 1928, he contended that students and teachers of public schools were being exploited by the propaganda of agents of the public utility corporations. Textbooks were constantly censured of all adverse reflections on privately owned utilities and of statements showing the benefits of municipally owned utilities. To counteract the influence of the privately owned corporations, he suggested that publicly owned plants combine their efforts in an aggressive program to teach the taxpayers the advantages of municipally owned utilities.[6]

Victoria N. McAlmon, a member of the Minnesota Federation of Teachers, recalled Stockwell's efforts to block outside interference of any kind in the classroom:

> We teachers pay little attention to the fact that organized commercial groups press upon our school educators, who in term dictate to sycophantic supervisors and they to terrified teachers.

Anyone who disobeys is in danger of losing his bread and butter and a very little jelly. It was for Mr. Stockwell's fight in this situation that the teachers of the public schools honor him.[7]

Inasmuch as Stockwell believed that education of the masses for democracy was crucial to the system's success, it is not surprising he was troubled by the lethargy of the electorate. As an offsetting measure he consistently maintained that schools should be open at night to give adults a chance to discuss public questions. Otherwise they would pay no attention to the ballot. If science, religion, economics, and history could not be taught to everyone, how could citizens be expected to participate intelligently?[8]

Stockwell added a corollary to the axiom that an educational system is no better than the quality of its teachers; he held that good teachers could flourish only within a democratic organization of their own making. He strongly supported the Minneapolis Federation of Teachers and was a familiar figure at its gatherings, ready to champion its cause and to speak out in the face of what he saw as injustice. He so spoke out in the case of Mae Snow.

Snow was a member of the executive board of a teachers' organization known as the Teachers Club, and she had been one of the leaders in a campaign for higher salaries. Teachers regarded eight hundred dollars' maximum annual pay as too low. Just before the Board of Education in 1907 finally raised the scale to a thousand dollars annually, Snow was transferred by the board from the position of principal of the ungraded school to a subordinate position in a small school in southeast Minneapolis. In an open letter to John A. Schiener, member of the Board of Education, published in the *Minneapolis Journal,* Stockwell protested:

> I read the article in the *Journal* of the 7th inst. headed "Teachers' Salary Raise is Granted" and having had something to do in the movement to secure higher salaries for the teachers, was somewhat surprised to learn that the board had been favorable to this movement. From some things that have come under my observation, I have been led to believe that the members of the board were decidedly lukewarm regarding the proposition. However, the attitude of the board on the salary question is not of as vital interest as its attitude on the work in the ungraded school.
>
> Diligent inquiry reveals the fact that every institution and individual actively interested in the delinquent, neglected and so-called "bad" boys, such as the Humane Society, the juvenile court, the Associated Charities, the probation officers, the settlement workers, the Improvement League and the police department, are strongly of the opinion that the board has made a serious mistake

in taking Miss Snow out of the work in the ungraded school. Surprise and regret are uniformly expressed that she should be taken from the work for which she has given such intelligent, unselfish and successful effort. Inasmuch as the work of Miss Snow has been remarkably successful, it is difficult to understand why she should be removed to make a place for a man, simply because he is a man.

The board of education seems to be suffering from an attack of "manitis." Apparently, sex rather than efficiency determines their appointments to responsible positions. That Miss Snow stood well with the school authorities is evidenced by the fact that she was last year offered the position of principal of one of the large buildings at an advanced salary. Her devotion to the boys and the far-reaching work of the ungraded school impelled her to continue this line of work rather than assume a position of greater remuneration and dignity.

Personal observation of the work of this school leads me to state that Miss Snow has never spared her strength, her time or her purse when one of "her boys" needed any service in her power to give at any time of the day or night throughout the year. She has been mother, father, counselor and friend to every child who has come within the range of her work, and her removal from this splendid service calls for further explanation than is contained in your statement to the *Journal.*

Your statement seems to imply that the board did not approve of the action of the grade teachers in their endeavor to secure an increase in salary. Just why the board should take this attitude is not clear. The failure of the board year after year to take any action along this line compelled the teachers to take the initiative in the matter. The board of education and the teaching force of the schools are supposed to be public servants, and of equal relative importance in the administration of the school work.

The teachers are citizens and taxpayers as well as the members of the board, and are just as much entitled to a hearing before the legislature and the board of tax levy as any other citizens. There are numbers of people who think from their observation of the fate of certain teachers who have evinced independence of thought and action, that Miss Snow's removal from the ungraded school has some connection with her activity in the salary matter and who are righteously indignant.[9]

Stockwell reached out to all young people, but like Mae Snow, he had special sympathy for the "so-called bad boys" and those in financial need. He quickly sided with the bad boys when T. W. Stout, pastor of Minneapolis's Calvary Methodist Church, wrote to the editor of the *Minneapolis Journal* about ruffians at school dances:

In view of the agitation concerning the use of public schools for dancing, it seems advisable for those who oppose such action to state some reasons for their attitude. The ministers have become the mouthpieces of this opposition . . . Who should lead rather than they, if there be a question of morals involved? As to medical inspection, we consult the physicians. As to curriculum we consult the expert in pedagogy. In matters of morals, ought not the physicians of the spiritual life to know the things that complicate their effort to fill their important place in society?

Consider carefully what the dance as a feature of the social center idea means. Parents are told "your child is better off dancing at schools than in downtown dance halls." Do you know that the school is the social center for the lowest character in the community as well as the best? In every community are characters you would not have your daughter dance with. But they have as much right there as you. Supervision will not prevent their insidious presence. A school dance is a public dance and they are always dangerous.[10]

Stockwell immediately replied:

I read with interest in yesterday's *Journal* the letter of Rev. T. W. Stout on the question of dancing in our schools. It occurred to me that I would like to ask Mr. Stout which he considers the greater influence for immorality, dancing under proper chaperonage, and under proper environment or the retention in the discipline of his church of a prohibition against dancing and then allowing it to become so dead a letter that it smells to heaven.

Did Mr. Stout ever hear of this provision of his church discipline being enforced against anyone in the last 50 years, and is it not true that the last general conference of his church held in this city attempted to remove this article from the discipline of the church because it is a dead letter and failed by a very narrow margin? He suggests that ministers are experts in matters of morality. I have been led to believe that orthodox ministers know nothing about "mere morality," that their long suit is "religion."[11]

Illustrative of his concern for young persons in financial need was Stockwell's meeting with Edmond Franklin—a brief but memorable encounter for Ed, who later told the story to this author. When Ed was growing up in Minneapolis in the 1930s, Boys Vocational High was used as a dumping ground for the least promising students. His parents were on relief. He attended Boys Vocational because no fee of any kind was required. He was the brightest boy in school, sweeping through in two-and-one-half years. His teachers, believing he must go on to college, discussed his further education with their counterparts at Central High, who were certain the University of Minnesota would not accept him without two years of academic courses. Ed then completed the two years at Central High and was named to the National Honor Society.

The University of Minnesota was still out of reach, however, because there were simply no family funds available for further education. Then, in the spring of 1935, Ed heard of a brand new agency established under the New Deal, called the National Youth Administration. It reportedly furnished scholarships for deserving students. The National Youth Administration, however, was enveloped in the mist of Washington bureaucracy. What to do? How to get an application? Someone at Central High suggested getting in touch with S. A. Stockwell in the legislature, and a meeting was arranged. Ed remembers the certainty of Stockwell's prompt assurance: "We're going to find out where we can get an application for you." Together, going from office to office, they circled the Capitol. Within days Ed received three separate applications in the mail. He was granted a scholarship and money for subsistence—more money than he had ever seen—as well as a job in the physics department library.

"I don't suppose this is very important," Ed added, "but it was important to me."

Helping young people from the sidelines was not enough, and Stockwell in 1910 entered the citywide race for membership on the Minneapolis Board of Education. Candidates were identified on the ballot according to party. Members of the board served six-year terms. In response to the *Minneapolis Journal's* request for information, Stockwell submitted the following personal data:

> Democratic candidate for nomination as member of Minneapolis Board of Education. Age 53; insurance: Member of two legislatures. Platform: special attention to sanitary conditions; individual instruction for backward pupils; industrial training; free night schools; school buildings as civic and social centers; teachers to get voice in school management; rigid economy; and sound business methods.[12]

Stockwell won the Democratic nomination. The Republican nominee, Harrington Beard, defeated him in the November election with 15,355 votes to Stockwell's 12,090.[13] In 1912 Stockwell was nominated again, only to lose the election to Republican Henry Deutsch, 12,250 to 11,150.[14] In 1914 he made a final try. Arthur Benson defeated him, 15,285 to 15,156. A court-ordered recount confirmed the result.[15]

In the fall of 1914 a world war was raging. Had Stockwell received just 130 votes more, he would have been elected. He was an outspoken opponent of the country's entry into a world war in 1917. What use, if any, might he have made of his forum with respect to the war issue had he been on the Board of Education during those years? Would he have used his post to speak out against the country's entry? What if he had called for a negotiated peace after Congress's declaration of war? Or protested a textbook committee's banning of any books in the schools showing a positive picture of life in Germany? As Carl Chrislock has demonstrated with examples in *Watchdog of Loyalty: The Minnesota Commission of Public Safety during World War I*, such conduct in 1917 and 1918 might well have led to Stockwell's removal from office by the governor on grounds of "malfeasance."[16]

References

1. Violet J. Sollie to William P. Everts, March 28, 1988. Sollie and the Stockwells were neighbors and close friends in the early 1930s, when she was a student at the University of Minnesota. Active in the ranks of the Farmer-Labor party, she became a specialist in state and local taxation. Acting in behalf of her own dream, she returned to school and was admitted to the practice of law in Minnesota in 1957 at age 50.

Several newcomers to the legislature in the 1930s gave Stockwell credit for valuable guidance when they first arrived. Among them were Hjalmar Petersen of Askov, who later became governor. Steven J. Keillor has written of Petersen's indebtedness in *Hjalmar Petersen of Minnesota: The Politics of Provincial Independence* (St. Paul: Minnesota Historical Society Press, 1987), 83:

> If the 1931 session did not yield any memorable accomplishments for the freshman legislator, it brought him into close contact with one memorable individual who had something to teach: Representative Sylvanus A. Stockwell of Hennepin County. Shortly after the session started, Petersen wrote, "My seat is just next to Mr. Stockwell's so I talk with him every day." Few if any liberal legislators were better qualified than Mr. Stockwell to instruct the rural representative in liberal principles and the ways of the Minnesota legislature.

2. Perhaps at Hull House (see Chapter 8), Beth learned about protecting the little one from the bully. When the author was about eight years old, a new house was being built on the vacant lot next door. Francis Neall, Peggy Barton, and he decided to explore it. Everything was wide open—just the flooring and joists were in place. As they were in full view on the second floor, Mr. Minnis, the gruff, dour neighborhood policeman, walked down the sidewalk on his regular beat. "Get down from there right away," he ordered, "before I have you arrested." Beth overheard his threat and upbraided him as few parents would have dared.

3. David H. Holbrook to Stockwell, June 6, 1927. References are to Stiles P. Jones and Sampson Reed Child. [The letters and speeches here referred to were collected in the Stockwell Complimentary Birthday book dated June 8, 1927, now in the author's possession.]

4. Louella B. Cook, "Tribute to the Memory of Sylvanus A. Stockwell," typescript of memorial service address, Minnesota Historical Society.

5. E. Dudley Parsons, Remarks, Complimentary Birthday Dinner; Binder, "The Stockwells of Minneapolis." Following Dorothy Walton's marriage to journalist Carol Binder, she wrote a prize-winning article: "The Stockwells of Minneapolis," appearing in the New Republic, December 22, 1937. A typescript copy is in the Stockwell Family Papers, Minnesota Historical Society.

6. *Minneapolis Tribune*, December 13, 1928.

7. Victoria N. McAlmon, Remarks, Complimentary Birthday Dinner.

8. Victoria N. McAlmon, Remarks, Complimentary Birthday Dinner.

9. *Minneapolis Journal*, August 9, 1907. Mae Snow overcame the setback to her career. In 1910 she was elected to the Minneapolis Board of Education with more votes than those of all her opponents combined. With that victory, she became the first woman in Minnesota to hold elective office. See Mary Dillon Foster, *Who's Who Among Minnesota Women* (St. Paul: No publisher, 1924), 303. She served on the board continuously until her death in 1918 at age 46. Her singular ability in dealing with boys at what came to be known as the truant school was a revelation to her coworkers as well as a source of admiration for Stockwell. His daughter Charlotte, later a social worker herself, shared his admiration. This poem by Lillian Marvin Swenson, dated February 28, 1918, was found in Charlotte's desk at the time of her death in 1973:

> In Memory of Mae Snow
> Framed in heroic mould, she early bent
> Her willing shoulders under Duty's yoke;
> Life's burden crushed her not, but rather lent
> A new occasion for courageous joke.
>
> Broadminded intellect, wherein there lay
> Goodhumored tolerance of another's right;
> Brave heart, that fighting bravely day by day,
> Winning or losing, knew not petty spite.
>
> If in his chalice, offered her to quaff,
> Life strewed no rose leaves on its foaming brim
> She scattered them herself with joyous laugh,
> Nor did the world ere see her eyes were dim.
> She lived, she toiled, she served, and now is free.
> Courageous heart, what better end for thee?

10. *Minneapolis Journal*, December 17, 1912.

11. *Minneapolis Journal*, December 21, 1912.

12. *Minneapolis Journal*, September 18, 1910.

13. *Minneapolis Journal*, September 26, 1910; November 11, 1910.

14. *Minneapolis Journal*, September 29, 1912; November 6, 1912.

15. *Minneapolis Journal*, June 17, 1914; November 4, 21, 1914; December 16, 24, 1914. Representing Stockwell in the recount matter was S. B. Child.

16. Carl H. Chrislock, *Watchdog of Loyalty: The Minnesota Commission of Public Safety during World War I* (St. Paul: Minnesota Historical Society Press, 1991), 133-56; Steve Trimble, "It's the Law," *Roots* 13 (Spring 1985): 17-22. During U.S. military involvement in Vietnam in the 1960s and 1970s, the Mill Valley, California, School Board unanimously adopted a resolution in the spring of 1970, a year when the author was its chairman, condemning President Richard M. Nixon's expansion of the conflict into Cambodia, an intervention seen as unconstitutional and unwarranted. While this was hardly a local matter in the usual sense, school board members nonetheless regarded the president's action a matter appropriate for address because they believed his disregard of law and justice sullied the teaching environment of Mill Valley's schools.

Chapter 15

"Sustained Activities"

The number and variety of his sustained activities in the fields of politics, religion, economics, and, above all, in the social field almost defy enumeration.

—Benjamin Drake

On June 8, 1927, his seventieth birthday, Stockwell's friends honored him with a dinner at the West Hotel in Minneapolis. Hundreds attended. The program listed speakers addressing many of Stockwell's interests and concerns.[1] Two of these, the Saturday Lunch Club and the First Unitarian Society, were assemblies for the discussion of public matters. Benjamin Drake saw them as closely linked:

> His enduring loyalty to each was based upon the same convictions. He regarded each as a free forum of discussion. Other avenues of discussion and consideration might be closed, but in these places, if the wisdom of the speaker permitted, one might hear and learn the truth. No matter how novel or unpopular the doctrine, in these places a speaker was free to express and maintain his views.[2]

A third forum, closely akin to these two, was the annual Stockwell cornfest.

The Saturday Lunch Club

Stiles P. Jones founded the Saturday Lunch Club in 1906. Born in New York State and educated at Harvard, Jones headed west to become a journalist, first in Duluth, then in St. Paul and Minneapolis. By 1906 he had served as secretary of the Voters' League for three years; his experience there and as a newspaperman showed him the need for an open club where political, social, and economic issues could be threshed out in free debate. He called together a few kindred souls; Stockwell was one. The Saturday Lunch Club was launched.[3]

Those who attended the early meetings and made up the club's nucleus included Jones, Stockwell, Sampson R. Child, Carl J. Buell, Sidney M. Owen, then a regent of the University of Minnesota, and several judges, attorneys, and members of the university faculty.[4] The club was formed as a loosely knit organization with no constitution or bylaws and remained that. An executive committee of five, of which Stockwell was long a member, formed the club's responsible managment. All of the committee's actions were subject to revision by the club. Resolutions introduced by members automatically went to the executive committee unless the club decided unanimously to act at the time of introduction.

The format called for lunch, a speaker and a discussion. (Occasionally several candidates running for the same office appeared— generally to be heckled). The workweek was five and one-half days for most downtown office workers, so it was an easy matter for members to meet for lunch and stay for the discussion before heading home.[5]

The first lunching place was the popular Grill, on the alley across from the Metropolitan Theater on Marquette Avenue. When the membership grew, meetings shifted for a time to the West Hotel. Other meeting places were Dayton's Tea Rooms, the Dyckman Grill Room, the Catholic Women's Cafe, the Elks Club, the Radisson Hotel, the YMCA Dining Hall, the Andrews Hotel, and Donaldson's Tea Room. The basement of the First Unitarian

The First Unitarian Society, Eighth Street and LaSalle Avenue, Minneapolis (Millett's *Lost Twin Cities*, page 185. Courtesy of the Minnesota Historical Society)

Stiles P. Jones, founder of the Saturday Lunch Club. (Courtesy of the Minnesota Historical Society)

Society at Eighth Street and La Salle Avenue was the meeting place for three years.

The club came to be recognized as an institution of the city; word was that Minneapolis had two universities, the University of Minnesota and the Saturday Lunch Club. The generally critical attitude of the club in political matters gained it the enmity of professional politicians. Some called it the Yellow Dog Club, a title that pleased Jones. He said that those who contended for what seemed to be the truth, without fear or favor, must expect to leave behind all hopes for political or social advancement. So vehement was the opposition in some corners that a political henchman of Republican Edward E. Smith, veteran Minneapolis political leader, once declared to a member that if he could have his way the club membership would be lined up against a wall and shot.

Jones, through his wide acquaintance in public life and journalism, was able to attract speakers of the highest caliber. Their names comprised an abbreviated list of the who's who of the liberal movement of the United States and several other countries.[6]

William Maxwell, the Scottish president of the International Cooperative Union, representing thousands of cooperatives, in 1910 spoke of what Great Britain, Germany, Sweden, and Denmark were accomplishing with cooperatives. The cooperative movement, much on everyone's mind, was later taken up by various other speakers.

Wilson S. Lewis, a Methodist bishop, in 1912 told of his twenty years of service in China. He said that, when he was struggling with the language, he made it a habit to attend popular gatherings of Chinese. Understanding but few words, he was often startled by the hearty applause that greeted the names of Washington and Lincoln.

Several militant ministers, including the brilliant Rabbi Stephen N. Deinard of the Reform Temple and the Reverend Wilson M. Backus of the First Unitarian Society, spoke to the club, too.[7]

William Jennings Bryan talked about the petit and grand larceny of the law and the "glorious larceny" of practical politics when someone steals a railroad or state legislature.

Louis D. Brandeis, who had just electrified the country by offering to save the railroads a million dollars a day if given personal and supreme control, spoke to the club before being named to the Supreme Court. At probably the largest meeting ever held by the club, Brandeis impressed everyone with his gentleness, modesty, and wide grasp of public affairs.

Oswald Garrison Villard, editor of the *Nation*, twice addressed the membership on the political signs of the times.

John Haynes Holmes, brilliant pacifist preacher of Community Church, New York City, always spoke to the club when in the Midwest. Following a visit to Russia, he talked of the religious situation in that country.

Among foreign speakers from countries such as France, Ireland, Persia, England, Finland, the Soviet Union, and India were Jean Longuet, labor leader of France after the war, and Professor Tutuskin of Moscow, who outlined the educational program of the Soviet Union.

Jane Addams, "the best loved and most hated woman in America," talked of peace.

Governor Oswald West of Oregon, author of the "Good Behavior System" at Oregon's State Prison, spoke on prison reform.

Stiles P. Jones spoke on the Nonpartisan movement in North Dakota, a topic of keen interest to the club from the movement's beginning. The Nonpartisan League was widely feared by many as a dangerous radical experiment, and after William Lempke, attorney general of North Dakota, spoke to the club in the YMCA dining hall, the club lost its eatery on the pretext that the room was engaged to someone else on Saturdays thereafter.

Joseph I. France, United States senator from Maryland, called for the recognition of Russia.

Zechariah Chafee, Jr. (Courtesy of Betty Thacher)

W. W. Folwell, first president of the University of Minnesota, spoke in 1924 at age ninety-one on the constitutional organization of the electorate.

Arthur E. Morgan, president of Antioch College, described Antioch's experiment in combining cultural and vocational work in the same college curriculum.

Joseph Fels, millionaire single-taxer and philanthropist of Philadelphia, spoke on the doctrines of Henry George and told why he was distributing his "unearned increment."

Zechariah Chafee, Jr., legal scholar and professor at Harvard Law School, spoke, in all probability, on freedom of speech and civil liberties.

Thomas Van Lear, socialist mayor of Minneapolis, spoke at a New Year's celebration in his honor following his election in 1916.

Two United States senators, W. D. Washburn and Thomas Schall, as well as John Lind and Floyd B. Olson, were among local political leaders to address the club. Olson, who was to become a club member, first appeared when he was attorney for Hennepin County. Stockwell later said of Olson:

> When I saw this young attorney who had nothing material to gain by joining this Saturday Lunch Club which was scorned by the corporations from which he could justly expect retainers, I knew him for a sincere liberal, and I have not changed my mind in regard to him.

Clarence Darrow, renowned criminal lawyer of Chicago, displayed compassion and tolerance in a talk on crime and criminals.

Raphael Zon, international authority on the forests of the world, lectured several times on conservation.

Lincoln Steffens came twice, speaking the last time on conditions in Mexico at the time of Woodrow Wilson's presidency.

Williams Pickens, Abram L. Harris of the city's Urban League, St. Paul attorney William I. Francis, and Reverend Robert W. Bagnall ably represented the National Association for the Advancement of Colored People in their talks.

Among the speakers in more recent years were historian Charles A. Beard; Boston reformer and merchant Edward A. Filene, who encouraged labor participation in managerial decisions to the dismay of fellow employers; and Margaret Sanger, founder of the birth control movement in the United States.

Stockwell spoke on economics. He often reported on legislative measures that he thought would benefit the people of the state. And he was called upon to pay tribute to Eugene V. Debs, America's best known socialist and a man beloved by the membership. The memorial meeting for Debs was the only one ever held for a nonmember.

The club often listened to and was always very cordial toward the Public Ownership League of America as represented several times by Carl Thompson, the league's secretary. In September 1923, Stockwell, Buell, and William E. Leonard represented the club at a conference of the league in Toronto. While attending the conference, they visited Ontario's great Hydroelectric Plant at Niagara Falls. The visit enabled Stockwell to speak from personal observation about the plan he deemed a model of public ownership.

As E. Dudley Parsons, public-spirited, liberal Minneapolis teacher, has pointed out, the club became closely integrated with the liberal movement in Minnesota. A rallying point for progressives, it was the storm center of a streetcar controversy that raged from 1915 to 1918. The street railway interests were pushing for a law that would divide regulatory authority over street railways between the Railroad and Warehouse Commission and the municipalities served. This proposal was anathema to the progressives of Minneapolis, who believed local units of government must solely control their own utilities. Club members strove for an equitable solution of the matter short of legislation, but, led by Jones, George B. Leonard, Child, David Swenson, and Stockwell, they failed to block passage of the Brooks-Coleman Act in 1921, which took away sole control of Minneapolis's street railway from the city.[8]

Successful or not in furthering one cause or blocking another, the club served the liberal movement well. The meetings, the debates, and the speakers were stimulus to a large band of public-spirited men who were given the courage and wherewithal to serve the public interest as they saw it, knowing friends were behind them, ready to offer help and counsel. One graduate was David Holbrook, who went on to New York well prepared to become the secretary of National Social Service League. Others moving onward were Lynn Haines, C. J. Buell, and A. W. Rankin, who from 1909 to 1925 voluntarily undertook the scrutinizing, analyzing, reporting, and publishing of the successes and failures of the sessions of the Minnesota legislature. Haines ultimately moved to Washington, D.C., where he continued as a reporter and scrutinizer with his *Searchlight on Congress.*[9]

John H. Dietrich, minister of the First Unitarian Society and leader of the humanist movement nationally, gained moral support from his associates in the club as his humanist teachings drew mounting criticism from other religious sects and the Unitarian Church's mainstream. The same can be said of members who reached high public office, including United States senators Henrik Shipstead, Ernest Lundeen, and Hubert H. Humphrey, and Minnesota governors Floyd B. Olson, Elmer Benson, and Harold Stas-

Rev. John H. Dietrich, minister of the Unitarian Society of Minneapolis, 1916-1933. (Courtesy of the Minnesota Historical Society) sen. And of Stockwell, who was to return to the legislature in 1923 knowing that, should spirits flag, Saturday was renewal time.

Women were not admitted to membership until 1918, but, from the beginning, they appeared as speakers, and they were always welcome as guests. Beth and Charlotte Stockwell often attended, and the discussion they heard may have influenced their decisions to become social workers. After Beth moved to Boston in 1914, Charlotte, Althea Heitsmith Atwater, and Dorothy "Tommy" Walton Binder seldom missed a meeting. Atwater recalled how they loved the meetings, went almost every Saturday, regretted missing one, and were proud to be there: "They were very intelligent people—all men—and they discussed everything under the sun. OM was prominent."

The First Unitarian Society

The First Unitarian Society of Minneapolis was established in 1881 by a small group of liberal-minded men and women who were united chiefly by a dissatisfaction with the orthodox religions of the day. A common bond was their agreement that many things in the Bible seemed to go against reason. The first board of trustees called Henry M. Simmons of Madison, Wisconsin, to be their minister. He had studied for the Presbyterian ministry but left the fold for reasons of conscience. Simmons served as minister until 1905.[10]

Maud and Albert Stockwell attended the society's meetings occasionally in the 1890s and joined the organization in 1902. They were drawn to Simmons, who, in the words of Maud Stockwell, was a

> man sincerely devoted to truth seeking, utterly fearless in proclaiming the truth as he saw it, a scholar of note, a pioneer missionary of the philosophy of evolution, especially in relation to the religious life . . . When the Spanish War came, he fearlessly

Members of the First Unitarian Society gathered at a picnic at the Stockwell farm. (Courtesy of the First Unitarian Society of Minneapolis)

preached not only against the war, but against the subjugation of a weaker race, and, Sunday after Sunday, condemned Imperialism with righteous indignation and eloquent tongue, although he knew that many in his congregation did not agree with him.

In addition to having hearty rapport with Simmons, Albert Stockwell liked the society's agenda—the informal group meetings with lay leadership, the spirited Sunday school, and the society's practice of opening its doors to lecturers with cultural messages—literary, artistic, and scientific—from across the country and abroad. Reformers of all types spoke from its dais. No church in the city was as available or used as often for conventions, conferences, and lectures devoted to worthy, humanitarian causes. Here was discourse and fellowship of high order.

The ministers who followed Simmons were E. Stanton Hodgin, Wilson M. Backus, and then, in 1916, John A. Dietrich. With Dietrich came the society's most exciting, if not finest, hour. He set the society's humanistic course. Unitarians had always stressed the free use of reason in religion, and from the beginning they had seen themselves as freed from traditions and committed to open inquiry and the advancement of scientific truth rather than to Christianity and the Bible. Dietrich went further. He saw human aspiration as fundamental to religion, and he emerged as the country's foremost preacher and pioneer of humanism. His 1931 address, "Religious Humanism," outlined a radical religious advance. He said in part:

> Humanism in religion is the shifting of emphasis from God to man, making the enrichment of human life, rather than the glorification of God, the object of our allegiance and consecration. . . . The biggest and best thing that man can conceive is a human life nobly and beautifully lived, and therefore his loyalties and energies should be devoted to the arrangement of conditions which make this possible. . . . The solid issue, therefore, is to make this world a place which is conducive to the living of a noble, human life, and then help people in every possible way to live such lives. When boiled down to its very essence, that is Humanism.[11]

During Dietrich's tenure (1916-1936) Stockwell gained special strength and sustenance from the First Unitarian Society. Each party was the gainer. As Stockwell was Dietrich's beneficiary, so, too, was Dietrich the beneficiary of his parishioner. Dietrich wrote of Stockwell:

> Associated as he has always been with every liberal and humane movement, we naturally find him one of the pillars of the

liberal and humanistic movement which I have the honor of leading in this city; and I should like to testify to the unfailing support of Mr. Stockwell in every phase of this kind of religion. The same undaunted spirit which he manifests on every occasion where human life is concerned is one of the motivating influences of the First Unitarian Society of Minneapolis, which places human life above everything else as the object of all aspiration and endeavor.

Not only has his support of this Society been of great value to the liberal religious life of this community, but his dauntless courage and persistent vigilance have been a real inspiration to me as a public teacher. I myself am braver and more honest because of his unfailing courage and integrity. When I contemplate his words and deeds, it is easier for me to be more firm and erect.[12]

Dietrich, like Stockwell, was a pacifist. Both men opposed the country's entry into World War I. In his letter, Dietrich doubtless was recalling Stockwell's courageous commitment to principle during the war years, when, standing fast, he was pilloried unmercifully. And Dietrich was also recalling a period when he himself had suffered a severe public beating.

When the Scopes trial in Tennessee ended in 1925 and the defendant was convicted of violating state law by teaching the theory of evolution in the public schools, the fundamentalists in Minnesota, led by the militant William B. Riley, proposed to introduce into the next session of the legislature a bill that would prevent the teaching of the theory of evolution in Minnesota's public educational institutions. Riley, called by William Jennings Bryan "the greatest statesman in the American pulpit," was the minister of the First Baptist Church in Minneapolis and president of the Christian Fundamentalist Association. Dietrich's congregation did not remain idle in the face of Riley's proposal—the question of academic freedom was vital to the society. In 1926 its members organized into a committee to foster an unfa-

William B. Riley, minister of the First Baptist Church in Minneapolis and fundamentalism's chief national organizer. (Courtesy of the Minnesota Historical Society)

"Monkey Business before the House." (*Minneapolis Daily Star*, January 5, 1927)

vorable reception of the bill in the legislature. Orthodox clergymen, who favored academic freedom, lent their voices as did leaders of the academic community like Lotus D. Coffman, president of the University of Minnesota. The bill was defeated in 1927.[13]

The battle was not confined to the legislature. Riley, whose church was a mere two block from the First Unitarian Society, relentlessly assaulted Dietrich and his work: The methods of science and divine revelation were hopelessly at variance and, in Riley's view, revelation must be the victor. He saw Dietrich as the devil incarnate, and in a series of fiery sermons he portrayed Unitarianism, particularly the humanist movement, as the most sinister influence on American life. In the face of broad attack, Dietrich, like Stockwell a decade earlier, held fast. He made no answer but merely suggested to the members of his congregation that they hear Riley speak on the other side of the question.[14]

Whether Stockwell believed in God is unknown. Perhaps he stood four square with Thomas Paine, "a filthy little atheist" in the eyes of Theodore Roosevelt but in truth a deist. In *The Age of Reason*, Paine proclaimed his own deism at the outset. "I believe in one God, and no more; and I hope for happiness beyond this life." In *The Age of Reason, Part II* (1796), Paine analyzed the Old and New Testaments, book by book, critically demonstrating in lawyer-like fashion that the Bible is inconsistent and, therefore, not infallible. He rejected orthodox Christianity but still looked to God. He saw God's power "apparent in the immensity of the creation" and God's wisdom "in the unchangeable order by which the incomprehensible whole is governed."[15]

Stockwell probably held similar views—though there is no substantial evidence. Perhaps his references to God in conversation afford a scintilla of evidence. Mercedes Nelson recalled that such references were not infrequent. Nelson was the president of the Promethean Club, an organization of young people within the society based on the principle of freedom of inquiry. Stockwell was the club's friend and mentor. In a speech made at his seventieth birthday banquet, Nelson said that the club, "nearly perfect," needed "his guidance, inspiration, and sometimes chastisement." She was especially mindful of how, again and again, he softened his criticism with the words, "whomsoever the Lord loveth, he chastens."[16]

Whatever Stockwell's views, there is no doubt that many of his fellow legislators saw him as an atheist. An interruption of proceedings in the house of representatives in 1937 underscored the perception.

The chaplain customarily opened the day's affairs with a recital of the Lord's Prayer. Stockwell, while respecting the rights of others, did not think that prayer had any place in legislative proceedings. Ordinarily he just stepped outside when prayer was said. Louis W. Hill, Jr., grandson of James J. Hill and a newcomer in the 1937 house, recalled a painful moment:

> Mr. Stockwell was such a perfectionist about keeping his record clean on this score that once he found himself in the chamber when the Lord's Prayer was about to be recited. He rushed out, tipping over the spittoon in his haste. This showed how clean-cut he was.[17]

175

Carl Erickson, also present, said it was standard procedure for legislators to be issued huge brass spittoons. Stockwell tipped his over "with a clang that echoed through the chamber." He recalled the incident as "an atheist's noisy retreat."

Such rigid adherence to separation of church and state was seen by some outsiders as dangerous radicalism. Hjalmar Petersen of rural Askov, who entered the legislature in 1931, learned this early in his political career. In his biography of Petersen, Steven J. Keillor wrote:

> Petersen's association with the liberal Stockwell subjected him to some political attacks back home. In a 1931 birthday greeting to "Dear Friend Stockwell," Petersen wrote, "I have not been 'reprimanded' since last fall for being friendly to you in spite of your non-appearance in the chamber when the chaplain offers prayer." During his 1932 campaign for representative, he complained that his opponent, Therrien, was trying to depict him as a radical, partly because of his friendship with Stockwell. Some of the rural people were offended by Stockwell's causes even if he did milk cows in his bare feet.[18]

The Cornfests

The annual cornfest was a sustained activity of the Stockwells' own making. These late-summer gatherings on their farm began in 1906 when some twenty families brought their lunches and were served corn from the garden. The cornfests later attracted as many as two hundred families, who came on the day the corn ripened to perfection.[19]

Judge Vince A. Day of Hennepin County District Court traced the cornfest's beginning to the nature of the founder:

> I like to think of him as a lover of the good earth, as one who loved his flowers and his plants. He loved the soil and all the creatures, great and small, upon the earth. He believed that Mother Nature had provided a bounteous feast for all mankind, and that this earth, on which men lived and worked, should be the common property of all.
>
> I sometimes think his greatest joy was to share the harvest of his field of corn with his family or friends and neighbors. It was typical of him that he desired to share with others the bounties of nature, believing as he did that all the earth's resources of whatever kind belonged to the people, and that to permit them to become the private property of specially privileged owners was an infringement upon the inalienable rights of man.[20]

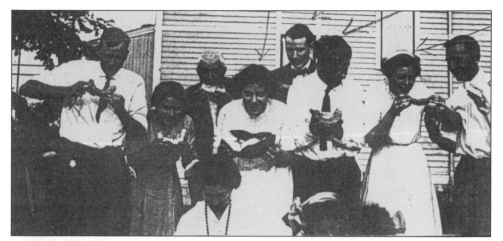

Unitarian cornfest at Stockwell's farm. (Courtesy of the First Unitarian Society of Minneapolis)

For grown-ups the cornfests were similar to the Saturday Lunch Club. Indeed, many of the same people came. After lunch there was a speaker, followed by discussion. The speakers ordinarily represented a minority group or an unpopular cause. There were single taxers and Negroes, Jews, Hindus, suffragists, and pacifists.[21] But how different from the downtown eateries of the lunch club was the setting of the cornfest—a picnic on spacious grounds, a touch of autumn in the air. (Genevieve McGraw, who clearly remembered Stockwell from her Sunday School days, recalled that it never rained). The attraction was the corn—fresh, sweet corn. "Corn never tasted so good," was the instant, spontaneous recollection of many participants. Husks and all, the corn was boiled in a washtub braced on an iron stand over a wood fire in a pit. The host was barefoot. There was a generous sprinkling of teachers who, protective of their Saturdays, were not apt to go to the lunch club. Conservatives came too; one was Frank Gleason, Irish Catholic undertaker who stood far to the right politically, and Andrew C. Anderson, bill collector for a law firm with an office

Stockwell speaking to guests at one of the cornfests. (Family photo.)

next to Stockwell's in the Andrus Building.[22] And here was the furnace repairman who fixed the coal furnace in the cellar of the Brin house. Ten-year-old Howard B. Brin had never before seen him out of uniform.

"Some who were there were called Bolsheviks," recalled Gerald Friedell, who came with his father, Aaron Friedell, Russian-born family physician of the Stockwells. Dr. Friedell had been called "a Communist, a Bolshevik" by the medical profession because he had instituted a prepaid and preventive health care system among his private patients.[23]

Children, in particular, added a happy dimension. Friends who had not seen each other all summer rejoined at the beginning of a new school year, to tell and retell of their summer's adventures. Howard B. Brin wrote:

> I suppose that I was 8 or 10 at the time—1927-1929. I remember the annual cornfest and picnic at the Stockwell farm. My mother was very active in the peace movement both locally and nationally, and that's how we got involved.
>
> Whole families were involved. There were activities for the kids, and I believe that they were supervised. Three-legged races and that sort of game, as well as just general running around through the corn fields. While the children were involved in their activities, the adults sat around, listened to speeches and heard about the state of the world and then had their discussion.[24]

Edward W. Harding wrote:

> I remember eating corn on the cob and other good things, and after the meal there were speeches by different people. This was in the early 1920s, and at that time my interest in speeches was not great. I played with the other kids after eating, the only rule being that we must not be loud enough to bother the speaker or the adults listening.[25]

Harry Levin, professor emeritus, comparative literature at Harvard, did not remember details of the cornfests, but he captured their essence:

> [S. A. Stockwell's] respected name rings a distant bell in my mind, which carries benignly liberal tintinnabulations . . . But I can now specifically remember, about that "socialist picnic" to which I was taken by my West High English teacher, E. Dudley Parsons, only a bustling and friendly occasion which took place somewhere near the banks of the Mississippi River. At all events, it seemed to be some distance from my Lake of the Isles background and my Republican manufacturing family.[26]

Althea Atwater, a regular attendee during and after her college years, was full of praise:

> The cornfests were wonderful. Everybody with any unanimity of feeling was invited. The corn was right from the stalk. Once I brought along a beau from Oregon. OM was in his bare feet. "There's a man after my own heart," my friend said to me . . . Another time the speaker was from North Dakota. He wanted to get the presidential nomination. He was very persuasive, and he got my vote if not many others.

A byproduct of the cornfests was political recognition and support. They gave Stockwell an opportunity to meet with his constituents. Another Minnesotan mindful of politics, former Governor Harold Stassen, some fifty years after attending a cornfest, credited Stockwell with "developing them into an institution . . . Everybody expected to come."

Hjalmar Petersen was among those who came. In a 1963 interview, Petersen recalled:

> The Stockwells used to have corn festivals . . . out at the end of town. My wife, Medora, and I were there several times. But on this one occasion (1931), Knud Wefald, the prominent Norwegian, a congressman from northwestern Minnesota, was the speaker and, by gosh, he came there with a swallow-tail coat—like the King of Norway and he gave his talk and then they started asking questions. Well, he wasn't used to that but he did pretty well. However, he was perspiring, it was a little warm anyway but he was kind of anxious and when the whole thing was completed, he came over to me and said, "I think this must be the intelligentsia of Minneapolis." It was a great revival. I've heard about it from children of Fanny Brin, who, as little children, would go.[27]

In his biography of Petersen, Keillor made further reference to the 1931 cornfest:

> Stockwell spoke on a wide range of issues, both foreign and domestic: The Irish republic, the Philippines, India, free trade, and American agriculture. Representative Petersen of Askov was present and took notes—on two comments in particular: "Our treatment of American Indian. Used most shamefully. Mpls. recently disgraced itself against the Negroes." These were issues not frequently discussed by local politicos of Pine County. The political education of Hjalmar Petersen was advanced by exposure to the causes and character of Sylvanus Stockwell.[28]

Activist Meridel Le Sueur, writer and teacher, who during the McCarthy era was blacklisted and barred from getting financial support from foundations, saw the cornfests as "a great communal celebration—a social, communal light. They were very political, but there was love and affection. Some Republicans came. The guests looked like vegetarians—they looked pure."[29] Le Sueur recalled that liquor was not served or seen at the cornfests. Stockwell was known to be an abstainer and prohibitionist. In his view—one doubtless held by most of his guests—the brewery-distillery complex embodied most of the evils against which progressivism was contending.[30]

The cornfest of September 1937 was the last. The thirty-one-year tradition ended when the Stockwells sold their house. It was a sad day for the Stockwells and their friends, as Violet Johnson Sollie remembered:

> I was sorry when I heard that the Stockwells were selling their home and told Mr. Stockwell so. He said the old house had gotten to be too much for Mrs. Stockwell. They had lived in an apartment during winter months when there was snow to shovel, and I thought they could continue, but he said it was time to sell and he had satisfied himself the buyers had some sense because they were going to save some of the magnificent old trees when they surveyed for the new contemplated buildings. While they lived there, the Stockwells had an annual cornfest, open to all it seemed, where their fresh corn raised on the land was the chief food . . . I had attended these. And now that tradition was over.[31]

References

1. Hundreds attended the dinner, and scores who couldn't come wrote letters. Stockwell's daughters, Beth and Charlotte, made the trip from Massachusetts. John Lind was a last-minute speaker. The participation of the Franklin Cooperative Creamery Association is noteworthy. The association had by 1922 become known as the showplace of the cooperative movement in the United States. Worker controlled, it functioned also as a consumers' cooperative. Stockwell was on Franklin's board of auditors and later represented the company as a delegate at national cooperative congresses. The association's thirty-five voice chorus sang at the dinner. Made up entirely of Franklin employees, it was thought to be the only milkman's chorus in the country; the company also furnished ice cream and cake for the party. Harold I. Nordby, president of Franklin, was scheduled to speak on cooperation but could not do so. His substitute, C. F. Sherman, vice president, knew Stockwell to be active at the creamery and in the cooperative movement generally and thought these were his main pursuits. He was dumbfounded to learn of the breadth of

Stockwell's other interests. For an excellent brief history of Franklin, see Steven J. Keillor, "A Remedy Invented by Labor: The Franklin Co-operative Creamery Association, 1913-1919," *Minnesota History* 51 (Fall 1989): pp. 259-269.

2. Benjamin Drake, "Tribute to the Memory of Sylvanus A. Stockwell," typescript copy of memorial service address, Minnesota Historical Society.

3. The material about the Saturday Lunch Club is taken in large part from two privately published pamphlets, William E. Leonard's *The Saturday Lunch Club of Minneapolis—A Brief History* (Minneapolis, 1927) and E. Dudley Parsons' *The Integration of the Saturday Lunch Club with the Liberal Movement in Minnesota* (Minneapolis, 1951). Marian Le Sueur joined Parsons in his undertaking, contributing *The Liberal Movement in the North Middle-West*. These pamphlets are available at Minnesota Historical Society.

4. Sampson Reed Child, a distinguished Minneapolis lawyer, was the father of Emily Child, who was Beth Stockwell's dearest childhood friend and a bridesmaid in her wedding.

5. Stockwell came for the speech and discussion, but he did not eat lunch. When Violet Sollie asked him why, he said the reason he could attend at all [in the early 1930s] was that he did not eat in the middle of the day.

6. The list of speakers enumerated by Leonard and Parsons is long but incomplete. The book of club notices and press comments from 1910 to 1918, authorized by the executive committee in 1914 and placed in Stockwell's custody, was stolen from his office amidst the war hysteria. His rooms were twice broken into and ransacked.

7. On September 16, 1914, Backus officiated at the marriage of Beth Stockwell and William Paine Everts.

8. See Leonard, *The Saturday Lunch Club of Minneapolis*, 9, and also Chrislock, *Progressive Era*, 187.

9. The legislative reports of these men covering the Minnesota capitol are available in pamphlet form at Minnesota Historical Society.

10. Here and below, "Our Debt to the Seventies," typescript copy of an address given by Maud Conkey Stockwell at the sixtieth anniversary celebration of the First Unitarian Society of Minneapolis on November 18, 1941, Minnesota Historical Society; Carleton Winston, *This Circle of Earth—The Story of John H. Dietrich* (New York: C. P. Putnam Sons, 1942), 136. See also Janet Salisbury, *First Unitarian Society of Minneapolis*, a brief history written in 1987, when Salisbury chaired the society's history committee. She placed the founding in perspective:

> In 1881 when Minneapolis was a "scattered, open frontier city of 50,000 without a foot of paved street but with an almost savage faith

in their ability to control their own destiny," a small group of liberal-minded men and women established the first Unitarian Society of Minneapolis. Establishment of the society "was an expression of that faith."

A copy of Salisbury's history is in the society's archives.

11. Winston, *This Circle of Earth*, 123; John H. Dietrich, *Religious Humanism—Excerpts from an Address by John H. Dietrich* (Minneapolis: The First Unitarian Society of Minneapolis, 1983).

12. Dietrich to William E. Leonard, June 8, 1927.

13. Mark A. Greene, "The Baptist Fundamentalists' Case Against Carleton, 1926-1928," *Minnesota History*, 52/1, Spring 1990, 16-25; Winston, *This Circle of Earth*, 175-177. While Bryan, who had assisted in the prosecution of the defendant Scopes, was high in praise of Riley, Clarence Darrow, chief defense counsel, was equally high in his praise of Dietrich. He declared that "the only church in the country that I would be willing to join is John Dietrich's." See Winston, *This Circle of Earth*, 190. Darrow also had words of praise for Stockwell in a letter of May 29, 1927 (errors in the letter were present in the handwritten original):

Chicago Ill.
May 29th

My Dear Mr Morris

Lest I will not be able to go so far away from home on June 8th I am replying to your letter. I was very sorry to get an invitation for Mr Stockwells 70th birthday. You may know that I just had a 70th birthday and likewise a dinner and it seems to me as if all the good men are dead or around 70 and it is really very sad.

I have long known and admired Mr Stockwell He has been a good fighter in the great cause of human liberty and I would dearly like to celebrate with you. It is however too bad that both he and I should be the same age. It would be better if one of us at least could have lived until some one else was ready to take up the fight. Still I am glad you are to show Mr Stockwell how much we admire and love him. Amongst his friends I am proud to be counted as one.

With all good wishes
Clarence Darrow

14. Winston, *This Circle of Earth*, 178-79.

15. *Dictionary of American Biography*, 7:159-66. *The Age of Reason, Part II* was sacrilege to R. Watson, D. D., F. R. S., Lord Bishop of Landaff and Regius Professor of Divinity at the University of Cambridge. With *An Apology for the Bible In a Series of Letters Addressed to Thomas Paine* (Philadelphia: "Printed for W. Young, Miller & Son, No. 52, Corner of Second and Chestnut Streets by W. Woodward," 1796), Watson sought to repair the damage worked by Paine. Stockwell somehow acquired a first edition of Watson's book (one Sarah Little had shown herself with flowing hand to be the owner in 1817), and he gave the book to the author with this inscription: "Well, Bill, we have made some progress in 141 years. Let's hope we make more in the next 141. October 3, 1937. S. A. Stockwell."

16. Remarks, Complimentary Birthday Dinner, June 8, 1927.

17. Hill added with warmth and candor, "I found him charming and good-natured. We got along well. I was a rich man and he was not, but this mattered not one whit. He was not a tin horn who talked one way and acted another. I am most happy to have had the chance to know him."

18. Keillor, *Hjalmar Petersen*, 84; Binder, "The Stockwells of Minneapolis."

19. *Minneapolis Tribune*, April 18, 1943.

20. Judge Vince A. Day, "Tribute to the Memory of Sylvanus A. Stockwell," typescript copy of memorial service address, Minnesota Historical Society. Desiring as he did to "share with others the bounties of nature," Stockwell gladly turned over his house and grounds—"the only farm nearby" in the words of E. Dudley Parsons, Jr.—to friends and relatives for their use. The First Unitarian Society often held Sunday school picnics on the land. Among many who held outdoor weddings there were Eugenia Day Gannsle; Marjory Child Husted (Betty Crocker of General Mills fame); Corelli Nelson Shupe, sister of Mercedes Nelson; Althea Heitsmith Atwater; and, Margaret Wagenhals Day.

21. *Minneapolis Tribune*, May 16, 1949.

22. Anderson, a Republican of conservative leanings who held a keen interest in world and national affairs, attended both the cornfests and the Saturday Lunch Club meetings. His wife usually stayed home. According to Janet Salisbury, his niece, he was extremely personable—ideally suited for bill collecting it would seem. The firm for which he worked let him go during the depression.

23. *Minneapolis Star and Tribune*, December 9, 1984.

24. Howard B. Brin to William P. Everts, March 25, 1988.

25. Edward W. Harding to William P. Everts, March 21, 1988.

26. Harry Levin to William P. Everts, March 3, 1990.

27. Papers of Hjalmar Petersen, Minnesota Historical Society, Interview with Russell Fridley and Lucile Kane, May 28, 1963.

28. Keillor, *Hjalmar Petersen*, p. 84.

29. Stiles P. Jones might have agreed vegetarians looked pure, but he would not have gone further. At one Saturday Lunch Club meeting, the speaker innocently referred to the gentleness of vegetarians. Jones bolted from his chair and cried, "So? Stockwell and Buell are all vegetarians." A great shout went up. Gentle or not, the Stockwells were vegetarians of long standing. Althea Atwater, who ate many meals with them, recalled that meat was never served, but she didn't miss it. "She could make anything out of nuts," Atwater said of Maud Stockwell. Atwater remembered in particular the time when another guest complimented Maud after din-

ner on the delicious turkey. Maud explained they hadn't had turkey.

Maud bestowed vegetarianism upon her daughter Beth, who in turn bestowed it sporadically on her own family. Beth did not inherit her mother's skill and interest in turning nuts into turkey or in cooking at all, for that matter. Nonetheless, for extended periods the family ate a canned product from Battle Creek, Michigan, called Nutelene, instead of meat. As prepared by household helper Bessie Houghton, it was passable fare.

30. Chrislock, *Progressive Era*, 31. Willis G. Underwood, a leading prohibitionist at the state and national level, told of Stockwell's stand on the liquor question at his seventieth birthday dinner:

> Whenever the gong sounded for a row or fight on the liquor question, you could always depend on Stockwell being in the ring. And more than that, you could always depend on Stockwell being effectively in the ring . . . He was peculiarly able to judge the situation, and to put the licks in where they would count for the most . . . He was always fair to his opponent. He gave some awfully hard knocks, but always above the belt, never below, no foul blows struck.

31. Violet Johnson Sollie to William P. Everts, April 11, 1988.

Chapter 16

Democratic Party Conventions 1910 and 1912

T he social activities that so absorbed Stockwell and to which he so gladly gave of his time and energy were plainly high priorities. Higher, it seems, than his everyday work at Penn Mutual. Yet, as general agent of the company, he had taken on a demanding job; he must have worked overtime at his desk in the Andrus Building. The population of Minneapolis soared during his years with the company: in 1890 there were 164,581 people; in 1900 there were 202,718. By 1910 this figure had risen almost 100,000 to 301,408, and in 1920 there were 380,582. The population of the city in 1930 had grown to 464,536. Penn Mutual grew with Minneapolis' population. About one-tenth of Penn Mutual's mortgage loans in the United States were placed in Minneapolis. In total amount, these loans exceeded the totals of any other insurance company

Ad from the *Blue Book of Minneapolis Clubs*, 1906.

doing business in the city. Much of that business was secured within the first twenty years of Stockwell's tenure as general agent, and nearly one-half of the business done by Penn Mutual in Minnesota was transacted through Stockwell's office.[1]

Although out of public office from 1902 to 1923, Stockwell stayed in the political arena and was frequently a delegate to state and county conventions of the Democratic party. The state convention in 1910 was memorable because the odds-on favorite did not choose to run. In 1912 Stockwell was a delegate to the Democratic national convention in Baltimore. Having earlier participated in so many losing battles, he must have gained special satisfaction in the triumph of Woodrow Wilson, candidate for the progressive wing of the Democratic party.

Democratic Convention, Minnesota, 1910

Upon the death of John A. Johnson in 1909, Adolph Eberhart, the thirty-nine-year-old Republican lieutenant governor, rose to the governorship of Minnesota. Again the Republicans were positioned to control both the executive and legislative branches of state government. Eberhart, however, demonstrated little leadership, and he failed to satisfy the progressives of either party. As the incumbent, he did win the Republican nomination in June 1910, despite progressive opposition, thereby presenting the Democrats with a golden opportunity to regain the governorship if they could come up with the right man. All eyes turned toward John Lind.[2]

Lind, who served three terms in Congress as a Republican before his single term as governor (1899-1901), returned to Congress as a Democrat for one more term in 1903. He found the Congress a much less interesting body than what it had been when he served previously, and he did not run for reelection. In a speech at St. Paul delivered on October 17, 1904, on behalf of newcomer John A. Johnson, Lind declared, "On the 3rd of March next my political career will end. I will never again seek or accept public office."[3]

As the Democratic state convention, scheduled for July 28, approached, pleas to Lind from Democrats and Republicans alike besought him to run once more for governor. He was acclaimed the one person who could rescue Minnesota from domination by the "interests." Nonetheless, Lind stated emphatically he would stand by his decision not to accept public office again. A few days before the convention he departed by train for Oregon.[4]

Despite Lind's statements that he would not accept a nomination, county delegation after county delegation was instructed to vote for him. Stockwell was a member of the Hennepin County delegation, as was Zed H. Austin, who had received a letter from Lind dated July 14 declaring positively that he would not accept the nomination if tendered. Stockwell and Austin, along with other

Political cartoon of John Lind. (*St. Paul Dispatch*, July 29, 1910)

of Lind's friends in the Hennepin delegation, believed he must be taken at his word and not be compelled to reject the nomination. The delegation adopted a resolution providing that,

> The services of Honorable John Lind to the state and nation clearly fix him as Minnesota's first citizen, worthy of any place of honor or service to which the people may call him . . . but we do not deem it wise to insist on his nomination for governor.[5]

187

The Hennepin delegation turned to John Jenswold, a dark horse from Duluth. The day before the convention was to open, Stockwell and Austin lobbied valiantly on behalf of Jenswold with the key Ramsey County delegation as well as other county delegations. They met no success. The hoped-for boom for Jenswold never developed. Jenswold bowed out, sought, and was granted the right to nominate Lind. The Hennepin County organizers for Jenswold had little to say as they watched the procession for Lind; they reluctantly joined in.[6]

"At the Headquarters of John Jenswold of Duluth." (From the *Minneapolis Journal*, July 28, 1910)

When the convention opened on July 28, the delegates shouted down those who sought to explain Lind's position. The *Minneapolis Journal* described the melee:

> Following Jenswold's speech half the delegates rose to their feet, yelling. There was an unsuccessful effort to make a demonstration. . . . The county roll call was resumed. Anoka, Beltrami, Benton. . . . Each one seconded Lind's nomination. J. M. Freeman of Olivia County moved that nominations be declared closed. This was carried *viva voce*, with only a few negative votes. It was then moved by Matt Fitzpatrick of Stewartville to make the nomination unanimous, but S. A. Stockwell took the platform to object. The delegates tried to cry him down, and he had hard work to obtain a hearing. "John Lind is a man of his word," he said, "and John Lind says he will not accept the nomination."
>
> Another roar from the convention drowned his voice. Before he could begin, Ed. A. Stevens arose to a point of order.
>
> "The nomination has been made," he said. "The only question before the house is whether the nomination shall be unanimous."
>
> Chairman Daley said the point was well taken, but Mr. Stockwell held the floor.
>
> Order was finally obtained by Chairman Daley when Mr. Stockwell promised to limit his speech to ten words.
>
> "I have too much hope for the future of the Democratic party, too much faith in John Lind, to think that he is either incompetent or a liar," said Mr. Stockwell. The remainder of his remarks were drowned in catcalls and yells of derision.[7]

True to his word, Lind refused the nomination. The Democratic central committee chose James Gray, who had served one term as mayor of Minneapolis, in his place. Eberhart won reelection decisively.[8]

President Wilson later chose Lind as his personal representative for an extended mission to Mexico. Lind never again sought public office. His biographer doubted any man could be found in the history of the country who could match Lind's record of dodging nominations and proposed nominations.[9]

Democratic National Convention, 1912

The Republicans held their 1912 national convention for the selection of a presidential candidate at Chicago in mid-June. William Howard Taft, Theodore Roosevelt, and Senator Robert La Follette of Wisconsin were the contenders. Animosity had arisen between Roosevelt and Taft, whom Roosevelt had handpicked to succeed him four years earlier. Despairing of Taft's rejection of pro-

189

gressivism, Roosevelt threw his hat back into the ring in February, four months before the convention. Party regulars renominated Taft but not without cries of thievery from the Roosevelt forces. The Republican party was split; the possibility of Roosevelt's running on a third-party ticket loomed large.[10]

In Minnesota, Stockwell was an early admirer of New Jersey governor Woodrow Wilson. As a member of the executive committee of the Hennepin County Democratic Committee, Stockwell organized a Wilson-for-president movement, and he was subsequently chosen as a delegate-at-large in Minnesota's delegation to the Democratic National Convention scheduled the last week of June in Baltimore, just days after the Republican imbroglio.[11] As the delegation shuttled through the streets of Chicago to change trains for Baltimore, its twenty-four members surely rejoiced at the political shambles left behind by the Republicans. Here was the chance to win the election in November—if only a progressive candidate could be put across. They were bound by instructions and by their own enthusiasm to cast all of Minnesota's votes for Wilson.

The leading Democratic candidate and choice of the party loyalists was Champ Clark of Missouri, speaker of the House of Representatives and a middle-of-the-roader. Governor Judson Harmon of Ohio had the support of Tammany Hall. Oscar Underwood of Alabama represented the "Bourbon Democracy of the South." Wilson commanded the progressive wing of the party.[12]

When the delegates reached Baltimore, they found the city jammed with visitors. The hotels were oversubscribed. The atmosphere, charged with excitement but laden by the humidity, was sweltering. The Minnesotans shared a hotel with delegates from several southern states. At once they began missionary work on behalf of Wilson and were pleased to discover a friendly feeling for him among Underwood delegates, who seemed more likely to go for him than for Clark.[13]

William Jennings Bryan led Nebraska's delegation. Despite his defeats in 1896, 1900, and 1908, he unquestionably dominated the convention. Bryan supported Champ Clark.

Another man whose presence would be felt was Thomas F. Ryan, of the Virginia delegation. A Wall-Streeter tied to the monied interests, he had been slipped by Democratic party machine leaders into the delegation by trickery. They believed his presence would be influential in bringing about results hoped for by conservatives.[14]

When the convention organized, Bryan and Alton B. Parker, his old rival who had led the Democratic ticket in defeat in 1904, were the contenders for temporary chairmanship. Pursuant to instructions to the Minnesota delegation to vote for Wilson as a unit on all matters, Stockwell drafted a resolution that was adopted by the delegation without dissent:

> That we demand a progressive candidate for temporary chairman of this convention and that if Alton B. Parker is presented as a candidate for temporary chairman, we will under our rules vote as a unit against him.[15]

Parker won the chairmanship by a margin of 579 to 510, but the reaction across the country to the choice of Parker was highly negative. Bryan's influence was enhanced in defeat. Stockwell took heart from Bryan's strong showing:

> "I am glad Bryan made the fight," said S. A. Stockwell. "I am glad that we know where we stand. I believe that many voted for Parker under protest and at any rate their margin is very small—nothing like enough to control the convention."
>
> Asked by Ray G. Farrington of Ortonville whether he thought there was a conservative majority out there, Stockwell said no.
>
> "Neither do I," said Farrington, "and I believe there will be a progressive candidate nominated."
>
> "That depends on what you call a progressive," said Stockwell. "I suppose you call Clark a progressive."
>
> "Yes, I do," said Farrington.
>
> "Well," said Stockwell, "That is where we differ, you see. Bryan has made an awful mistake in not opposing Clark from the start. Clark is not a progressive and I would not vote for him if he is nominated."
>
> Stockwell, usually a fire eater, was the most unperturbed of all during and after the vote yesterday. "I had it all figured out that we would lose," he said. "I only wanted to see how well Ryan's attorney could earn his fee."[16]

The close Parker-Bryan contest was quickly followed by another boost for the Wilson forces:

> The progressives claimed a notable victory last night when they carried a motion abrogating the rule by which some state delegations were bound to cast their votes as a unit. The fight for and against the unit rule was waged particularly about the state of Ohio, where 18 district delegates had been instructed by primaries to vote for Wilson but where the state convention, controlled by Harmon forces, had invoked the unit rule binding all Ohio delegates to the Ohio governor, Harmon.[17]

Here was a discernible move for Wilson; it was likely other states would follow. Victory over Tammany Hall on the Ohio question, which coincided with remarks by Senator William Stone, head of Missouri's delegation, seen as linking Clark with Tammany Hall, brought joy to the Minnesota contingent:

> Nimble, dancing joys have chased the glooms from Minnesota headquarters. The delegation from the gopher state had an informal jubilee today to rejoice over the victory on the Ohio vote last night.
>
> "I yelled last night for the first time," said S. A. Stockwell. "You can tell the folks at home that the houn' dawg is dead. 'Gum Shoe Bill' Stone killed him with Tammany rough on rats."[18]

Before the balloting got under way, Bryan fired a salvo at Thomas F. Ryan and Wall Street: "I resent Ryan and [August] Belmont coming here with their paid attorneys and conferring with their party leaders." He then proposed a resolution declaring the convention opposed to the nomination of any candidate for president under obligation to J. Pierpont Morgan, Ryan or Belmont, or any other member of the privilege-seeking class. His challenge and resolution hit the convention hall like a bombshell. Over strenuous protest, the resolution passed, 899 to 196.[19]

When the nominating process began, the roll call on the first ballot gave Clark the lead: Clark 444½, Wilson 324, Harmon 148, others 173. New York voted for Harmon from the outset. Underwood would have been acceptable. On the tenth ballot, however, New York transferred its ninety votes from Harmon to Clark. Charles F. Murphy, the Tammany boss, gambled that the switch would signal a surge to the Speaker of the House. Clark was torn between accepting or rejecting. In the end he accepted. Wilson, disregarding the advice of William F. McCombs, his campaign manager, stated flatly that he would not accept the nomination if it depended upon the Tammany vote. Bryan, already half won over to Wilson, released the Nebraska delegates from their pledges and cast his own vote for Wilson because he felt Clark would be beholden to Tammany Hall.[20] The tide turned in Wilson's favor. On Monday, July 1, he took the lead 460 to 455, on the thirtieth ballot. The next day Underwood withdrew. Clark delegates were released. On July 2, on the forty-sixth ballot, Wilson was finally nominated by the necessary two-thirds majority.

Weary from night-long sessions, worn down by unremitting heat and humidity, the Minnesota delegation, which never wavered but voted forty-six times for Wilson, was ready to return home. "The Houn' Dog is for Wilson now," a member of the Missouri delegation shouted to the Minnesotans as they prepared to depart.[21]

Stockwell actively campaigned for Wilson. On November 5, 1912, Wilson was elected president with 435 electoral votes. Roosevelt received 88 votes, Taft only 8. Minnesota's electoral votes were cast for Roosevelt in one of the rare instances when Minnesota did not vote for the winning presidential candidate.

On July 24, 1914, Austria declared war on Serbia, beginning World War I. On September 17, 1914, the headline for the *Minneapolis Journal* read: "3,000,000 Men in Battle in Aisne, Raging for 150 Miles."

On the same day, the paper reported on page 10:

> Miss Elizabeth Stockwell, daughter of Mr. and Mrs. Sylvanus Albert Stockwell, and William Paine Everts of Boston, Mass., were married last evening at 8:30 o'clock at the home of the bride's parents, 3204 East 51st Street. Rev. Wilson M. Backus of the First Unitarian Society officiated. Miss Charlotte Stockwell was her sister's maid of honor and the bridesmaids were Miss Christine Everts of Boston, a sister of the bridegroom, Miss Eugenia Day, a cousin of the bride, and Miss Emily Child. Ward Paine of Boston, a cousin of the bridegroom, was the best man . . . Mr. Everts and his bride will be at home after November 1 at 41 Pilgrim Road.[22]

Beth had met William P. Everts, a Boston lawyer fourteen years her senior, in Burlington, Wisconsin, while visiting Conkey relatives. She and Everts, on business in the Midwest, met and fell in love at a house party. They courted long distance (the author has possession of poems written to her during and after their courtship), and on September 12, 1914, they married at the Stockwell home, when Beth was twenty-one.

On the day of the wedding, Maud suddenly missed Albert. He had disappeared. Althea Atwater found him in tears, leaning against a tree in the orchard. "She's so young, she's so young," he cried.

References

1. *History of Minneapolis and Hennepin County*, 495. Stockwell's grandchildren never heard him utter a word about his business life. They knew he was associated with Penn Mutual, but there was always the feeling

that his was just a job to keep body and soul together. Althea Heitsmith Atwater, who attended the University of Minnesota at the same time as Charlotte Stockwell did, told the author in 1985 that Albert "never talked business or about business." After graduation, she took a job paying sixty-five dollars per week and went to Sauk Center to buy an insurance policy. When she requested a thirty-five-dollar loan of Stockwell to pay the premium, he asked, "Why didn't you buy it from me?" She had not even known he was in the insurance business! "He said he would make me the loan but declined my offer to pay interest," she concluded.

2. Chrislock, *Progressive Era*, pp. 37-40.

3. Stephenson, *John Lind*, pp. 192, 197.

4. Stephenson, *John Lind*, pp. 199, 201.

5. *Minneapolis Journal*, July 23, 1910.

6. *Minneapolis Journal*, July 28, 1910. St. Paul lies in Ramsey County.

7. *Minneapolis Journal*, July 29, 1910.

8. Chrislock, *Progressive Era*, p. 39.

9. Stephenson, *John Lind*, p. 203.

10. Morison and Commager, *Growth of the Republic*, 2:416-20.

11. *History of Minneapolis and Hennepin County*, p. 496.

12. Morison and Commager, *Growth of the Republic*, 2:422.

13. *Minneapolis Journal*, June 26, 1912.

14. *Minneapolis Journal*, June 27, 1912.

15. *Minneapolis Journal*, June 25, 1912.

16. *Minneapolis Journal*, June 26, 1912.

17. *Minneapolis Journal*, June 27, 1912. The Minnesota delegation was not affected by the ruling. The ruling applied only to states where the delegates were chosen under state primary law by congressional districts.

18. *Minneapolis Journal*, June 27, 1912.

19. *Minneapolis Journal*, June 28, 1912.

20. *Minneapolis Journal*, June 29, 1912.

21. *Minneapolis Journal*, July 2, 1912; Maud Stockwell to William P. Everts, May 13, 1958.

22. *Minneapolis Journal*, September 17, 1914.

Chapter 17

The World War

Long before the country's involvement in World War I, Stockwell was addressing the question of war or peace. Europe had been preparing for war from the early days of the twentieth century. Peace was precarious.[1] What could an American citizen 4,500 miles away do about all this? What tiny step could one take? How best to air the problem? Write letters to the editor? Would that help, even imperceptibly? At the time of the Spanish-American War, Stockwell had sought to counter imperialist jingoism by telling the other side of the story. As a private citizen in 1912, in a country that was not at war or on the verge of war, he chose another way—to focus the eyes of the younger generation on the grave question of war or peace. He instituted an annual essay contest on some subject connected with peace for pupils in the five high schools of Minneapolis.

The first prize in the contest was $15.00 and a plaque. Second prize was $10.00. A panel of three judges determined the winners. In 1912 Olga Auran of South High School tied Madelyn E. Wilcox of North High School, and each received $12.50. Auran, valedictorian of her class, wrote an essay calling for immediate disarmament of the United States.[2]

Two years later Stockwell offered cash prizes for the best essay on another subject: "Would Intervention in Mexico by the U.S. Be Conducive to Worldwide Peace?"[3] In 1915, Ruth Sevon, a seventeen-year-old junior at North High School, won first prize for her essay on the subject "Is the Maintenance of a Large Army and Navy Conducive to World Peace?" Clinton Loehlin of East High School came in second. Three students tied for third, for which there was no prize. The local *Chronicle* extended heartiest congratulations to Sevon and called her victory as worthy of public attention as a winning football team.[4] She wrote in part:

When our boys are old enough, we teach them the stories of the famous deeds of great military patriots. We buy them guns and tin soldiers and encourage them to play that they are real soldiers. . . . Their trade once established, they are not going to give it up without a conflict. . . . They want to try out their guns and test their new maneuvers. . . .

Furthermore, who desire standing armies and navies? Why, the armament works, contractors, sabre rattlers. . . . The Krupp gun works in Germany was by all means the chief factor in arousing this war and making it possible. . . .

In 1910 two-thirds of all our expenses were for war, and in 1907 the four nations of United States, Great Britain, Russia and Germany spent $1,184,000,000 on their army and navy. This great expense has also moral effects on the people. Unnecessary poverty menaces the lives in the state, while relieving it would do a work of collective character building. The best way to grasp the effects of such great expenditure is to see what would happen if we had 100 percent of the country's revenue instead of only 28 percent which is now available. We might irrigate dry plains, restore forests, build waterways for heavy traffic, and build beautiful roads and highways. We could stamp out tuberculosis, hookworm, cancer and rabies and put an end to the introduction of plagues. We could build more schools, universities and encourage the study of art. On the whole, where would our country be in the point of well-being if this would be done?[5]

Two years later the *New York Times* announced that the National Board of Historical Service, as if not to be outdone, was conducting a contest among high school and elementary school teachers for the best war essay. A first prize of seventy-five dollars was promised to the winner.[6]

Stockwell was indignant about military matters. His indignation was reflected in a letter to the *Minneapolis Journal* written three years before the outbreak of war:

As a citizen and taxpayer, I would like some member of the Board of Tax Levy to explain to me by what process of reasoning they reached the conclusion that it was wise and desirable to allow $25,000 to an institution that is worse than useless—the armory—and could not find money to properly support night schools and adequately care for our city hospital.

It would seem quite as important to educate the future citizens of the city and care for the sick and unfortunate as to enlarge the place where young men are taught to strut and to kill each other.[7]

Nothing in the years to come changed his views. If anything, the advent of war only reaffirmed them. He deplored the glorification of war. A resolution before the state house of representatives in 1925, to which Stockwell had returned two years earlier, requested that the secretary of war aid Minnesota in obtaining the colors of the Fifty-fourth Infantry, then held in New York, so that they could be placed in the rotunda of the Minnesota capitol alongside other flags representing the state's part in previous wars. In an effort to defeat the resolution, Stockwell told the house:

> I would take the flags out of the Capitol and put them out of sight and in their place I would paint a picture of what war really is.
>
> I want to stop this glorification of war, and if I had my way about it, I would paint a picture of the battlefield with its mud and mire, its death and its dire.
>
> I would paint a picture of 40,000 young men who are in the madhouse, there to remain for the rest of their lives.
>
> I would put in the rotunda of the Capitol a picture of the blind, countless thousands of them who will never again see the light of day, the other thousands who are dying in hospitals from tuberculosis.
>
> I would paint a picture of the real monster to show you what war really is and not the picture that is put up before you.
>
> I would write the story of the cost of the war and put it in the Capitol where everyone could see it. In the story I would tell how 92 cents out of every dollar paid in taxes goes to the past, present and future support of this demon.
>
> I would tell them of the outrages committed by American marines in the island of Haiti, where 3,000 youths of that country were put to death in cold blood by our troops.

Various members of the House sprang to the defense of the flags resolution. All, except Stockwell, voted in its favor.[8]

Robert Haagenson, who became a member of the First Unitarian Society in 1936 and thereafter a friend of Stockwell's, attributed Stockwell's outlook towards those in uniform to his deep-seated belief in the equality of all people. Haagenson, who had been severely wounded in the war and placed on total disability, recalled:

> He was good to all of us. He didn't care whether you were black or white or brown. It mattered not at all who you were. He was independent. He had no special respect for the military. It didn't mean a thing to him if you were a five-star general or what. He wouldn't stand up.

Although Europe was engulfed in war by midsummer of 1914, hardly anyone thought the United States would be drawn in.

There was wide determination to stay out. The sinking of the *Lusitania*, torpedoed off the coast of Ireland on May 7, 1915, brought clamors for war against Germany from Theodore Roosevelt and several other public figures. Some of the press took up the cry. Still, general opposition to entry into the war held firm. The country was mindful of Washington's advice to avoid entangling alliances. The press generally favored President Wilson's stand of nonintervention; in 1916 he was reelected, though narrowly (277 electoral votes to 254), on a platform proclaiming that he had kept the country out of the war. Stockwell campaigned for him in 1916 as he had in 1912.[9]

By 1917 the antiwar sentiment had shifted in Minnesota and across the nation. Germany's submarine warfare against merchant shipping, which, up until that time, had varied in intensity, mounted. When Germany informed the United States on January 31, 1917, that henceforth Germany would sink on sight all merchant vessels, armed or unarmed, within a military zone around the British Isles and in the Mediterranean, diplomatic relations between the two countries were severed. War was imminent.[10]

Conservatives representing business interests and supporting increased military preparedness tended to favor entry into the war, while liberals tended to oppose it. By early 1917, the press in Minneapolis and St. Paul had become intolerant of those unwilling to recognize the need to discipline Germany. Targeted in particular were trade unionists, socialists, and German-Americans. Trade unionists, at least in the early stages of the war, saw it as but another advantage for capital at the expense of labor. Socialists similarly saw capitalism as demanding war for its own gain at the expense of the working class. In their view, capitalism was dictating war for the protection of its trade with Great Britain and the further acquisition of new fields for industrial exploitation. Socialist doctrine in its most extreme form denied any justification for war. The antiwar attitude of German-Americans, who constituted a major segment of Minnesota's population, typically was based on sympathy for the fatherland. Swedes, another significant block, were pacifist by nature and generally opposed to war.[11]

Charles A. Lindbergh, Sr., outgoing member of the Sixty-fourth Congress from the Sixth Minnesota District, and Ernest Lundeen of Minneapolis, were among the congressmen opposing entry into the war.[12] Thomas Van Lear, socialist mayor of Minneapolis, was in accord. A gifted public speaker, Van Lear rose through the ranks of labor to become mayor in 1916. His determination to stay out of the war meshed with Wilson's position in 1916. Ban-

Thomas Van Lear. (Sussman photo, courtesy of the Hennepin History Museum)

ners for the elections of Wilson and Van Lear were widely displayed on the streets of Minneapolis. Stockwell campaigned vigorously for both. Early in 1917, when U.S. entry into the war seemed inevitable, Van Lear declared he would not back Wilson's war policy. When Wilson severed diplomatic relations with Germany, Van Lear called a mass meeting in the Minneapolis Auditorium to protest.[13]

An enormous crowd attended. Throngs spilled over into the street. Prowar observers estimated the number as "probably five or six thousand." The *Socialist New Times* reported an "immense throng of nearly 25,000."[14] Van Lear, the principal speaker, assailed the munitions manufacturers who, he asserted, were seeking to plunge the country into war. When he launched into an attack on the *Minneapolis Tribune* and "patriots for revenue only," the audience went into an uproar.[15] Stockwell was among the speakers:

> Mr. Chairman, women, and men: I count it the greatest honor to address this splendid audience tonight in behalf of peace. We are assembled to exercise the free man's right of free speech and peaceable assemblage. We are not here to throw bricks at the administration, nor to place anything in its way. We are here to protest against war. [Long continued applause and rising.] In these hours what can a free man do when the press and the pulpit desert it? If they will not consider our nation's welfare, where can we be heard?
>
> I hold in my hand a copy of *The Minneapolis Tribune*. [Hisses.] The public press is attempting to stampede the American people into war. That paper—read its headlines. Every sentence for the purpose of stampeding us and we are here to protest.
>
> I want briefly to pay my respects to the custodians of canned patriotism. When our ancestors came to this country in 1628—I claim to be an American but I insist that that fact does not make any reason why I should be expected to settle these questions any more than the last man who has settled on our

"A crowd marched through downtown St. Paul in a loyalty parade during World War I."
Minneapolis Star Tribune article about World War I, November 13, 1991. (Photo courtesy of
the Minnesota Historical Society)

shores. These men who shed great briny tears whenever the
Stars and Stripes are displayed, but yet who spit upon, who
drag in the dust, the ideals for which that flag exists. Such
patriotism!

My friends, I am here because I stand with Thomas Paine.
"The world is my country; to do good is my religion." We are here
tonight to extend the hand to brothers across the Atlantic in the
war-torn countries of Europe, and to ask them to desist from
their struggle, to meet as brothers and settle these difficulties.

My friends, I congratulate Minneapolis that it is able to defy the
organized interests of this and every state, and we stand here
tonight to express our ideas, and to advocate peace at any cost.[16]

At the close of the meeting, resolutions denouncing the
press, urging citizens to keep out of banned war zones, and that
"our land be kept at peace" were unanimously adopted by the audience for delivery to President Wilson and Congress. One in particular reflected Stockwell's view, if not his hand:

We desire to respectfully recall the fact that in the elections of
November, the citizens of this country strongly favored our
keeping out of the war in Europe and the administration then

200

elected was committed to a policy of peace. To now abandon that policy and plunge us into war, we hold, is to make a solemn mockery of the great American principle of the consent of the governed.[17]

The rally infuriated local war enthusiasts. Determined "to restore Minneapolis' good name," they answered with meetings of their own throughout the city. A Minneapolis Loyalty League under the presidency of Cyrus Northrop, the highly regarded president emeritus of the University of Minnesota, was created.[18] The country was not at war, but the truth of a prediction made by Wilson as he agonized over the decision he faced was already evident:

> Once lead this people into war and they'll forget there ever was such a thing as tolerance . . . to fight you must be brutal and ruthless, and the spirit of ruthless brutality will enter into the very fibre of our national life, infecting Congress, the courts, the policeman on the beat, the man in the street. Conformity would be the only virtue . . . and every man who refused to conform would have to pay the penalty.[19]

At the Saturday Lunch Club, the question of war or peace overshadowed all else on the agenda. Lunch meetings broke up at suppertime. On March 24, the club was expected to record its stand on the question of loyalty to President Wilson pursuant to a

Liberty Loyalty Day Parade, October 1917. (Courtesy of the Minnesota Historical Society)

resolution proposed by J. Lynn Nash. The resolution had been referred to the executive committee, of which Stockwell was chairman. Stockwell asserted that he was a "loyal pacifist" but did not intend to stand in the way of a free and full discussion by loyal militants.[20]

Three hours of heated discussion followed, finally leading to the adoption of a rising thirty-three to nineteen vote on a watered-down version of Nash's proposal:

> Resolved, that much as we deprecate war, we do affirm and reaffirm our undivided support to our government in this crisis, and that to the full extent of our liberty, our lives, and our property.

There were calls for the vote to be made unanimous but Stockwell, presiding, declared the vote should stand at thirty-three to nineteen; he objected to any attempt to force something down the throats of members who had voted against the resolution.[21]

Stockwell spent all his energies during the days leading to America's entry into the war in trying to avert it. He never gave up. The night before Congress declared war on Germany he was chairman of a mass antiwar meeting at the Lyceum. If the course was irreversible, still he would try to reverse it. The very attempt would have meaning, if not in changing the result, in the purity of one's heart. And the final count of right and reason, as he saw it, would be closer on the day of reckoning because of his vote.

Tirelessly Stockwell sought to hold others to the cause and to enlist new supporters—persons willing to write letters, stamp and seal envelopes, send telegrams, attend rallies, speak out in protest. His vehicle was the American Neutrality Society, which had been active in Minnesota since 1915. The society flooded the state with this petition in late March:

> Petition
>
> We . . . the undersigned citizens . . . exercising our constitutional right of petition respectfully urge our president and congress not to plunge our country into the European war. . . . The present war is not our war and we are opposed to extending military or financial aid to either side to continue the struggle . . . The sending of our armed merchant vessels, loaded with ammunition and arms, through the war zone is certain to provoke war, a useless war that can and ought to be avoided.[22]

The society's plans called for establishing branch societies throughout the state, which in turn were to hold mass meetings for the adoption of resolutions calling for peace. Smaller gatherings were to be held in churches, clubs, schools, business organizations, factories, private homes, on the streets—"everywhere you can get together a few friends of peace." Copies of resolutions as adopted were to be mailed to the president, his cabinet, and members of Congress. After resolutions were mailed, there should be follow-up with a letter or telegram—"The personal touch counts."[23]

In addition to cultivating and harnessing grass-roots support for the cause of peace, the society cooperated with the Emergency Peace Foundation of New York in organizing a peace march to Washington. Stockwell recruited delegates for the march and was the society's spokesman. He told the *Minneapolis Journal* that every effort would be made to arouse sufficient enthusiasm for the "On to Washington" movement planned for April 2 by the Emergency Peace Federation of New York, to insure a big Minneapolis representation. His predictions were highly optimistic:

> I am sure that at least 25 peace advocates will go to Washington to be present when congress convenes. . . . We hope to have many more. It is planned to have 50,000 members of the federation in Washington, and we are going to stay until congress hears us. David Starr Jordan will be the chief speaker. We are going to tell congress that peace is preferable to war, no matter what Germany does.[24]

On April 1 Stockwell reported from New Ulm, a Minnesota town German in speech and custom, that the members of the Minnesota delegation would be in Washington the next day to protest against the war. "They are paying their own expenses," he said.[25]

On April 6, Congress passed a joint resolution declaring war on the German empire. On April 7, Stockwell was asked to give up the offices he had occupied in the Andrus Building for twenty years.

When war was declared, the fortieth session of the Minnesota legislature was all but over. The legislature would not meet again until 1919. To fill the vacuum in time of crisis, the legislature hastily established the Minnesota Commission of Public Safety (Laws 1917, Chapter 261), a seven-member body made up of the governor, secretary of state, and five persons appointed by the governor. Joseph A. A. Burnquist, Republican, was the governor. John Lind became a commission member.[26]

The emergency statute directed the commission to insure the protection of persons and property, the defense of state and nation, and the application of the state's resources toward successful prosecution of the war. It was empowered to authorize the arrest of anyone who sided with Germany or who criticized the government of the United States. In an early step the commission

1917 meeting of the Nonpartisan League with Charles A. Lindbergh, Sr., as speaker against United States involvement in the war. (Courtesy of the Minnesota Historical Society)

banned from Minnesota schools any textbooks placing Germany in a favorable light.[27]

The commission regarded the suppression of disloyalty and the preservation of public order as its primary responsibilities. Members of the Nonpartisan League, the Industrial Workers of the World (IWW), socialists, and pacifists were particularly suspect. So, too, was anyone refusing to contribute to war fund drives or publicly opposing government policies. Indeed, anyone who sought a negotiated peace was questioned. In its zeal to suppress any disloyalty, the commission hired six hundred "peace officers" to watch for suspicious activity.[28] A witch hunt ensued. Suspect files were filled with notes on activities such as these: "Organized Nonpartisan League," "Socialist," "Spent Some Time in New Ulm," "Local Secretary of IWW," "Raised German Flag," "Socialist But OK." Another note read: "Peterson [James A.] is very radical and would bear watching." And the mayor of Minneapolis was not above surveillance: "June 17, 1917. Speaking against conscription in various parts of state, said to be behind Worker's Council." And, "June 14, 1917, Mayor of Minneapolis radical and unpatriotic."[29]

Trade union spokesmen complained that the commission included no labor representation. And they saw the prominence

"Smoking Him Out" Law and Order vs. IWW agitators in the northern Minnesota lumber camps, 1917. (Courtesy of the Minnesota Historical Society)

attached to protection of property and preservation of public order in enabling legislation as yet another weapon against the union. To organize, strike, or picket was to act at one's peril. While the Wilson administration recognized the need for labor's full cooperation and support in the war effort and had no objection to the formation of new unions, Minnesota's policy was just the opposite. In fact, the state blocked the formation of unions. Commissioner John F. McGee, in particular, was vehemently anti-union, and he shamelessly used the commission to smite his enemies, including

The Minnesota Commission of Public Safety during World War I. (Courtesy of the Minnesota Historical Society)

moderate trade unionists. The commission created the Home Guard "to protect private property in this period of unrest and disorder." Author and columnist Harrison Salisbury's father was a member; as a boy, Salisbury watched his father in action:

> My father's finest hour came when the Home Guard was ordered to break a streetcar strike in 1917. Issued a long oak ax handle and nickel-plated pistol, he rode with strikebreaking motormen and, as he swore, cracked the skulls of strikers who tried to interfere. Put him in uniform, give him a weapon, issue an order, and even a gentle man like my father obeyed.
>
> After the war, case after case came to light in which the Home Guard had led mobs against supposed traitors, particularly A. C. Townley's Nonpartisan League and the IWW. I grew up believing that the Nonpartisan League was a branch of the Kaiser's war apparatus and that the initials IWW stood for "I won't work."
>
> So it was that the liberal state of Minnesota was transformed into a pre-fascist fief. The powers vested in the Minnesota Public Safety commission were totalitarian powers; the commission established a dictatorship in Minnesota; the ideology of hatred, racism, xenophobia, was as naked as in Nazi Germany.
>
> As a child, I understood nothing of this. Nor, so far as I can see, did my father and mother and their friends. They believed the propaganda.[30]

The People's Council of America for Democracy quite spontaneously came into being in the early summer of 1917. The council was a loosely knit body of persons and organizations joined to work for an early, democratic, and universal peace based on no annexation, no punitive indemnities, and the right of all nations to determine their own destiny; to urge upon the government a concrete statement as to the terms upon which it would conclude peace; and to work for the repeal of the draft law and for the preservation of all democratic liberties including free speech, free press, and free assemblage. All individuals and organizations in harmony with these aims were eligible for membership.[31] As Chrislock has pointed out, several notable American reformers joined, believing that peace negotiations on these terms warranted exploration:

> At its inception the People's Council claimed the affiliation and support of several distinguished citizens, including David Starr Jordan, naturalist and president of Leland Stanford University; ex-Senator John D. Works of California; Florence Kelly, a prominent social worker; and Senator La Follette. In Minnesota it won the backing of local Socialists, a few German-American spokesmen, and a number of prominent progressive politicians such as James Peterson and Sylvanus A. Stockwell, a long-time state legislator from Minneapolis.[32]

In early August, leaders of the People's Council gathered in Chicago to plan a national convention scheduled for the first week of September, at which time the People's Council was to be formally organized. Thousands from all over the country were expected to attend. The *Minneapolis Journal* reported:

> If plans announced today by the Minneapolis members of the People's Council of Americans for Democracy and Terms of Peace are successful, the council is expected to place Minneapolis before the world as the center of anti-draft and anti-war propaganda . . . A Minneapolis branch of the council was to be organized . . . National headquarters were to be opened in Minneapolis' Majestic Hotel on Friday by Louis P. Lochner of Chicago, national secretary. Minneapolis was selected for the national headquarters and for the first convention of the People's Council. S. A. Stockwell announced to the press that the national meeting was brought to Minneapolis as a result of a conference in Chicago attended by a member of Mayor Van Lear's staff and "others from here." He said he supposed "this city was selected for the headquarters because it is known there is a great deal of sentiment here for early peace, and with the idea that this is as congenial an atmosphere as we

Marchers (top) carrying the American flag during an evening parade through downtown Minneapolis, April 19, 1917. (From the *Minneapolis Journal*) Street Railway Company strike (bottom), 1917. (Courtesy of the Minnesota Historical Society for reproductions)

can get for the meeting" . . . Leaders frankly avowed that the movement was being directed with a view of combining all dissatisfied elements for the next political campaign, drawing for support on former pacifist organizations, the Socialist party, farmers' organizations, labor unions, and on persons who before the United States entered the war were known as of pro-German tendencies . . . Lochner was of German ancestry . . . and had been a lecturer and author on peace subjects.[33]

As September approached, sponsors of the People's Council meeting encountered difficulty in finding a suitable meeting place. As the YMCA deemed the Saturday Lunch Club suspect and closed its dining room doors to the club, so did the owners of halls and auditoriums in Minneapolis rebuff the People's Council.

On August 18, the *Minneapolis Journal* reported that Stockwell, "in charge of the council of Minneapolis," had said he did not know where the meeting would be held.[34] By this time, Stockwell was probably considering making his own land available.

Even as Stockwell spoke to the press, Governor Joseph A. A. Burnquist was making himself heard in a different vein at the Stars and Stripes Parade:

> Governor Burnquist addressed a parade of 50,000 which jammed Nicollet Avenue in a surge of patriotism. . . . He touched a popular chord when he stated plainly that the pacifist agitation had gone far enough and henceforth would be checked with a firm hand . . . Gibes at Mayor Van Lear, James A. Peterson and other pacifist leaders were frequent. "What shall we do with the copperheads?" cried Fred Snyder. "Shoot 'em!" "Hang 'em!" came calls from the crowd.[35]

Governor Joseph A. A. Burnquist, 1917. (Courtesy of the Minnesota Historical Society)

Looking back at the Stars and Stripes Parade, which seemed "right as rain" to him as a child, Salisbury recognized that it was "not just an ordinary flag-waving demonstration" but one that "touched off—and was designed to touch off—a violent wave of xenophobic, pro-war vigilantism in Minneapolis and in the State of Minnesota."[36]

On August 20, the *Minneapolis Journal* reported that Minnesota, "selected by the People's Council of America for its antiwar national conclave," might not be the situs after all. The state might bar the organization from holding any public gathering within its borders. Governor Burnquist, the *Journal* reported, had said the Public Safety Commission was investigating the matter and would promptly decide whether the meeting could take place. "All anti-American meetings must cease," he said. Lochner, the *Journal* reported, would not say where the meeting would take place: "We are going to keep the public guessing."

The next day's paper added:

> Excluded from halls and auditoriums in Minneapolis by loyal hall owners, the People's Council will meet, if it is permitted to meet at all, in tents on the outskirts of the city, it was announced today. Louis P. Lochner, the secretary, said that two large tents will be erected on land belonging to S. A. Stockwell, Minneapolis antiwar leader, near Minnehaha Park.
>
> One tent was to be used for the meeting of the "constituent assembly" or delegate body of the People's Council and the other for mass meetings.[37]

On August 28 the paper reported that Mayor Van Lear had declared he would give the meeting police protection to ensure that it wouldn't be disturbed and to see that the law was not violated. Van Lear said he would tolerate no efforts to break up the meetings of the People's Council by people hostile to the purposes of the council and promised to fulfill his oath of office and uphold the constitutions of the United States and Minnesota, which guaranteed the rights of free assembly and free press.[38]

Stockwell forged ahead with the plans. In the doing he must have wondered whether the tents would be delivered as assured. And if delivered, would they be erected? Still, the corn was ripened to perfection; might not this gathering be the biggest and grandest cornfest of all?

In the meantime, there was growing insistence that the People's Council be banned from meeting anywhere. As Stockwell knew, his neighbors had turned against him:

> The Twelfth Ward of Minneapolis is loyal and it wants the whole city to know. It wants the citizens of Minneapolis to know that it looks with disfavor upon the proposal of the so-called People's Council to hold its circus within the ward.
>
> A meeting of the Minnehaha-Nokomis Improvement Association, of which S. A. Stockwell is president, will be held at the Minnehaha School. The members say they are going to depose Mr. Stockwell on account of his connection with the peace-at-any-price organization. C. F. Maurer, one of the members, says that he has found no one who is willing to keep Mr. Stockwell as president.[39]

The membership of the Minnehaha-Nokomis Improvement Association ousted Stockwell as predicted. And another neighborhood group, the Twelfth Ward Equality Club, joined the chorus:

> The Twelfth Ward Equality Club yesterday sent a letter to the Public Safety Commission, asking that the meeting of the People's Council be prohibited.
>
> "The nature and character of the meetings are well understood," says the letter to the commission, "and we believe at the present time and under present conditions they will be a means of spreading a feeling of discontent and distrust and even sedition against our recognized form of government."
>
> To further emphasize their spirit of loyalty, there will be a patriotic meeting on the Minnehaha schoolhouse grounds Friday night.[40]

Another rebuff came in the person of Walter Stockwell, living in North Dakota, who sought to further distance himself from his brother Albert with a letter to I. A. Caswell, in charge of the Loyalty Lyceum, saying he wanted the privilege of speaking at Minnesota loyalty meetings.[41]

The *Minneapolis Tribune* rebuked Stockwell and Lundeen in its editorial of August 31:

> S. A. Stockwell busied himself energetically in helping make plans for the conference of the People's Council of America here, even offering to house the body in a tent on land he owns after hall after hall was denied to it. Mr. Stockwell's old neighbors—many of them his personal friends—have now ousted him from the presidency of the Nokomis-Minnehaha Improvement Association. It is a plain case of sufficient cause and logical effect. These old-time friends felt that neither they nor their community could afford to have their Americanism challenged by keeping Mr. Stockwell in the office to which they had chosen him. Mr. Stockwell is intelligent enough to know that this sign of disapproval of his attitude toward a citizen element whose influence, if not its intent, is pro-German and anti-American, is exactly the kind of thing that might have been expected under the circumstances.
>
> Ernest Lundeen, representative in Congress from the Minneapolis district, has challenged the wisdom of the President and Congress by introducing a bill for repeal of the draft act.
>
> Perhaps neither Mr. Stockwell nor Mr. Lundeen is concerned about these evidences of popular displeasure. Apparently, it has no weight with them that an overwhelming majority of the people stand back of the overwhelming majority of Congress

211

which voted for the draft act and approved the plans they are making to send American troops abroad to fight for democracy, liberty and humanity.[42]

Then came the Public Safety Commission vote to determine whether to allow the People's Council to meet on Stockwell's land. Of special interest was how Lind would vote. He was committed to the war effort. At the August 16 Stars and Stripes Parade, he had said, "If there were a mad dog running amok, I wouldn't stand idle." But he wanted to build the broadest possible coalition in support of the war's furtherance and sought to win Stockwell and Van Lear over so as to include them in that base. He voted against banning the assembly. McGee, on the other hand, wanting mainly to smite his enemies—pacifists, socialists, trade unionists, pressed to ban the assembly. McGee's stridence prevailed over Lind's moderation, and the commission voted to prohibit the meeting.[43]

John F. McGee, 1918. (Courtesy of the Minnesota Historical Society)

Governor Burnquist then banned the People's Council from meeting anywhere in Minnesota. On September 1, the *New Times* denounced Kaiser Burnquist for suspending the United States and Minnesota constitutions. The conservative press applauded the governor's action.[44]

In the course of war, Stockwell's office was twice broken into and ransacked, and pressure was brought to oust him as general agent of Penn Mutual. The company, rooted as it was in the land of Quakers, remained supportive, and he kept his job. But he and Maud Stockwell were attacked and persecuted unmercifully. "It was brutal what he took," said Edward Peet. For weeks in 1917, police guarded the Stockwell house. Threats were made to tar and feather him and paint his house yellow. As Althea Atwater recalled, "they did paint his house yellow." He was charged with being a German spy and a traitor to his country. Super-patriots sought his arrest, all without effect.[45]

Stockwell never wavered from his opposition to war as a means of settling disputes. The fact of war did not lessen his hostility to it. Years later, Fanny Fligelman Brin looked back on his stand:

With regard to war and peace, nothing has impressed me more than the remark of President Faure of France: "War is old; pathetically old, hopelessly antiquated, tragically futile. Peace alone—heroic and sacrificial—is the ideal which only the young can believe."

Unfortunately, very often in the course of events in the last few years it has been increasingly difficult to remain young, and to believe in this great ideal. But there is one . . . who remained youthful, ardently, enthusiastically, consistently youthful throughout all of these difficult years. And, while we speak of the ideal of peace as being one that is heroic and sacrificial, we are here tonight to pay tribute not only to the heroism and sacrificial qualities of that ideal of peace, but to the heroism and sacrificial service which Mr. Stockwell has paid to his ideal. And he has served that great cause and movement not only when it became safe and acceptable and approved, but when it was taboo and unpopular and dangerous.[46]

References

1. Morison and Commager, *Growth of the Republic*, 2:445.

2. *Minneapolis Journal*, June 23, 1912.

3. *Minneapolis Journal*, April 17, 1914.

4. *Minneapolis Daily News*, May 21, 1915.

5. *Minneapolis Daily News*, May 22, 1915.

6. *New York Times*, July 28, 1917.

7. *Minneapolis Journal*, October 9, 1911.

8. *St. Paul Pioneer Press*, March 18, 1925. A young man, driven mad by his war experience, lived in a tree house near Stockwell on East Fifty-first Street. He thought he was Jesus.

9. Morison and Commager, *Growth of the Republic*, 2:446, pp. 458, 459, 463. Minnesota's electoral votes were cast for Charles Evans Hughes, who defeated Wilson in Minnesota by the narrowest of margins.

10. Morison and Commager, *Growth of the Republic*, 2:469-470.

11. Keillor, *Hjalmar Petersen*, p. 40; Franklin F. Holbrook and Livia Appel, *Minnesota in the War with Germany* (St. Paul: Minnesota Historical Society, 1932), 1:6, 36, 39.

12. Chrislock, *Progressive Era*, pp. 126, 130, 135.

13. Chrislock, *Progressive Era*, p. 130. For an excellent account of Van

Lear's political rise, see David Paul Nord, "Minneapolis and the Pragmatic Socialism of Thomas Van Lear," in *Minnesota History* 45 (Spring 1956):2-10.

14. Chrislock, *Progressive Era*, 131.

15. *Minneapolis Tribune*, February 11, 1917.

16. *Minneapolis Tribune*, February 11, 1917.

17. *Minneapolis Tribune*, February 11, 1917.

18. Chrislock, *Progressive Era*, p. 131.

19. Keillor, *Hjalmar Petersen*, p. 40; Arthur S. Link, *Wilson, Campaigns for Progressivism and Peace, 1916-1917* (Princeton, New Jersey: Princeton University Press, 1965), pp. 367-368, 398-399.

20. *Minneapolis Journal*, March 24, 1917.

21. *Minneapolis Journal*, March 25, 1917.

22. *Minneapolis Journal*, March 29, 1917.

23. *Minneapolis Journal*, March 29, 1917.

24. *Minneapolis Journal*, March 29, 1917.

25. *Minneapolis Journal*, April 1, 1917.

26. *Minnesota, Laws, 1917*, Chapter 261; Chrislock's *Watchdog of Loyalty* is an objective, comprehensive account of the trampling on civil rights in Minnesota occurring when the Commission of Public Safety held sway in 1917 and 1918. The book serves as an alert for future generations about what can go wrong when a governmental agency is given near-dictatorial powers.

27. "Laws That Limit Rights," Roots 13, No. 3 (Spring 1985): pp. 17-20.

28. "Laws That Limit Rights," p. 18.

29. Public Safety Commission Files, Minnesota Historical Society; Chrislock, *Watchdog of Loyalty*, pp. 130-131.

30. Harrison E. Salisbury, *A Journey for Our Times* (New York: Harper and Row, 1983), pp. 13-14. According to Hyman Berman, during the course of the transit strike, the Public Safety Commission refused even to allow federal negotiators to come in, saying that would be tantamount to treason.

31. *Minneapolis New Times*, July 29, 1917.

32. Chrislock, *Progressive Era*, p. 138.

33. *Minneapolis Journal*, August 14, 1917. The sympathetic attitude of Mayor Van Lear was doubtless a factor in the selection of Minneapolis. See Chrislock, *Progressive Era*, p. 138.

34. *Minneapolis Journal*, August 18, 1917.

35. *Minneapolis Journal*, August 17, 1917.

36. Salisbury, *A Journey for Our Times*, p. 12.

37. *Minneapolis Journal*, August 21, 1917.

38. *Minneapolis Journal*, August 28, 1917.

39. *Minneapolis Tribune*, August 28, 1917.

40. *Minneapolis Tribune*, August 28, 1917.

41. *Minneapolis Journal*, August 30, 1917.

42. *Minneapolis Tribune*, August 31, 1917.

43. Chrislock, *Watchdog of Loyalty*, pp. 147-150, 200. Lind resigned from the commission in December 1917 following his sharp differences with McGee over whether to prosecute Van Lear.

44. Chrislock, *Progressive Era*, p. 138; Chrislock, *Watchdog of Loyalty*, p. 149.

45. Binder, "The Stockwells of Minneapolis."

46. Remarks, Complimentary Birthday Dinner, typescript copy in the possession of the author.

Chapter 18

The Nonpartisan League
and Postwar Years

As Stockwell's political fortunes ebbed in Minnesota, an agrarian uprising in North Dakota served to revive them. Farmers simply were not sharing in the prosperity enjoyed by the rest of the country, and they rebelled. Their wrath found vent in the Nonpartisan League, an organization formed in 1915 in the tradition of the Grange and Farmers' Alliance. The league was a forerunner of Minnesota's Farmer-Labor party, the instrument of Stockwell's return to elective office.[1]

The immediate origin of the league was the wheat farmers' revolt against the closely held management of the grain trade. The farmers directed their anger chiefly against the Minneapolis Chamber of Commerce, which they saw as exercising monopolistic control over the pricing, buying, selling, storage, and transportation of their products. North Dakota's Governor Louis B. Hanna triggered the revolt when, in 1915, he refused to carry out plans for a state-owned terminal elevator twice approved by the voters.[2]

Arthur C. Townley, Socialist party organizing genius and himself a bankrupt flax farmer, launched the league with Socialist party help and the aid of the American Society of Equity. The latter organization had formed several coop-

Arthur C. Townley, Socialist Party genius who organized the Nonpartisan League. From *Twin Cities: A Pictorial History of St. Paul and Minneapolis* by L.M. Kane and A. Ominsky. (Courtesy of the Minnesota Historical Society)

A. C. Townley speaking at outdoor meeting of farmers. From *Twin Cities: A Pictorial History of St. Paul and Minneapolis* by L.M. Kane and A. Ominsky. (Courtesy of the Minnesota Historical Society)

erative elevators in North Dakota, but their operation was blocked at every turn by the urban power structure. The cooperatives fought endless battles just to get needed railroad sidings. The league's program called for state-owned terminal elevators, flour mills, packing houses, and cold storage plants, state inspection of grain and grain dockage, exemption of farm improvements from taxation, state hail insurance, and state rural credits. Its political strategy was to capture the primaries of the dominant party.[3]

The anger of the farmers, harnessed by men in the field skilled in the art of organizing, brought sweeping political victory to the league in 1916. Their candidates captured the Republican party primaries and fared extremely well in the elections. The league was again successful in the 1918 elections, and by 1919 its entire program was enacted into law.[4] With these successes, the league spread into neighboring states. Headquarters were moved from Fargo to St. Paul. In states such as Minnesota, which embraced large blocks of industrial workers in Minneapolis, St. Paul, Duluth, and on the iron range, leaders broadened their program to include workers' demands such as the legal right to organize and bargain collectively, the eight-hour work day, and old-age pensions.[5] Organizers were able to effect a coalition of farmers and laborers, a move that dismayed the Public Safety Commission and other conservative forces in Minnesota, which were horrified by the socialism of the league's platform and deplored the prospect of any such alliance.

Charles A. Lindbergh joined the nonpartisan movement in 1918 and became the league's candidate for governor. The June Republican primary was seen as the avenue to the governorship.

Lindbergh had opposed entry into the war up to the last minute, but in 1918 he endorsed Wilson's war aims. In his campaign he pledged full support of all war activities. Nonetheless, he faced incessant accusations of pro-Germanism and disloyalty.[6] In the words of Charlotte Hamlet, Stockwell's niece, Lindbergh and Stockwell were Minnesota's two most persecuted men.

The incumbent Joseph A. A. Burnquist defeated Lindbergh in the primary with 199,325 votes to Lindbergh's 150,626. The conservative press saw this as a great victory for loyalty and patriotism.[7] But Lindbergh surely had made a respectable showing, and the strength of a farmer-labor alliance had been demonstrat-

Charles A. Lindbergh, Sr. (Photo by Lee Brothers. Courtesy of the Minnesota Historical Society)

ed. Further, Republican Congressman Ernest Lundeen, who had not supported the declaration of war, made a reasonably good showing in his bid for renomination. These relative successes at the polls showed Stockwell that an anti-war stand did not necessarily signal political oblivion. Perhaps a degree of tolerance for differing views was returning to society even as the war continued. In June 1918 Stockwell may have decided that before long he would run again for office.[8]

While Burnquist was reelected governor, he did not receive a majority of the votes cast. The Democrats had chosen conservative Fred E. Wheaton, a man who inspired little enthusiasm, as their nominee. The Nonpartisan League, sidetracked in the primary, departed from the preferred strategy of focusing on and winning in primaries by entering an independent ticket headed by David Evans, heretofore a progressive Democrat. Evans had worked tirelessly in the war effort, and there was no room for charge of disloyalty. He filed by simple petition only to have the Secretary of State rule that election laws precluded filing for the governorship as an independent. To meet this technicality—almost on the spur of the moment—he tendered the designation "Farmer-Labor." Two years later the Minnesota Farmer-Labor Party was officially organized.[9]

Wheaton's poor showing in November 1918 underscored the moribund state of the Democratic party in Minnesota. Burnquist polled 166,515 votes, Evans 111,948, and Wheaton 76,793. The Democratic party was in for a long postwar eclipse.[10] Carl Chrislock has attached historical significance to the election:

> The 1918 election signaled the end of the Progressive era in Minnesota. The old bipartisan coalition of moral reformers, small-town business and professional men, and farmers that had sustained the progressive movement was shattered beyond repair. Out of the wreckage, the Nonpartisan League appropriated progressivism's rhetoric, much of its crusading spirit, and the support of its left wing. In addition, the league gained the allegiance of organized labor and a substantial segment of the German-American community, two elements whose affiliation with progressivism had been limited. This coalition of radical progressives, trade unionists, and German-Americans constituted the voting base which the Nonpartisan League would pass on to its successor, the Minnesota Farmer-Labor party.[11]

The strength of the Nonpartisan League itself declined after 1920. A postwar depression, particularly severe in agricultural states, made payment of membership dues difficult. Internal difficulties compounded the problems, and, by 1924, the league as a separate entity had almost disappeared, though not without an enduring legacy.[12]

The loyalty question was not the key issue in the 1920 election as it had been in 1918—another development that boded well for Stockwell. The extremism of the Public Safety Commission had tarnished Burnquist; indeed, it was widely believed that if he had faced a single, strong opponent in 1918, he would have been defeated. To the relief of Republican party leaders, who realized "the McGee-Burnquist image was creating a backlash," Burnquist decided not to run again in 1920.[13] The Republicans turned instead to Jacob A. O. Preuss. Henrik Shipstead, who had made a strong run against Preuss in an attempt to seize the Republican primary, became the Farmer-Labor candidate for governor. Farmers and laborers had convened separately, but, further cementing the coalition, they agreed on the same candidate to represent their common cause.

Shipstead lost to Preuss, who was to hold the governorship until 1925, and Republicans remained dominant in Minnesota for the balance of the decade. In 1922, however, Shipstead came back to upset the widely respected Frank B. Kellogg to win a seat in the U.S. Senate, and the young Farmer-Labor party made other significant inroads in the state senate and house. With the 1922 election, the Farmer-Labor party established itself as the second party of the state.[14]

In the nation at large, as in Minnesota, the Republican party remained dominant in the 1920s. Stockwell found little to cheer about in Washington or in St. Paul. Steps taken by Republican leadership in two international matters following the armistice were particularly troubling. He was saddened by the failure of the Senate to ratify the Treaty of Versailles and thereby become a member of the League of Nations. In his view any hope of a sane, new world order, with the United States playing a leading and constructive role, had vanished. Henry Cabot Lodge led the opposition to the League of Nations in the Senate. Again, as with the issue of imperialism twenty years before, Stockwell's views were directly opposite to the Massachusetts senator's.

In a second distressing development, Stockwell was able to lend help from afar. In 1917, Russian Bolsheviks had overthrown the monarchy and, led by Lenin, seized control of the government. In the civil war that broke out thereafter, lasting from 1918 to 1920, the communists (or reds) prevailed over anticommunist forces (or whites), and the Union of Soviet Socialist Republics was formed. As these events unfolded, fear of Bolshevism became a burning question in the United States. Typical was the country's approach to near hysteria in 1919, a year of great labor unrest when a wave of strikes swept the country and caused irrational fear of a Bolshevist uprising.[15] Then in 1921, at a time when the United States was unwilling to recognize a government deemed ideologically unacceptable, a great famine struck southern Russia.

Trade relations between the countries had been closed earlier when the United States imposed an economic blockade aimed at forcing the Russian people to change their form of government. The harshness of the policy drew ire from trade unionists. The American Federation of Labor and the Minneapolis Trades and Labor Union Assembly, seeing their working-class brothers starving, demanded that the United States lift the embargo while urging recognition of Russia.[16]

Stockwell was of the same mind. He saw the embargo as cruel, inhumane, outside interference. Throughout the famine he served as treasurer of the Friends of the Soviet Union. He and Maud Stockwell combined to collect funds and supplies for the people of southern Russia.

The famine lasted until 1923. Despite ideological differences between the countries, the United States, led by Herbert Hoover, who became Secretary of Commerce, saved the lives of millions with shipments of food to Russia. But prejudice against Russian Bolshevism was so great as to make even relief work suspect in the eyes of many. Stockwell, undeterred, strove to help. Yet with equal conviction he roundly condemned Communist oppression.[17]

On the domestic front in 1920, Stockwell was disappointed but scarcely surprised by the choice of candidates of the two major parties for the presidency. Warren G. Harding of Ohio, favorite of the old guard, won the Republican nomination. Calvin Coolidge of Massachusetts, who gained national fame when he said in breaking a Boston police strike that there was "no right to strike against the public safety by anybody, anywhere, any time," joined Harding on the ticket. The Democrats chose James Cox, "not himself a man of any strong liberal principles," as their standard-bearer. Franklin D. Roosevelt was named his running mate, presumably to balance the ticket and mollify Wilsonian progressives.[18]

The temper of the times was reactionary. Harding was elected with 16,152,200 votes to Cox's 9,147,353. His margin in the electoral vote was 404 to 127. Yet for Stockwell there was a bright spot in the election. Socialist Eugene V. Debs, "intellectually the most respectable of the three candidates," achieved something of a moral victory, amassing nearly a million votes as he served a term in the Atlanta penitentiary for alleged sedition. Three times earlier he had run as a Socialist candidate, gaining 94,768 votes in 1900, 402,460 in 1904, and 897,011 in 1912. The 1920 run was his finest—and final—try.[19]

Stockwell almost certainly voted for Debs, although single-taxers fielded a national ticket in 1920. Macauley, the Single Tax candidate, received 5,825 votes.[20] By this time Stockwell had left the Democratic party and joined the Socialist party. Millard L. Gieske of the University of Minnesota's Department of Political Science, in describing the makeup of the early converts to the Farmer-Labor party, has written:

> Members of the state Socialist Party, particularly those active in the organized labor movement, were already in or close to Farmer-Laborism. They included William Mahoney, Arthur and Marian Le Sueur, S. A. Stockwell . . . and Benjamin Drake. Other proponents of Farmer-Laborism, like Henry Teigan, had started in the Nonpartisan League but had come to question Townley's capacity to lead the movement; or, like James Manahan, they had moved to the League from the Progressive Movement and were now ready to support a third party.[21]

Elsewhere Gieske has referred to the "veteran Farmer-Labor legislator S. A. Stockwell (a socialist)."[22] The Reverend Raymond Bragg of the First Unitarian Society, however, in a 1943 memorial address, recalled an introduction he had arranged between Stockwell and British reformer George Lansbury and made this distinction between the men who otherwise had much in common: "Lansbury [was] a lifelong socialist, which Mr. Stockwell had never been."[23] The statement must have puzzled a number of those in attendance. In any event, when Stockwell returned to the legislature in 1923, he would not be running as a Socialist, Farmer-Laborite, Democrat, Single Taxer, or Republican because the legislature in 1913 had enacted a statute providing for the election of members without party designation.

References

1. Larry Remele, "The Nonpartisan League: The Courage to Stand Up for Farmers," *Plowing Up a Storm: The History of Midwestern Farm Activism* (No city: Nebraska Educational Television Network, 1985), p. 21; *Dictionary of American History*, 5:106. Robert L. Morlan's *Political Prairie Fire: The Nonpartisan League, 1915-1922* (St. Paul: Minnesota Historical Society Press, 1985), with a new introduction by Larry Remele, is the standard work on the Nonpartisan League.

2. *Dictionary of American History*, 5:106.

3. *Dictionary of American History*, 5:106.

4. *Dictionary of American History*, 5:106-107.

5. George H. Mayer, *The Political Career of Floyd B. Olson* (St. Paul: Minnesota Historical Society Press, 1987), p. 22.

6. Chrislock, *Progressive Era*, pp. 164-171.

7. Chrislock, *Progressive Era*, pp. 171-181.

8. Chrislock, *Progressive Era*, pp. 171-181.

9. Chrislock, *Progressive Era*, pp. 171-181. While the Farmer-Labor party entered candidates on ballots beginning in 1920, the farmers' Nonpartisan League and labor's counterpart, the Working People's Nonpartisan Political League, were not fully integrated but simply cooperated and worked along parallel lines until 1924 when the Farmer-Labor Federation was established. Its constitution provided for a single organization based upon the affiliation of labor unions and township clubs among the farmers. The federation was to be the educational arm of the party and the controlling agency from which would come the leadership and the policy decisions binding upon the party and its candidates. Communist inroads prompted a name change in 1925 from Federation, seen as tainted, to Association. See Arthur Naftalin's unpublished Ph.D. dissertation, "A History of the Farmer-Labor Party of Minnesota" (University of Minnesota, 1948), pp. 30-121.

10. Mayer, *Floyd B. Olson*, p. 99; Chrislock, *Progressive Era*, p. 179.

11. Chrislock, *Progressive Era*, p. 181.

12. *Dictionary of American History*, 5:107.

13. Chrislock, *Progressive Era*, p. 185.

14. Chrislock, *Progressive Era*, p. 183, quoting historian Arthur Naftalin, "The Farmer-Labor Party," p. 84.

15. Keillor, "Franklin Cooperative Creamery Association," p. 260.

16. Labor continued to urge recognition of Russia as a stimulus to foreign trade and a step that would open the way to a promising new consumer market. Typical was the stand of the Minneapolis Labor Defense Committee expressed at a May 1925 meeting to raise funds for Sacco and Vanzetti. The assemblage of nearly five hundred overwhelmingly adopted a resolution calling on the government to recognize the Soviet Union. See *Minneapolis Journal*, May 11, 1925. The United States recognized the Soviet Union after Roosevelt took office in 1933.

17. *Dictionary of American Biography*, Supplement 7, p. 357; Binder, "The Stockwells of Minneapolis."

18. Morison and Commager, *Growth of the Republic*, 2:516.

19. Morison and Commager, *Growth of the Republic*, 2:517; *Dictionary of American Biography*, 3:183-185.

20. Morison and Commager, *Growth of the Republic*, 2:665.

21. Gieske, Millard L., *Minnesota Farmer-Laborism: The Third Party Alternative* (Minneapolis, Univeristy of Minnesota Press, 1979), p. 240.

22. Gieske, *Farmer-Laborism*, p. 240.

23. "Tribute to the Memory of Sylvanus A. Stockwell," typescript of memorial service address, Minnesota Historical Society.

Chapter 19

Return to the Legislature

Five years after Stockwell's attempt to provide a forum for the People's Council in the fall of 1917, he ran again for the legislature. His stand on the war would have rendered futile any campaign for office in 1918 or 1920. But in 1922, public memory of the earlier years was fading.[1] And perhaps some of his neighbors and constituents for the first time felt there was some merit in what he had said and stood for. In any event, the issues of patriotism and radicalism had lost much of their old power. An impaired economy for the agricultural sector—continuing and worsening—boded well for Farmer-Laborism. This was the time to run.

Years later Stockwell gave a specific reason for the move: "In the twenties, I became very greatly interested in the destruction that was going on in the northern part of the state, caused by drainage ditches, and I went back into the legislature for the sole job of trying to do something to stop that devastation."[2]

Running for the legislature after an absence of twenty years, Stockwell campaigned under a changed election practice decreed by the 1913 law providing for election of members without party designation. The law was intended to encourage the electorate to vote for the candidate and not the party and to encourage candidates to appeal to voters across party lines. Once in office, it was thought, legislators would be more apt to exercise their best judgment, unrestricted by party allegiance. The law also worked a change in organization of the legislature. Heretofore the house and senate had been organized along party lines. Under the new practice, two coalitions were established—a coalition of liberals on the one hand and a coalition of members opposed to radical theories of government on the other.[3]

The new law suited Stockwell. At a later time, he voted against a bill that would have returned the election process to the old party basis. He had always been his own man anyway. As A. W. Rankin recalled, "He never followed any party if he felt they were not right. The Farmer-Labor Party could not count on his vote if he thought they were wrong."[4]

Sam Bellman, still practicing law in Minneapolis in 1993 at age eighty-seven, spoke in the same vein. He had served in the house with Stockwell in 1935 and 1937, and he remembered the counsel Stockwell gave him. Bellman had been meeting with the governor for the vote on a bill allowing liquor sales in the suburbs. He didn't want to vote at all but could not then leave. Politically, it was in his interest to vote to extend the boundaries of permissible sale. He turned to Stockwell. "How does one vote in this situation?" he asked. Stockwell replied, "Vote your conscience." Bellman voted not to extend the limits. Thereafter he always heeded that advice.[5]

In the June 1922 primary, six candidates declared for the two house seats from the Thirty-second District. The *Minneapolis Journal* warned that Norwegian-born Otto D. Nellermoe, the incumbent, a member of the Teamsters and Chauffeurs Union, and S. A. Stockwell, who had served "some twenty years ago," were endorsed by the Nonpartisan League. On the safe side, implied the *Journal*, were Oscar C. Christianson and Herman Moe, "anti-Socialists."[6] Nellermoe, Stockwell, Christianson, and R. H. Wheeler survived the primary—an election affording Maud Stockwell her first opportunity to cast a vote for her husband in a legislative contest.

In early November, the *Minneapolis Journal* again wanted to make certain the voters knew just who the radicals were. The newspaper printed this alert in large type:

> There is so much confusion among voters as to just what candidates in tomorrow's election are being supported by the socialists and other radicals that the *Journal* herewith publishes the complete list of candidates [partially set forth below] endorsed by the Working Peoples' Nonpartisan Political League of Minnesota:
>
> U. S. Senator:
> Henrik Shipstead, Minneapolis
>
> For Congress:
> Seventh District—Ole J. Kavale, Benson
> Ninth District—Knud Wefald, Hawley
>
> Governor:
> Magnus Johnson, Kimball
>
> Representatives:
> 32nd District—Otto D. Nellermoe, Minneapolis
> S. A. Stockwell, Minneapolis[7]

Shipstead defeated the incumbent Kellogg in a stunning upset. Preuss survived a strong bid by Magnus Johnson with a plurality of just 14,277 votes. The Democratic party candidate, Edward Indrehus, was a distant third. Victories by Kavale and Wefald in the congressional races shocked the opposition.[8] Stockwell and Nellermoe were winners in the Thirty-second District: Nellermoe 7,399, Stockwell 7,095, Christianson 6,007, and Wheeler 3,088.[9] Four women were elected to the house for the first time. None were seated in the senate.

It was a Farmer-Labor victory, in substance if not by party designation, that reached to the core of the legislature. Buell regarded the ouster of incumbents as a "political revolution" and attributed it to the number of unpopular measures passed by the 1921 legislature. (The Brooks-Coleman street railway bill was the most hated.)[10] Chrislock has given this account:

> This impressive achievement did not signal a wholesale conversion of Minnesota voters to Farmer-Labor radicalism. Rather, it reflected the need for an opposition party capable of representing aggrieved grain farmers, trade unionists, and ethnic groups victimized by wartime and post war nativism.[11]

Thirty-one-year-old Floyd B. Olson, who had not yet cast his lot with the Farmer-Labor party, ran for election as Hennepin County attorney, a position he previously held by appointment. He won decisively—a significant political victory for the party's future leader. Born in the northside slum area of Minneapolis of humble Scandinavian stock, Olson was a young man of rebellious nature, attributable at least in part to his mother's aspirations for improved economic status and his own lasting sympathy for his neighborhood's underprivileged. After a lackluster year at the University of Minnesota, where he alienated authorities by refusing to accept compulsory military training, Olson went west. He worked as a salesman in Alberta, a fisherman and miner in Alaska, and a longshoreman in Seattle, where he joined the IWW, "absorbing something of their smoldering indignation against capitalistic exploitation of workers." He returned to Minneapolis at age twenty-two, entered night law school, and, after graduating in 1914, started out in private practice with the firm of Larrabee and Davies. There he quickly gained recognition as a skilled and persuasive trial lawyer. In 1918 and again in 1920 he ran for Congress as a Democrat. He was defeated twice, but he established a strong block of support from both major parties. A public career became his objective.[12]

Floyd B. Olson. (Courtesy of the Minnesota Historical Society)

When Stockwell returned to St. Paul on January 2, 1923, to begin the forty-third legislative session, he took his seat in a new capitol building. Designed by architect Cass Gilbert and completed in 1905 after nine years of construction, the building drew national acclaim. Though his surroundings were different, Stockwell picked right up where he had left off and, within weeks, was in the middle of the bitterest fight of the session. C. J. Buell, author of *The Minnesota Legislature* for 1913, 1915, 1917, 1919, and 1921, described the fray in his 1923 edition, which proved to be his last:

> The House had under consideration a report of the rules committee to pay employees who had performed services before the opening of the session and to reimburse members who had served on the committee to draft farm legislation.
>
> This committee had been appointed by Mr. Nolan who was expected to be speaker, though not yet elected, and had drafted the rural credits bill and other measures.

228

The Minnesota State Capitol (top), 1905. The transfer of the Civil War flags (bottom) from the old Capitol building on Tenth Street to the new building on Capitol Hill, June 14, 1905. (Courtesy of the Minnesota Historical Society)

The committee was composed of one member from each congressional district, and it was charged that all were of the "old guard" faction.

The proposal to pay back to these men the money they had spent in connection with this work met with strong opposition, led by Representative Stockwell, who insisted that all such unofficial work was gratuitous and a pernicious meddling with the regular work of the session.

No speaker had been elected. The members had not been sworn in. They had a perfect right to consult, to do any work they pleased, to frame proposed bills; but they had no right to ask the state to compensate them for their expenses.

Many other members had spent much time preparing bills. They, too, had served the state according to their light and their ideas of what laws should be enacted, but they had asked for no refunding of their expenses, and no one would think of paying them if they had asked it . . .

The amount involved was small, only $238.11, all to go to the committee on farm legislation.

Only a few had voted against paying the employees. They were wholly innocent. They believed themselves legally employed. But the house members themselves—that was different.

The vote to pay them for money expended was close—only two more than enough to pass.[13]

Stockwell's ire flared again when he discovered a gaping omission in the *Legislative Manual,* a handbook known as the *Blue Book,* which contained the federal and state constitutions, information about state government, election results, and so forth. Legislators and others used it for convenient reference. The Declaration of Independence had always been included. Stockwell discovered that the Declaration of Independence had been omitted from the 1923 edition. Outraged, he reacted with this resolution:

Whereas, the *Legislative Manual* for 1923 published by authority of this legislature does not contain a copy of the Declaration of Independence, and

Whereas, the omission of this immortal document from a publication of this nature by this state is most unfortunate to put the matter mildly, and

Whereas, if this omission was due to carelessness on the part of an official of the Secretary of State, the official responsible therefore should be severely censured, and

Whereas, if the omission is due to premeditated design, the person or persons in the office of the Secretary of State responsible therefor should be dismissed from the service of the state and debarred from further official connection in any department of the state government.

Now, Therefore, Be It Resolved, That the Secretary of State be requested to inform this House at once why this omission occurred, as to who was responsible therefore, and any other material facts in connection with this most unfortunate accident.

And Be It Further Resolved that it is the sense of this House that all future issues of the Legislative Manual published under the authority of this state should contain an unabridged copy of the Declaration of Independence, one of the greatest and most fundamentally sound state papers ever penned by man.

Stockwell's resolution, somewhat toned down, passed the House.[14] Buell, too, questioned the motives of the censors:

The Declaration of Independence is a very radical, revolutionary document and a dangerous document in the eyes of some, and many of our rich would like to have us forget it.

Many who toady to privilege, though poor, feel the same way.

"The young and the immature should not be given such strong mental stimulant."

Is that why the Declaration was kept out? To protect the Legislature?

Stockwell wants to know.[15]

Stockwell scrutinized legislative proposals with the same watchful eye. One measure referred to "the Philippine Insurrection" of twenty-five years previous. He moved to strike out the word "insurrection" in the interest of historical accuracy. This was done with no member objecting.[16]

In the political vernacular of the day, legislation seeking to secure some special favor or advantage for one or a few to the disadvantage of the great common mass of the people was known as a "woodchuck." Buell credited Stockwell with killing a number of woodchucks in the course of the session, one being his derailment of a proposal to tax all public bonds.

According to Buell, representatives of the great public service corporations for some time had been active in denouncing tax-exempt securities. They contended that rich men buy these bonds, thereby escaping all taxation, and they demanded that all bonds should be taxed—school bonds, road bonds, town, county, village, city, state, and national bonds. The drift toward publicly owned utilities, it was argued, would be ended.

Their campaign had been very successful. Chambers of Commerce, commercial clubs, city councils, the National Tax Conference, state legislatures, and even one branch of Congress had passed resolutions denouncing tax-exempt securities and proposing a constitutional amendment to tax all public bonds. The Minnesota senate had unanimously passed such a resolution and sent it to the house, where it was referred to the tax committee.

Stockwell was a member of the tax committee. He prepared and introduced a counter-resolution pointing out, as summarized by Buell:

> First—just what influences were behind this movement to tax all public bonds.
>
> Second—how, if public bonds were taxed, it would inevitably increase the rate of interest that the people must pay.
>
> Third—That the same rich men would buy these bonds as before, and would really make a bigger profit than ever.
>
> Fourth—It would greatly hamper all public activities by making it more difficult to finance them.
>
> Fifth—It would tighten the grip of the public service corporations, and make them more powerful than ever.
>
> Well, this resolution set members to thinking, and the Senate resolution against tax-exempt securities died in the House Tax Committee.
>
> Stockwell had killed the woodchuck.[17]

Two military bills had been passed in the senate, and they came up in the house on April 10 on special order. The first one attempted to permit the armory commission, the armory board, or the armory officer in charge to increase the fund for the maintenance of each unit of the National Guard from $250 to $750 dollars annually and required every county auditor to levy the amount on the taxpayers of the county. Stockwell protested, and the bill was killed, twenty for and eighty against.[18]

The second bill would have greatly increased the number of armories that could be built each year. The house stood by Stockwell and killed the bill with only twelve for and sixty-four against. Buell noted the real militants were not so many when they had to go on record.[19]

A bill to tax mining royalties had passed in the house in 1921 (103 to 14), but lost in the senate (28 to 34). Voters were angered by the senate's vote. Twenty-two of the thirty-four senators voting against it did not return, and at least twelve of them were defeated for reelection. A virtually identical bill, described by Buell as "just a very small tax (six percent) on the net royalty received by those who were fortunate enough to hold title to these very valuable free gifts of nature—supposedly a gift of nature to all the people—not to a favored few" was introduced in the 1923 session by C. M. Bendixon. Attempts were made to increase the rate to eight percent and ten percent. Stockwell explained that he regarded even ten percent as ridiculously low. In his view, the state ought to have all of the royalty—100 percent: "These people have no moral right to any of it." When attempts to increase the tax failed, the bill passed 104 to 16. Stockwell voted yes even though he believed six percent was ninety-four percent too little.[20]

A bill doing away with the indeterminate sentence and thereby virtually eliminating the parole board was introduced. Prisoners would have had little hope of getting out before the end of their terms. The bill was strongly opposed by prison authorities at public hearings and by Stockwell on the floor of the house. He made an extended speech pleading that even from a business standpoint the parole system pays by restoring to society a large percentage of offenders. The bill was decisively defeated.[21]

A bill to provide a system of physical education with instruction in dietetics and the laws of health was introduced in the house near the close of the session. Representatives from county districts opposed the measure, regarding it as a fad or frill quite unnecessary for farmers' children, whose chores kept them in good physical condition. Farmer though he was, Stockwell stood solidly behind the measure: "A strong body is needed to house a strong mind. Let us develop all children into strong, healthy, intelligent men and women," he urged, "not a few athletes, as now, with all the others as audience and applauders for the few heroes."[22]

Stockwell had decided not to run again for the legislature after his defeat for reelection to the senate in 1902 because he wanted to enter the fight against the Minneapolis Gas Light Company at the municipal level. In 1922, he chose the legislature as the preferred battleground in the fight against the public utilities, whose operations were severely damaging the public domain Buell stated the problem:

> Minnesota, the land of 10,000 lakes, has vast water power. In 1923 much of it was still on undeveloped state land. The policy of the state for some years had been to retain title to its great natural resources of minerals and timber and not to dispose of them to private ownership.
>
> Not so with water power. Much of it was already in private hands. As fast as private companies could get possession, more and more of it was going the same way. An amendment to the constitution was required to put the state into a position where it could protect the rights of the people by conserving and developing such water as still remained unappropriated. To give the

people a chance to amend the constitution with this end in view, Stockwell introduced a bill for a constitutional amendment "to permit and authorize the state to engage in the acquisition, development, and operation of water power resources within the state and on the boundaries thereof, and to negotiate bonds and certificates of indebtedness therefor." In developing water power sites, the state could use the power or sell it as it saw fit. Bonds could be issued up to $50,000,000 to carry on such projects. As a practical matter, the State of Minnesota could be given the right to buy Northern States Power Company for $50,000,000 taking over an existing power system by right of eminent domain.[23]

Faced with Stockwell's bill, attorneys for the waterpower interests argued strenuously before the Public Utilities Committee against the idea of letting the state go into industry—private industry, as if, noted Buell, conservation of the common inheritance were not the very first duty of government. By a seven-to-five vote, the committee reported on the bill for indefinite postponement. Friends of conservation got busy. The minority report was defended by Stockwell, who moved that it be substituted for the committee report. The minority report was overwhelmingly adopted, yeas eighty-two and nays thirteen. But it was too late for the matter to be reached on general order, and nothing further could be done in the 1923 session.[24]

Neither could the Stockwells do much about their second daughter's inevitable departure from Minnesota. Charlotte loved her social work and enjoyed activities with her friends, and she had marched in suffragist parades and distributed literature in support of causes backed by her father. But as she sewed a wedding dress for her friend Althea Heitsmith's wedding in 1920, Charlotte, who was maid of honor, probably wished she could do the same thing for herself. As Althea Heitsmith Atwater recalled, Charlotte was unhappy during those years, and she didn't like living on the outskirts of Minneapolis:

> There was no city water, there was nothing. OM kept a cow but no horse or automobile, a variation from the norm, and Charlotte worried about that. When she could have been having beaux, she was isolated. It was a long ride on the streetcar from downtown to her house.

In the summer of 1923, Charlotte made an extended visit to Boston to see her younger sister Beth, who had moved to Massachusetts after her marriage to William P. Everts in 1914. Beth was expecting another child—Elizabeth (Libby) had been born on December 23, 1915, and William (this author, called Bill) on June 24, 1918. That same year Bessie Houghton, just a few days after stepping off a boat from Ireland, had come to live with the family.

Beth had also given birth to a stillborn child in 1921, and Charlotte meant to help run Beth's household during July and August; the Everts family had taken a cottage at Lake Winnepesaukee in New Hampshire for the summer. Stockwell (Stocky) Everts was born in Boston on July 29, 1923. Libby and Bill, under the loving care of Charlotte and Bessie, flourished at Boulder Cottage.

Charlotte was much happier in Massachusetts than she had been in Minneapolis. There she met Hamilton Wallace Baker, a client of Beth's husband, and within the year, she moved to Boston permanently, to live on Beacon Hill and again ply the trade of a social worker. Charlotte and Hamilton married in 1925 and lived, after a few years in Cambridge, in Brookline just two blocks from the Everts home. Charlotte gave birth to no children, but she loved her niece and nephews and looked upon them almost as her own. Hamilton Baker, who had been married previously, was a successful businessman. He established and became the first president of the American Locker Company—"The key is your check"—which he successfully marketed across the country for use in railroad stations and bus terminals. He was more conservative politically than Charlotte's father, and she lost her liberal leanings, doubtless under Baker's influence, as she felt he could do no wrong. (Hamilton Baker died in 1946. Charlotte lived until 1973 but never really recovered from the loss of her husband.)

Beth continued her involvement in the social welfare movement after her marriage, but raising her children was clearly her uppermost concern. Prison reform was a continuing interest, heightened by the shocking living conditions for inmates at the Charlestown prison. The couple's attention riveted on that institution during the period Sacco and Vanzetti spent on death row there, before their execution on August 23, 1927. The Evertses, convinced of their innocence, raised funds and did all in their power to save them from the electric chair. When Massachusetts erected an additional, more humane facility at Norfolk, Beth sometimes corresponded with inmates there—a course set by her father.

Through the years, Beth retained the liberal political bent of her parents. Maud served on the lay advisory board of the Minnesota Birth Control League (forerunner of Planned Parenthood) and associated with Margaret Sanger on a national level, for instance.

Beth was active in the Planned Parenthood League of Massachusetts, her husband serving as president during the organization's most bitter conflict with the Roman Catholic Church. (William P. Everts died from pneumonia on September 15, 1970, in Cambridge. Elizabeth Stockwell Everts died at Massachusetts General Hospital on August 21, 1971, from pancreatic cancer.)

Back in Minnesota, Stockwell successfully ran for reelection in the fall of 1924. He was the Thirty-second District's front runner, leading with 8,917 votes to Nellermoe's 8,897. Conservatives, however, comprised the majority in the upcoming session.[25]

Also running for office was Floyd B. Olson, who had by 1924 joined the ranks of the Farmer-Labor party and won its nomination for governor. His wit, charm, boyish good looks, keen mind, and excellent record as county attorney all served him in good stead. His opponent was the formidable Theodore Christianson, who replaced the unpopular Preuss at the head of the Republican ticket. Olson ran strongly but lost, 406,692 to 366,029. Carlos Avery, Democratic candidate, polled 49,353 votes as the Democratic party in Minnesota continued to sink. Olson's defeat can be attributed in part to a communist infiltration of the Farmer-Labor party and his acceptance of communist support. Republicans pounced on Olson's miscalculation. But Olson learned from the experience. The following year communists were expelled from the Farmer-Labor movement, though expulsion did not end suspicion of their presence and the "Communist problem" remained.[26]

Running for office nationally were Calvin Coolidge, seeking election for a full term in his own right, and conservative Democrat John W. Davis, born in West Virginia and, by 1924, one of New York's most prominent lawyers. Unhappy with their choices, liberal leaders from the ranks of labor and agriculture, with strong socialist support, turned to Robert La Follette to organize a third party—the Conference for Political Action. La Follette was to run on his own platform. Like Stockwell, he was a strong supporter of the cooperative movement. His platform, "pledged to secure such legislation as may be needful or helpful in promoting and protecting cooperative enterprises," included public ownership of waterpower, downward revision of the tariff and railway rates, farm relief, and a federal child labor amendment. Stockwell almost certainly supported him. La Follette ran third, but his nearly five million votes demonstrated a significant undercurrent of liberal sentiment in the country. Coolidge won easily with 15,725,000 popular votes, nearly twice the number received by Davis, whose 136 electoral votes all came from the then-solid south.[27]

In Minnesota, outlook for the passage of Stockwell's agenda was not promising as he took his seat in the forty-fourth session on January 6, 1925. The conservative mood of the country, epitomized by Coolidge, called for perpetuation of the status quo, and such was the mood of the legislature. Thus defeats of Stockwell's proposals outnumbered the victories. Typical was the fate of his attempt to increase the amount of the occupation tax. For years the mining companies had been protected from

Wisconsin Senator Robert M. La Follette. (Courtesy of the Minnesota Historical Society)

paying their fair share of taxes by legislators beholden to the steel industry. Finally in 1921 the legislature enacted a law levying "an occupation tax equal to six percent of the valuation of all ores mined or produced . . . in addition to all other taxes provided for by law." Stockwell regarded the six-percent tax on the mining industry as woefully inadequate, just as he regarded the six-percent tax on royalties received by owners of mineral rights as much too low. Minnesota simply was not getting a just share of the taxes. When the occupation tax was enacted in 1921, Farmer-Labor members of the legislature began talking about raising the tax; talk was the extent of activity. Scant attention was paid to the question in 1923 because at that time an awaited U.S. Supreme Court ruling on the constitutionality of the occupational tax had not yet been handed down. By 1925, the court had upheld it. Stockwell introduced a proposal to increase the rate from six to ten percent. While his proposal received general support from the Farmer-Labor faction, the bill represented Stockwell's individual efforts and was not a party bill.[28] Opponents contended that a larger tax would be a case of killing the goose that laid the golden egg. The committee on taxation, of which Stockwell was again a member, killed the bill by a twelve-to-one vote for indefinite postponement.

Stockwell was the lone dissenter. Thereafter, before the full house, he moved to have the minority report substituted for the committee report. F. H. Holladay moved a call of the house. Stockwell's motion was defeated, yeas thirty-five and nays eighty-four.[29]

It was Stockwell's willingness to stand alone in the face of defeat, pressing onward when he believed he was right, to which A. W. Rankin, former professor at the University of Minnesota and Buell's successor as observer of the legislature in 1925, referred when he said:

> I am reminded of the story of the jury foreman who was asked by a caterer if he should send up twelve dinners. "No, eleven dinners, one bale of hay," the jury foreman replied. Stockwell would say, "Eleven bales of hay, one dinner," —so confident was he in his cause.[30]

References

1. Memories did continue to be jogged by the press. On June 15, 1922, the *Minneapolis Journal* reported that Burnquist had testified in a trial in Chicago that Stockwell was known for being pro-German. Burnquist grouped him with others said to be traitors and disloyal.

2. Deposition of S. A. Stockwell, *J. E. Foster v. Al P. Erickson, County Auditor,* Supreme Court File No. 32676, 1940, Minnesota Historical Society.

3. Hitchcock, *Issues of the Minnesota Legislature—Regular Session 1935, and Special Session, 1935-1936,* p. 7.

4. Remarks, Complimentary Birthday Dinner, June 8, 1927.

5. Bellman also admired Stockwell's "calm, collected way of thinking." Elected by narrow margins in 1934 and 1936, he was defeated in 1938. "Hitler's anti-Semitism was being felt in Minnesota," he told the author in an interview in 1988.

6. *Minneapolis Journal,* June 18, 1922.

7. *Minneapolis Journal,* November 6, 1922.

8. Chrislock, *Progressive Era,* pp. 183, 187, 188.

9. *Legislative Manual,* 1923, p. 462.

10. C. J. Buell, *The Minnesota Legislature of 1923* (St. Paul: [Buell], 1923), p. 7.

11. Chrislock, *Progressive Era,* p. 183.

12. Mayer, *Floyd B. Olson*, pp. 7-11.

13. Buell, *Minnesota Legislature of 1923*, pp. 14-15. Much of this chapter is taken from the *Minnesota Legislature of 1923*. In the frontispiece Buell wrote, "This book is not copyrighted. Quote as much as you please but give credit." The author has taken him at his word.

14. *House Journal, 1923*, pp. 766-777. The Declaration of Independence no longer appears in *The Minnesota Legislative Manual.*

15. Buell, *Minnesota Legislature of 1923*, p. 35.

16. Buell, *Minnesota Legislature of 1923*, pp. 35-36.

17. Buell, *Minnesota Legislature of 1923*, pp. 34-35. Stockwell served on the Corporations, Crime Prevention, Insurance, Public Health, and Hospitals Committees in addition to the Committee on Taxation.

18. Buell, *Minnesota Legislature of 1923*, p. 36.

19. Buell, *Minnesota Legislature of 1923*, p. 36.

20. Buell, *Minnesota Legislature of 1923*, pp. 7, 49-50.

21. Buell, *Minnesota Legislature of 1923*, pp. 45-46; *Minneapolis Journal*, March 25, 1923.

22. Buell, *Minnesota Legislature of 1923*, p. 76.

23. Buell, *Minnesota Legislature of 1923*, p. 60.

24. Buell, *Minnesota Legislature of 1923*, pp. 60-61; *House Journal*, 1923, p. 587.

25. *Legislative Manual, 1925*, p. 492.

26. Mayer, *Floyd B. Olson*, 10, 17, 31; Gieske, *Minnesota Farmer-Laborism*, p. 92; *Dictionary of American Biography*, Supplement 2, p. 503.

27. Morison and Commager, *Growth of the American Republic*, 2:519-521; see also *Minneapolis Cooperator* 4 (16) (October 10, 1924), quoting La Follette speech.

28. *Minneapolis Tribune*, March 17, 1925.

29. *House Journal, 1925*, p. 841.

30. Speech, Complimentary Birthday Dinner, June 8, 1927.

Chapter 20

Never Give Up

Defeat of Stockwell's fifty-million-dollar power bill of 1923 did not put the state-owned power system matter to rest. Rankin's *Minnesota Legislature of 1925* describes his attempt two years later to revolutionize the distribution of hydro-electric power in Minnesota:

> House file 310 . . . introduced by Mr. Stockwell was referred to the Committee of Public Domain and was by bare majority vote recommended out for passage. On its return to the house, however, the speaker ruled that, inasmuch as it carried a prospective appropriation, it should have gone in the first place to the committee on appropriations, and it was accordingly sent to this committee, which ruled that it be indefinitely postponed. The ruling by the speaker that it was the province of the committee on appropriations to consider the bill was based on a rule of the house that all appropriation bills must be referred to the committee on appropriations. As a matter of fact, the bill carried no appropriation but simply provided for a condition which might in the future enable a legislature to involve the state in indebtedness, provided the amendment to the constitution was ratified by the people.
>
> Mr. Stockwell moved to reject the report of the committee and that the bill be placed on general order without recommendation.
>
> To place a bill on general orders after its rejection by a committee is infrequently done. Some members consider a rejection of a bill by a committee as prima facie evidence of its undesirability.[1]
>
> A role call was ordered on Stockwell's motion, and the motion was rejected. (Yeas 52, Nays 70).

Rankin's further commentary, having named the voters for and against, expressed Stockwell's views explicitly:

I give the roll call because it comes nearer than any other to show the strength of the opposition to Public Ownership. Also, because opposition to handing over to private interests of our available water power is likely to be an issue in the future. Hydro-electric power is considered of vital interest to control the life of generations ahead. Enormous aggregations of capital and unlimited combinations of private owners of hydro-electric power are being formed day by day. These movements will enable the owners of this power to exercise a greater monopoly and control than the world has ever known. Some day the people may see that it was a mistake to give over to private interests such control. Then the roll call over this question will have significance.

Stockwell, absent from the legislature in 1927, reintroduced the power bill in 1929 and 1931. Each time he met defeat.[2] He tried again in 1933, when he was a member of the Committee on Public Domain. R. M. Aalbu, successor to Buell and Rankin in coverage of the legislature, reported on the mounting pressure against Stockwell's proposal in *The Minnesota Kaleidoscope of 1933*:

Perhaps no legislation ever introduced has been contested more bitterly. . . . Members were bombarded with letters and telegrams from bankers, professional men, chambers of commerce. It was noticeable that the letters from each locality bore practically the same date and were of similar wording, indicating that they had been inspired by some central agency interested in defeating the bill. . . . It is evident that the people of the state are rapidly awakening to the fact that public or municipal ownership is the only means of protection against the usurpations of the power trust. The extortionate rates charged in many places and the shameful watering of stock, as revealed by the Federal Trade Commission, proves that it is the only means of protection . . . The power amendment was H.F. 79 and reached the House calendar about March 1st. The sponsors, knowing that it would take all the strength they had to pass this bill, delayed action on it for several days because some of the supporters were gone to Washington to attend the presidential inauguration. By the time they returned, the House was so swamped with special orders that the calendar was never reached again.[3]

Stockwell continued to fight the power trust with "tooth and claw," Aalbu's words.[4] In 1934, when the country was in the depths of economic depression, Stockwell's plan for a state-owned power system was advanced as a key plank in the Farmer-Labor party's platform, along with other public ownership projects—a state bank, state workmen's compensation insurance, state printing of textbooks, even some key industries. Olson, then running for a third term as governor, pushed for Stockwell's proposal throughout his campaign. Martin A. Nelson, the Republican candidate, spoke against the plan. Stockwell sought to set the record straight in a letter to the editor, *Thief River Forum*, dated October 20, 1934. Stockwell's reliance on economics to present his argument makes the letter similar to what has come to be known in the law as a "Brandeis brief":

Dear Sir:

On a number of occasions the Republican candidate for Governor has attempted to discredit the Farmer-Labor Platform because it declares in favor of introducing the Ontario system of electrical production and distribution into Minnesota. He says, in substance, that "the Ontario system is a failure and that it would be the height of folly and very destructive to attempt its introduction into our State."

Just what is the Ontario system? And what has it accomplished?

About thirty years ago the Parliament of Ontario created an Electrical Commission to study and investigate the desirability of a Public Ownership Power and Light system of production and distribution of electricity. The Commission reported favorably on the project, and a permanent Hydro-Electric Commission with Sir Adam Beck, a wealthy and prosperous businessman of New London, Ontario, as Chairman, was appointed. This Commission acquired for the people a small plant of 100,000 h.p. at Niagara Falls. From this small beginning a wonderful system covering all of Ontario has been developed. The people of Ontario now own a property worth $334,661,542.90. The generating and distribution system is worth $285,003,959.26, and the municipal distributing systems are valued at $109,657,573.64. The total reserves of the production and distribution system are $69,453,260.25 and the reserve of the municipal systems stands at $59,736,619.76. The total reserves $129,170,050.01. This splendid property never cost the people of Ontario a single cent in taxes. It has been built up out of rates, the lowest on this continent. There are many rates for light and power in important centers as low as two cents top rate, 1 and 1/4 cents second rate, 3/4 to 7/8 cents third rate. Our neighbor city of Fort William, Ontario, has a rate of 8 mills per k.w.h.

It is interesting to note that before public ownership was adopted by Ontario the rates were just as extortionate as they are in the United States today. What has caused this remarkable change?

The answer is the Public Ownership System adopted 30 years ago.

The Ontario System is a perfect system in that it provides for the cheapest possible production and distribution and preserves local self-government in the municipalities and districts.

The Republican candidate for Governor has out of his own lips told the people of Minnesota whose candidate he is. It is plain that the Power gang [is] interested in his candidacy. Nothing could be more certain. He has, in my judgment, perhaps wilfully [sic] misrepresented the system of our friendly neighbors in Ontario. It is outrageous that he should deceive the people of Minnesota and attempt to discredit the perfectly sound and solvent institution of a neighboring people, and all for a few votes. Mendacity could hardly stoop lower. Public ownership is the only way to handle a natural monopoly, if you expect to secure justice for the people. Regulation of a natural monopoly has utterly failed and, in my judgment, always will. It is so in the very nature of the case.

I have received a letter from the Chairman of the Hydro-Electric Commission, who states there has been a decline in the income of the Commission due entirely to the depression but all of this decline has been absorbed by a contingent rate and stabilization fund set up for just such an emergency as we are passing through. Not a penny has been charged against taxes, as there was no occasion for it. As a matter of fact some of the municipalities were entirely free from debt on their distribution system and have reduced rates during the depression. That all electric light and power companies have had a decline in revenue is well known. . . .

An item in the *Minneapolis Tribune* on October 9 has this:

Northern States Earnings Drop

New York, Oct. 8 (AP) Net earnings of the Northern States Power Co. (Minnesota) and subsidiaries during the fiscal year ended June 30 totaled $12,031,713, compared with $12,723,502 in the preceding 12 months.

The people of Ontario are proud, and justly so, of their "hydro." And such wild statements as are made by the Republican candidate for Governor lead them to think that the people of the United State are just plain liars. Ontario is not the only country blessed with low rates. Our neighboring city of Winnipeg has a domestic rate of .89 of a cent per K.W.H. as against an average rate of 5 and 1/2 cents per K.W. for domestic service in this country. . . . The Farmer-Labor people of Minnesota, if given control of the government at the coming election, will take a forward step in bringing this marvelous servant of mankind to the homes and farms of the people of the state of Minnesota at rates that they can afford to pay. A vote for the Farmer-Labor candidate is a vote to introduce into the homes and farms of Minnesota the most useful servant of humankind so far developed.[5]

Olson defeated Nelson in 1934 but his victory did not necessarily mean success for the Farmer-Labor program in the legislature. Stockwell's bill, HF84, was considered early in the 1935 session as both sides agreed to prompt consideration after brief hearings. Battle lines were drawn over a minority report signed by Stockwell alone of the public domain committee. The majority voted to kill the bill.

Stockwell forged ahead, launching his attack on power interests, which he accused of dominating the educational system, getting particular textbooks into schools "from kindergarten to university." He charged that the electrical engineering department of the University of Minnesota was "more or less dominated" by the power industry. "Electric rates are at least twice what they ought to be on the basis of fair valuation and honest administration," he contended. "I don't want a communist state nor a dictatorship . . . I plead with you to let democracy have its say . . . give the people the right to vote on this."[6]

He was met from all corners with familiar arguments about the evils of the state entering private business. The *Minneapolis Journal* took poignant note of the odds against him:

> Stockwell, now a man of 77, who fought this battle almost alone for years, enlisted the Farmer-Labor movement in his program, but went down to another sweeping defeat. He knew he was licked before he started, but he stood up to take his rejection with the promise that he would be back again "until it succeeds . . . I am not discouraged . . . I know we must struggle for reform, and it will take time."[7]

Back he came in 1937. After "another supreme effort," he had to sit by and see the house crush the measure (HF3) once more by a vote of sixty-seven to fifty-three. He "held the floor for more than an hour, delivering the longest speech of the session. He pleaded with his fellow liberals—whose majority in the house had given him confidence of success—to pass the bill," and closed by berating the power companies "for propaganda which he said even insinuated itself into the church." The debate raged all afternoon and into the evening. S. T. Severtson, a minister and one of the leaders of the opposition," stressed the fact he had not been influenced by any sinister propaganda."[8]

On the roll call, despite support of the measure by Governor Elmer A. Benson in his inaugural message, twenty-eight liberals kicked over the traces and voted against it.

After the roll had been called and Stockwell realized he had lost again, he rose and said, "The time will come when this measure will prevail, and you'll be sorry you didn't vote for it."

Following Stockwell's defeat, Clara Ethyl Dickey Parsons, wife of the author of the history of the Saturday Lunch Club, sought to console him. "Oh, that's all right," said Stockwell. "It was defeated by fewer votes this time."

He simply refused to be dismayed by defeat. And so it was with all commitments—in all forums. He strove to save Sacco and Vanzetti until the day the Commonwealth of Massachusetts electrocuted them. He strove somehow, some way, to keep the country out of war right up to the moment Congress declared war. Participating in seven different home-rule campaigns, he strove for the passage of a new charter for Minneapolis that would give the city complete power of local self-government. His method? "Oh, house meetings and campaigns from soap boxes and any other old way that would get the attention of the public."[9] With others from the Saturday Lunch Club he strove to block the infamous Brooks-Coleman law; after the law was enacted in 1921, he strove to have it repealed through public debate and by legislation.[10] Again and again in the legislature, he strove to increase the "woefully inadequate" occupation tax on the mining industry.[11]

Through it all Stockwell remained optimistic. His daughter Charlotte took special note of his abiding faith in the ultimate triumph of good over evil, confident as he was that right must in time prevail: "How often I heard him say, 'I shan't live to see it, but you may.'"

Near the close of his career, Vivian Thorp of the *Minneapolis Journal* saluted Stockwell's staying power:

> Mr. Stockwell's dream has been that the people of this state and nation shall repossess their fine heritage of natural resources which slipped away from them when the doctrines of individualism ruled the country. From selfless efforts to make this dream come true, he has never swerved. While men with more "practical" aims (or so they are called) would have abandoned the fight, this man has held on and still holds on in the patient certainty that his dream will become reality.
>
> In watching his fight through the years, his patience has seemed an amazing thing, for he is not a patient man. He has a caustic tongue and biting gift of satire which have been used

as weapons in this long struggle. But even these have been subdued to a belief in his fellow citizens which has made it seem to him worthwhile to carry on, almost alone, in our law-making body, with faith that the economic soundness of his contention will be proved. It is safe to say that as long as there is breath in his body, he will continue steadfastly in the course.[12]

Stockwell gave a personal explanation:

I think one of the reasons why I am always hopeful is that I have seen so many occasions when causes that seemed to be dying or hopeless have finally come to fruition. I recall the fight that was made to save Rudowitz and Pouran (which George Leonard will remember) from extradition at the behest of Czar Nicholas of Russia. He was attempting to establish the precedent that this nation should no longer be an asylum for the oppressed of the world. Rudowitz and Pouran were on the verge of extradition. There did not seem to be any hope. Jane Addams, Raymond Robins—a splendid group of people over the United States—had done everything they could, but I was determined, with the rest of our friends here in Minneapolis, that one final effort should be made. I went to Harry Mead after the meeting of our society at 8th Street and LaSalle Avenue, and suggested that we call a meeting after the morning address, in order to have something done about this situation.

Some of the brethren objected, said we didn't know anything about the question, thought it was not any of our business anyway, etc. But the meeting was called, and from that meeting we had a larger meeting in the First Baptist Church, addressed by Wm. Henry Eustis, Rev. G. L. Morrill, and others, and a resolution was adopted, drawn by Willis M. West, that ought to be read every morning in the public schools of this and every other city. That resolution was carried to President Cyrus Northrop, who was so impressed by the resolution and the action taken that he immediately took the matter up personally with President Roosevelt and Elihu Root. Out of that work came the force that kept Rudowitz and Pouran from being extradited.

I think we can by that little incident prove to ourselves, at least, that there is never any use in giving up. We must keep at it . . . So, friends, it seems to me that if we love our fellow men and the principles for which this government stands, we should never surrender.[13]

References

1. Here and below, A. W. Rankin, *The Minnesota Legislature of 1925* (Minneapolis: Voters Research League of Minneapolis, 1925), pp. 27-28.

2. *House Journal, 1929*, HF314, pp. 509-511; *House Journal, 1931*, HF88, pp. 435-436, 451, 1372.

3. R. M. Aalbu, *The Minnesota Kaleidoscope of 1933* (Thief River Falls: Forum Publishing Company, 1933), pp. 72-73.

4. Aalbu, *Minnesota Kaleidoscope*, p. 1.

5. Letter from S. A. Stockwell to the editor, *Thief River Forum*, dated October 20, 1934. See Quetico-Superior Council files, correspondence between Ernest Oberholtzer and Stockwell, Minnesota Historical Society. In the 1920s and 1930s, Republican Senator George W. Norris of Nebraska was the leading figure in political life favoring the public production, transmission, and distribution of hydroelectric power. His crowning achievement was the creation of the Tennessee Valley Authority (TVA) in 1933 and construction of a dam on the Tennessee River at Muscle Shoals in northwestern Alabama. TVA brought the federal government into the business of manufacturing and selling electric power. Norris successfully shepherded enabling legislation through Congress and into the statute books after Coolidge and Hoover had vetoed his earlier bills. President Franklin D. Roosevelt was highly supportive. Additional dams were constructed after Muscles Shoals, and by 1972 TVA was selling low cost electric power to two million residential consumers and to industry at a price per kilowatt hour equivalent to half the national average.

Aalbu has noted in *The Minnesota Kaleidoscope* of 1933 that Stockwell was often called the Norris of Minnesota. Views of the two men on other issues besides hydroelectric power were parallel. Norris, a Republican, supported much of the Populist program, and he was one of six senators who voted against the country's declaration of war in April 1917. They were also in accord on ethical questions. Upon first being elected to Congress in 1906, Norris returned his free railroad pass to the Chicago, Burlington, and Quincy Railroad, which he had represented in private law practice. A minor step, perhaps, but one not universally followed by elected officials. (See "George William Norris" in *Dictionary of American Biography*, Supplement Three, p. 557; "Tennessee Valley Authority" in *Dictionary of American History*, Vol. VII, p. 27; Aalbu, *Minnesota Kaleidoscope*, p. 1; Morison and Commager, *Growth of the Republic*, pp. 538-39).

6. *Minneapolis Journal*, February 22, 1935.

7. *Minneapolis Journal*, February 22, 1935.

8. Here and below, *Minneapolis Star*, February 19, 1937. On February 23, 1937, a resolution was received and read to the house from the Farmer-

Labor delegates of the Eighth Congressional District convention protesting and condemning "so-called Liberals and Progressive members" of the legislature who voted against HF3. See *House Journal*, 1937, p. 540.

9. *Minneapolis Charter Commission, A Brief Explanation of the New Charter* (1913), Minneapolis History Collection, Minneapolis Public Library; Stockwell Deposition, *J. E. Foster v. Al P. Erickson, County Auditor*, Minnesota Historical Society; Buell, *Minnesota Legislature of 1917*, p. 27.

10. *House Journal, 1923*, p. 105; *House Journal, 1925*, p. 251; *House Journal, 1929*, p. 235; Aalbu, *Minnesota Kaleidoscope of 1933*, p. 97; Chrislock, *Progressive Era*, p. 187; *Minneapolis Tribune*, December 2, 1928.

11. See Chapters 19 and 31.

12. *Minneapolis Journal*, March 29, 1937.

13. Speech, Complimentary Birthday Dinner, June 8, 1927.

Chapter 21

Political Prisoners

A s the Declaration of Independence was dear to Stockwell's heart—"one of the greatest and most fundamentally sound papers ever penned by man"—so was another of Jefferson's declarations—his admonishment to the nation in its infancy: "If there be any among us who would wish to dissolve this union or change its republican form, let them stand undisturbed as monuments of the safety with which error of opinion may be tolerated, where reason is left free to combat it."[1]

Stockwell, who had personally felt the impact of popular hostility toward radicalism, saw such hostility rise again after World War I. Jefferson's admonishment was all but forgotten. Morison and Commager have described the mounting intolerance of the 1920s:

> Busily engaged in getting and enjoying wealth, and sure that they were at last on the road to Utopia, Americans were peculiarly intolerant of criticism or heresy. The seeds of intolerance had been planted during the war; in the post-war years they sprouted strange and noxious weeds. Nationalism took on an especially virulent form, manifesting itself in the "revision" of history and history textbooks, teachers' loyalty oaths, compulsory military training in state schools, the persecution of pacifists, criminal syndicalist laws, "red" baiting, the purging of legislative and other bodies of Socialists, the deportation of aliens, and the judicial lynching of radicals.[2]

Sacco and Vanzetti

The judicial lynching of Nicola Sacco, "a good shoemaker," and Bartolomeo Vanzetti, "a poor fish peddlar," philosophic anarchists and labor organizers, outraged Stockwell as no other event on the world stage.

On April 15, 1920, at the Slater and Morrill shoe factory in South Braintree, Massachusetts, Frederick A. Parmenter, paymaster, and Allesandro Berardelli, his guard, were shot, killed, and robbed of $15,776.51. Two men were seen running from the scene to a getaway car. Sacco and Vanzetti, Italian immigrants, were charged with the crime. The money was never recovered. The evidence presented against them in trial was flimsy at best. Testimony brought out by a hard-hitting if less-than-scrupulous prosecutor showed that the defendants were philosophical anarchists and atheists. Judge Webster Thayer, presiding in superior court in Dedham, was shockingly biased. His extreme prejudice against the defendants was expressed outside the courtroom and was implicit in his behavior on the bench. The defense was badly mismanaged. Pervasive and dominating was the political climate of the times, which made it appear that anyone holding an unpopular opinion was a red, a radical, a Bolshevik, a terrorist, a threat to all that was dear. The social mind of the jury was simply unfit to deal with issues involving hysterical passions.[3]

On July 14, 1921, the jury found the defendants guilty of the crime. Immediately, anti-American rioting broke out abroad. Protests against the verdict in the United States, Latin America, and western Europe were loud, furious, and unrestrained. In America the demonstrations brought increased red-baiting. Protesting loudly and furiously in Minnesota was Stockwell. From that day forward, until their executions, he worked tirelessly on behalf of Sacco and Vanzetti, hoping to see justice done.[4]

Typical of Stockwell's effort was the organizing of a meeting called by the Minneapolis Labor Defense Committee at Minneapolis City Hall on May 10, 1925. He was chairman and one of the speakers. Two of the speakers were Communists. His political opponents surely would seek to gain advantage from such association. But what possible difference could that make?

The *Minneapolis Journal* covered the event:

Class War Lauded in City Hall Rally

Overthrow of the existing order and the substitution of "rule by workers" in America and over the world was urged last night at a meeting in the assembly room of the Minneapolis City Hall. The meeting was called to raise funds for the defense of Sacco and Vanzetti, convicted of murder in a Massachusetts court. $100 was raised.

"This case is just another frame-up like the Tom Mooney trial in California and just another example of the need of workers to organize for defense," Dan E. Stevens, communist, told the meeting. "Not only must we organize for defense, but on the basis of the class struggle eventually to establish world rule by the workers. Denizens of the underworld were paid to perjure themselves to send Sacco and Vanzetti to the chair" . . . J. Louis Engdahl, editor of the communist organ, *The Daily Worker*, of Chicago and formerly of Minneapolis, also spoke.[5]

Sacco and Vanzetti poster, from *Twin Cities: A Pictorial History of St. Paul and Minneapolis*, by L. M. Kane and A. Ominsky, published in 1983. (Courtesy of the Minnesota Historical Society)

Sacco and Vanzetti remained in prison for seven years. In 1925 a condemned criminal, Celestino Madeiros, gave evidence that the murders had been committed by a group known as the Morelli gang. Judge Thayer declined to reopen the trial. Governor Alvin T. Fuller appointed a special committee headed by A. Lawrence Lowell, president of Harvard, to review the case. The committee upheld the governor's refusal of clemency. Edmund M. Morgan and G. Louis Joughin in *The Legacy of Sacco and Vanzetti* regarded the committee's report as bearing heavier responsibility than Judge Thayer for the deaths of two innocent men. Heywood Broun, in a stinging commentary on the commission's finding that the men were guilty and had received a fair trial, asked, "Is Harvard to be known hereafter as Hangman's House?" The article led to Broun's firing from the *New York World*.[6]

In June 1927, Stockwell was still optimistic: "I believe that the effort that has been put forth by the friends with whom I am glad to be associated, to save two innocent men, Sacco and Vanzetti, is going to result in their being saved."

Sacco and Vanzetti were executed minutes after midnight in Charlestown prison on August 23, 1927. The reaction to their deaths among the fair-minded was one of unbearable anguish. In Boston, on August 28, their caskets were at the head of an eight-mile cortege; 10,000 mourners were at the cemetery; 200,000 lined the streets of Boston from the North End to Hanover Street to Tremont Street from Scollay Square and on to Roxbury Crossing.

Thousands mourned in the circles, squares, and plazas of New York, London, Paris, and Rome, as well as in other cities and towns around the world.[7]

There was mourning, too, in Beth's house in Chestnut Hill. She and her husband had done everything they could—attended meetings, written letters, given money to the cause—as all the while neighbors and acquaintances were heard to say, "Guilty or not guilty, give 'em the chair." One of the earliest childhood recollections of the author is picking up the *Boston Herald* from the front porch on Tuesday morning, August 23, to be greeted by the headline: "SACCO AND VANZETTI ARE EXECUTED."[8]

And there was mourning in Minneapolis. How Stockwell must have wept as he read Bartolomeo Vanzetti's last words to the court that condemned him:

> If it had not been for this thing I might have lived out my life talking at street corners to scorning men.
>
> I might have died, unmarked, unknown, a failure. Now we are not a failure.
>
> This is our career and our triumph. Never in our full life could we hope to do such work for tolerance, for justice, for man's understanding of man, as now we do by accident. Our words, our love, our pain—nothing.
>
> The taking of our lives—lives of a good shoemaker and a poor fish peddlar—all.
>
> The last moment belongs to us—that agony is our triumph.[9]

Never again was it business as usual for Stockwell. He was simply unwilling to put the matter behind him.

Maud C. and S. A. Stockwell extend a cordial invitation to the
Annual Corn Fest, Sunday, September 8, 1929,
at their home, 3204 East 51st Street

———

There will be a basket lunch at 1 o'clock
and a program at 3 o'clock.
The program will be in the nature of a memorial for
Sacco and Vanzetti
Mr. Lewis C. Duncan will read the play
"Gods of the Lightning."

———

Take the 34th Avenue South and North Bryant car to East 51st Street.

The anguish did not diminish. Ten years later, Stockwell, unhappy, distraught, and removed, attended the author's graduation from Harvard College. Not only had he reluctantly departed from a self-imposed decision never to set foot in the Commonwealth of Massachusetts again, but at Cambridge he found himself in "Hangman's House."

Jefferson's plea to the nation to permit the free exchange of ideas had, of course, been scorned before the 1920s. In 1886, disclosures of philosophic belief in anarchism at the time of the Haymarket riots unleashed the passions of those who maintained that radicals ought to be hanged on general principles.[10] With the hanging of four anarchists in November 1887 for "constructive" conspiracy to incite murder, and Governor John P. Altgeld's courageous pardoning six years later, in the face of outraged public opinion, of defendants still in jail, Stockwell's sympathy for and determination to help political prisoners became forever ingrained. He would thereafter and throughout his life act as bondsman for men unjustly imprisoned during labor troubles or threatened with deportation. When the American Civil Liberties Union was founded in 1920 to defend constitutional freedoms, especially freedom of expression, due process, the right to privacy, and equal protection under the law, he rushed to join.[11]

Charles N. Beum

Stockwell's assistance to Charles N. Beum in an earlier case paralleled his later efforts on behalf of Sacco and Vanzetti. In February 1912, Beum, business agent and secretary of the Minneapolis Building Trades Council, was arrested by federal agents of the Department of Justice as one of several labor leaders named in indictments returned by an Indianapolis grand jury charging the transportation of explosives from one state to another in passenger cars.[12] Labor leaders and friends quickly organized a relief committee in Minneapolis to raise funds for Beum's defense. The committee, made up of forty-five members, arranged a huge "Public Hearing and Entertainment" to take place at the Shubert Theatre on March 2. Theater managers furnished acts free of charge and performers donated their services. Stockwell was among those in charge of the entertainment.

About a thousand people attended, according to the *Minneapolis Journal*, hundreds more, according to labor's estimates. Stockwell and Thomas Van Lear, then on the rise, were principal speakers. Van Lear said:

253

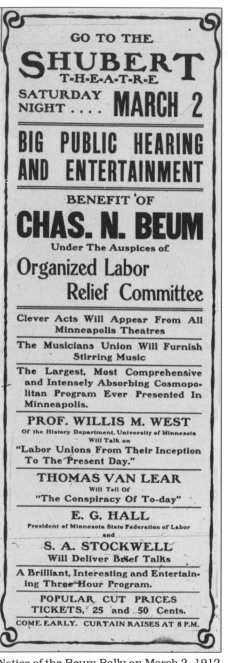

GO TO THE

SHUBERT
T-H-E-A-T-R-E

SATURDAY NIGHT .... MARCH 2

BIG PUBLIC HEARING AND ENTERTAINMENT

BENEFIT OF

CHAS. N. BEUM

Under The Auspices of

Organized Labor Relief Committee

Clever Acts Will Appear From All Minneapolis Theatres

The Musicians Union Will Furnish Stirring Music

The Largest, Most Comprehensive and Intensely Absorbing Cosmopolitan Program Ever Presented In Minneapolis.

PROF. WILLIS M. WEST
Of the History Department, University of Minnesota
Will Talk on
"Labor Unions From Their Inception To The Present Day."

THOMAS VAN LEAR
Will Tell Of
"The Conspiracy Of To-day"

E. G. HALL
President of Minnesota State Federation of Labor
and
S. A. STOCKWELL
Will Deliver Brief Talks

A Brilliant, Interesting and Entertaining Three-Hour Program.

POPULAR CUT PRICES
TICKETS, 25 and 50 Cents.

COME EARLY. CURTAIN RAISES AT 8 P.M.

Notice of the Beum Rally on March 2, 1912, in the *Labor Review*, March 1, 1912.

I honestly believe there is a conspiracy against organized labor in the United States. The ruling class wants the people to think that organized labor is organized crime and all because labor dared to demand better conditions. . . . In the wake of the Haymarket riots, five men were hanged and three sentenced to long prison terms for daring to attempt to organize labor in Chicago. Wasn't that conspiracy?[13]

Stockwell spoke on a topic uppermost on labor's mind nationwide. In the textile city of Lawrence, Massachusetts, at precisely the moment he spoke, hundreds of employees of the American Woolen Company—men, women, and "pallid, thin children"—were engaged in a great and a bitter strike. At its outset, the strike suffered from lack of strong leadership. Then the "aimless wandering of disorganized workers, seeking but a living wage and tolerable working conditions" was galvanized when the IWW took charge. The IWW "displayed to the shocked middle-class red banners with lawless mottos."[14] The state militia responded with brutality. According to testimony presented to a Congressional committee in Washington, as the strike was in progress, pregnant women were clubbed by the authorities. Children of employees being sent away from the city by train for reasons of safety were blocked in their attempts to leave.

Stockwell's remarks were a protest against the conduct of the state police. "No Russian methods are demanded by conditions

"SOME OF THOSE WHO TOOK PART IN BEUM BENEFIT PROGRAM." Stockwell and others at the Beum Benefit, March 2, 1912. (From the *Minneapolis Journal*, March 3, 1912)

in the United States," he declared. "Localities can best take care of their own police." He proposed resolutions condemning the action of the authorities of Lawrence during the textile strike, while demanding that the state "punish those responsible for the outrages and if United States laws were violated by the prevention of the taking from Lawrence of the children of strikers, that the president immediately begin prosecution of the offenders." The audience unanimously adopted the resolutions.[15]

Tom Mooney and Warren K. Billings

Another miscarriage of justice that grieved Stockwell and spurred him to action was the imprisonment of Tom Mooney, whose daring to be a labor leader wiped out twenty-five years of his life. During a strike in San Francisco in 1913, Mooney was arrested and charged with the unlawful possession of explosives. He was acquitted. Warren K. Billings, also arrested, was imprisoned for two years. Three years later, on July 22, 1916, a bomb exploded on a San Francisco sidewalk along the course of a Preparedness Day parade. Ten persons were killed and forty others wounded. Mooney and Billings were among those charged. Mooney was sentenced to death, Billings to life in prison. The case against Mooney was extremely weak, some of the evidence so questionable that the presiding judge, convinced the trial had been unfair, joined in the fight to save Mooney. In 1918, at President Wilson's request, Governor William Stephens of California commuted his sentence to life imprisonment. Mooney finally was pardoned in 1939; Billings was released through commutation.[16]

Labor unions and other organizations had fought steadily on Mooney's behalf. So had Stockwell. As W. E. Leonard put it in 1927, "Sacco and Vanzetti have personal acquaintance with him, and Tom Mooney must be a personal friend in his lonely cell in San Quentin."[17]

In 1923, before Mooney's pardon, Stockwell, as in the past, harnessed the legislature to further a cause outside Minnesota. HF587, proposed by Stockwell and others, was a concurrent resolution memorializing Congress

> to select a committee to investigate the present status of Mooney and Billings cases . . . and, if necessary, recommend the enactment of legislation which will enable the President of the United States to issue pardons if it is found by congressional investigation that there has been a miscarriage of justice.

The resolution was adopted.[18]

In befriending Sacco, Vanzetti, Mooney, and Billings, whose names were household words, Stockwell was in cosmopolitan company. The ordeals of these men stirred not only the radicals of varying degree but also the conservatives who, disliking the men's opinions, nevertheless defended their constitutional right to a fair and impartial trial.[19] Stockwell's special gifts, perhaps, were in befriending the less-well-known and in a rare sense of timing.

Violet Johnson Sollie recalled the time when an innocent man in Minneapolis known to the Stockwells as a likely political prisoner was in danger of arrest. What to do? They decided he must be smuggled out of town. Maud Stockwell came up with some women's clothing. He escaped successfully. "He was a small man and easy to fit," said Albert Stockwell.

Less ingenious but no less daunting was a trip Stockwell took on Armistice Day 1940. The Armistice Day Blizzard of that year set an all-time Minneapolis snowfall record for November. Even today, old-timers recall precisely where they were and what they were doing the day that storm paralyzed the city. Sollie (whose remarkable memory and clear grasp of facts must have delighted the judges before whom she appeared) recalled not only her own activities but also those of Stockwell:

> Mr. Stockwell knew a Russian named Georgian living out near Minnetonka who was in danger of being deported. He owned a small store, and the plate glass front of his store had been bashed in, apparently by neighbors trying to speed him on his way to Russia. Mr. Stockwell, then eighty-three, always preferred the street car, but on out-of-the-way trips he was sometimes driven by Robert Alexander. In the face of the great Armistice Day storm Mr. Stockwell and Robert Alexander drove to Minnetonka with food for Mr. Georgian.

The author has since talked with Robert Alexander, Jr., who also drove Stockwell on occasion. "No, it wasn't me that day," he said. "It must have been Dad."

On one occasion, probably the only one, Sollie and Stockwell found themselves on opposite sides of an issue. She had held responsible positions in state government in the 1930s and was familiar with Communist activities in the Farmer-Labor party. Along with nine other Minnesotans in late October 1938, she was subpoenaed to appear and testify before the Dies Committee, a congressional committee investigating communism in government. Stockwell deplored the prospect yet knew full well she must appear or be held in contempt. Nonetheless:

> He disapproved very much. He had no love for Communists; he had dealt with them in Minneapolis in the 1920s and found them unreliable. Their word, he discovered, was worthless. Yet he felt one should not be helping witch hunters. Despite his disapproval of my testifying, we continued to be friends.[20]

Stockwell ran unsuccessfully for reelection in 1926. Walter Lundeen was the top vote-getter in the Thirty-second District, and Stockwell fell to third: Lundeen 6,843; Nellermoe 6,326; Stockwell 6,177.[21] Perhaps Stockwell's willingness to sit on a platform with Communists Stevens and Engdahl cost him his seat. In the ensuing session he was missed by some, if not his adversaries. One of the reporters for United Press pleaded when things were going stale and nobody was saying anything, "God, please send Stockwell back again."[22]

References

1. Morison and Commager, *Growth of the Republic*, 2:546.

2. Morison and Commager, *Growth of the Republic*, 2:545. Schlesinger has cited an unnamed English observer of the times who wrote of America: "Property was in an agony of fear and the horrid name 'Radical' covered the most innocent departure from conventional thought." See *Rise of Modern America*, p. 305. Future historians may see a similarity in the nation's state of mind in the 1980s, particularly as reflected in the 1988 presidential contest when "Liberal" was the horrid name.

3. G. Louis Joughin and Edmund M. Morgan, *The Legacy of Sacco and Vanzetti* (New York: Harcourt, Brace and Company, 1948), pp. 94-107, 117-126, 137-157, 201-220; *Dictionary of American History*, 6:182.

4. Binder, "The Stockwells of Minnesota."

5. *Minneapolis Journal*, May 11, 1925.

6. Eugene Rachlis, "Sacco, Vanzetti, Hammett and Boyer," a review of Rick Boyer's *The Penny Ferry* (Boston: Warner Books, 1984), in *Rights* (July-September 1986), pp. 3-5; Joughin and Morgan, *Sacco and Vanzetti*, pp. 509-510.

7. Rachlis, "Sacco, Vanzetti, Hammet and Boyer."

8. According to the *Herald*, "Vanzetti was perfectly cool and collected as he entered the chamber at 12:20:38. Before he had quite reached the chair, he started to shake hands with the two guards with whom he had become well acquainted during his stay in the death house. Just as he had seated himself Vanzetti said: 'I wish to tell you that I am innocent and never committed any crime, not only this one, but all. I am an innocent man.'"

9. Rachlis, "Sacco, Vanzetti, Hammett and Boyer."

10. Schlesinger, *Rise of Modern America*, p. 305; Kennedy, *Profiles in Courage*, pp. 233-234.

11. Binder, "The Stockwells of Minneapolis;" *Dictionary of American History*, 1:100.

12. *Minneapolis Labor Review*, February 16, 23, 1912.

13. *Minneapolis Journal*, March 3, 1912; *Minneapolis Labor Review*, March 8, 1912.

14. Morison and Commager, *Growth of the Republic*, 2:165; *Minneapolis Journal*, March 3, 1912; *Minneapolis Labor Review*, March 8, 1912.

15. *Minneapolis Journal*, March 3, 1912; *Minneapolis Labor Review*, March 8, 1912.

16. *Dictionary of American History*, 4:406.

17. Speech, Complimentary Birthday Dinner, June 8, 1927.

18. *House Journal*, 1933, pp. 248, 862.

19. Schlesinger, *Rise of Modern America*, p. 306.

20. Violet Johnson Sollie to William P. Everts, March 28, 1988. See also, Gieske, *Minnesota Farmer-Laborism*, p. 271. From 1938 until 1944, Congressman Martin Dies of Texas was chairman of a temporary Special Committee on Un-American Activities, a forerunner to the House Committee on Un-American Activities that came later. See Victor S. Navasky, *Naming Names* (New York: The Viking Press, 1980), p. 21.

21. *Legislative Manual, 1927*, p. 357.

22. Remarks of A. W. Rankin, Complimentary Birthday Dinner, June 8, 1927.

Chapter 22

Two against the Curriculum

T he Stockwells worked as a team in support of chosen causes. Together they campaigned for the initiative and referendum, supported the American Civil Liberties Union, and
helped raise money for Sacco and Vanzetti. Together they created
the forum that was the cornfest; together they fought for women's
suffrage. During World War I, they faced public ridicule and threats
as one, without blinking. Dorothy Binder put it succinctly: "In
Minneapolis they talk of the Stockwells as a unit, for one thinks of
them always as fighting the good fight together."[1] Their commitment to the cause of disarmament generally and to the abolition of
compulsory military training at the University of Minnesota in particular is illustrative.

Women and peace movements throughout the world were
inextricably bound early in the twentieth century. In 1915, even as
World War I was raging, more than one thousand women from
twelve countries, neutral and belligerent alike, convened at the
Hague, seat of the government of the Netherlands and capitol of
the province of south Holland, to protest the war and discuss ways
of ending it. At a second international congress held in Zurich,
Switzerland, in 1919, the Women's International League for Peace
and Freedom was formed. Jane Addams became the first president, and, under her leadership, sections of the league were organized in many countries. In the United States, the league functioned on both national and state levels. As a national body it
sought to secure the passage of peace legislation in Congress; state
sections of the league were left to choose their own local causes
and pursue them as they saw fit.[2]

After the passage of the women's suffrage amendment,
Maud Stockwell turned her attention to the cause of disarmament.
She became active in the Minnesota Women's Disarmament

Committee, a group formed in 1921 that, among other things, sent organizers into Minnesota small towns to mobilize women's support for the cause of disarmament. In 1922, she and her colleagues made up the nucleus of the Minnesota section of the league. Their objective was but a restatement of goals of the parent: "To promote that peace between nations, races and classes which is based on justice and good will; to outlaw war; to substitute law for war and to cooperate with women working for the same ends."[3]

Maud Stockwell was chosen the first president of the Minnesota section, a position she held for eleven years. The job took her as far away as Dublin, where, in 1926, she was one of twenty delegates to the league's biennial congress. Looking back on those eleven years, she said, "We fought for the League of Nations and the World Court. We supported conferences at London and Locarno and Geneva. We lived through the exciting days of the Kellogg-Briand pact to outlaw war."[4]

Closer to home, in a notable early skirmish with the Minneapolis Board of Education in City Hall, Maud Stockwell and other members of the Saturday Lunch Club succeeded in getting the program of military training in the Minneapolis public schools largely changed into physical drill.[5] Thereafter, the Minnesota section's overriding local concern was the abolition of compulsory military training at the University of Minnesota, a curriculum requirement that stemmed from passage of the Morrill Act in 1862. Under the Morrill Act, the federal government donated public land to states and territories upon condition that the land be sold and the proceeds placed in a perpetual fund with income to be used for

> the endowment, support, and maintenance of at least one college where the leading object shall be, without excluding other scientific and classical studies, and including military tactics, to teach such branches of learning as are related to agriculture and the mechanic arts, in such manner as the legislatures of the States may respectively prescribe.[6]

The act did not make any of the courses compulsory, but administrators of many land-grant institutions, including the University of Minnesota, believed they would lose the federal funding if they did not make military training a required course. Thus, all able-bodied male students at the university were required to take thrice-weekly military drill during their freshman and sophomore years. Organized opposition to compulsory training was almost nonexistent in the early 1920s. Then began the league's work and its enlistment of other organizations to help bring about nullification of the requirement: a steady flow of letters, the distribution of educational materials, and the lobbying of legislators. Attitudes in some quarters began to shift.[7]

On February 4, 1925, the executive board of the Minnesota section voted to ask Stockwell to bring the military training question before the legislature. Six days later he introduced HF559:

> Section 1. All schools and colleges of the University of Minnesota in their respective departments and class exercises shall be open without distinction to students of both sexes, and any able-bodied male student therein may, at his option, receive training and discipline in military tactics.
> Section 2. All acts and parts of acts inconsistent herewith are hereby repealed.[8]

A public hearing on the proposal before the house Committee on University and State Schools was scheduled for the evening of March 16 at the capitol. Maud Stockwell had earlier issued a statement of the league's position:

> That is the one university course that is compulsory—the one that every man must take although many do not care for it. They must waste two years of their time studying military tactics which will never be of any use to them. . . . Then, too, it perpetuates the idea of war. Outside the university the idea is being replaced by the thought that law must take the place of war and the universities should follow in the new way.[9]

The house chamber was packed the night of March 16. Feelings ran high and could not be contained. While the worst of the red scare was over, the atmosphere of hate and distrust it had engendered, still lingering in the nation, exploded in the confines of the chamber.

Proponents of HF599 included representatives of the league, the Minnesota Women's Christian Temperance Union, John Dietrich of the First Unitarian Society, and university students including young Edward Peet, grandson of James Peet. Dietrich charged that the Board of Regents was "passing the buck" to avoid abolishing compulsory military training by its own order. The students declared the training did them no good, that it was a "joke" and not necessary to college education. A. J. McGuire, secretary of the Minnesota Cooperative Creameries Association, favored making the training optional because it detracted from studious pursuits. Stockwell stated that even if the bill he introduced served no other purpose, he hoped it would show the people of Minnesota that compulsory military training was not stipulated in the Morrill Act.[10]

Opponents of the bill included E. E. Nicholson, dean of student affairs at the university; Major Bernard Lentz, ROTC commandant; and representatives of the Minnehaha Federation of Women's Clubs, the Minnesota Daughters of the American Revolution, and the American Legion Auxiliary. Nicholson said that eliminating military training would throw a burden on the physical education department that would tax its facilities. O. M. Leland, dean of the College of Engineering, said that regardless of any legal interpretations of the Morrill Act, the university was morally obligated to have compulsory military training in return for federal funding. Colonel E. E. Watson contended that the ROTC was the backbone of the national defense act and practically indispensable.

Marion D. Shutter saw the Third Internationale in Moscow as the real party in interest: "There is one group in the world that is preeminently interested in our total disarmament. The object of that group, after we shall be completely disarmed and helpless, is the violent and bloody overthrow of the government of the United States."

One Amy Ware, chairman of international relations for the Federation of Women's Clubs, declared that the move to abolish compulsory military training was Communist-inspired. Hisses greeted her when she stated that the move to do away with military training at the university was a move to disarm the whole country—a move with its foundation in the Third Internationale in Moscow.

A Mrs. Hubbell, representative of the American Legion, sprang to Ware's defense: "There are only two creatures that hiss, a goose and a snake."

In a final thrust, Maud Stockwell's former pastor got up and accused her of accepting "Moscow gold." Years later she recalled with a smile, "The reaction there in the House chamber was the most wonderful thing I can remember. The room echoed with laughter."[11]

Stockwell's bill came up for a vote in the house in April, where it was defeated, sixty-nine to forty-two.[12] In the senate, it died in committee. But Maud Stockwell was not discouraged, stating in her report for 1925 that, although the bill had failed to pass, it had served an educational purpose. The Minnesota section of the Women's International League for Peace and Freedom, she wrote, planned a similar bill for the next session. An identical bill, HF146, was introduced two years later. It was defeated by a vote of sixty-seven to fifty-four. In a newsletter she reminded members that "inasmuch as the vote of the last session of the legislature was 70 against 41 in favor [sic], decided gain has been made at this session."[13]

Absent though he was from the legislature in 1927, Stockwell stayed in the struggle. On June 30, 1927, he was elected permanent chairman of the Minneapolis anti-war conference as 105 delegates held their first general meeting in the assembly room of the courthouse. Maud Stockwell was among the speakers.[14]

Voters in the Thirty-second District returned Stockwell to the house for the 1929 session. He promptly reintroduced his bill, now HF391. It was referred to the Committee on University and State Schools and thereafter routed to the Committee on Judiciary, where it died.[15]

Efforts to make military training optional were shifting from the capitol to the campus itself at about this time. Dictum in *University of Minnesota v. Chase*, a decision of the Minnesota Supreme Court in a case arising out of a wholly unrelated dispute, stated broadly that such matters as curriculum were not within the jurisdiction of the legislature but solely within the jurisdiction of the Board of Regents.[16] With this development, other groups entered the fray, and the Women's International League for Peace and Freedom, while assisting and supporting student dissent, assumed a lesser role. The Jacobin Club, a student organization of which the young Eric Sevareid was an active member, took the lead in fighting compulsory military training on campus.[17]

With the election to the governorship in 1930 of Floyd B. Olson, the league and the students found a friend in high places. As a student, Olson had refused to participate in military drill and, perhaps even more unforgivable, insisted on wearing a derby hat, a right traditionally reserved for seniors. In his 1933 inaugural speech, Olson, then at the peak of his popularity, came out in favor of change: "Private institutions have a right to maintain a military cadet system, but a compelled drilling of students in public institutions of learning is not only contrary to the objects of peace, but is unfair to them from an American standpoint." Soon afterwards Olson had the opportunity to appoint four progressive Farmer-Laborites to the Board of Regents. In June 1934 the board voted six to five in favor of making military training optional.[18]

The Women's International League for Peace and Freedom, together with friends in the legislature, had laid the groundwork.

Vivian Thorpe took note of Maud Stockwell's contribution:

> Long years ago Mrs. Stockwell took up the fight for the franchisement of women and pursued it unweariedly, day in day out, also with faith that its justice must win out. So fine a fight-

er was she that when there came a time when it seemed best that the women who did the pioneering should make way for a younger and different group to take the reins, she and the women who were associated with her stepped aside, let others take command, and to a large extent get the credit for final victory. Many people achieved an admiration for her fine and intelligent gesture that nothing has ever shaken. That long fight for the right of women to participate in the government might have been enough to win her lasting gratitude of the people of Minnesota. But it was not enough for Mrs. Stockwell. She turned her energy and her fine mind toward the crusade for world peace. Never frittering herself on smaller issues and lesser reforms, she has undeviatingly, for years, fought for peace as she fought for suffrage. She is still fighting.[19]

References

1. Binder, "The Stockwells of Minneapolis."

2. Much of the material in this chapter is taken from Carol Laseski's excellent paper "The Minnesota Section of the Women's International League for Peace and Freedom and the Abolition of Compulsory Military Training at the University of Minnesota," written in 1982 at the University of Minnesota; copy in possession of author.

3. Laseski, "Compulsory Military Training."

4. *Minneapolis Tribune,* June 20, 1926, and May 16, 1949. Frank B. Kellogg, after losing to Henrik Shipstead in a bid for reelection to the U.S. Senate, became Secretary of State in 1925 under President Calvin Coolidge. The Kellogg-Briand Pact, signed by sixty-two nations, renounced war as an instrument of national policy. The pact seemed to assure significant disarmament and was widely viewed as a highly promising achievement.

5. Leonard, *History of the Saturday Lunch Club,* p. 15.

6. Land Grant Act (Morrill Act), U.S. Code, Vol. 7, Sec. 4 (1862); Laseski, "Compulsory Military Training."

7. James Gray, *The University of Minnesota: 1851-1951* (Minneapolis: University of Minnesota Press, 1951), pp. 367-370; Laseski, "Compulsory Military Training."

8. *House Journal, 1925,* p. 333.

9. *Minneapolis Journal,* March 15, 1925.

10. Here and below, *Minneapolis Journal,* March 17, 1925; *Minneapolis Tribune,* March 17, 1925.

11. *Minneapolis Tribune*, May 16, 1949.

12. *House Journal, 1925*, p. 1276.

13. *House Journal, 1927*, p. 102; Laseski, "Compulsory Military Training." Following defeat of Stockwell's bill in 1925, Maud Stockwell wrote and privately published a succinct, seven-page pamphlet entitled *Some Facts Concerning Military Training at State Universities* (1925). The pamphlet became something of a bible for those opposed to compulsory military training in state universities and was widely distributed in other states where the same battle was being fought.

14. *Minneapolis Journal*, July 1, 1927.

15. *House Journal*, 1929, pp. 205, 1257.

16. See *University of Minnesota v. Ray P. Chase*, 175 Minn. 259 (1928). The question before the court was whether the legislature could deprive the regents of the whole or any part of the management of the university. The court held that the entire power to govern the university was placed in the regents under the state constitution by the people. No part of it could be put elsewhere except by the people themselves. It seems likely that in 1929, HF391 was sent from the Committee on University and State Schools to the Committee on Judiciary in light of this decision.

17. Laseski, "Compulsory Military Training." Sevareid was one of the founders of the Jacobin Club, a progressive, academic association of campus leaders that flourished for much of the 1930s. It was partly because of Sevareid's prominent role in the drive to end compulsory military training that he was denied the position of editor of *The Minnesota Daily*. See *St. Paul Pioneer Press*, July 10, 1992, and Eric Sevareid, *Not So Wild a Dream* (New York: Atheneum, 1976), pp. 53, 60, 61-68, 181, 182, 201, 224.

18. Laseski, "Compulsory Military Training."

19. *Minneapolis Journal*, May 29, 1937.

Chapter 23

The People's Money
and His Own

W hile Stockwell's activities were many—Chrislock has written in his most recent book, *Watchdog of Loyalty*, that Stockwell "had been identified with virtually every important reform movement since the 1890s"[1]—in one pursuit he was not at all interested: making a lot of money. Neither did he save or keep track of what he did make. His testimony under cross-examination in a judicial proceeding is the story of his personal financial life.

In 1940 Stockwell decided to run for a vacancy in the state senate instead of seeking a return to the house. Three months before the November election, J. E. Foster, another candidate for senator from the Thirty-second District, took legal steps to try to keep Stockwell's name off the ballot, contending that he was no longer a legal resident of the district. The Stockwells had sold 3204 East Fifty-First in 1937 and taken an apartment outside the Thirty-second District, but they retained a small parcel with a modest garden and dwelling on Keewaydin Place within the district. Foster, at the behest of Stockwell's enemies, or so Stockwell contended, challenged his jurisdiction. Foster's attorney, Joseph J. Granbeck, delved into the question of homesteading in a deposition.[2]

> Q. Mr. Stockwell, you are the owner of the premises at 3129 Keewaydin Place, Minneapolis, Minnesota, are you not?
> A. Yes, sir.
> Q. And you filed an application for a reduction of taxes because of a claim of homestead at those premises in the year 1938, did you not?
> A. I did file an application for reduction—for homestead reduction, yes.
> Q. Yes. And you were later apprised that reduction in taxes was denied, were you not?
> A. No, sir.

Q. When did you find it out?

A. Found it out yesterday.

Q. Well, you paid taxes on that place since that application was made in 1938.

A. Yes.

Q. Didn't you observe when you got your next year's tax state ment, that the taxes were still the same?

A. No, I didn't. Mrs. Stockwell takes care of the taxes.

Q. She didn't tell you about it?

A. No, not that I recall.

Q. Did you know that your taxes had not been reduced the year following your application?

A. No, I don't think that I did.

Q. And you made no effort to find out?

A. None whatever.

Q. You signed the application for tax reduction, didn't you?

A. Yes, I did.

Q. And it was for the purpose of lowering the taxes on those premises?

A. Well, I wanted to find out what it was like.

Q. So that is the only reason you did it?

A. Yes, sir, precisely.

Q. You weren't interested whether the taxes were reduced or not?

A. No.

Stockwell simply had no interest in money. If money came his way, he gave it to a needy student for the first installment of tuition, to Russian famine relief, to the fund for defense of Sacco and Vanzetti, to the owner of a hall for half a day's rent so that a suffrage meeting could be held, to post bond for the release of a union member unjustly imprisoned during a labor dispute, or to an international threatened with deportation. Why keep it when others were in greater need?

During the Spanish Civil War, which lasted from 1936 until 1939 when Francisco Franco overthrew the Spanish democratic republic, Albert's sympathies were with the children victimized by the war. When Maud told him she had ordered ice cream and cakes to serve at their fiftieth wedding anniversary celebration, he looked up in amazement and said, "When little children are starving in Spain, how can you think of buying ice cream?" When Eugene Day gave the Stockwells five hundred dollars in gold pieces to be used for travel as an anniversary present, Stockwell promptly declared the money would go to Spain.

Maud never knew what money she had for household use.

Though Stockwell disbursed his own funds almost at random and paid no attention to the family budget, casual expenditures of public monies were an entirely different matter. Here he was a self-appointed guardian and had been from the start of his career. As a newcomer to the legislature in January 1891, he moved to strike from an omnibus resolution a provision whereby two daily newspapers would be furnished free of charge to members. Later he opposed paying journalists $150.00 each for covering the legislature. In return for what? Wasn't that their job? Legislators were fiduciaries. To give public money away, to fail to exercise accounting safeguards, or to show favoritism in an expenditure was the breach of a sacred trust.

In 1923, Stockwell strenuously opposed paying legislators for time spent on legislative matters before being sworn in. He added a corollary four years later when he advocated a divided legislative session, with a thirty-day intermission to permit study of bills under consideration, as a means of improving the legislature's efficiency. At a meeting of the Commonwealth Club at the West Hotel in Minneapolis, he declared that such an arrangement would obviate the onrush of measures of the last fortnight of a session and

> do away with passage of bills by nerve-wracked lawmakers too weary to know what it is all about. . . . It is a wonder more treachery is not practiced and more harmful bills forced through under such circumstances. . . . Citizens themselves are the best factors for cutting down taxes. There is plenty of room for economy, even at the statehouse. There could be a savings of $100,000 every legislative session without encumbering the work of that body.[3]

Stockwell believed the entire house should be kept informed of expenditures incurred during the course of a session. Otherwise how could it properly exercise the duties of trustee? Thus on the third day of the 1925 session he moved to amend Rule 50 of the Permanent Rules of the House, which provided:

> The Chief Clerk of the House shall be the agent of the House for the purchase of supplies. Before making any purchases, however, it shall be his duty to submit to the Rules Committee a list of necessary supplies, together with the prices for which the same can be secured, which supplies shall then be purchased only upon the approval of the Rules Committee.

Stockwell wanted to add "and said Rules Committee shall report to the House at the end of each ten days of the session the kind, amount, and cost of such supplies." And so it was.[4]

Unwarranted as it might be to appropriate public monies for the issuance of two daily newspapers to members of the legislature, at least the expenditure was authorized by the members. Representative government was at work here, and the voters were standing by ready to curb significant excesses by ballot. What was totally repugnant to Stockwell was a legislator's acceptance of a gift proffered by an outsider. Samuel H. Bellman recalled his strict adherence to principle:

> Of the total membership of the House and Senate, I believe he was the only one that found it necessary to return the pass that was offered and sent to each member of the Senate and House admitting them to all movie houses free and, in addition, to baseball games and wrestling matches. Needless to say, in those days of shortness of economic ability to buy things, that was quite a premium to have, and he felt that it may in some way control his vote in any matters affecting these enterprises.[5]

Senator M. J. Galvin of Winona recalled an example of generosity towards legislators in a practice originating with the special session of 1936 that Stockwell would have deplored. The session had been called in December by Governor Hjalmar Petersen, successor to Olson, who died in August of that year. Minnesota needed to enact special appropriations before January 1, 1937, to meet the eligibility requirements of the recently passed Social Security Act. The house had primary responsibility for appropriations, and there was little if anything for senators to do. Galvin conceived the idea of inviting a number of fellow senators to the Winona Country Club, one-hundred miles to the south, for a day-long outing. All expenses were paid by either the railroad or the club. The trek then became an annual golf outing in the spring. Clearly, even if he had been a scratch golfer, Stockwell would have declined.

Stockwell's aversion toward any practice that smacked of influence was matched or nearly matched by his aversion to nepotism, an abuse that flourished in the house in the 1920s. According to Rankin the 1925 legislature hired more employees than needed.

> Some 20 of these were near relatives of members. Probably these were as good or better than the average, but good policy would have prevented what looks like favoritism. The 1925 session was held in a time of general unemployment. A legitimate practice in some states is to carry on public works at such a period in order to give employment to the needy. To give work is better than to exercise charity.[6]

Rankin expressed Stockwell's views accurately if in more restrained terms. By 1929 more than one hundred such employees appeared on the house payroll. Stockwell greeted them with a resolution that set off a storm of protest:

Whereas there is widespread and serious unemployment in this state at the present time; and

Whereas, there are many persons who deem it unjust that married women having no one dependent upon them for support should be given employment in the public service, and

Whereas, nepotism is believed by all right-minded persons to be conducive to bad government—not to say correct government, and

Whereas, nepotism has reached scandalous proportions at this session of the legislature,

Therefore, be it resolved that the speaker and committee on rules are hereby directed to remove from any salaried connection with this body all employees who are related by blood or marriage to any member of the house;

Be it further resolved that these positions, where necessary and it is possible, be filled from the ranks of the disabled veterans of the World War.[7]

The resolution triggered a storm of protest against the administration's forces in the house. It was the first time the administration had been defied since the session began. The target was W. I. Norton, the chairman of the rules committee, who suffered withering criticism for loading the payroll, even from members of his own delegation. In a page-one story under a banner headline, the *Minneapolis Tribune* covered the row:

When the Stockwell resolution was read, Norton rose to say he could not believe the resolution was intended for anything but a joke—nothing but a gesture. He demanded to know why the resolution had not been introduced earlier, defended the patriotism of appointees, and finally sat down after "waving the bloody shirt" until he grew hoarse.

Willis I. Norton, detail from a group photograph of 1927 Minnesota House of Representatives 45th Session. (Photo by Forseen. Courtesy of the Minnesota Historical Society)

Stockwell rose and, shaking his finger at Norton, declared that the resolution was neither a joke nor a gesture. "The conditions in this house have become so notorious that they demand action. In presenting this resolution, myself and others felt that the members of this house have been unfaithful when they have allowed a system to grow up here and become so serious."

"What makes it serious?" Norton demanded.

"Serious unemployment in this state," Stockwell said. "This is the most serious situation in public service. Members of the house bring their wives who give practically no service to the state. At the last legislature one member had three members of his family employed here. I don't think we should have twice as many employees as we need just to pay political debts. Some clerks have not had a pencil in their hand for seventeen days."

"As for Mr. Norton," said Stockwell, "his program in this body is doing more to undermine the democracy of this state than Mussolini. The stigma on the house of representatives which has become a hissing and a by-word should be removed."

Norton arose to say that he had not heard of any corruption or indolence in the house or among the employees.

"All you have to do is to use your eyes and look around you," retorted Stockwell. "Do you think this house needs 120 servants? Do you think we should have twice as many as we need just to gratify a political whim?"

Norton said there were only 103 employees coming under the patronage classification and resorted to a routine of heckling Stockwell but "the minority member from Hennepin only waited for a second wind and then continued to lash away at the administration leader with all the fury at his command."

Representative Joseph A. Kozlak of Minneapolis, while not condoning the Norton defense, took issue with Stockwell in his contention that disabled veterans were being discriminated against. He recited that both his brother and he participated in the war and that "he was a better patriot than a lot of Socialists of the calibre of Stockwell."[8]

At the close of the debate, a voice vote was taken. The resolution was rejected.

J. A. Mann, allied with Stockwell, introduced HF413, a bill that would have provided that no officer or employee of the legislature or any of its committees shall be elected or employed by blood or marriage to any member of the house or senate. The Committee on General Legislation reported the bill back with recommendation that the bill do pass, which was adopted. But the bill was not enacted.[9]

An aftermath of the Stockwell-Norton showdown was the circulation around St. Paul of a song to be sung to the tune of Gilbert and Sullivan's "Pinafore":

I am a member of the lower house,
Before the boss as meek as a mouse.
If on the payroll you will glance,
You'll find my sisters and my cousins and my aunts,
My sisters and my cousins,
I have them by the dozens,
My sisters and my cousins and my aunts.
With Norton by my side,
My bosom swells with pride,
And I snap my fingers at Rockne's taunts,
So do my sisters and my cousins and my aunts;
My sisters and my cousins,
I have them by the dozens,
My sisters and my cousins and my aunts.
For when I need the dough,
I know just where to go,
To get the job that Norton grants.
So do my sisters and my cousins and my aunts;
My sisters and my cousins,
I have them by the dozens,
My sisters and my cousins and my aunts.[10]

Norton almost had the last laugh. Charlotte Granger (later Hamlet), daughter of Stockwell's sister, badly needed a job in 1933. She had typing skills and was hired as a secretary by a member of the legislature. Stockwell ran into her in the halls of the capitol. "He was not welcoming. He was shocked. His opponents were looking for a weakness and here I was!" Hamlet admired him but admits she was afraid of him.

Charlotte Granger landed her government job in spite of her uncle rather than with his help. But back in 1905, Stockwell did intervene on behalf of his brother William, who was a candidate for postmaster in Anoka. William gained the appointment, though it was not easy. In a letter to his brother Walter, dated February 13, 1905, Stockwell wrote:

Dear Brother Walter:
I hope that the appointment that Will has gotten will be of service to him. Two or three persons in Anoka made a very savage fight on him, one that was entirely unwarranted as far as I can see, and had it not been for the very cordial relations existing between Governor Johnson and myself, it would have been impossible to have landed him.
With love,
Al

A merit system of employment based on nonpartisanship and on technical expertise, as determined by competitive examinations, would have ruled out the nepotism in the legislature and other branches of state government prevalent during the 1920s. Governor Harold E. Stassen established a model civil service program in Minnesota in 1939. Stassen remembered Stockwell's strong advocacy of civil service and his frustration with the Farmer-Labor party stand on this issue. "He didn't support me for governor, but he came out loud and clear for my civil service program," Stassen said.

References

1. Chrislock, *Watchdog of Loyalty*, p. 148.

2. *J. E. Foster v. Al P. Erickson, County Auditor*, Minnesota Supreme Court File Number 32676 (1940), Minnesota Historical Society.

3. *Minneapolis Tribune*, July 8, 1927.

4. *Journal of the House*, January 8, 1925.

5. Sam Bellman to William P. Everts, March 21, 1988.

6. Rankin, *The Minneapolis Legislature of 1925*, pp. 9-10.

7. *Minneapolis Tribune*, February 6, 1929.

8. *Minneapolis Tribune*, February 6, 1929.

9. *Journal of the House, 1929*, pp. 215, 470, 472, 1570.

10. *Minneapolis Tribune*, February 7, 1929.

Chapter 24

Working with the Black Community

Silvanus and Charlotte Bowdish Stockwell, staunch abolitionists by heritage and conviction, had departed Sutton,
Massachusetts, in 1856 for a region where few blacks lived
and little abolitionist sentiment existed. Abolitionism simply was
not a powerful movement in the Minnesota territory or the state.
Whereas the underground railroad scarcely operated in Minnesota,
the town of Sutton had been a key link in operation. (Still standing is the Asa Waters house, with its escape tunnel under the road
to Delia Torrey's place, where slaves seeking freedom were fed and
kept in hiding.) Perhaps the plight of blacks in the South seemed
less pressing to Minnesotans because blacks numbered so few;
according to the 1860 census only 259 blacks lived in the state.
Uniform opposition to slavery and the extension of slavery, however, did exist—the holding of slaves within the borders of Minnesota,
which occurred when southerners visited the area accompanied by
slaves, was particularly repugnant. But, by and large, Minnesotans
showed no active desire to eliminate slavery elsewhere. Minnesota
was Republican in 1860. Her four electoral votes went to Abraham
Lincoln. The Republicans, though hostile to the extension of slavery, did not propose to interfere with it in the southern states.[1]

Minnesota was never in the mainstream of black migration
to the north, either of free men before the Civil War or of freed
slaves in the decades following the Emancipation Proclamation.
The black population in such states as Ohio, Indiana, Illinois,
Michigan, and Wisconsin grew much more rapidly. The 1880 census showed 1,569 blacks living in Minnesota; in 1900 there were
4,959; in 1910, 7,084; in 1920, 8,809; and in 1930, 9,445. During
this fifty-year period, blacks made up between three and four
tenths of a percent of the state's population. Nearly all settled in
three main urban areas: St. Paul, Minneapolis, and Duluth.[2]

Many blacks who finally settled in Minnesota had moved to other northern states first. Tela Burt's roundabout route to Minneapolis was typical. Doubtless his loneliness upon finding almost no members of his race in Minneapolis was also typical for other black newcomers. Burt, lucid and articulate at age ninety-six, with a very good memory, was born in South Carolina in 1892, the son of a minister. His father wanted him to stay in the South and become a minister, but Burt headed for New York instead, living in Harlem, then in Philadelphia, before finally settling in Minnesota in 1912. He tried to enter the University of Minnesota, but his schooling did not qualify him, so he attended MacPhail School of Music instead. When he first arrived, Burt found almost no blacks in the city. He was so lonesome for his own people that he frequently walked over to Nicollet and Third Street just to look at a black man who had been hired by a dentist to stand in front of the office shouldering an ad. Burt said he was a "fine looking, tall man, straight as a soldier."

Frances McHie, a native black woman, was born in Minneapolis in 1912. Her father was black and her mother German, according to McHie, but "Mother took the position she was black. She was active in St. Peter's African-Methodist Episcopal Church. The members of the church adored her. When mother died, that church was loaded." To McHie, her mother was God.

Her father was born in Virginia. He completed only the third grade, but he taught himself and went on to become an avid reader. He was a contractor. A vocal, positive man, he didn't allow any alibis, was afraid of no one, and "there was no stopping him." He was against what a lot of people believed, but he spoke his mind just the same. It nearly cost him his life.

McHie's mother liked to go to the movies. On movie nights, her father stayed home with the children. One night her mother returned from a movie to find the door wide open. She rushed upstairs. Her husband was gone. Desperately she called friends. No one had seen him. Late that night she got a telephone call: "He had escaped from captors who broke into the house, dragged him away, and were about to hang him. A rope was around his neck."

Life returned to normal. Frances excelled in school. There were about thirteen blacks in her high school. She was accustomed to being the only black person in class; "colored" was what they called it then. But she didn't feel isolated, and she encountered no serious social problems.

Mary Burns, McHie's homeroom and civics teacher, felt Frances had great promise and wanted her to be a social worker.

McHie's father wanted her to be a teacher; her mother didn't care what career she chose but said she didn't think social workers ever got married, so Frances ruled that out. She ruled out teaching too because she had assisted Burns in class and didn't enjoy it enough to make it a career. When her teacher said nursing was about the only other field open to a young black woman, McHie decided to be a nurse.

She completed her high school requirements in three-and-one-half years, finishing in January 1929. Commencement would not be held until June, but she was "dying to go to college." She applied in March to the School of Nursing at the University of Minnesota with top recommendations from her teachers. The director of the school, Marion L. Vannier, however, rejected her application for the express reason that she was black. Vannier suggested that McHie consider applying to Kansas City General Hospital #2, a black hospital.

The McHies were stunned. Burns, outraged, turned to Gertrude Brown, director of Phyllis Wheatley House and a close friend of the McHie family.

Phyllis Wheatley House, named after a Senegal slave girl living in Boston who became a poet, was a settlement house established in 1924 by the Women's Christian Association for the betterment of the lives of those living in a blighted, predominantly black, north Minneapolis neighborhood. The building acquired had been used as a factory at one time:

> It was surrounded by houses in every stage of dilapidation and buttressed with junk yards where piles of old tires filled the air with the pungent smell of hot rubber on hot afternoons. The little old building, renovated and furnished by its Negro and white friends, was a hospitable and pleasant spot with its gay, flower-filled boxes.[3]

Earl Spangler in *The Negro in Minnesota*, has called Phyllis Wheatley House central in the history and progress of African Americans in the state. Gertrude Brown deserves most of the credit for its remarkable success. Educated at Scotia Women's College and Hampton Institute, where she did graduate work, she was in all respects admirably suited to be its director.[4]

The programs she instituted were summarized in a tenth-anniversary report:

> Phyllis Wheatley offers a leisure time program for the Negro. This program includes opportunities in drama, music, recreation, and opportunities for education and work. It has helped

the boy and girl without food, shelter or friends. It has helped the boy and girl who need only encouragement and recreation. It has been a meeting place for associate groups. It has served as a bureau of information on race questions.[5]

Among Phyllis Wheatley's friends and supporters was Mabeth Hurd Paige, lawyer and legislator who played a key role in its founding, and S. A. Stockwell. They had served side by side in the legislature since 1923. Although Paige was a political conservative, on matters of health, the environment, and public welfare, she and Stockwell were fully in accord. They were good friends and Phyllis Wheatley House was an important, common interest.

When Gertrude Brown learned of the discrimination against Frances McHie, she turned to Stockwell for help. It was a natural choice. His heart was with the young, and he had standing in the legislature. His public support for the causes of blacks, dating back at least as far as 1899 when as a senator he defeated a plan to pay black janitors at the state capitol less than white janitors, was widely known. Further, as recalled by Raymond Cannon, former prominent black Minneapolis lawyer and a Phyllis Wheatley House board member now in his nineties, Stockwell counted many blacks among his personal friends. According to Cannon, Stockwell had first become acquainted with the black community through the Minneapolis Sunday Forum, organized by a group of civic-minded blacks in 1908. There were no dues. Speakers came to twice monthly meetings at St. Peter's and St. James' churches.

When Gertrude Brown told Stockwell of Frances McHie's rejection, he was enraged and astounded. The legislature was in session, so he moved quickly. At the first opportunity he stepped to the floor of the house chamber and reported to the members on the state of things at the School of Nursing. They couldn't believe what they heard. Stockwell must be mistaken. How could this be? Two blacks were enrolled in the medical school. Andrew Hilger, the first black to graduate from the university, received his degree back in 1887. Scottie Davis had followed as the first black woman to graduate, in 1904.[6]

Stockwell went by the book. As reported in the *Journal of the House* for April 9, 1929:

> Mr. Stockwell rose to a question of personal privilege, his statement having been challenged with regard to a letter from the University of Minnesota, declining to permit negroes entering the Nurses Training School, and prepare for the work of a trained nurse. Mr. Stockwell sent to the desk the letter, which was read, and made brief remarks in regard to the situation as

to the attitude of the University toward permitting the negroes to have the full benefit of the institution.[7]

Stockwell then arranged to have Gertrude Brown come to the legislature, bringing Frances McHie with her. Gertrude Brown told the whole story. Seventeen-year-old McHie sat quietly by, not saying a word.

"The impact was like a firecracker; everyone started running," McHie said. The members then voted overwhelmingly to write to the Board of Regents directing that Frances McHie be immediately admitted, *University of Minnesota v. Chase* to the contrary notwithstanding.

Stockwell and George Leonard, a lawyer who also served for a time on the Board of Regents, pursued the matter at the university level. They forced the university to reverse its stand, and Frances McHie was admitted to the School of Nursing in October, a month after her classmates had started.

She was nervous and afraid. Her home life had been sheltered; in her word she was a "retiring" person; she cried and cried. Her mother told her she had to go and kept talking to bolster her courage. Her father was the one who took her to the campus to register on the first day. According to McHie, "Mr. Stockwell put up the money for books and tuition. Ultimately, he was paid back."

When Frances McHie started school, the other students were "very nice," lent her their notebooks, and helped her with the assignments she had missed. She loved nursing and, generally

The 1931 student nurse graduating class from the School of Nursing at the University of Minnesota. Frances McHie is standing in the last row, second from the right. (Taken from the *Gopher*, the University of Minnesota Yearbook of 1931)

speaking, got along very well. But there were some trying aspects of hospital training. The regular staff regarded her as an oddity and would "jump out" in the hallway to look at her, then disappear. Everyone wanted to see what she was like. Patients sometimes asked whether they might feel her arm. They wondered if the black would rub off.

Frances McHie graduated and went on to become superintendent of a training school for nurses in New Orleans. She is now Frances McHie Rains and lives with her husband, a physician, in Long Beach, California. She remains profoundly grateful to those who helped her enter nursing school. Clifford Rucker, a black who knew Stockwell intimately as a friend and co-worker in the legislature, looked back on the incident many years later: "Mr. Stockwell's only reward came in the satisfaction of having fought for that which was honest and right."[8]

Stockwell opened the door of the house chamber to the black community on two other occasions that spring of 1929.

A. Philip Randolph, international president of the Brotherhood of Sleeping Car Porters and national president of the Negro American Labor Council. (Courtesy of AP/Wide World Photos)

For some years he had followed with interest A. Philip Randolph's work on behalf of black workers in the U.S. labor movement. Randolph was the general organizer of the Brotherhood of Sleeping Car Porters, established in 1925. Headquarters of the brotherhood were in New York City; Stockwell did what he could from afar to help the brotherhood to achieve its stated goals: more wages, better hours, better working conditions, pay for overtime, pay for "preparation time," abolition of "doubling out," conductor's pay for conductor's work, and manhood rights.[9] Randolph sent a wide-ranging letter of thanks to Stockwell on November 10, 1927:

> Just a word of remembrance and to express to you my sincere appreciation and thanks for the great work you did on behalf of

the Brotherhood of Sleeping Car Porters in the Twin Cities. I assure you that the Organization as a whole and I personally are deeply grateful to you for your generous attitude toward the Movement. The meetings you arranged have done much to awaken a new interest in the Movement and to extend the truth about it to a larger section of the Twin Cities populace. May I say that it certainly has been a pleasure to know you and to feel your fine, pulsing, spiritual soul, fighting for the liberty which all men crave but for which few men will dare to achieve. It is a pleasure to meet the spirit you typify in different sections of the country. There are but a few here and there, but they are the salt of the earth. After all, the fight of the Pullman porters is only one segment of the circle of struggle for economic democracy of the world, and the council of true lovers of liberty cannot be limited by race, creed or color. It must embrace the peoples of the world, for therein lies the only hope of the future.

By the spring of 1929, Randolph had become president of the brotherhood. His work took him to Minneapolis and St. Paul when the legislature was in session. On April 4, Stockwell moved that the house of representatives recess for ten minutes for the purpose of listening to Randolph. His motion prevailed. Randolph spoke in advocacy of a living wage for Pullman car porters and for the abolition of the tip system.[10]

Later in the session Stockwell was instrumental in arranging to have the Phyllis Wheatley glee club sing at the capitol. By 1929 Phyllis Wheatley House had come to be known for contributing music to civic functions of all sorts in Minneapolis. Members of the glee club, like the members of the glee club at Hampton Institute who sang throughout the country, became local messengers of good will. Even the most bigoted and prejudiced seemed to welcome and enjoy their music.[11] After the entertainment, Stockwell thanked them for their performance, not by letter but by resolution of the house. They posted the resolution, envelope and all, on the bulletin board in their small, frame building:

> Whereas, the Phyllis Wheatley Glee Club under the leadership of Mrs. Mason, who rendered solos, were so very kind and generous in entertaining us on Wednesday evening, April 24,
> Therefore, Be It Resolved, That the members of the House of Representatives extend their heartiest thanks and appreciation of the Phyllis Wheatley Glee Club and that the chief clerk of the House be instructed to send a copy of this resolution to them.
> Which was adopted.[12]

The success and popularity of the programs instituted by Gertrude Brown meant that the small, frame building was soon too small. Stockwell and others joined the struggle to secure funds for a new building, raising money primarily through private donations. A new, more spacious facility, with eighteen bedrooms upstairs, was completed in 1930. The bedrooms were put to good use. In those days blacks were not permitted to live in dormitories at the University of Minnesota, nor were they welcome in Minneapolis hotels. Black students from out of town, and such distinguished visitors as Roland Hayes, Marian Anderson, W. E. B. Du Bois, Ethel Waters, and Langston Hughes, made Phyllis Wheatley House their Minneapolis home.[13]

Another opportunity arose for Stockwell to be of service to the black community in the 1930s when the Farmer-Labor party was dominant. As Clifford Rucker recalled:

> It was Stockwell who insisted that the Farmer-Labor party, of which he was a founder, extend to its Negro adherents some of the patronage which all successful political parties fall heir to. As a result, under Farmer-Labor administrations, Negro citizens held more important jobs and a larger number of positions than ever before in state history.

Rucker himself was among the beneficiaries:

> A few years ago thru the efforts of Mr. Stockwell, I was appointed to a very responsible position in the State Legislature at the State Capitol, and I can recall how Mr. Stockwell found it necessary to battle with those who felt that any position of importance should be reserved for members of a race other than mine.[14]

In the closing days of the 1939 session, the last in which he served, Stockwell engaged in a final parliamentary battle. Fittingly he fought for the black cause; ironically the opposition was a lineup of spokesmen for an industry that had been his livelihood.

For some years, blacks in Minnesota had found that collision and liability insurance policies on their vehicles, as well as policies protecting them from other risks, were being arbitrarily canceled by insurance carriers. Requests for policy renewals made by insureds, ready and willing to pay full premiums, were being denied without adequate explanation. The legislature entered the controversy. Senator B. G. Novak introduced a bill in the upper house providing that:

> No insurance company or its agent shall refuse to issue a policy of insurance or make discriminations in the acceptance of risks, in rates, premiums, dividends or benefits of any kind on account of race, and on request of any person whose applica-

tion for insurance has been rejected, the company shall furnish him in writing the reasons therefor and that such rejection was not for any racial cause.[15]

Penalties for violation were provided.

Backers of the bill in the senate cited flagrant examples of discrimination against blacks seeking insurance. Opponents strained to support their right to be selective. Seeking to justify the dropping of one black's automobile policy after seven years, a State Farm Mutual of Illinois representative blandly asserted that blacks do not get fair trials in courts when involved in accidents.[16]

Following a conference with Clarence Mitchell of the St. Paul Urban League and Cecil Newman, publisher and editor of the *Minneapolis Spokesman*, the area's leading black newspaper, Stockwell on March 9 introduced HF1054, a measure identical to Novak's. Stockwell's bill was referred to the Committee on Insurance, of which Carl Erickson of St. Cloud was chairman.[17]

In spite of an "eloquent plea" by Stockwell, Erickson's committee simply refused to vote on the bill. It was considered by the committee in executive session only.[18] Using a rule requiring that, on request of the author, a bill that has been unreported for more

Cecil E. Newman. (Courtesy of Instructional Fair • TS Denison)

than fifteen legislative days must be brought out, Stockwell got HF1054 to the floor of the house. He then moved to have it voted on as a special order.[19] Such a motion required unanimous consent of the house for passage. Erickson raised an objection—enough to keep the motion from being granted. Twice more, when Erickson was not present, Stockwell attempted to have his motion accepted. Lawrence Hall, speaker of the house, from St. Cloud, sent out for Erickson so that objection could be made.[20]

The bill passed in the senate, forty-four to five. Insurance interests prevented it from coming to a vote in the house.

Erickson said with some pride fifty years later that when Stockwell's bill reached him he "sent it to a subcommittee, and that is where it stayed." In his view, the basis of insurance must be selectivity of risk. A company must reserve the right to accept or reject an applicant. It is a matter of freedom of contract, he said. Thus, it should be possible to turn down a Swede's application for life insurance if Swedes can be shown to have proclivity to a given serious disease. The same should hold true for blacks who may be prone to contract certain diseases or who, for other reasons, are poor risks.

In the course of the contest, John Lundquist of St. Paul wrote to the editor of the *Spokesman*:

> The state owes a vote of thanks to the people who are trying to get a bill passed in the legislature to keep the insurance companies from arbitrarily refusing to write liability insurance for colored people. It is a dirty shame and it will affect the white people as well as your race. I am happy that we have people like Senator Novak and S. A. Stockwell in this state.[21]

Cecil Newman was disappointed but gracious:

> The defeat which comes when victory seemed assured should not silence our praise for Senator Novak and Representative Stockwell, our most sincere friend member of the House, who fought for the passage of the bill.[22]

After Stockwell's death in 1943, Newman paid him tribute in a *Spokesman* editorial:

Stockwell, Advocate of Men's Rights
1857-1943

Saturday, April 18, death took Sylvanus A. Stockwell, known the country over as an advocate of man's inherent right to "life, liberty, and the pursuit of happiness." He was Minnesota's most widely known liberal and humanitarian. As an evidence of Mr. Stockwell's stature as a public servant, a prominent financial figure, in a moment of frankness, once told the writer that if Stockwell had not "been so interested in the Indians, Negroes, co-operatives, public ownership, labor and other similar causes he could have been governor of Minnesota and could have ended his years as a member of the United States Senate."

It is certain that Stockwell had unlimited opportunities for personal aggrandizement which he turned aside, to fight the battles of the common people. He courageously chose to serve as best he could the needs of the people without regard to his own chances for personal profit or gain.

Serving the state in the legislature for many years, he was the chief voice in that body for many sessions for the liberals. He was a liberal before it was politically popular to be one, and he was a true liberal till the day of his death.

Not the least of his many interests was his intense devotion to the cause of the Negro. His family before him, hailing as it did from New England, were real friends of the Negro. Every campaign to advance the economic, social and civil rights of the Negro people, found a staunch, unrelenting champion in Sylvanus A. Stockwell and his good wife, Maud Conkey Stockwell, who survives him.

Several months ago, as he was wont to do, he visited this newspaper office. As the years crept on, his step grew faltering, but his spirit and mind were as strong as ever. When he came into the office for the last time, it was to inquire how he might help in a problem facing the Negro community. When we told him the part he could play, he was pleased and left us, with a hearty, cheerful goodbye, to do the job assigned him.

We did not see him again.

Among the Negroes of Minnesota as among other groups Sylvanus A. Stockwell was an institution . . .

We shall miss our good friend Stockwell. The people and their causes will miss him more.[23]

At a memorial service for Stockwell, Clifford Rucker spoke in the same vein: "The name of the late Sylvanus A. Stockwell is revered by every colored citizen of the State of Minnesota." Frances McHie Rains, Tela Burt, and Raymond Cannon said the same thing. Stockwell would have disagreed with all of them. But he would not have disagreed when Clifford Rucker went on to say that Stockwell had "proudly" shown him an autographed copy of a book by the late George Washington Carver.[24]

References

1. Earl Spangler, *The Negro in Minnesota* (Minneapolis, T. S. Denison & Company, Inc., 1961), pp. 27-28, 40-42, 62-67, 97-98; Morison and Commager, *Growth of the Republic*, 1:531; Blegen, *Minnesota*, pp. 236-37.

2. Spangler, *The Negro in Minnesota*, pp. 62-67, 97-98.

3. Alice B. Fraser, *Twenty-Five Years a Neighbor: The Story of Phyllis Wheatley Settlement House* (Minneapolis: No publisher, 1949), p. 2.

4. Stockwell descendants have held a long-standing interest in Hampton Institute. When Hampton's glee club came to Boston, Beth Stockwell Everts, the author's mother, was always an active sponsor. The author first encountered discrimination against blacks during a visit to Hampton Institute in 1937, when a downtown restaurant manager would not let him eat with his new friends. He went back to teach at Hampton in 1980 and 1981.

5. W. Gertrude Brown, *Ten Years a Neighbor: Phyllis Wheatley Settlement*

House, 1924-1934, [Minneapolis: no publisher, 1934], available at Minneapolis Public Library.

6. Spangler, *Negro in Minnesota*, p. 76.

7. *House Journal, 1929*, p. 964.

8. "Tributes to the Memory of Sylvanus A Stockwell," Minnesota Historical Society.

9. Sleeping car porters traveled approximately 11,000 miles per month. This usually meant 400 hours of work, excluding preparatory time and time spent at terminals. Working conditions were outrageous. Men assigned to regular runs began work at $67.00 a month. Tips increased actual earnings, but the cost of uniforms, shoe polish, meals, and so forth was deducted from wages. To aggravate the situation, porters often "doubled out" or ran "in charge" of a car, taking increased responsibility under unfavorable physical conditions for added pay at a diminishing rate. "Manhood rights" included the right to organize one's own union and to receive a living wage without reliance on a slavish shuffling for tips. See Philip S. Foner, *Organized Labor and the Black Worker 1619-1973* (New York: Praeger Publishers, 1974), pp. 177-187.

10. *House Journal, 1929*, p. 873.

11. Fraser, *Story of Phyllis Wheatley Settlement House*, p. 4.

12. *House Journal, 1929*, pp. 1523-1524.

13. Langston Hughes, poet and playwright who came to the family residence on occasion, was a friend of the author's father, William Everts. Poetry was a special interest of Everts, and he organized a poetry club that for a long time met monthly, with members reading aloud poems they had written or other poems to their liking. Established poets were invited, Langston Hughes among them. Sometimes as a boy, the author perched, out of sight, at the head of the stairs, listening. He vaguely remembers Langston Hughes reading "Mother to Son." Or maybe he dreamt it:

Mother to Son
by Langston Hughes

> Well, son, I'll tell you:
> Life for me ain't been no crystal stair.
> It's had tacks in it,
> And splinters,
> And boards torn up,
> And places with no carpet on the floor . . .
> Bare.
> But all the time
> I's been a-climbin' on,
> And reachin' landings
> And turnin' corners,

And sometimes goin' in the dark
Where there ain't been no light.
So boy, don't you turn back.
Don't you set down on the steps
'Cause you finds it's kinder hard,
Don't you fall now—
For I's still goin', honey,
I's still climbin',
And life for me ain't been no crystal stair.

14. "Tributes to the Memory of Sylvanus A. Stockwell," Minnesota Historical Society.

15. *Minneapolis Spokesman*, March 10, 1939.

16. *Minneapolis Spokesman*, March 10, 17, 1939.

17. *Minneapolis Spokesman*, March 10, 17, 1939; *House Journal, 1939*, pp. 706-707.

18. *Minneapolis Spokesman*, March 31, 1939.

19. *House Journal, 1939*, p. 1652.

20. *Minneapolis Spokesman*, April 21, 1939.

21. *Minneapolis Spokesman*, March 24, 1939.

22. *Minneapolis Spokesman*, April 21, 1939.

23. *Minneapolis Spokesman*, April 23, 1943.

24. "Tributes to the Memory of Sylvanus A. Stockwell," Minnesota Historical Society.

Chapter 25

The Emergence of Floyd B. Olson

F armer-Labor candidates met with surprising success at the polls in the 1920s, but the party's legislative achievement was marginal at best. For Stockwell, however, the party was a total success—a forum on which to further long-championed causes and institute wide-ranging statutory reform measures, while adding nearly two decades to his political career.

Floyd B. Olson's entrance to the party was quite different. At first he remained curiously aloof from Farmer-Laborism. Lacking any apparent interest in reform politics, in 1918 and 1920 he unsuccessfully sought a seat in Congress as the Democratic nominee. By 1924 he had turned to Farmer-Laborism and won the party's nomination for governor, but even then he was seen by many as a carpetbagger who had wrested the nominaton from deserving Nonpartisan Leaguers and bona fide Farmer-Laborites. Nontheless, though defeated by Christianson in the 1924 election, he had made a strong showing, and he became the party's favorite son from that time forward.[1]

In political terms, 1928 was a quiet year for Olson. Leader of the Farmer-Labor party and odds-on choice for governor, he decided not to be a candidate because he saw the incumbent, Republican Theodore Christianson, as unbeatable. The Democrats, meanwhile, showed signs of resurgence. The gubernatorial candidates of the minority parties were defeated in the November elections by nearly identical margins:[2]

Theodore Christianson	Republican	549,857	(51.4 percent)
Andrew Nelson	Democrat	213,734	(20.0 percent)
Ernest Lundeen	Farmer-Labor	227,193	(21.2 percent)

Olson stayed on as Hennepin County Attorney, winning case after case.

Governor Floyd B. Olson, 1932. (Courtesy of the Minnesota Historical Society)

Stockwell was without any paying job in 1928. He had retired two years earlier from Penn Mutual and had lost his seat in the legislature in the previous election. Freedom from these responsibilities may have prompted him to write a rare letter to his granddaughter Libby Everts:[3]

January 19, 1928
My darling Elizabeth,

It is most kind of you to write so often and not get any answers. I have intended to answer your letters but it is hard to drive myself to write letters. I notice a great improvement in your handwriting. I am glad you have such a good school. It is most fortunate that Nanna is in California tonight as it is storming and blowing like mad—a real blizzard in fact. I enclose letters received since I wrote Charlotte. I hope Nanna will find California kinder than Minnesota. She could not enjoy life here at all. Do you have birds with you during the winter? I have a feeding box and some suet out. I have seen a nut hatch and a downy woodpecker feeding on the suet. They are bright little fellows and seem to enjoy life. There are about six or more blue-jays at the feeding box every morning. I put out sweet corn—the kernels are so large they can not get them down so they come and get a kernel and take it over to the apple tree, get it into a hole in the bark and then proceed to pick it till it is small enough to swallow.

The grey squirrels come every morning for their share and between the jays and the squirrels they eat about 20 ears a week. I am most glad to feed them even if the jays have a bad reputation. I suppose it is true that blue jays do rob nests of other birds but they stay here all winter and help cheer up during the cold snow. That helps take the curse off . . .

I am glad Bill is learning to play the clarinet. Tell him I will give him a job in my next campaign if I have one, playing on the street corners to drum up the crowd.

Ask your adorable mother if she has heard this yarn. It goes this way. Someone says I understand there is to be a shortage of maple syrup this spring. The other fellow says, How is that? The answer is, Because the sap from Vermont does not choose to run. See?

Well, my dear, it is bed time for little folks. Did you ever hear that? I have several times. It is too bad I can't see you often but I love you just the same.

OM[4]

"OM" did have a next campaign. In November 1928 he was elected to the Forty-sixth Session of the legislature, finishing ahead of Otto D. Nellermoe, who had defeated him in 1926.[5] Thus began a succession of six straight victories at the polls. Running without party designation, he was widely known as a member of the Farmer-Labor's party's inner circle—liberal but not militant or extremist. Nearly thirty years after his first try, he did weigh another run for Congress. At the urging of other party leaders, he filed in a June 1929 primary for the vacancy created by Congressman Walter Newton's resignation, but he withdrew the next day when Farmer-Laborite Ernest Lundeen filed at the last minute.[6]

The 1929 legislative session, dominated by conservatives, was noted more for what it rejected—reforestation, small-loan regulation, university expansion—than for what it approved.[7] With HF430, Stockwell again sought repeal of the Brooks-Coleman law, which divided regulation of street railways between the Railroad and Warehouse Commission and the municipalities served, and he proposed a measure providing for the establishment of a state printing press (HF485) but got nowhere. He tried to assist young blind persons with a bill providing for the necessary expenses of blind students in the university, college, and conservatories of music in Minnesota (HF1223). He had the votes, but time ran out before HF1223 could be enacted.[8]

On the national front, Calvin Coolidge, favorite son of Plymouth, Vermont, held fast to his decision not to run. Times were good, Coolidge was popular, and the country insisted on regarding his disclaimer as equivocal. But the country was mistaken. He had served as president since Harding's death in 1923. Five and one-half years in the White House was enough.[9]

So the Republicans in 1928 turned to Herbert Hoover, the mining engineer who had succeeded so brilliantly in administering relief organizations in Belgium during the war and in Russia during the famine of 1921-1923. The Democrats chose Alfred E. Smith, Irish Catholic governor of the state of New York. Hoover won easily.[10] Stockwell may have voted for Norman Thomas, Socialist party candidate.

The stock market crashed the following October. In one month's time, stocks overall declined forty percent in value, marking the beginning of the Great Depression. The people of Minnesota turned to Floyd B. Olson and the Farmer-Labor party in 1930. The nation turned to Franklin D. Roosevelt and the Democrats two years later.

It has commonly been supposed that Olson chose 1930 for his reentry into state politics because of the depression: hard times signaled need for change. The notion is not borne out by the chronology of events. At a time of national prosperity, a full month before the October 1929 stock market crash, Olson had indicated his willingness "to serve the party in any way it demands." And he had begun to campaign actively before the Wall Street panic was translated into the devastating agricultural price break of May 1930.[11]

Olson dominated the March 1930 biennial meeting of the Farmer-Labor Association, guiding the debate and supervising the drafting of the platform. The party's mission, as he saw it, was restoration of the fundamentals of good government, not replacement of the capitalist system; he sought to identify with old-fashioned progressivism, stationing the party as an acceptable alternative to the one in power. The platform combined several mildly reformist planks, including repeal of the Brooks-Coleman law and opposition to labor injunctions. The most drastic proposal called for public works to ease unemployment. Socialist principles such as public ownership, found in the constitution of the Farmer-Labor Association, were avoided to blunt the charges of radicalism. As a result, the platform was not nearly as radical as the extremists would have liked, but Olson was confident they would not defect. He was nominated in the primaries without opposition.[12]

The break in agricultural farm prices in the spring of 1930 produced widespread unrest. The situation worsened as election day approached. Minnesota farmers, who typically voted a straight Republican ticket, were wavering. Further, Christianson was not running for reelection, having opted to seek his party's nomination for the U.S. Senate. Ray P. Chase, less formidable, became the

Republican standard-bearer. These factors, coupled with labor's solid support and the likely vote of the unemployed, all inured to Olson's benefit.[13]

And yet, but for his remarkable effectiveness as a campaigner, Olson might well have lost. A student of economics, he marshaled the facts and presented them in straightforward, convincing, understandable terms. He was witty, persuasive, quick on his feet. Typical of his resourcefulness was his response to Chase's keynote address, in which Chase professed great concern about the seeming repudiation of socialist doctrine in the Farmer-Labor platform. "The Farmer-Labor party is dead. Its soul fled when its principles were abandoned," declared Chase. He invited the rank-and-file to rejoin the Republican party, claiming that the Farmer-Labor leadership was a faction of disgruntled Minneapolis politicians and job hunters.

Olson's retort became famous. "If the Farmer-Laborites have a bandwagon of job hunters," he said, "it would be just another handful added to the hundreds of thousands walking the highways of the nation hunting jobs under a Republican administration."[14]

When the votes were tallied, Olson received 473,154, Chase 289,528, and Democrat Edward Indrehus 29,109.[15]

Olson called for significant reforms in his inaugural speech. Among them were blue-sky laws to tighten regulation of securities and a statewide old-age pension law. Conservative majorities, however, controlled both houses, accounting in large measure for the legislature's failure to follow most of his recommendations. The legislature did enact a modest statute regulating securities. And a public works program calling for highway and state building construction was undertaken, strengthened by Olson's order to the Highway Department that contracts on state-financed jobs include a minimum wage of forty-five cents an hour, a forty-eight-hour work week, and extra pay for overtime. In terms of tangible legislative achievement, however, Olson's first term was not highly productive. Soundings of public opinion told Olson the public would not support a sharp turn to the left.[16]

Stockwell, easily reelected in 1930 with 8,659 votes, the most received by any candidate running for the house from the Thirty-second District, did what he could for Farmer-Laborism in the 1931 session.[17] He sponsored bills called for, if not strenuously supported, by Olson; he resubmitted bills he had proposed earlier only to see them crushed; and he submitted new proposals on matters he believed must be addressed.

Floyd B. Olson speaking at a dedication of the Christopher Columbus statue at the Capitol. (Courtesy of the Minnesota Historical Society)

On January 28, he filed HF269, an old-age pension bill. Absent intervention by Olson, it got nowhere.[18]

HF189 was yet another attempt to gain "home rule" rather than any state regulation of street railways by the repeal of the Brooks-Coleman Law. Again, conservative forces combined to defeat him.[19]

Bill HF88, the Stockwell fifty-million-dollar power bill, was blocked by the opposition until time ran out with the session's adjournment. Progress was made, however, on a less ambitious related measure. In 1931 some ninety percent of Minnesota farms were still without electric power. Stockwell submitted HF299, calling for an act to permit municipalities to extend municipally owned electric service beyond city limits. His proposal was passed by the house on March 30 (111 to 2), only to be stalled in the senate. Two years later it was enacted.[20]

HF114, a bill proposing an amendment to the constitution that would reserve to the people the direct power of the initiative and the referendum as an additional means to secure and control legislation, was indefinitely postponed by the Elections Committee.[21]

HF185, calling for an increase in the occupation tax from six percent to ten percent, was voted down.[22]

HF490 sought to bolster existing laws prohibiting discrimination on account of race or color in public conveyances, theaters or other places of amusement, hotels, barber shops, saloons, restaurants, or other places of entertainment or accommodation. The house, sitting as a committee of the whole, indefinitely postponed the measure.[23]

F1439 was a concurrent resolution asserting that "there is and has been for many years last past a great deal of destitution and unemployment among the Indian citizens of our state" and that "the welfare of all citizens of our state is of paramount importance to the state." It called for a survey of unemployment and living conditions among Indians of Minnesota. It died in committee.[24]

Economic conditions worsened for farmers and wage-earners in 1931. Farmers cried out for a special session of the legislature to ease their plight by enacting legislation providing for tax reduction, easier access to credit, and a floor under plummeting farm prices. With foreclosures, unemployment, and descent to poverty for thousands of families came dissatisfaction with Olson's administration. Official Farmer-Labor doctrine prescribed large-scale government intervention to cure society's ills, and Olson favored state appropriations to relieve the unemployed, but past practice was against him. Traditionally, responsibility for relieving destitution rested with county governments. Pump-priming to relieve unemployment, which was to come nationally under Roosevelt, was a policy that had not reached individual states. Yet in 1931, most counties lacked sufficient funds to care for the destitute. The solution of the Republican majority in the legislature was directly opposite that of Farmer-Labor's. The Republicans favored spending cuts and encouraged retrenchment.[25]

Olson's opponents controlled enough votes to block appropriations for relief. Olson became convinced that contributions for relief from private donors would have to be sought and found wanting before government relief could command needed public support. He turned to Frank T. Heffelfinger, Minneapolis socialite and civic leader, to head a state committee of 275 to collect money and clothes for distribution through existing relief agencies. They performed their job well, but the resources made available proved woefully inadequate.[26]

Stockwell, like Olson, believed that the circumstances demanded vigorous government intervention: Hoover's contention that relief must be left in private hands was poppycock. But he could not just stand by. As recalled by Violet Sollie, he joined the ranks of volunteers:

I do not remember just when I started walking from 52nd and Minnehaha to 51st Street and 32nd Avenue, but it became something of a habit, and always there was a cordial reception. Mr. Stockwell would sometimes be helping Mrs. Stockwell clean up after supper, and they were both interesting and stimulating. I also found Mr. Stockwell to be remarkably honest—no fudging. In the fall of 1931, before any of the welfare programs we take for granted today, there was a great deal of unemployment, the depression was worsening, and the local community fund put on its annual drive with the message we must feed the hungry. I got a copy of their proposed allocation of funds to be raised and on the basis of the information in their own publication, it did not appear much of the money would go to reduce starvation. Besides, the drive's directors were coercive—allocating quotas to be raised in various businesses and institutions, and individuals did not feel free to refuse to give. On top of that, the executive secretary of the fund organization was paid $15,000 per year—which was twice what the governor of the state was getting.

I had discussed this with a little group I belonged to one Sunday night and they told me we should still support the fund raising as there was nothing to put in its place. I really intended to abide by that decision but I got a three-page letter from this executive secretary telling me I was wrong, and I replied with another long letter listing the figures I had compiled from their reports and asking him to indicate any errors.

The next thing I knew the mayor of Minneapolis, William A. Anderson, who was also a Saturday Lunch Club member, called me and said the chairman of the drive had called on him and urged the mayor to use his influence to stop me from spreading derogatory material about the fund. This drive chairman was Rufus Rand, whose family had owned the Minneapolis Gas Company and who was also a member of the Board of Regents at the University. I was working on a tax study at the University under the direction of Roy G. Blakey. The mayor listened to my criticism and called a public hearing on the matter in the Mayor's reception room asking both Mr. Rand and me to present our points of view. It was a time when many people were not working, and there was quite a crowd, and a large dispute developed after our respective presentations. The newspapers picked up the topic, as they had reporters at the courthouse then, regularly, and when I got back to the office, Mr. Blakey was on the phone talking with someone demanding I be fired. Mr. Blakey got several more calls in the next couple of days, and he was not too happy with me. He told me he wished I would just paint my cheeks green and walk down the street, if I wished attention, but when I asked if I should leave, he told me to get back to work on the matter I had been working on. A couple of days later a student died outside our office door at the head of the stairs on the second floor of the old Eddy Hall, and was pulled into our office. After the student health service and the coroner had done their work, the death was attributed to a heart attack induced by malnutrition—which I insisted was a fancy term for starvation—and this took the spotlight off my anti-community fund posture, but we were still criticized for not doing anything positive, so we organized a Direct Relief Committee to deal with this extreme poverty—and the organization functioned until the New Deal programs began to operate. We depended exclusively on contributions—of goods as well as cash and we needed a treasurer whose honesty was unquestioned and Mr. Stockwell became that treasurer.[27]

In Minnesota and the nation, 1932 was a key election year. Olson framed the Farmer-Labor platform with a free hand as he had two years before, but this time there was a tilt to the left. Thus the 1932 platform incorporated Stockwell's long-standing proposal for state ownership of water and electric power. Other planks called for compulsory unemployment insurance, statewide old-age pensions, an income tax, low interest farm loans, and national minimum farm support prices.

The Democratic party, its fortunes still at low ebb in Minnesota and its ranks depleted by Farmer-Labor's appeal, nominated John Regan for governor. He aroused little enthusiasm and was seen by some as an unmitigated joke. Earle Brown, the Republican nominee, was a gentleman farmer and, allegedly, a tax-dodger. Dirt farmers didn't like the former; taxpayers didn't like the latter. But the campaign was not a walkaway for Olson; his personal life became a major issue.[28] Violet Sollie remembered asking Stockwell about the matter:

The opposition called him reckless, and a red, but there was also a definite smear campaign spreading innuendoes about drinking and womanizing. Mr. Stockwell was a prohibitionist and an upright man and I remember asking him if there was any foundation for these stories. He said one could never prove a negative—but he had met with Olson at various times, with and without previous notice, and he had never seen him drunk, nor had he ever seen him in an embarrassing situation with women. Some Olson supporters had told me Olson had been known to drink and he had not denied it, but Mr. Stockwell said

"Earle Brown's Horses Under Different Skies," Cartoon from the *Farmer Labor Leader*, August 15, 1932.

he never displayed any indication of being drunk—and that convinced me.[29]

The positive side was that Olson received a gracious boost from Roosevelt. He had met the New York governor at the 1931 governor's conference in French Lick, Indiana, and the two men found their approaches to economic problems remarkably similar. When Roosevelt came to Minnesota for the Jefferson Day rally on April 18, 1932, he first met privately with Olson. At the St. Paul Auditorium that night, where 1,500 dined and 5,000 jammed the galleries, Roosevelt began his address with a cross-party reference to "My colleague and friend, Governor Olson." As the next day's *Minneapolis Journal* reported:

> That was all, but it was enough for the Olson supporters, who rose to cheer while the speaker made a dramatic point. It was only a courteous gesture, perhaps, but in the eyes of fusion democrats and other partisans of Governor Olson, it was an accolade, endorsement of the Farmer-Labor governor by the democratic chieftain.[30]

Roosevelt went on to be nominated on the fourth ballot at the Democratic National Convention, winning out over an embittered Alfred E. Smith.

In the course of his campaign, Olson shifted further to the left. In the words of his biographer, George H. Mayer, "He set out for a promised land halfway between Populism and Socialism." In the doing, as he crisscrossed the state tirelessly, shaking hands with thousands, he skillfully incorporated national issues in his speeches, underscoring Hoover's indifference to the plight of farmers and unemployed.[31]

Said Stockwell when the campaign was over:

In my opinion, Olson is the greatest and ablest leader of a progressive movement that I have seen in my forty years or more of political activity in this state. On the closing night of the campaign he rose to heights which, in my mind, neither Ignatius Donnelly, nor for that matter William Jennings Bryan, ever attained.

Olson won reelection by an outright majority over his two opponents: Olson 522,438; Brown (Republican) 334,081; Regan (Democrat) 169,851. Roosevelt's victory over Hoover was equally impressive.[32]

Hennepin County had become a left-wing stronghold. As the leading vote-getter in the Thirty-second District, Stockwell received 15,188 votes, nearly twice the number he received in 1930.[33]

Violet Sollie recalled the aftermath of the election:

These were turbulent times, and when our tax study was completed I was out of a job. I worked hard in the 1932 campaign for Olson's reelection and for the election of a liberal House of Representatives. . . . Mr. Stockwell needed no particular election help because his vote was solid but other candidates did. After the election it appeared the liberals might organize the House. At that time there was no party designation for members of the Legislature, so one could not just count the results. Each caucus, the conservative or Republican, and the liberals, sent out invitations to the newly elected for a meeting to select the candidates for speaker. Only 55 legislators showed up at the Republican caucus and 65 at the liberal caucus. It took 66 votes to elect. Some people were "sitting it out." Olson addressed the liberals and that caucus selected Charles Munn as their candidate for speaker. If the liberals prevailed, they would control committee assignments and also appoint the legislative employees—clerical, doormen, pages. Mr. Stockwell asked me if I would be interested in employment and in late 1932, with no job, I certainly was. I wanted to be clerk of the tax committee but Mr. Stockwell indicated that might not be possible—the incoming chairman of the committee would have a voice here—and I told him I would be glad to get anything. Mr. Stockwell was part of an inner circle setting up the machinery for the 1933 session and he did have two appointments—myself, a woman, and Clifford Rucker, a black man who lived in his district and was appointed a clerk instead of to one of the janitorial jobs usually reserved for black people. I was designated a stenographer—and that rating paid 50 cents a day less than the clerk's title. Before the formal beginning of the session I went over to watch the newly assembled legislature being sworn in and then proceed to elect a speaker. One young legislator from rural Hennepin County, Allen Johnson, refused to vote. There were 74 votes for Mr. Munn as against 56 for the conservative candidate, Mr. Finstuen, so his vote was not deciding, but Mr. Stockwell called on Mr. Johnson to vote, and Mr. Johnson persisted in abstaining which angered Mr. Stockwell, but someone then made a motion to escort the new speaker to the chair and the matter was dropped. When the vote was called for Chief Clerk, the next order of business, Allen Johnson voted for the liberals' choice.[34]

References

1. Mayer, *Floyd B. Olson*, pp. 12-14; Russell W. Fridley, Introduction to the 1987 reprint edition of George H. Mayers's biography, pp. xiii-xiv.

2. Mayer, *Floyd B. Olson*, p. 42; Gieske, *Farmer Laborism*, p. 120.

3. Albert almost never wrote to his grandchildren. Maud was the family letter-writer, sending long letters on birthdays and at Christmas, with short ones in between. Rarely did the grandchildren receive birthday or Christmas presents. Others were in greater need, and Christmas was not a time for celebration in Minneapolis.

4. See also *J. E. Foster v. Al P. Erickson, County Auditor*, Stockwell deposition, wherein Stockwell described his activities during seven different campaigns for revision of Minneapolis's charter as "house meetings, campaigning from soap boxes, and any other old way that would get the attention of the public."

5. Results of the voting in 1926 and 1928 for representatives from the Thirty-second District were: 1926—Walter S. Lundeen 6,843, Otto D. Nellermoe 6,326, S. A. Stockwell 6,177, and John A. Johnson 5,533; 1928—Walter S. Lundeen 12,636, S. A. Stockwell 11,025, Otto D. Nellermoe 10,863, and John A. Johnson 8,893. See *Legislative Manual, 1927*, p. 357, and *Legislative Manual, 1929*, p. 379. Nellermoe contested Stockwell's right to the seat after the 1928 election but declined to pursue the matter in view of a decision from the office of the attorney general that a special election would be necessary. *St. Paul Post-Dispatch*, January 8, 1929; *House Journal, 1929*, pp. 15, 190-91, 248.

6. *Minneapolis Tribune*, June 4, 1929; *Minneapolis Journal*, June 4, 1929.

7. Gieske, *Farmer-Laborism*, p. 123; *Minneapolis Journal*, April 21, 1929.

8. *House Journal, 1929*, pp. 235, 283, 822; Chrislock, *Progressive Era*, p. 187.

9. Morison and Commager, *Growth of the Republic*, 2:521; *Dictionary of American Biography*, Supplement 1, pp. 191-98.

10. Smith was scoffed at in Chestnut Hill. An Irish Catholic president? Never. Furthermore, he couldn't even pronounce the word radio. He thought the r-a-d rhymed with bad. The author's ten-year-old classmates at Pine Road School thought he was out of his mind to be wearing an Al Smith button.

11. Mayer, *Floyd B. Olson*, p. 42.

12. Mayer, *Floyd B. Olson*, pp. 43-49; Chrislock, *Progressive Era*, pp. 193-194.

13. Mayer, *Floyd B. Olson*, pp. 49-52.

14. Mayer, *Floyd B. Olson*, p. 53.

15. Gieske, *Farmer-Laborism*, p. 140.

16. Mayer, *Floyd B. Olson*, pp. 67-68, 76-77; Chrislock, *Progressive Era*, p. 194.

17. *Legislative Manual, 1931*, p. 376.

18. *House Journal, 1931*, p. 146.

19. *House Journal, 1931*, p. 117.

20. *House Journal, 1931*, pp. 87, 164; Gieske, *Farmer Laborism*, p. 175.

21. *House Journal, 1931*, p. 95.

22. *House Journal, 1931*, p. 114.

23. *House Journal, 1931*, p. 651.

24. *House Journal, 1931*, p. 264.

25. Mayer, *Floyd B. Olson*, pp. 107-108; Bjornson, *History of Minnesota*, 1:493.

26. Mayer, *Floyd B. Olson*, p. 90. Frank Totton Heffelfinger was the younger brother of Yale's legendary running guard W. W. "Pudge" Heffelfinger, who played football in the days when a lineman could carry the ball.

27. Violet Sollie to William P. Everts, March 28, 1988.

28. Mayer, *Floyd B. Olson*, pp. 109-112; Aalbu, *Minnesota Kaleidoscope of 1933*, p. 5.

29. Violet Sollie to William P. Everts, March 28, 1988.

30. *Minneapolis Journal*, April 19, 1932.

31. Mayer, *Floyd B. Olson*, pp. 109, 115.

32. Mayer, *Floyd B. Olson*, p. 116; Aalbu, *Minnesota Kaleidoscope of 1933*, p. 7. In a biography of Olson published the year after his death, authors John S. McGrath and James J. Delmont included twenty-six of

his greatest speeches, including the keynote speech for his 1932 reelection campaign and a campaign speech given November 5, 1932, before a "Victory" rally held in the Minneapolis Auditorium. See *Floyd Björnsterne Olson: Minnesota's Greatest Liberal Governor* (No city: no publisher, 1937).

33. *Legislative Manual, 1933*, p. 380.

34. Violet Sollie to William P. Everts, March 28, 1988.

Chapter 26

Minnesota's New Deal

W ith the 1932 election, Olson's political alliance with Roosevelt broadened to a cross-country linking of their political parties. Farmer-Laborites supported the Democrats nationally, and Democrats supported Farmer-Laborites in Minnesota elections. Olson's policies already had anticipated, and now would generally reflect, those of the New Deal. Implementation of those policies, however, was not an easy matter, even with the overwhelming victory that voters had given Olson. While liberal

President Roosevelt and Governor Floyd B. Olson at a conference in Washington. (Photo from McGrath and Delmont, *Floyd B. Olson: Minnesota's Greatest Liberal Governor*, reproduced courtesy of the Minnesota Historical Society)

candidates were mostly successful in election bids to the house, there was no change in the makeup of the senate. Its members were in a holdover status and remained hostile.[1]

Stockwell was raring to go when the Forty-eighth Session began on January 3, 1933. Nearly seventy-six years of age, he had the zeal of an incoming freshman. A kindred spirit would be entering the White House and another returning in triumph to the governor's office. Roosevelt's vigorous leadership and election brought excitement, high purpose, and commitment to government service felt far beyond Washington: there was work ahead, the nation's ills could and would be cured. One of the first matters the Minnesota legislature would address, however, had nothing to do with struggling from the depression. The issue was prohibition.

The Eighteenth Amendment forbidding the "manufacture, sale or transportation of intoxicating liquors" had been submitted to the states for ratification in December 1917. It was ratified by the requisite three-quarters of the states in a year's time and proclaimed in effect in January 1920. The Volstead Act, authored by Minnesota congressman Andrew Volstead, whose sponsorship gave Minnesota a bone-dry reputation, defined intoxicating liquor as any beverage containing over one-half of one percent alcohol. Strict federal enforcement regulations were established. States in turn passed enforcement regulations of their own.[2]

Then the mood of the country changed. In the 1920s, Americans in increasing numbers openly flouted the Volstead Act. Smith in 1928 proposed virtual abandonment of federal enforcement, urging return of the problem to the states. Roosevelt in 1932 called for repeal of the Eighteenth Amendment. In February 1933, Congress passed the Twenty-First Amendment which repealed the Eighteenth. The question of ratification fell to the states.[3]

Minnesota in 1915 had adopted a system of county option, which enabled the voters of each county to determine whether liquor licenses should be issued in their jurisdiction. Chrislock has credited the progressives for adoption of the system:

> By 1908 most Minnesota progressives had embraced the concept of county option . . . Enthusiasm for the measure did not rest solely on the presumption that it would reduce drinking. The brewery-distillery complex seemed to embody most of the evils against which progressivism was contending. Allegedly it built and maintained corrupt political machines, bought and sold legislators and conspired against the general welfare. Why not give the people an opportunity to vote against such a monstrous evil?[4]

Stockwell was a prohibitionist long before it became fashionable. His mother campaigned against the saloon on religious, social and moral grounds. Stockwell, blaming liquor and saloon interests as he blamed the railroads and the public utilities for political corruption, carried on the fight. He was against repeal.

Even before the new Congress convened to cope with the question of repealing the Eighteenth Amendment in 1933, those in favor of repealing the Volstead Act in the Minnesota house introduced HF33, a bill calling for the repeal of Minnesota's enforcement acts. Repeal was urged:

> because Minnesota must be in a position to take advantage of any modification of the Volstead Act. Our industries must be allowed to start manufacture of beer at a moment's notice. It means employment for thousands of men. It means a market for Minnesota grains.[5]

The wet or dry issue was not a party issue. Many progressive men were "wets" while some of the legislature's most reactionary members were "dry." Stockwell and W. I. Norton, adversaries on the question of nepotism and virtually all other issues, were aligned in opposition against HF33. When the bill reached the house floor on January 26 for consideration on the merits, debate raged all afternoon. The *Minneapolis Journal* covered the proceedings:

> Then came speakers who sit a few feet from each other but almost never agree, but on this issue spoke for the same cause—Mr. Norton and S. A. Stockwell. Stockwell, radical . . . old, white haired, declared that "until the eighteenth amendment is taken from the constitution in a legal way, I'll support it to the last ditch." Asked how many voters in his district Otto Nellermoe (an ardent wet) represented, Stockwell replied, "About 30 percent, I think."[6]

Norton pleaded for further consideration and offered his services to help draw a bill that would accomplish what the proponents professed to seek—namely, to leave the way open for Minnesota brewers to start manufacturing beer if and when federal law was modified. To this proposal Representative Ray J. Quinlivan retorted, "I'm afraid you would put a woodchuck in it."[7]

Placed on final passage, the vote was seventy-two yea, fifty-four nay. Governor Olson refused to be stampeded and let it be known he would veto such a bill unless some other regulatory legislation was set up in its place. The senate withheld any action until after a beer regulatory bill had been passed.[8]

After Congress passed the Twenty-first Amendment to repeal federal prohibition in February and submitted it to the states for ratification, Congress modified the prohibition laws to permit, in specified circumstances, sale of beer with an alcoholic content of 3.2 percent by weight. Wets in the Minnesota legislature seized the opening. They declared, simplistically, that 3.2 percent beer was not intoxicating. Such a declaration, it was contended, was the only thing needed for compliance with the Eighteenth Amendment.

The drys, upstaged, pointed out that the beer of preprohibition days was no stronger than that being legalized. Alcoholic content of preprohibition beer had been: Budweiser 3.8, Blatzwiener 3.7, Blatz Munchener 3.5, Old Style Lager 3.4, Cream City Pilsener 3.33, Edelweis 3.3, Weber Superb 3.2, Schlitz Pale 3.15, Pabst Blue Ribbon 2.9, Jung Pilsener 2.8, Graff Weiss Bier 2.8, Red, White and Blue 2.75, Husting Weiss Bier 2.6, and Bohemian 2.5 percent.[9]

But the wets prevailed.

A senate bill calling for an election of delegates and a convention for the purpose of repealing the Eighteenth Amendment was the last of the wet platform bills introduced. The drys put up a strong fight, but the measure swept through the senate without a dissenting vote. In the house, twenty-four members, including Stockwell and Norton, voted against it.[10]

On December 5, 1933, Utah became the thirty-sixth state to ratify the Twenty-first Amendment, and repeal was achieved.

Stockwell's stand on other social and moral legislation introduced in the session was in keeping with his stand on prohibition. He voted with the minority against HF85, a statewide boxing bill that sanctioned unfettered, fifteen-round prize fights, anywhere in the state, with or without police protection, and without regard for the training, experience, or ability of the boxers. He voted with the minority against HF175, a pari-mutuel horse-racing bill that Aalbu deemed the most iniquitous measure of the whole session. Stockwell in all probability would have agreed with columnist Arthur Brisbane's contemporaneous assessment of pari-mutuel horseracing:

> Florida notes the fact that these horse racing and seven day racing associations have paid to the state this year $710,000 in commissions on betting. That is gratifying. But to get the $710,000 men and women in Florida had to bet at least $23,000,000, practically all of which went to the gambling promoters and betting operations. Race track betters do not leave with profits. They stop when they must because their money is gone. That is not gratifying.[11]

HF1071 called for a sales tax on cigarettes. Hearings on the measure brought out the fact that cigarettes were already taxed at fifty-seven percent of their retail price. During discussion of the bill, Stockwell, a member of the Committee on Taxes and Tax Laws and a nonsmoker, said, "I think it is about time we got away from the idea of taxing people upon the basis of what they consume." The committee handed the bill back to its authors.[12]

Stockwell also faced the issue of child labor in the 1933 session. Congress sought to prohibit child labor by legislation, first in 1916 under the guise of regulation of interstate commerce and again in 1919 through the medium of taxation. The Supreme Court found both laws unconstitutional. Opponents of child labor thereafter successfully chaperoned through Congress a constitutional amendment giving Congress the power to limit, regulate, and prohibit the labor of persons under eighteen years of age. Ratification by the legislatures of three-quarters of the states was needed. In Minnesota the mechanism was HF477.

Stockwell, Hjalmar Petersen, and Roy Wier led the battle for ratification in the house. They brought out that three million children from nine to sixteen years of age were employed in mines, canning factories, and textile mills in the United States. Proper child labor legislation, they contended, would give parents an opportunity to support their children rather than to be supported by them, which had become the case in many households where, standing idle, were twelve to fifteen million unemployed adult wage-earners. When the roll was called on HF477, there were eighty-four yeas and thirty-six nays. The bill died in the senate.[13]

Taxes and tax reductions, wage cuts, and salary reductions were critical questions of the day. One hundred seventeen such bills were referred to the House Committee on Taxes and Tax Laws alone. The committee held thirty-five meetings, some of them three to four hours long. The Stockwells had taken an apartment that winter within walking distance of the Capitol; it was a prudent move.[14]

Salary cuts for public employees were a particularly sensitive issue. During the 1932 campaign the public had been told its troubles were due to the high cost of government and waste in the conduct of the state's affairs, and there was a determined demand from many districts for a reduction of county and state salaries. Some newly elected legislators favored dispensing with many if not all functions of government—particularly a government administered by the Farmer-Labor party. High-salaried representatives of the power, steel, railroad, and telephone industries appeared, hat in hand, before the Committee on Tax and Tax Laws, pleading for tax reductions while urging wage and salary cuts for employees in the public sector. Counsel for the mining companies, pressing for a tax-limitation measure that would have deprived villages and school districts in the Iron Range of major revenues, contended that mines had been forced to close "because of the excessive burden of taxes." An auditor's report showed those closures occurring in 1922, 1925, and 1930, due to being mined out, or closures were attributable to low-grade ore. But the mining companies were heard sympathetically, particularly in the senate.[15]

Typical of the cost-cutting measures considered by the legislature was Senator Claude H. MacKenzie's salary reduction bill, SF638. MacKenzie's bill cut by ten to twenty percent the wages and salaries of every person in state, county, city, village or school employ, starting with the governor. The senate passed the bill with fifty-two yeas and fifteen nays. A companion house measure, HF1725, only slightly less drastic, was passed with seventy-six yeas and fourteen nays. The members seemed to feel they were under obligation to pass some kind of wage-cutting bill. Stockwell was among the handful of veteran Farmer-Labor members who voted against it. When the bill was repassed by both houses, Olson vetoed it. He denounced the action of the legislature as

> on a par with the performance of the so-called captains of industry who have been slashing wages and destroying buying power, and who seem to expect that by some species of magic their business will improve despite the destruction of buying power in the people.[16]

Adoption of a state income tax had been called for in Farmer-Labor's 1932 platform and again by Olson in his second inaugural address. The Committee on Taxes and Tax Laws, with assistance from the dean of the University of Minnesota Law School, combined on a well-drafted income tax measure that became the house bill. Hundreds of representatives of chambers of commerce, taxpayers' leagues, and employee association protested, at hearing after hearing, against any kind of income tax. Ultimately the legislature enacted the house bill after compromises had been reached.[17]

A blue-sky law establishing a Securities Commission had been enacted in Minnesota before 1933, but several important categories of securities were exempted from regulation, and adequate enforcement authority was lacking. Stockwell introduced a bill intended to restrict the sale of the then-exempt securities, and his colleague, Representative Fred A. Curtis, introduced a bill putting teeth in the existing law. Their bills were combined and, relatively intact, passed in the house. The senate judiciary committee drastically weakened it. Deeming it the best that could be obtained, both houses finally passed it, putting Minnesota ahead of the country. Congress passed the Securities Exchange Act in June 1934.[18]

A continuing, troubling problem for Olson's administration was the surge of mortgage foreclosures, causing violence, particularly in western rural areas, where farmers were demanding that mortgage payments be suspended. Olson's sympathy for their plight was unbounded, yet he knew that the federal courts had always strictly interpreted the constitutional prohibition against impairment of contracts. To attempt statutory relief or proclaim a mortgage moratorium seemed useless. Nonetheless, in the face of spreading violence, Olson issued a proclamation halting all mortgage foreclosure sales until May. "I am doing that which I could do under martial law without declaring martial law to halt impending riots and insurrection. It is my duty as governor to preserve law and order in the state."[19] His action, hailed by many and deplored by others, led to the passage of mortgage moratorium legislation

Thousands of farmers gather in St. Paul Capitol to listen to Governor Floyd B. Olson speak to them on farm relief. (Courtesy of the Minnesota Historical Society)

that provided a measure of relief until the federal government could institute a large-scale program to help the nation's farmers. The law was challenged on the ground that it violated Article I of the U.S. Constitution, which prohibits any state from passing a law impairing the obligation of contracts, but it was upheld by the state and federal supreme courts.[20]

Another major plank in Olson's program was unemployment insurance. As finally drafted in committee, again with help from university faculty, a house bill was proposed providing that employers make contributions of four percent of total payroll to an unemployment fund. Strange bedfellows joined in opposition to the bill. Capitalists and employers on February 12 marched from all parts of the state to St. Paul to protest against any interference with profits. A noisy Communist delegation also opposed the bill; the Communists wanted nothing to interfere with the disintegration of the capitalist system. They literally invaded the capitol as more than four hundred men and women carrying "Down With Capitalism" banners filed into the house chamber, filling the galleries and every aisle and corner of the house floor. The members hastily recessed. Governor Olson stepped forward with a ringing speech:

> We do not claim that this bill as drawn is perfect. There may be changes necessary, but we must start somewhere, and this is a starting point. If you gentlemen do not favor this plan—then what is your plan? Bring your plan before this committee so that it may be heard and considered—something must be done to prevent a recurrence of the want and misery caused by unemployment during this depression. We stand committed to the idea of patching up this so-called capitalistic system. My friends down here . . . will say that it can't be done—that the capitalist system must perish. Perhaps they are right. But nevertheless—wisely or unwisely—we stand committed to an effort to try, to make it possible for mankind to exist under the present economic order.

With a number of faint-hearted Farmer-Laborites in the House joining the opposition on a first vote, the measure failed. Forces then girded up, and on reconsideration the bill passed, with sixty-seven yeas and fifty-five nays. But it died in the senate.[21]

Charles B. Cheney of the *Minneapolis Journal* concisely explained the legislature's dilemma in an appraisal of the Forty-eighth Session:

> The legislature was between two fires. On the one hand was a distressed population, unemployment, institutions in distress,

counties and communities unable to meet obligations. These conditions demanded that the state open its pocketbook. But the cupboard was bare. State funds were running in the red. Revenues available from corporate taxes were drastically down . . . The legislature was expected to perform miracles.[22]

Chrislock views Olson's second term as more productive in terms of tangible legislative achievement than his first or third despite strong conservative opposition in the senate. In addition to crediting Olson with passage, among other measures, of an income tax and the enactment of the mortgage moratorium law, Chrislock points out that two of the administration's most enduring achievements were in the field of conservation. Further power development and continued logging operations on state lands in the border lake region to the north were outlawed. And thirteen state forests were created on tax-delinquent lands in northern Minnesota.[23]

And it was as a conservationist, as we shall see, that Stockwell made a significant and enduring contribution.

"Grand Old Man." Dedication as found in Aalbus' *Minnesota Kaleidoscope of 1933*. (Courtesy Minnesota Historical Society)

References

1. *Dictionary of American Biography,* Supplement 2, p. 503; *Legislative Manual, 1933,* p. 380.

2. Morison and Commager, *Growth of the Republic,* 2:528-529.

3. Morison and Commager, *Growth of the Republic,* 2:529-530.

4. Chrislock, *Progressive Era,* pp. 31-32.

5. *House Journal, 1933,* p. 38; Aalbu, *Minnesota Kaleidoscope of 1933,* p. 13. Much of the information in this chapter has been taken from *Minnesota Kaleidoscope,* a book dedicated to Stockwell, "The Grand Old Man of Minnesota."

6. *Minneapolis Journal*, January 27, 1933.

7. Aalbu, *Minnesota Kaleidoscope of 1933*, p. 13.

8. Aalbu, *Minnesota Kaleidoscope of 1933*, p. 14.

9. Aalbu, *Minnesota Kaleidoscope of 1933*, pp. 25-26.

10. Aalbu, *Minnesota Kaleidoscope of 1933*, p. 23.

11. Aalbu, *Minnesota Kaleidoscope of 1933*, pp. 15-18.

12. Aalbu, *Minnesota Kaleidoscope of 1933*, p. 62.

13. Aalbu, *Minnesota Kaleidoscope of 1933*, pp. 23-25; Morison and Commager, *Growth of the Republic*, 2:168-169. In the 1930s the child labor issue was frequently discussed in the Everts household as it was across the land. A poem that his father recited still rings in the author's memory:
> The mill so near the golf course lay,
> The little children working there
> Could look up and see the men at play.

14. Aalbu, *Minnesota Kaleidoscope of 1933*, p. 54. The Stockwells' address that winter was 309 Dayton Avenue, St. Paul. A pleasant walk to work it must have been, past St. Paul's cathedral, then up a gentle slope to the capitol. Interstate 94 now divides the city, cutting that path in half.

15. Aalbu, *Minnesota Kaleidoscope of 1933*, pp. 57-59.

16. Aalbu, *Minnesota Kaleidoscope of 1933*, pp. 64-67; Mayer, *Floyd B. Olson*, p. 138; *Minneapolis Journal*, April 23, 1933.

17. Mayer, *Floyd B. Olson*, p. 139; Aalbu, *Minnesota Kaleidoscope of 1933*, pp. 59-61.

18. Aalbu, *Minnesota Kaleidoscope of 1933*, pp. 80-81; Mayer, *Floyd B. Olson*, pp. 69-70.

19. *Minneapolis Journal*, February 25, 1933.

20. Mayer, *Floyd B. Olson*, pp. 123-127; *Blaisdell v. Home Building & Loan Association*, 189 Minn. 422, 448 (1933) and 290 U.S. 398 (1934).

21. Aalbu, *Minnesota Kaleidoscope of 1933*, pp. 94-97.

22. *Minneapolis Journal*, April 19, 1933.

23. Chrislock, *Progressive Era*, pp. 194-195.

Chapter 27

Conservation

In addition to being an early, brave defender of civil liberties and social justice, Stockwell was an early conservationist, staunch defender of the environment. The *Minneapolis Journal* credited him as one of the first to advocate a public conservation policy in Minnesota.[1] Just how early in life he came to appreciate the consequences of the violation of nature's laws by the misuse of her resources and saw the need for a state policy of protection is uncertain. As a boy of ten, arching and twisting to keep his balance on logs flowing down the Rum River, he would not have questioned the forestry practices lying behind the sport. As a circuit school teacher traveling upriver from Anoka, he probably observed forest devastation along the way. Central to a growing concern about forestry practices would have been his belief, held as a young man, that nature's resources belong to all the people.

Protection of the environment was not a political issue when Stockwell entered politics in 1890. No political party took a stand for conservation until 1892, when the Populist party advocated planned management of forests, called for concerted efforts to prevent destruction of forests by fire, and favored state surveillance of water resources and checks to prevent private exploitation of Minnesota's wealth of trees.[2] These were Stockwell's views. Doubtless Theodore Roosevelt's enlightened views on conservation were one of the reasons Stockwell said in 1902 that he would vote for Roosevelt over David B. Hill, a hopeful whom the Democrats never nominated.

The environmental concerns that first spurred Stockwell to action were local. In 1902 he sought passage of a law to protect the waters of Lake Calhoun from contamination from the use of oil-spilling, ice-cutting machinery. Later he helped organize the Minnehaha Improvement League for the purpose of ridding the district

312

near Minnehaha Falls of objectionable buildings and business enterprises. And he was instrumental in starting public improvements along the shores of Lake Nokomis, not far from his home. In 1908, he became interested in a movement to supply Minneapolis with an artesian well supply and was active in a club organized to further the scheme. He outlined plans in a letter to the *Minneapolis Journal:*

Water for Parks and Schools

To the Editor of the *Journal:*

Public ownership is in operation in Minneapolis so far as our water supply is concerned. The city has undertaken the work of supplying us with water, and no private party is permitted to lay water mains in the streets. If the city water is not fit for use, suitable water must be obtained overland or from private wells. There can be no question but that the city is in duty bound to furnish pure water. This duty has been neglected. There has been much complaint, and the result is that there are more than a hundred artesian wells in the city, sunk by private parties for commercial and business purposes. These wells are furnishing water free to all families within convenient carrying distance, except in the case of water companies, which peddle it about the city in bottles. Our citizens, having gotten a taste of this water, have compelled the school board to furnish it to school children at an expense, I am informed, of $3,500 annually.

Not long ago I noticed an advertisement of a land company which proposes to drill artesian wells and lay water pipes so as to supply all residents upon lots in their addition, holding this out as an inducement to buy these lots.

I also saw recently an advertisement of a laundry company in this city that it was using artesian water, and the advertisement says: "Soft artesian water means no chemicals."

The president of one of the spring water companies says that private parties in Minnesota are paying a quarter of a million dollars every year for drinking water, a large part of which comes from the ground underneath the city.

Now, because the shallow park wells have been closed, Superintendent [Theodore] Wirth of the park board has recommended that the board establish a system of artesian wells to furnish water for all the parks.

I am also reliably informed that a contractor stands ready to supply an artesian system which will supply the city with all the water it needs for all purposes, using the piping system now in use, for about half the estimated cost of a filtering plant. That the only change in the water distribution would be that we would take the water from the wells instead of from the river, and that the contractor would give a bond to guarantee the amount needed for all purposes.

The city is losing water rents on account of the private supplies, while in some cases private citizens are paying the city for water, and supplying themselves besides at a private expense for drinking water.

The foregoing facts show that the people of this city have expressed themselves most emphatically in favor of artesian water, and are supplying themselves with it at private expense while paying the city to do the job.

Is it not bad business policy to force private citizens to supply themselves with artesian water at great private expense; force the school board to buy artesian water at great expense; and force the park board to maintain a separate artesian system at the taxpayers' expense, when money is so greatly needed for other park improvements, and when at a comparatively small expense the city can supply every one with the same water for all purposes?[3]

S. A. Stockwell

As the years passed Stockwell became increasingly dismayed about damage to Minnesota's wilderness. In his own words, he returned to the legislature in 1923 "in the interests of conservation for the sole job of trying to do something to stop that devastation."[4] But the political climate of the Harding-Coolidge era

Horse-drawn log sled of the Alger Smith and Company, Lake County, 1916. (Photo by William Roleff. Courtesy of the Minnesota Historical Society)

Interior of E. W. Backus Wholesale Lumber Company. E. W. Backus is standing in the door-way. (Courtesy of the Minnesota Historical Society)

was not conducive to the enactment of programs protecting the environment and little could be accomplished. In 1929, Stockwell was named to the Public Domain, Reforestation, and State Park committees of the house. The climate was unchanged, and the legislature rejected a modest reforestation proposal that was "remedial only and hardly to be described as reckless or socialistic, as viewed by some."[5]

While conservationists at the capitol were accomplishing little, to the north was emerging a citizens' coalition of conservationists prepared to challenge the unlimited exploitation of timber and water resources in the beautiful, unspoiled border lakes region lying between Minnesota and Canada. In 1925 the question of developing the Rainy Lake watershed, a vast area drained by river systems in the border lakes region, had been referred by the federal government to an organization known as the International Joint Commission, previously established for the purpose of adjudicating differences between Canada and the United States. Edward W. Backus, an industrialist associated with the Minnesota and Ontario Paper Company, among other companies, had produced a general plan for waterpower development in the watershed. His plan called for construction of seven dams and it would have flooded the lowlands while raising the water level of a number of lakes as much as eighty feet. Other lakes would be drained to mere mud flats just to supply water for power plants. Rivers would be rerouted. Proposed operations included the generation of electrical power, extensive lumbering, and the establishment of newsprint and papermaking plants. Backus himself had acquired far-flung holdings in the region. Though he lived on Rainy Lake, he saw no harm in flooding: damage to scenic beauty, which he could not concede, must give way to industrial expansion.[6]

Conservationists sounded the alarm and rose in opposition to the Backus plan, objecting to the industrialization of the region, the inundation of forest lands, the creation of fire hazards, and the disturbance of fish and wildlife. The Izaak Walton League set up a special organization, the Quetico-Superior Council, to fight for the maintenance of the border lakes in their natural state.[7] The council chose Ernest C. Oberholtzer as president. He, too, lived at Rainy Lake, by himself on a tiny island, but that was all he had in common with Backus. "I didn't want to get into the controversy," he said later, "but I couldn't stand by and see all that beauty destroyed."[8]

Born in Iowa in 1884, Oberholtzer studied landscape architecture under Frederick Law Olmsted at Harvard and settled at Rainy Lake in 1909 at

Ernest C. Oberholtzer, 1940. (Courtesy of the Minnesota Historical Society)

about the time the Superior National Forest in Minnesota and Quetico Provincial Park in Manitoba were established. His dream was for a joint international park dedicated to peace, extending eastward all the way to Lake Superior, never to be maimed or sullied.[9]

In the course of lining up opposition to the Backus plan, Oberholtzer met Stockwell. They at once became allies. Though the men were a generation apart, the alliance developed into a fast friendship. Predictably, Stockwell invited Oberholtzer to the Saturday Lunch Club. At a June 1928 meeting of the club, Stockwell, ever the single-tax proponent, gave Oberholtzer a volume of selections from Henry George's *Progress and Poverty*. In a letter of thanks to Stockwell, Oberholtzer registered disappointment at labor's predilection for the dams called for in the Backus plan. "How best can we offset this?" he asked. Oberholtzer was the main speaker at the cornfest that September.[10]

The Quetico-Superior Council lobbied for protection of the northern lake area at the grass roots, state, and national levels. Due in large part to the council's efforts, Congress in 1930 passed the Shipstead-Nolan Act, which prohibited the leasing of lands in the Superior National Forest for private use.[11] In a letter on September 26, 1930, Stockwell congratulated Oberholtzer on the success he had attained in Congress with the international forest movement and closed with the assurance that "if I am returned to the legislature this session, I will cooperate with you to the limit in any legislation or movement that will strengthen our position."

Both men recognized that the Shipstead-Nolan Act did not afford complete protection for the Superior National Forest. The International Joint Commission was still studying the Backus proposal, and if the commission approved waterpower development in the Rainy Lake watershed, in all probability the United States and Canada would implement the commission's recommendation with a treaty extinguishing Shipstead-Nolan benefits. Further, the Minnesota Power and Light Company had already flooded the Gabbro Lake area owned by the state and was trying to legalize its trespass. Recognizing that it could do nothing to control the International Joint Commission decision, the Quetico-Superior Council turned to the Minnesota legislature for the enactment of a Shipstead-Nolan Act for Minnesota, outlawing private exploitation of state lands in the area.[12]

Oberholtzer wrote Stockwell on October 18, 1930:

> For my own enlightenment will you please let me have your own estimate of Mr. Olson for governor. I'm sorry I have never met him and have not had an opportunity to talk over our conversation with him. I may not be back in Minneapolis until after election, for I am yet to visit many places in the vicinity of Superior National Forest . . . It is only by constant plugging that we can hope to protect the northern lake area. Aside from all the public work, it is necessary to study all the voluminous engineering and legal documents with minute care, for we are up against experts who are looking for a chance to discredit us.

On January 8, 1931, Oberholtzer wrote again:

> As soon as possible, I am hoping to have the opportunity to see you. I read Governor Olson's inaugural message last night with much pleasure and appreciation. What he says about conservation could not have been better . . . I hope you and Mrs. Stockwell are very well this winter. I know you are all ready for the fray and will really enjoy making the sparks fly in the public interest over at the legislature. All power to you.

Olson had called for a unified conservation department in his inaugural message. Stockwell, serving on the same committees as before, did what he could for the administration and for Oberholtzer, alerting him to moves by the Minnesota Power and Light Company and Backus interests. Also, Stockwell coauthored with Mabeth Hurd Paige a bill for an act to protect the levels of lakes and adjacent lands owned by the state in the border lakes region. Opposition kept the measure, HF1380, from a vote. Olson could have given valuable help, but he remained inactive for fear of jeopardizing his proposal for a unified conservation department. Olson's proposal was enacted, and he regarded the law, under which all conservation activities were united under a five-member commission appointed by the governor, as the most important achievement of his first term.[13]

In response to a letter from Oberholtzer inquiring about a possible meeting with Governor Olson, Stockwell wrote on September 29, 1932:

> We are sorry that you could not be at the Corn Fest . . . I think I shall probably be in the next House of Representatives and if we organize the House, as I hope we may, I will try to be made chairman of the Committee of Public Domain. Then we would be in a position to handle the situation in the interest of the public good . . . It is not necessary for me to tell you that I will die in the last ditch for the Quetico-Superior Council and its secretary . . . I am sure that I can arrange for an interview with Governor Olson.

To which Oberholtzer replied on October 3, 1932:

> One letter a week like yours of September 29 would be just the tonic I need. Well as I know your militant loyalty to our work, I cannot help but get renewed exhilaration out of your further assurance of support. I only hope it is true that you will be the next chairman of the Committee of Public Domain in the House. There could be no better fortune for us.

Stockwell did become chairman of the Public Domain Committee for the 1933 session. More interest was shown in legislation relating to waters of the state than ever before, and Olson actively joined the conservationists in their fight to outlaw further power development on logging operations on state lands within the Shipstead-Nolan area.[14]

Stockwell's answer to the Backus interests was HF892, a committee bill that provided the same protection for state lands within the Superior National Forest as Shipstead-Nolan did nationally. It also provided for the protection of Gabbro and Bald Eagle lakes, which had been illegally dammed by the Minnesota Power and Light Company. The legislation was bitterly contested; the power company spent money without stint to kill it. Stockwell rallied support for HF892 within and without the legislature. Typical was his April 10 letter to a constituent:

> Replying to your letter of April 7th, I must say I will go to the limit in support of House File No. 892. You cannot be more in accord with this bill than I am, and I urge you to get in touch with as many representatives, either in Minneapolis or elsewhere, as you can, taking the matter up with them personally, as that is the best way to exert influence at this time.[15]

When it was finally realized that HF892 stood an excellent chance of passage, the opposition offered a compromise—to withdraw further opposition if their past steals could be legalized. Proponents and opponents then reached an accord. The company was allowed to hold Gabbro and Bald Eagle Lakes but could not raise the water level of the lakes another thirteen feet as urgently requested, was required to clear the flooded land, pay triple damages for trees killed, and pay rental to be fixed by the commissioner of conservation. The bill, as amended, reached the house floor on the evening of April 17. The house voted to pass it, yeas ninety-five, nays two. The senate passed it without a dissenting vote.[16]

Thus, a fight started nearly nine years earlier by a small group of conservationists ended in victory for the state. But Stockwell's struggle to protect the environment from marauders was not limited to the border lakes region. His committee also introduced a bill to establish thirteen state forests, four of which did lie within the Shipstead-Nolan area, from tax-delinquent lands in different parts of the state. HF1293 passed both houses virtually without dissent, and 2,500,000 acres were added to the state forest. The forestry and land utilization programs provided for were the most extensive ever undertaken in Minnesota. Enactment so augmented Minnesota's participation in Roosevelt's forest employment program as to make possible the employment of five thousand members of the Civilian Conservation Corps on state lands.[17]

Stockwell and Oberholtzer each placed a high priority on facilitating federal control of the entire Shipstead-Nolan area. The Superior National Forest would be more valuable if the federal government acquired state lands within that area. Land-for-land exchange was an equitable, mutually advantageous method of consolidating control, with the state ceding land within the area to the federal government in exchange for federal lands of comparable value outside. Such outside lands, in turn, could be set up as state forests.

A proposed amendment to the state constitution, strongly supported by Stockwell and Oberholtzer, authorizing Minnesota to exchange state lands for land owned by the United States or by private parties, was submitted to the people at the general election of November 1934. The amendment netted 468,617 yes and 216,000 no votes, but because the yes votes were not a majority of all votes cast at the election, it was not adopted. Opposition was based on the questionable contention that the amendment might open the way for juggling state lands to the disadvantage of the state.[18]

The measure failed again at the general election of 1936, but Stockwell remained optimistic. At a 1937 dinner honoring the Stockwells on their fiftieth wedding anniversary, he forecast concerted action by Minnesota citizens to elect legislators and officeholders who would work for reforestation and the rebuilding of levels of state lakes. The big answer to these problems, he added, would be an amendment to the state constitution enabling the exchange of state lands inside the forest areas for federal lands outside. He pointed out that efforts towards this solution had failed in the past. But he said prospects were bright.[19]

His optimism was warranted. In 1938 an amendment to the state constitution authorizing the legislature to exchange state public lands for federal lands was adopted with 609,046 yes votes to 259,007 no votes.[20]

References

1. *Minneapolis Journal*, June 8, 1927.

2. Blegen, *Minnesota*, p. 405.

3. *Minneapolis Journal*, July 27, 1908.

4. Deposition, *J. E. Foster v. Al P. Erickson, County Auditor*, Supreme Court File No. 32676 (1940), Minnesota Historical Society.

5. Gieske, *Farmer-Laborism*, p. 123.

6. *Minneapolis Tribune*, April 28, 1967; A. Newell Searle, *Saving Quetico-Superior: A Land Set Apart* (St. Paul: Minnesota Historical Society Press, 1977), pp. 34, 35, 39-41, 59, 94, 104, 165.

7. Mayer, *Floyd B. Olson*, p. 140.

8. *Minneapolis Tribune*, April 28, 1967.

9. Searle, *Saving Quetico-Superior,* pp. 62-70, 108, 201, 206, 215.

10. Correspondence between Stockwell and Oberholtzer quoted herein is contained in the Quetico-Superior papers, Minnesota Historical Society. Another of Oberholtzer's friends was William P. Hapgood, who owned a nearby island on Rainy Lake and hired Oberholtzer to landscape it. Through him, Oberholtzer met Norman Hapgood, editor of *Collier's Magazine.* Norman Hapgood's son-in-law, Sewell T. Tyng, who vacationed at Rainy Lake in the 1930s, was a junior partner in a large Wall Street law firm. Tyng loved the region, deplored the Backus plan, and for the next twenty years gave indispensable legal advice to Oberholtzer, sharing his dream of an unspoiled international wilderness. Norman Hapgood was a good friend of the author's father, and Hapgood visited the Everts family at Petersham, Massachusetts, in the summers. See also Searle, *Saving Quetico-Superior,* pp. 56, 62.

11. Mayer, *Floyd B. Olson,* p. 140.

12. Mayer, *Floyd B. Olson,* pp. 140-141.

13. Mayer, *Floyd B. Olson,* p. 69.

14. Aalbu, *Minnesota Kaleidoscope of 1933,* p. 72; Chrislock, *Progressive Era,* pp. 194-195.

15. S. A. Stockwell to H. E. Berreau, April 10, 1933, Quetico-Superior papers, Minnesota Historical Society.

16. Aalbu, *Minnesota Kaleidoscope of 1933,* p. 75; Mayer, *Floyd B. Olson,* p. 141.

17. Mayer, *Floyd B. Olson,* p. 141; *Minneapolis Journal,* April 18, 1933; Searle, *Saving Quetico-Superior,* p. 112.

18. R. W. Hitchcock, comp., *Issues of the Minnesota Legislature, Regular Session 1935 and Special Session 1935-1936,* p. 65.

19. *St. Paul Pioneer Press,* March 31, 1937; *Minneapolis Tribune,* March 31, 1937.

20. *Legislative Manual, 1991-1992,* p. 52.

Chapter 28

The Great Truck Strike

S tockwell expected far-reaching accomplishment for the 1933
session of the legislature. Farmer-Laborites were ascendant.
Roosevelt's leadership and proposals for the economy had
everywhere buoyed hopes that remedial action by the federal government could lift the country from economic depression. If ever
there was a time for Minnesota'a governor and legislature similarly to intervene to help cure society's ills, that time had come.

But accomplishments were disappointing in many respects.
The 1933 session did see enactment of an income tax and mortgage moratorium law as well as tangible achievement in the field of
conservation, but benefits for labor were disappointing. Newly
elected house members proved no more liberal than most of their
predecessors when it came to labor legislation. Scores balked at
the unemployment insurance bill introduced by Stockwell and others. It finally passed in the house on reconsideration, only to die in
the senate. With limited exceptions, measures designed to protect
labor, even in small ways, were emasculated or killed. Roy Wier of
Minneapolis, selected to pilot labor bills through the house, along
with Stockwell and other like-minded members, ran into frustrat-
ing opposition at every turn.[1]

But Washington treated the blue-collar worker more kindly.
Lasting benefits to the labor movement in Minnesota stemmed directly and indirectly from Roosevelt's administration.[2]

One of the New Deal's key measures was the National Industrial Recovery Act. Enacted in mid-1933, the law in Section 7(a)
specifically guaranteed employees "the right to organize and bargain collectively through representatives of their own choosing . . .
free from interference, restraint, or coercion of employers." Not
since Woodrow Wilson's day had labor known such an ally in the
White House. With the passage of the National Industrial Recovery

Act, vigorous drives to organize unions sprang up across the country.[3]

Business leaders in Minneapolis simply ignored the National Industrial Recovery Act. They lived in a city that for more than two decades had neutralized organized labor by working through a loose but effective local trade organization called the Citizens' Alliance. Minneapolis had a long-standing reputation, bolstered in practice by the Minnesota Public Safety Commission during the war years, of being open to business but closed to unions. The Citizens' Alliance was determined to keep things that way, Section 7(a) of the National Industrial Recovery Act to the contrary notwithstanding.[4]

The depression of the 1930s had facilitated the neutralization of organized labor in Minneapolis by creating a vast pool of unemployed. Men who did hold jobs, concerned about providing at least a few dollars for their families, were generally unwilling to risk their employment by becoming union activists. Among those hardest hit in the depression were transportation workers. Taxi drivers in 1934 received anywhere from $6.66 to $12.00 for an eighty-four-hour work week. Truck drivers never got more than $18.00 for the same period. William Brown, veteran driver and a born leader, courageously took on the task of organizing the truck drivers. He opted for an industrial union rather than the traditional craft variety and selected Carl Skoglund and the three Dunne brothers—Grant, Miles, and Vincent—to spearhead the organizing. They were competent, resourceful, and devoted to the labor movement. Local 574 was in the making.[5]

Vince Dunne was perhaps the ablest. All three belonged to the Trotskyist wing of the Communist party. While this did not detract from their effectiveness in winning recruits for Local 574, identification with communism became ammunition for the Citizens' Alliance, eager to obscure economic issues at any cost. The Employers' Committee, a "respectable front" for the Citizens' Alliance, would thereafter accuse Local 574 of providing a shield for the operations of Communists seeking to subvert American institutions. In time a full-page ad appeared in the *Minneapolis Journal*, charging the union with a plot to set up a local Soviet Republic. The tactics of class warfare emerged.[6]

On April 15, Local 574 held a mammoth rally at the Shubert Theatre. Olson, fully in sympathy but unable to attend, was represented by his secretary and confidant, Vince Day, who read a letter from Olson commending the membership for their activities and asserting that any group of workers refusing to take advantage of the right to organize, as protected by the National Industrial Recovery Act, was blind to its own welfare.[7] Two weeks later, Local 574 demanded from employers a closed shop, shorter hours, an average wage of $27.50 a week, and extra pay for overtime. The Citizens' Alliance, astounded, saw the demand as a declaration of war. Attempted negotiations led nowhere. The Employers' Committee totally rejected union demands and spurned efforts of the Regional Labor Board, newly established under the National Industrial Recovery Act, to mediate. In refusing to recognize or deal with union leaders, the employers with near certainty assured an outbreak of violence.[8] The union then withdrew its demand for a closed shop, agreed to arbitrate disputes over wages, and demanded only a promise of compliance with Section 7(a). The Employers' Committee, which had previously declared the closed shop to be the stumbling block, shifted ground and refused as before to recognize or deal with union leaders. Its objective was the destruction of Local 574.

On May 16 the union voted to strike, taking a step that placed Olson in a dilemma. If he called out state troops to keep the streets open and maintain orderly movement of truck traffic—typically the response of state leaders in the past—he would crush the strike. He did not wish to do so. Yet he was responsible for the safety and well-being of the general public.[9]

Within hours, pickets sprang up at key points in the city. Truck transportation was reduced to a trickle. Only trucks carrying food, milk, and ice were permitted to move. Pitched battles

Minnesota National Guard troops arrested Vincent Dunne, leader in the Minneapolis truckers' strike of 1934. (*Star Tribune*, September 7, 1987)

between the police, employer hirelings, pickets, and union suppliers broke out in the city's market area, a focal point because it was to the market that nonunion farmers sought to deliver their produce. Two persons were killed, one of whom, C. Arthur Lyman, a prominent business leader, was for many years attorney for the Citizens' Alliance. Olson finally called out the National Guard, but only to insure the distribution of food. To the anger and disgust of the Employers' Committee, he made clear that troops were not to be used to convoy employer trucks. Finally in May, through personal, round-the-clock, shuttle diplomacy, Olson successfully worked out a temporary settlement.[10]

The quiet was short-lived. Piece by piece the Employers' Committee dismantled the settlement, and on July 16 the union voted to renew the strike. On July 20, fifty local police officers, under orders from Minneapolis police chief "Bloody Mike" Johannes to end the strike, attempted to breach a picket barricade while escorting a delivery truck. The pickets carried no weapons. With little or no warning the police opened a shotgun barrage. Sixty-seven persons were wounded, including thirteen bystanders; two died. Some were shot in the back while fleeing.[11]

The employers charged Olson with obstructing rather than aiding local authorities in maintaining law and order. Olson fired back:

> I do not agree that the plea for a living wage by a family receiving only $12.00 a week is answered by calling him a communist. Neither am I willing to join in the approval of the shooting of unarmed citizens of Minneapolis, strikers and bystanders alike, in their backs in order to carry out the wishes of the Citizens' Alliance.[12]

Ultimately Olson did call out state troops to stop the bloodshed, but he remained determined that troops should not be used to help either employers or strikers. Their task was to protect the citizens of Minneapolis from both sides, if necessary. His action, nonetheless, nearly broke the strike, and leaders of Local 574 who had hoped Olson would join them in the fray objected strenuously. Brown, Miles, and Vince Dunne were arrested for a brief period, leaving striking truck drivers leaderless and dismayed.[13] The standoff continued until, somewhat surprisingly, on August 21 an agreement favorable to the union was finally reached. The strike, and with it Minneapolis' open-shop policy, came to an end. Other unions grew in size following Local 574's success. Roosevelt had given his friend Olson a boost. Through the Reconstruction Finance

Corporation, the administration exerted pressure on banks and businesses in Minneapolis to moderate their stand by threat of cutting off all further loans.

Olson received outside help, to be sure, yet he deserves credit for the victory. Local 574 soon came to recognize this even though Olson had called out state troops and acquiesced in the arrest of its leaders.[14]

Where was Stockwell during these four months of conflict? M. J. Galvin, who served in the senate at the time, recalled in general terms that

> Stockwell supported the efforts of organized labor. . . . He supported all of the liberal provisions of the unemployment compensation laws and opposed bills that made it hard for labor to organize. He would have been involved in the truck strike, I am sure.

How would a seventy-seven-year-old legislator, unable to drive any motor-driven vehicle, support a truck strike? He probably attended every major union rally, beginning with the great rally of April 15 at the Shubert Theatre where Vince Day read Olson's message of support. As he could be counted on to appear at meetings in black churches where but a handful might be seated, only to let them know someone cared, so would he have appeared at crowded union rallies just to let the members know they had one more friend—an amicus curiae.

Stockwell and Day were on the closest terms. Stockwell likely offered counsel at the capitol. Or took him to the Saturday Lunch Club for moral support and a high-powered exchange of ideas.[15] In addition, both the Stockwells probably aided the strikers and their families by bringing them food and medical supplies. The union had converted an abandoned garage at 1900 Chicago Avenue into strike headquarters where leaders received progress reports, dispatched pickets, and held rallies to keep the rank-and-file posted on developments. Some strikers ate and slept in the garage with their families. Even the sick and wounded received medical care on the premises.[16] Certainly the Stockwells, with regularity, took the street car to 1900 Chicago Avenue, bearing vegetables and flowers from their garden, along with medicines and medical supplies from some nearby pharmacy. Then they returned to their farm on the outskirts of the city in time to milk the cow.

References

1. Aalbu, *Minnesota Kaleidescope of 1933*, pp. 93-94.

2. Olson's sympathy for the cause of labor is not surprising given his youthful poverty and early association with longshoremen and the Industrial Workers of the World. More surprising was the sympathy for labor's cause demonstrated by Roosevelt, a patrician. On taking office in 1933, he named Frances Perkins, labor reformer and friend of the worker, to be Secretary of Labor. The appointment triggered a cry of alarm from his critics. "A woman for that post? Good God, man! Has he gone mad?"

3. Arthur A. Sloane and Fred Witney, *Labor Relations* (Englewood Cliffs, New Jersey: Prentice-Hall, Inc., 1977), pp. 78-80, 106-107: Mayer, *Floyd B. Olson*, pp. 139-142. The National Industrial Recovery Act was declared unconstitutional by the Supreme Court early in 1935, but Congress quickly replaced it with a law that was even more to labor's liking, the National Labor Relations Act, better known as the Wagner Act. Senator Robert Wagner of New York was its prinicpal draftsman.

4. Gieske, *Farmer-Laborism*, p. 195; Mayer, *Floyd B. Olson*, p. 185. Berman sees another factor as contributing to the neutralization of labor in Minneapolis and St. Paul. In his view, the labor experience was made distinct by the community's relative economic isolation. It gave business a monopoly of power so complete only radical action would break it. See *Minneapolis Star Tribune*, September 7, 1987.

5. Mayer, *Floyd B. Olson*, pp. 187-188. See also, Charles R. Walker, *American City* (New York: Arno & *The New York Times*, 1971) for an excellent account of the whole subject.

6. Mayer, *Floyd B. Olson*, p. 188; Gieske, *Farmer-Laborism*, p. 195.

7. Maycr, *Floyd B. Olson*, p. 189; *Minneapolis Labor Review*, April 20, 1934. Lee and J. J. Shubert dominated American theatrical management and production from 1906 until after World War II. Their holdings included theaters and industrial real estate in New York, Philadelphia, Baltimore, Buffalo, Cincinnati, Minneapolis, Boston, and other cities. William Everts, father of the author, was the Shuberts' Boston lawyer for much of this period. Complimentary tickets given to him for opening nights were a bonus for all the family, who likely were applauding such as "Of Thee I Sing" at Boston's Shubert Theatre while Stockwell applauded Local 574 from a front-row seat in Minneapolis. For a monograph about the Shuberts, see *Dictionary of American Biography*, Supplement 5, pp. 626-628. Agnes DeMille has written in *Portrait Gallery* (Boston: Houghton Mifflin, 1990) a scathing commentary: "I think Lee would rather have lost a leg than a bargain. . . . He possessed a genuine talent for greed. He was a rapacious man (as was Jake) through natural instincts. Where money was concerned, he knw no mercy and he knew no generosity." All we

knew as children about his business was that he was demanding on our father.

8. Mayer, *Floyd B. Olson*, p. 194.

9. Mayer, *Floyd B. Olson*, pp. 192-193.

10. Mayer, *Floyd B. Olson*, pp. 194-201.

11. Mayer, *Floyd B. Olson*, pp. 201-210; Walker, *American City*, pp. 166-168.

12. Mayer, *Floyd B. Olson*, p. 211.

13. Mayer, *Floyd B. Olson*, pp. 207-214.

14. Mayer, *Floyd B. Olson*, pp. 220-222. See also Richard M. Valelly, *Radicalism in the States: The Minnesota Farmer-Labor Party and the American Polictical Economy* (Chicago: University of Chicago Press, 1989), pp. 103-118.

15. Olson rarely convoked general meetings of his staff to debate and hammer out a program or decide on specific action. No major overall advisor stood by his side. He enlisted many special talents in the preparation and execution of his policies. See Mayer, *Floyd B. Olson*, p. 234.

16. Mayer, *Floyd B. Olson*, pp. 194-195.

Chapter 29

"I Am a Radical"

While Olson's economic and labor policies aligned him with the New Deal, his rhetoric from 1934 until his death placed him well to the left of Roosevelt and affected the political fortunes of all who supported him, including Stockwell. Olson's leaning corresponded to a growing dominance within the Farmer-Labor movement of its radical socialist wing. Chrislock attributes the Farmer-Labor movement's turn to more radical solutions for society's ills, at least in part, to "the innovative spirit and permissive political milieu of the early New Deal years." Political leftists came to believe that deliverance was at hand.[1]

But Olson's unbridled political rhetoric almost led to his party's undoing.

The March 1934 Farmer-Labor Association convention came at a time when Olson's prestige and popularity were at an all-time high. He had assured his followers he would run for reelection. Political observers unanimously agreed he was unbeatable. Nonetheless, he seemed to lack firmness. Some believed he was becoming careless and experimental. Weary of the endless mediation of intraparty disputes, continuing demands of spoilsmen for appointment to office of friends and party faithful, and suffering from what proved to be precancerous ulcers, Olson gave thought to seeking a seat in the U.S. Senate. Work there would surely be less onerous.[2] In the eyes of convention delegates, nonetheless, he could do no wrong. Carried away, perhaps, by the adulation, Olson made a surprising speech, declaring the party's goal to be:

> a cooperative commonwealth wherein the government will stifle as much as possible the greed and avarice of the private profit system and will bring more equitable distribution of the wealth produced by the hands and minds of the people . . . I am frank to say I am what I want to be. I am a radical.[3]

He had already captured the convention. Led by extremists, who were willingly joined by moderates under Olson's spell, the entire throng stood and roared approval. Stockwell, loyal and ever courteous, would have risen. But, he must have wondered whether Olson, ablest leader of a political party he had seen in some forty years of political life, was making a serious blunder. If Stockwell clapped, he clapped cautiously.

When Olson finished his speech, without adding any note of caution, he serenely departed the premises to keep an engagement in Washington, leaving the platform's drafting to others instead of masterminding the sessions as he had in 1930 and 1932. This was his second miscalculation.[4] The convention drafted a platform forecasting that "palliative measures" would continue to fail and "only a complete reorganization of the social structure into a cooperative commonwealth will bring economic security and prevent a prolonged period of future suffering." Among the planks was a sweeping public ownership clause embracing banks, insurance companies, and factories, as well as mines, public utilities, and transportation. Only bona fide cooperatives were exempt.[5] The convention adopted the most extreme platform ever drawn up by a party in power in the United States.[6]

Surely Stockwell was deeply troubled. The platform transgressed his own standards of practical reform, could not be achieved, and would only alienate moderate voters in all parties. While William Watts Folwell had said that Stockwell "wants the Kingdom of heaven right away," the description fit the younger man. Now, a seasoned legislator, Stockwell was the realist who told his daughter Charlotte, "We must move slowly; I shan't live to see the day, but you may." How distressing now to see Olson standing on a platform proclaiming the failure of capitalism and the advent of a cooperative commonwealth—Olson, who but a year before had told protesting Communists and capitalists alike in the chamber of the house, "We are determined to try and fix the capitalist system."

Russian immigrant George Leonard quickly saw the danger, too. He thought the blunder "had resuscitated the Republican corpse." Republicans and Democrats, momentarily stunned, could scarcely believe their good fortune. Within hours they opened a barrage of denunciation that lasted until the election. Typical was R. W. Hitchcock's condemnation of the platform: "An attempt to substitute the Russian for the American system." Farmers, small bankers, merchants, and manufacturers fled that wallowing ship.[7]

The uproar reached Olson in Washington. He knew at once he should never have gone and sought to control the damage with an immediate statement: "I interpret the public ownership plank as approving federal and state ownership of public utilities and key industries. It does not contemplate any general ownership and operation of business beyond that."[8]

He hastened back to Minnesota. In a radio address on April 12, he adroitly shifted emphasis from socialistic planning to voluntary cooperation. Yet, more was needed to avoid total disaster. Vince Day urged reworking of the platform, eliminating its socialistic features, and emphasizing the development of private cooperatives. This step, however, would have required a second convention. Finally, in May, the original platform was amended by "analysis" without the calling of a second convention. Essentially it was an outline of the Farmer-Labor legislative program, calling for (1) operation of idle factories, (2) extension of the mortgage moratorium law, (3) exemption of homesteads from taxation, (4) additional taxes on large incomes and inheritances, (5) unemployment, sickness, and accident insurance, and (6) extension of municipal authority to sell power outside the city limits.[9]

Stockwell was running again from the Thirty-second District. For his part, he said, "I am for the platform as interpreted by the state committee of the Association and by myself." He had already been endorsed by the Farmer-Labor party in his district and was standing on its platform. But he was worried; the opposition never allowed the voters to forget the platform as adopted. Outcome of the election was in grave doubt.[10]

The campaign was Olson's most formidable. His convention speech, the platform, and the time-consuming trucking ordeal, wherein he had been so bold as to use troops to protect the rights of strikers as well as the rights of property owners, forced him to the defensive. To the dismay of socialists within party ranks, he tabled radicalism and allied Farmer-Laborism with the New Deal. To the dismay of conservative Democrats and to the reassurance of liberal Democrats who had been won over to Farmer-Laborism, Franklin Roosevelt gave him a boost. On a visit to Minnesota in August, Roosevelt, not himself a candidate in that off-year, declined to endorse Democratic candidates. This tacit approval of Olson was strengthened by his remark in Rochester that Olson should join him in Washington and leave a secretary to govern Minnesota.[11]

Olson had returned to the mainstream of New Dealism and found a welcome. Instead of directing his campaign against Martin Nelson, Republican candidate for governor, and John Regan, running again for the Democrats, he took aim at the chain stores,

Floyd B. Olson (right) with Secretary Vince Day. (Photo by *St. Paul Daily News*. Courtesy of the Minnesota Historical Society)

banks, the steel industry, monopoly, and the Republican party's inept response to crisis. At the close of the campaign he virtually ignored Nelson and Regan, striking out instead at the Citizens' Alliance, the *Minneapolis Journal*, and the *Minneapolis Tribune*.[12]

Ever the resourceful campaigner, Olson won election as governor for a third time. He held labor's vote and that of the unemployed. Further, many industrial leaders had come to recognize that his rhetoric outdistanced his expectations and that, in reality, his remedies were not unreasonable. In the privacy of the election booth, such men voted for him. But much of the support of farmers and small business had vanished. His margin of victory was considerably smaller than in 1932:[13]

CANDIDATE	No. of Votes	% of Vote
Floyd B. Olson (Farmer-Labor)	468,812	44.0
Martin Nelson (Republican)	396,359	37.2
John Regan (Democrat)	176,928	16.6
A. C. Townley (Independent)	4,454	.4
S. K. Davis (Communist)	4,334	.4[14]

Hjalmar Petersen of Askov, who had served in the lower house in 1931 and 1932, was elected lieutenant governor. Vince Day saw him as the best available man to succeed Olson as governor. Henrik Shipstead, the aloof Farmer-Laborite, was reelected easily to the U.S. Senate. Three of the party's nine congressional candidates were reelected, and five of eight state offices were won by Farmer-Labor candidates.[15]

The labor vote and forces of reform remained dominant in Hennepin County. Stockwell won reelection handily but with fewer than the 15,188 votes he received in 1932:

THIRTY-SECOND DISTRICT—HENNEPIN COUNTY

S. A. Stockwell	13,912
Otto D. Nellermoe	11,165
Henry G. Young	10,853
Lewis D. Peterson	9,099[16]

In the legislature as a whole, conservative candidates prevailed. A coalition of Republicans, Democrats, and independents organized both the senate and the house. Once again Stockwell would be aligned with the minority.[17]

References

1. Chrislock, *Progressive Era*, p. 195.

2. Mayer, *Floyd B. Olson*, pp. 168-170.

3. Mayer, *Floyd B. Olson*, p. 171; Gieske, *Farmer-Laborism*, pp. 187-188.

4. Mayer, *Floyd B. Olson*, p. 171; Gieske, *Farmer-Laborism*, pp. 187-189.

5. Mayer, *Floyd B. Olson*, pp. 171-172.

6. Mayer, *Floyd B. Olson*, p. 171.

7. Mayer, *Floyd B. Olson*, pp. 172-173.

8. Mayer, *Floyd B. Olson*, p. 175.

9. Mayer, *Floyd B. Olson*, pp. 177-179; Gieske, *Farmer-Laborism*, pp. 191-193.

10. *Minneapolis Journal*, June 8, 1934; Gieske, *Farmer-Laborism*, p. 93.

11. Mayer, *Floyd B. Olson*, pp. 240-241.

12. Gieske, *Farmer-Laborism*, pp. 197-199.

13. Mayer, *Floyd B. Olson*, pp. 249-251.

14. Gieske, *Farmer-Laborism*, p. 200.

15. Gieske, *Farmer-Laborism*, pp. 199-201.

16. *Legislative Manual, 1935*, p. 387.

17. Hitchcock, *Issues of the Minnesota Legislature, 1935*, p. 7.

Chapter 30

O Captain!

When Stockwell, nearly seventy-eight, took his seat in the Forty-ninth Session of the legislature on January 8, 1935, he enjoyed good health and remained as energetic as ever. Living on Dayton Street in St. Paul for the winter, he strode to work—couldn't wait to get there—and was ready in all respects to carry the load in store for a member of the committees on public domain, reforestation, drainage, taxes and tax laws, and insurance. Perhaps more than ever he looked forward to the association with young men and women just entering public service. The *St. Paul News* took note of his grace as a senior on opening day in a page-one story:

> On meeting Representative Ralph W. Severson, the youngest member of the House of Representatives [twenty-five years old at the beginning of the 1935 session], Stockwell, the oldest, said, "I'm old enough to be your great grandfather, but I welcome you to the legislature just the same. . . . You'll no doubt be disillusioned in many respects, yet I think you'll find your experience worthwhile, despite the fact that your best efforts in trying to serve the public will be more or less thankless and often misunderstood.[1]

Two other newcomers, Sam H. Bellman in the house and M. J. Galvin, a young senator from Winona, later recalled that Stockwell was not a bystander. Neither felt that age impeded him. "In the 1930s," said Bellman, "I had the opportunity to serve with him in the Minnesota House and I sat next to him in my first session. All listened when he spoke . . . He had a calm, collected way of thinking. As a speaker he was quiet. But he had the facts and people listened." Bellman also remembered that Stockwell went afield when he saw a need, and he harked back to Stockwell's appearance at a huge public barbecue near Lowry Bridge: "In those

days Farmer-Labor ward clubs were integral to the party structure. Our club had been given eight steers by a man who couldn't
afford to feed them. Fifteen thousand people came. Stockwell
spoke even though the gathering was outside his district."

Galvin did not agree that Stockwell spoke quietly: "He
always talked loud enough so that everyone could hear. Some
thought he was a shouter. He sat in the back and participated in
all the welfare discussions. He was known to be sincere. Some of
his opponents on the utility issues sought to belittle him."

Carl Erickson, who served with Stockwell two years later,
held a different view. Adversaries on the issue of selectivity of risk
by insurance companies, the men held few close conversations.
Stockwell gave Erickson the feeling he was old: "He didn't take an
active role in the 1937 and 1939 sessions. He was not on his feet
making speeches."

When Olson, thirty-six years younger than Stockwell,
returned to the capitol in January to begin his fifth year as governor, he was suffering serious health problems. He had recuperat-
ed from an incapacitating attack of ulcers in the summer of 1931,
but his health began deteriorating again early in 1934. He spent
more and more time at a retreat near Gull Lake. His physical
decline was particularly noticeable during the 1934 campaign. In
the 1932 campaign he had worn out subordinates with his killing
pace, but he finished the 1934 campaign "on nerve alone." By his
account he didn't spend a single day in 1935 entirely free from
pain.[2]

Return to the legislature for Stockwell at a time when the
conservative coalition made up a majority of the house meant loss
of chairmanship of the Committee on Public Domain. It also signaled yet stronger opposition to oft-introduced favorite measures
such as his power bill. Return for Olson meant confrontation. Both
houses stood poised, determined to block him. But when the conservative coalitions heard his opening address to the legislature,
determination turned to rage. Challenging all they stood for, Olson
managed to endorse every radical panacea the Farmer-Labor party
had ever advocated, including public ownership of key industries.
The legislature had expected militancy, but nothing like this.[3]

Olson's abandonment of the moderate stance that saved his
campaign has since puzzled many. Why antagonize? Why invite
hostility? In Mayer's view, Olson did not mind the prospect of a
standoff:

It relieved him of the responsibility for implementing a platform
which had bred discord in the party and violated his own stan-

dards of practical reform. It permitted him to advocate whatever he deemed politically advantageous without assuming the risks of fulfillment. And it enabled him to transfer the blame for mounting deficits and tax levies to other shoulders.[4]

The outlook for legislative achievement was grim except in one area—the public appropriation of funds for relief. Here Olson had wide outside support. The public by this time had come to accept relief appropriations as a government responsibility. Roosevelt's administration established a policy of making federal funds available to states, provided the states supplied part of the outlay. It was one thing to harass Olson by blocking social legislation, but to refuse appropriations where refusal meant shutting off federal aid was political suicide. Thus 1935's legislative appropriations, totaling $43,932,987.74, were the highest ever made in the history of the state to that time.[5]

In addition to supporting the governor's request for appropriations along with most members, Stockwell did what he could to further relief in other areas. Typical was his sponsorship of a measure to promote the public welfare by providing low-cost housing (HF615) and of a proposal prohibiting the maintenance of actions for deficiency judgments in all cases where real estate mortgages were foreclosed by sales of property (HF309). The bills died in committee. His power bill (HF84) lost again, as did a renewed attempt to gain repeal of the Brooks-Coleman law (HF754) and his proposal for a constitutional amendment permitting initiative and referendum (HF82). With Sam Bellman, he introduced another public ownership measure that would have authorized cities, villages, and towns to acquire, construct, own, operate, maintain, and lease public utilities (HF1015). The Committee on Municipal Affairs returned it to the authors.

On issues of conservation, Stockwell met with more success. HF1581, a Public Domain Committee proposal, called for the establishment of thirteen new state forests. The house adopted it by near unanimous vote (ninety-three to one) and it was enacted as Chapter 372, Laws of Minnesota, 1935. But HF686, filed along with several others on the Public Domain Committee, authorizing the Commissioner of Conservation, by proceedings in the district court, to establish and maintain uniform stages of water in lakes and other bodies of water in Minnesota, was referred to the full Public Domain Committee, where it died.

Stockwell was not alone in such defeats; Farmer-Laborites were thwarted all along the line. In Mayer's view,

The dismal record of deadlock reflected little credit on either side. Beyond extending the mortgage moratorium two years, exempting household goods and farm machinery from the personal property tax and authorizing thirteen new state forests, the legislature accomplished nothing noteworthy.[6]

Noteworthy as a sign of the times, however, was Olson's request, carried out by Stockwell and Representative Roy W. Wier, for the introduction of a concurrent resolution (HF1729) opposing the spread of fascistic, un-American doctrines in Minnesota and elsewhere in the United States. The house took no action. Perhaps the tabling of this resolution was attributable in part to the undercurrent of anti-Semitism that would lead to Sam Bellman's defeat for reelection in 1938.

By early 1935 it was widely believed that Olson would run for the U.S. Senate the following year. He would have served six years as governor, and a Senate seat would free him of the thankless task of mediating intraparty disputes and contending with patronage demands. Furthermore, he had a hearty dislike for the incumbent, Republican Thomas Schall, who would be running for reelection. The feeling was mutual. The Senate looked especially appealing, and Roosevelt's backhanded invitation to Washington seemed to assure a warm welcome.

Who should succeed him as governor? Hjalmar Petersen, lieutenant governor who served two terms in the legislature, had the experience. He was eager. Party insiders of radical bent disliked Petersen. He was cold if not pompous. Worse, he was independent and could not be counted on to heed their advice. Their choice was Elmer Benson, a progressive forty-year-old banking commissioner, an amiable man of limited experience. He had never been elected to any office, but he would take their advice.[7]

Olson formally announced his candidacy for the Senate at the end of the summer, remaining neutral as to choice of a successor.

On December 22, 1935, fate interceded. Senator Schall, who was blind, was killed by a hit-and-run driver while crossing a street in Washington. His death abruptly changed the political mix. Olson declared he would not appoint himself or resign to permit Petersen to appoint him; he wanted the people to speak. Benson supporters saw an interim appointment to the Senate as virtually guaranteeing Benson's election to the governorship in November, and they frantically sought to persuade Olson to name him to the vacancy. While not ruling him out, Olson did not wish to appoint anyone as inexperienced as Benson. He vacillated between Stockwell, state senator Victor Lawson, and former congressman Henry Arens, pioneer Farmer-Laborites with long records of unselfish devotion to the party.[8]

Rebuffed, the Benson supporters did not give up. Counting on their ability to persuade Olson to name their man, they went so far as to prepare a special edition of the Farmer-Labor party newspaper, *The Minnesota Leader*, headlining the appointment of Elmer Benson to the Senate. The paper was sent to distribution points throughout Minnesota. C. D. Johnston, managing editor, unsuccessfully tried three times to reach Olson by telephone to clear the announcement. On orders from superiors, Johnston released the paper on the morning of December 27.

Olson, unaware of the preemption, had finally decided on Vince Day, his former secretary recently appointed to the bench. Day resisted, suggesting others, but then he relented. Poised to announce his choice to the press on December 27, Olson learned about the special edition heralding Benson's appointment. According to Olson's biographer, George H. Mayer, "When his eye caught the *Leader* headline, he turned white and paced up and down a full five minutes. Finally, in glacial tones, he said, 'Get that son-of-a-bitch on the phone.'"

Abe Harris and his cohorts had erased Olson's options. If he disavowed the announcement, he would splinter the party. He simply did not have the stamina to seek to rebuild the party in the days ahead. Olson capitulated, appointing Benson.[9]

On December 31, 1935, the Mayo Clinic announced in a terse bulletin that Olson had undergone major abdominal surgery. There was no mention of malignancy, but after Olson's release from the hospital, his health rapidly declined. Loss of weight revealed the seriousness of a condition he himself was unwilling to accept. Tenaciously he directed affairs of state and party during a period when pleas arose from the left to convert the Farmer-Labor party into a national third party. Olson would have been the logical presidential candidate of such a party, but he resisted the draft and instead supported Roosevelt as he had in 1932.[10]

In early August, drastically ill, Olson was driven from Gull Lake, where he had been trying to recuperate, to the Mayo Clinic in Rochester. News that Roosevelt would make a special trip to visit him in Rochester on August 31 cheered him. On Saturday, August 22, 1936, Governor Floyd B. Olson died of pancreatic cancer at age forty-five.[11]

Violet Sollie has recalled learning of his death:

The 1933 legislative session passed Minnesota's first income tax and I went to work in the new income tax department. The liberals lost the 1934 legislative election and the 1935 legislature passed an omnibus tax bill which included a sales tax that the governor vetoed. It also passed a bill for a constitutional amendment which would abolish the state's right to levy property taxes, and this amendment was not subject to the governor's veto, and was designed to force a sales tax. Mr. Stockwell told me early that year, if I did not want to see a sales tax I had better get busy in marshalling arguments against this amendment—Amendment No. 2 in 1936—otherwise known as the Youngquist amendment. I did, and I campaigned vigorously against it, and I had been out speaking against it on August 22, 1936 the day Olson died, and was out again the next day, Sunday, at a picnic held near Rochester. When I went to work on August 24, I found the office was closed—all state offices were closed—and with some of my co-employees, one of whom had a car, three or four of us drove out to see Mr. Stockwell. I think by this time we had feared Olson's death, but we were young and we were devastated. Mr. Stockwell was like a rock. He disapproved of the closing of state offices but allowed little work would probably have been done. He said he had seen many good people die but one had to go on—and he remarked at least we could be part of the roadbed over which one day great movements would travel. He impressed us that morning, and I continued the campaign against the Youngquist amendment and we staved off a sales tax for Minnesota for a generation (until 1967).[12]

References

1. *St. Paul News*, January 10, 1935.

2. Mayer, *Floyd B. Olson*, pp. 78, 143-145, 289-291.

3. Mayer, *Floyd B. Olson*, p. 259.

4. Mayer, *Floyd B. Olson*, p. 258.

5. Mayer, *Floyd B. Olson*, pp. 266-268; Hitchcock, *Minnesota Legislature, 1935*, p. 18.

6. Mayer, *Floyd B. Olson*, p. 272.

7. Mayer, *Floyd B Olson*, pp. 280-283.

8. Mayer, *Floyd B. Olson*, pp. 284-286.

9. Mayer, *Floyd B. Olson*, pp. 286-288. See also Charles B. Cheney's account in the *Minneapolis Journal*, March 10, 1936. Mayer does not suggest Olson knew in advance of the preparation of a special edition of *The Minnesota Leader* announcing Benson's appointment to the Senate. Steven Keillor's account is more charitable towards the "King Makers." (Mayer's Chapter 7 is entitled "The Spoilsmen Turn King Makers.") He writes that the Benson backers—Abe Harris, George Griffith, Joseph Poirier, and Roger Rutchick—apparently persuaded Olson to permit advance preparation of the special edition of the *Minnesota Leader*, provided that Olson give final approval before publication. Keillor believes the real explanation is that Olson, in poor health and awaiting surgery, had allowed the lobbying for Benson to get out of control, thereby allowing Benson's backers to feel convinced of victory, which they innocently announced in the *Leader*. See, Keillor, *Hjalmar Petersen*, pp. 124-125. Gieske's view is close to Mayer's. He called the plan a conspiracy. *Farmer-Laborism*, pp. 212-215.

10. Mayer, *Floyd B. Olson*, pp. 289, 295-297.

11. Mayer, Floyd B. Olson, pp. 300-301.

12. Violet Sollie to William P. Everts, March 28, 1988. Thelma Selander was among those who drove out to see Stockwell. She knew him to be a friend of youth in the region—"he was their mentor"—but had not previously met him. She said, "This was one of life's vignettes. It was not 'Nice to meet you.' It was—the facts. He put things in perspective. I knew I was in the presence of wisdom. He generated this feeling in me; I sensed this wisdom."

Chapter 31

Descent

O lson's death brought forth an extraordinary outpouring of public grief. Much as the nation would plunge into mourning when Franklin Roosevelt died in April 1945, Minnesota mourned in August 1936. The common man had lost his champion. What did the future hold? Where to turn? What to do? At least one could pay respects. Thousands of Minnesotans stood in a line more than a mile long, inching forward to file past Olson's bier in the rotunda of the capitol. Thousands jammed the Minneapolis auditorium to hear Wisconsin Governor Philip La Follette's funeral oration. Thousands clustered along the funeral route to Minneapolis's Lakewood Cemetery.[1]

Hjalmar Petersen (left), detail of painting by Carl Bohnen, 1937. Elmer A. Benson (above), 1936. (Courtesy of the Minnesota Historical Society)

Lieutenant Governor Hjalmar Petersen became Minnesota's twenty-third governor. Even as he was sworn in he knew he could serve but four months because Benson, as calculated by party insiders, had won Farmer-Labor endorsement and gained the party's nomination for governor in the primary. Following a bitter party contest, Petersen had been forced to settle for nomination as railroad and warehouse commissioner.

Hostility between Petersen supporters and the Benson camp did not subside with Petersen's elevation to governor. Instead, hostility mounted, leading to a split in Farmer-Laborism that would steadily widen. Many observers saw the split as an opportunity for Democrats and Republicans to improve on their 1934 showings at the polls and perhaps even regain control of the executive branch. Optimism was not warranted, for Minnesota was still in mourning. Devoted Olson followers saw a vote for Olson's party, cast in the quiet of a voting booth, as a final tribute to the man they so admired. Another factor contributing to the party's success in the November elections was the platform—more moderate than in 1934 and requiring no embarrassing reinterpretation. Many who had left the ranks rejoined. Roosevelt was winning in a landslide, and the surge helped the liberal candidates in Minnesota from Benson on down. In a surprising, highly questionable move, the Democratic candidates for governor and U.S. Senator withdrew entirely.[2]

Roosevelt received 698,811 votes in Minnesota to Republican Alf Landon's 350,421. Ernest Lundeen, Farmer-Laborite, defeated Republican Theodore Christianson in the U.S. Senate race with 663,363 votes to Christianson's 402,404. Five Farmer-Labor congressmen were elected. Benson defeated Republican Martin A. Nelson with 680,342 votes to Nelson's 431,841. Hjalmar Petersen, with 557,614, polled more votes in the contest for railroad and warehouse commissioner than his Republican and Democratic opponents combined.[3]

The Thirty-second District gave Stockwell a resounding endorsement, with the largest number of votes he ever received: Stockwell 16,983 (elected), Henry G. Young, 13,435 (elected), Maurice O. Jacobson 13,305, and Otto D. Nellermoe 10,412.[4]

Benson, once in office, presented the legislature with thirty major proposals, "an omnibus undertaking which was an outline for a beginning state social welfare system." Except for Stockwell's long-standing public ownership plan for electric power and a call for public ownership of a cement plant and liquor dispensary, Benson sought relatively modest reforms—of a sort that other liberal state governments were then pursuing. Within two weeks some seventy-five bills were introduced in the legislature to carry out Benson's program. But given the brevity of the session, the conservative makeup of the senate, and Benson's political inexperience, the outlook for adoption of his agenda was not promising. Some of his proposals were enacted, including fair trade legislation, extension of the mortgage moratorium, workmen's compensation, aid to dependent children, a teachers' tenure bill, and reduced farm loan interest rates of four percent. Rejected or mired in committee were an anti-lobbying bill, an income tax on the mining industry, a bill calling for return to the practice of party designation of legislators, a state Wagner Act patterned after the National Labor Relations Act to guarantee the right to organize and bargain collectively, civil service reform, a loan-shark bill, most welfare legislation, and all state ownership proposals. A relief bill and compromise tax bill were adopted in special session.[5]

Stockwell, who held a near-proprietary interest in much of the program, supported and furthered most but not all of it. He continued to oppose the idea of party designation of legislators. Vince Day credited him with enactment of the teachers' tenure law. Among the measures he sponsored in line with Benson's recommendations was a bill to facilitate municipal ownership of public utilities, defined to include street railways, bus transportation systems, telephone systems, waterworks, artificial or natural gas works, electric light, heat or power works, public docks, union depots and terminal systems, ice plants, stone quarries, and public markets. Stockwell explained to the Municipal Affairs Committee of the house that his proposal would eliminate a multiplicity of elections under present laws to acquire and operate public utilities. Under city home-rule charters, a majority vote of sixty percent or more was necessary to acquire a public utility. Under Stockwell's bill, a simple majority would suffice. Citing Minneapolis's experience, Stockwell charged:

> We had been so unmercifully gypped, bled and tortured by the machinations of the Minneapolis Gas Light Company, we felt there ought to be relief from that. So former Mayor Anderson appointed a committee to draft a bill to cover the situation in Minneapolis and throughout the state.[6]

Heated debate followed. Northern States Power Company led the opposition, claiming that home-rule charters, which enabled cities to conduct their own business, would be abrogated in every community in the state under the provisions of Stockwell's bill. The proposal was killed in committee.

Benson's program called for civil service reform, but Benson did not work wholeheartedly for enabling legislation. He seemed unable to cope with the patronage problem, concededly a thorny issue that had proved troublesome for Olson from the earliest days, when hard-working volunteers felt entitled to take over state jobs regardless of the competence of incumbents.[7] When Petersen succeeded Olson, he contributed to the patronage problems Benson would inherit by making a number of independent appointments without consulting the party professionals. This show of independence worsened the party split, and civil service reform got nowhere under Benson. Some observers attributed the defeat of his proposed reform plan to his inability to work with key legislators. Gieske offered another explanation: "Veteran Farmer-Labor legislator S. A. Stockwell (a socialist) and Hjalmar Petersen declared Benson had doomed civil service reform with the questionable insistence that the act take effect one year after passage, or in sufficient time to 'grandfather in' as many Farmer-Labor replacements as possible."[8]

Rightly or wrongly during Benson's administration, Minnesota voters gained the impression that a corrupt political machine had achieved domination of the Farmer-Labor party for the sake of patronage. The impression was bolstered by a practice whereby Farmer-Laborites holding state jobs were required to pay three percent of their salaries to the party war chest—funds to be used to publish the *Farmer-Labor Leader* (party newspaper later published under the less partisan title of *Minnesota Leader*) and finance a weekly radio broadcast.[9]

Benson's decisive election victory simply did not lead to strong, effective leadership. Grim, strained, seldom relaxed, his personality proved a political liability. He lacked Olson's easy way with rich and poor alike. Chrislock cites an example:

> The marked difference between Olson and Benson is aptly expressed in an often-repeated tale, possibly apocryphal but nevertheless illuminating. It tells of a businessman discussing militant Farmer-Labor rhetoric shortly after the 1936 election. He complained that "Floyd Olson used to say these things but this son of a bitch believes them."[10]

The fortunes of the Farmer-Labor party sank along with Benson's popularity. Even before Benson took the oath of office, Petersen let it be known he would seek to oust him in 1938. In particular, two disturbing factors, each disruptive, worked in Petersen's favor.

First, according to Carl Erickson, three Jewish Farmer-Laborites ran the state of Minnesota—Abe Harris, editor of the *Minnesota Leader*; Art Jacobs, secretary to the speaker of the house who reportedly controlled the house and told Farmer-Laborites how to vote; and Robert Rutchick, secretary to Governor Benson. In a wave of anti-Semitism, these men became targets of Petersen supporters; the anti-Semitism fueled hostility against Benson as well as the triumvirate. Although Petersen himself was not guilty of slander, the ugly charges inured to his benefit in the 1938 primary.[11]

Second, the infiltration of Communists damaged the party. Experience had taught Olson to cope with that problem, but Benson believed that redbaiting was a thing of the past, and he did not address it promptly or decisively. Voters gained the impression that the Farmer-Labor party had been taken over by extreme radicals. The impression would be bolstered on the eve of the 1938 election when the House Committee Investigating Un-American Activities, or Dies Committee as it came to be known, took testimony from ten Minnesotans, including Violet Sollie, about Communist activity in the Farmer-Labor party.[12]

Gieske has declared in *Minnesota Farmer-Laborism* that "if posterity demands a date" marking Farmer-Laborism's decline and fall, the date must be April 4, 1937.[13] The day began with a protest march on the capitol. Militant John Bosch engineered the protest, recruiting marchers from Farmer-Labor clubs and a radical group known as the People's Lobby. Hundreds of persons, frustrated with what they deemed the legislature's unwarranted delay in taking action on remedial legislation, saw the senate committees as especially obstructive. They believed "rattling legislative cages" would benefit the governor. Benson gave them a send-off in which he faulted reactionary legislators for, among other things, blocking his tax program. Thoughtlessly he added, "It's all right to be a little rough once in a while." Little happened during the day except for speeches, mostly moderate. Late in the day after many had left, Communists and other extremists took over. They burst through a locked door and poured into the room where the senate tax committee was in session, frightening many senators. At about five o'clock, some two hundred extremists preempted the senate chamber. Only after an appeal from Benson at 9:30 the next morning did they leave. Benson told the demonstrators they had "done a good job."[14]

Carl Erickson, apparently not mindful of Stockwell's respect for democratic institutions, gave this version of the events:

Tacticians of the Farmer-Labor party, including Harris, Jacobs, and Rutchick, had formed the People's Lobby. They picked up bums to march on the capitol. S. A. Stockwell was in support of this. These people took over the legislature for a day—a regular day. This was supposed to be democracy at work. They spent the afternoon in the senate, threatening and harassing senators, while demanding them to "Bring out these bills." At two o'clock in the morning I went to the capitol. There I saw Governor Benson and Abe Harris. They were concerned the situation was getting out of hand. They told the sitdowners they had better go home. There was defecation on the floor of the senate chamber.

Benson and Farmer-Laborism never recovered.

The legislature had enacted a state income tax law in 1933, but mining companies were exempt because the industry was subject to a modest occupation tax expressly tailored to cover the mining of iron ore. Benson, dissatisfied, called on the legislature to extend the income tax to the industry. The regular 1937 session proved to be another chapter in the industry's history of escaping payment of its fair share of taxes.

During the first quarter of the century, session after legislative session became a battleground on the mining tax issue. Several times tonnage tax bills were passed, only to receive gubernatorial veto. When the legislature appeared to have the votes to pass a significant tax measure, members who had been counted on for support would absent themselves or vote against it. Finally came the breakthrough. To Carl J. Buell goes credit for ending the industry's immunity. He took his case directly to the people. Armed with a list of the members of the house and senate who consistently furthered the companies' attempts to gain special treatment and another list of those in support of equitable taxation for all business enterprises, he traveled up and down the state, in season and out, urging ouster of the industry's pawns. His proposal was the placement of a tax on iron ore before it was shipped by vessel to blast furnaces in the East, a passage that in the past had left Minnesota both scarred and empty-handed. He contended a tax should be placed on the value of the ore at the mouth of the mine less stipulated costs of bringing it to the surface. He also proposed a parallel plan of taxing royalties received by the owners of mining properties. In a very real sense he sought adoption of at least a measure of the single-tax doctrine that he and Stockwell had espoused all their lives.[15]

In 1921, Buell's persistence was rewarded. The legislature adopted the proposal he had conceived, which came to be known as the occupation tax, that is, a tax on the business of mining, with the enactment of a law levying "an occupation tax equal to 6% of the valuation of all ores mined or produced in addition to all other taxes provided for by law."[16] As noted earlier, a companion bill taxing mining royalties failed to pass in 1921 but became law in 1923. No sooner had the 1921 law gone into effect than Farmer-Labor members of the legislature began talking about raising the tax from six to ten percent, but the proposal was crushed in committee. A bill to that effect was introduced at the 1923 session, but little was done because at that time an awaited decision of the U.S. Supreme Court, which ultimately would uphold constitutionality of the occupation tax, had not yet been handed down.[17] In 1925 Stockwell proposed an increase in the tax from six to ten percent, but his proposal was crushed in committee. The tax remained at six percent for the next ten years. When new sources of revenue were urgently needed in 1935, Olson recommended an increase in the occupation and royalty taxes to fifteen percent. The legislature passed an omnibus tax bill that would have raised the amount to eight percent, but Olson vetoed it because it contained a three-percent sales tax that would have fallen heavily on those least able to pay. In his view, eight percent was too favorable to the mining industry.[18]

The 1937 session was one of bitter controversy about taxes, particularly mining industry taxes. The house demanded a jump from six to ten percent in occupation and royalty taxes, while the senate refused to go higher than nine percent for the first year and eight percent thereafter. There was a push to put mining companies under the income tax law, but, by April 23, when the regular session ended, both sides had given up on the idea.[19] Benson called for a special session to begin on May 24. Two months were spent wrangling over taxes and the size of a badly needed relief bill. Finally, on July 20, 1937, an accord was reached on the mining question. HF75, covering the occupation tax, and HF76, relating to royalties, raised taxes to ten percent for 1937 and eight percent thereafter. Representative Theodore S. Slen, chairman of the house conferees, said that while the compromise was not what the house wanted, he believed it was the best that could be obtained.[20]

The house voted a hundred yeas and one nay to pass HF75. Stockwell was the holdout.[21]

Ralph Youngdale, historian and one-time editor of the *Minnesota Leader*, was a close friend of Governor Benson. In 1985 the author asked Youngdale whether he might seek from Governor Benson any special recollections of Stockwell. Youngdale called on him in the hospital and reported back that Benson praised Stockwell, but there was one thing he just couldn't understand: "He voted against our bill during the special session of 1937 to raise taxes on the iron ore companies. I never could figure out why he did that."[22]

Governor Benson died at age eighty-nine on March 13, 1985, two days after Youngdale's visit.[23]

In the spring of 1937, while Benson's program foundered, Petersen campaigned against him, and the Farmer-Labor party was breaking open, one particularly gladsome event took place. On March 30 the Stockwells were honored at a testimonial banquet at the Curtis Hotel in Minneapolis, commemorating "Fifty Golden Years of Valuable Service to Mankind." The dinner was held under the auspices of the Federation of Progressive Clubs. Sponsoring organizations included the Business and Professional Men's Club of Minneapolis, Social Science Study Club, Saturday Lunch Club, Men Teachers Federation, Minneapolis Women Teachers Federation, Social Workers Club, Social Relations Club, Unitarian Women's Alliance, Federation of Arts and Professions, Minneapolis Theatre Union, Vacation Month League, League for Political Progress, Women's Minneapolis Artists Union, Cooperative Oil Association, Emergency Teachers Association, Women's International League for Peace and Freedom, and the Amalgamated Clothing Workers Union.

More than a thousand attended. John P. Devaney, former chief justice of the Minnesota Supreme Court, was master of ceremonies. Benson was the principal speaker; Petersen and two Supreme Court justices were among the guests of honor. Judge Day was there and so was Abe Harris. Elizabeth Stockwell Everts and Charlotte Stockwell Baker took the train out from Boston. Other relatives came from afar. The Saturday Lunch Club arrived en masse and presented the Stockwells with a portrait of Albert painted by Cameron Booth.[24] Speakers included Jack Kurtz, M.D., president of the Federation of Progressive Clubs, and Clara Ethyl Dickey Parsons of the Women's International League for Peace and Freedom. Walter Stockwell, who declined to attend the dinner honoring his brother on his seventieth birthday, deigned to come this time, as well.[25]

Vivian Thorp of the *Minneapolis Journal* was not among the speakers, but, it seems clear, in her column of the day before that she spoke for the guests:

Friends of State Representative and Mrs. S. A. Stockwell will honor them at a dinner tomorrow night and honor themselves in so doing. If I were asked to pick the two "first citizens" of Minneapolis, my choice would fall on these two fine people. There seems to be so many things which make them the logical candidates for that position, which they would undoubtedly vigorously disclaim. One guesses that they would disclaim such a title for the reason that through all their long years in this community they have asked of it nothing for themselves—except the right to serve it . . .

A "covered wagon" pair, these two. They have always pioneered for the good of all the people. There is another kind of wagon with which neither of them has ever had any concern—the "bandwagon." They have never demeaned themselves by last minute climbing on the back seat of a popular winning cause. Critics might say that they were espousing lost causes—such criticism had no meaning for either of them. For them no cause was lost that was essentially right and just. What a record! It fills one with envy. And, last, if a personality may be permitted at this time, what a picture they present of the finest kind of marriage. All those years of undeviating loyalty together; of oneness of purpose; of give and take; of tolerance and understanding of each other's aims. Surely the Stockwells illustrate the real meaning of the phrase, "the marriage of true minds." Minnesota is fortunate to have them still with her and still working for her.[26]

In his remarks at the dinner, Stockwell retold the story of the fight for liberal causes in Minnesota from Ignatius Donnelly, Sidney M. Owen, and John Lind to Floyd B. Olson and Governor Benson. Looking ahead, he called for the election of legislators who would restore Minnesota's forests and lakes to their natural state.[27]

Political differences were cast aside on March 30, 1937. The banquet was a great surge of affection and respect for the Stockwells. The oneness of affection and respect for the guests of honor and Stockwell's reminder of the singleness of high purpose in the long fight for liberal causes in Minnesota restored solidarity to Farmer-Laborism on March 30, 1937. But the solidarity was not to last.

References

1. Mayer, *Floyd B. Olson*, p. 301.

2. Chrislock, *Progressive Era*, p. 196.

3. Gieske, *Farmer-Laborism*, p. 230.

4. *Legislative Manual, 1937*, p. 392.

5. Gieske, *Farmer-Laborism*, pp. 238-240.

6. *St. Paul Pioneer Press*, January 21, 1937.

7. Mayer, *Floyd B. Olson*, pp. 278-280; Gieske, *Farmer-Laborism*, pp. 142-149, 177-178, 182-182, 208-209.

8. Gieske, *Farmer-Laborism*, p. 240; see also Petersen release, March 13, 1937, Petersen papers, Minnesota Historical Society.

9. Chrislock, *Progressive Era*, pp. 196-197; Mayer, *Floyd B. Olson*, pp. 260-262, 264.

10. Chrislock, *Progressive Era*, p. 196.

11. Gieske, *Farmer-Laborism*, pp. 215, 245, 253-254.

12. Gieske, *Farmer-Laborism*, p. 271.

13. Gieske, *Farmer-Laborism*, p. 242. See also Valelly, *Radicalism in the States*, pp. 141-142.

14. Gieske, *Farmer-Laborism*, pp. 241-242.

15. Parsons, *Integration of the Saturday Lunch Club with the Liberal Movement in Minnesota*, p. 10; Leonard, *The Saturday Lunch Club of Minneapolis*, p. 14.

16. Chrislock, *Progressive Era*, p. 187. As Violet Sollie has pointed out, the main objection to the occupation tax was not so much that the tax would be measured by value of product less cost of producing it as that the base was fictitious. The so-called Lake Erie price—the price of ore "at rail of vessel" at lower lake ports—was the standard. Deducted from the Lake Erie price was the cost of transportation via the steel company's railroad from mine to Lake Superior port and cost of shipment by vessel to eastern ports. The result was value at the mine. Critics complained that the Lake Erie price was set arbitrarily between subsidiaries of the steel companies. A true free market did not exist. See letter from Violet Sollie to William P. Everts, July 26, 1990. See also Roy G. Blakey and Violet Johnson, "Minnesota Iron Ore Tax Valuation Problems," in *Minnesota Municipalities*, February 1941. The tax, small as it was, nonetheless yielded Minnesota considerable income. Jack N. Birk, longtime executive with the Duluth, Mesabi and Iron Range Railroad, has noted that in this pre-taconite era before vessels were self-unloading, ore was sold based on

natural iron ore at 51.5 percent iron. Ores usually varied from sixty-eight percent iron to fifty percent. Contained moisture was usually over six percent. Each ore shipment was priced by adjustment for iron and water content.

17. *Oliver Iron Mining Co. v. Lord, et al.*, 262 U.S. 172, 43 S.Ct. 526, 67 L.Ed. 929, decided May 7, 1923.

18. Hitchcock, *Minnesota Legislature, 1935-1936*, pp. 32-34.

19. *Minneapolis Journal*, April 23, 1937.

20. *St. Paul Pioneer Press*, July 21, 1937.

21. *House Journal-Extra Session 1937*, pp. 511-512. HF76 passed unanimously with 103 yes votes. Stockwell did not take part in the voting. See p. 513.

22. James M. Youngdale to William P. Everts, March 27, 1985.

23. *Minneapolis Star Tribune*, March 14, 1985.

24. *Minneapolis Tribune*, March 28, 1937. Cameron Booth's portrait of Stockwell is now in the possession of the Minneapolis Historical Society.

25. An unidentified newspaper clipping in the possession of the author contains a detailed account of a reception held for family and close friends at the Stockwell home as part of the golden wedding celebration.

26. *Minneapolis Journal*, March 29, 1937. The Stockwells' lives also filled Carol Laseski with envy. In a letter to the author on March 19, 1988, transmitting her unpublished paper about the abolition of military training at the University of Minnesota, she wrote: "As I poured through the records of the Minnesota Historical Society and read old newspaper clippings about your grandparents, I found myself longing to have been part of their just, progressive circle. What brave and visionary people!"

27. *St. Paul Pioneer Press*, March 31, 1937; *Minneapolis Star*, March 31, 1937.

Chapter 32

A Matter of Jurisdiction

The 1936 elections had produced the largest Farmer-Labor vote in the history, but two years later the triumph was abruptly reversed. The party suffered a catastrophic defeat. A bitter contest in the 1938 primary shattered what remained of party unity, virtually insuring defeat in November.[1]

Petersen yearned to be governor; he had waited impatiently for the chance, and he started his campaign for the primaries early. Publisher of a small town newspaper, the *Askov American*, he knew how to generate and disseminate news. His attacks began with broadsides against the party machine. He charged Benson with pitting class against class and claimed that he had encouraged Communist membership in the party. Petersen took no positive steps to stop the continuing racist slander against Benson strategists.[2] In the face of mounting attacks Benson became cautious. He retreated from public ownership issues and sought to shed his socialist image, shifting towards the center while defending his Farmer-Labor program. He deplored the mounting anti-semitism but refused to acknowledge any Communist problem.[3]

Benson retained the party's endorsement but just barely survived in the primary. Campaigning on a shoestring—Petersen had garnered $6,800 for the contest—Petersen almost won: Benson received 218,235 votes to Petersen's 202,205. And Petersen's attacks crippled Benson's chances for reelection.[4]

Harold Stassen, a thirty-one-year-old Dakota County attorney, was the beneficiary of Farmer-Labor infighting. As head of the Young Republican League, he challenged the Republican old guard in the primary, appealing to young progressives with the promise of extending New Deal reforms while shunning the more dangerous remedies of Farmer-Laborism. Stassen won the nomination with forty-seven percent of the Republican vote. The Democrats, who had lost by default in 1936, saw 1938 as a chance to come back; they nominated Thomas Gallagher.[5]

In the campaign against Benson, Harold Stassen, following Petersen's lead, charged the governor with corruption and scored him for Communist infiltration of his party if not adoption of Communist goals and methods. He promised immediate civil service reform. Petersen declined to endorse Benson, and Benson was unable to unite the Farmer-Labor party. Stassen overwhelmed him in the election with 678,839 votes (59.3 percent) to 387,263 (33.8 percent) for Benson. Gallagher received 65,875 votes (5.9 percent). The Democratic party in Minnesota had not yet come back to life, but its presence on the ballot hurt Farmer-Laborites. Republicans won all state offices and full control of the legislature while unseating four out of five Farmer-Labor congressmen.[6]

As Chrislock has pointed out, Benson should not bear all the blame. Several factors beyond his control weighed heavily against him. He inherited contentious problems from Olson, who failed to resolve continuing conflict between the faction that wanted an appointment policy based on merit and the spoilsmen who insisted that state jobs be allocated to deserving Farmer-Laborites. And the Farmer-Labor movement's radical image had been reactivated by the 1934 platform. Finally, there was a strong Republican surge across the nation. Republicans gained seventy-five seats in the House of Representatives and seven in the Senate. Governor Philip La Follette, who headed a progressive third party in Wisconsin, met like defeat.[7]

Stockwell was among the survivors. Voters in the Thirty-second District returned him to the legislature as the leading vote-getter. During the campaign, Stockwell spoke out in favor of Stassen's proposal for civil service for state employees, as Stassen later recalled, while noting that Stockwell was against the Communists but didn't support him for governor.[8]

Within days after the Thirty-second District constituents voted to return Stockwell, retention of his seat became an issue. It was a question of jurisdiction. The Stockwells had sold their house at 3204 East Fifty-first Street in the Thirty-second District in October 1937 and moved to 2103 Garfield Avenue, in the Thirty-fourth District. They retained a small portion of their land and a cottage facing adjacent Keewaydin Place.[9]

The Conservatives, or Independents as they became known, were in clear control of the new legislature. In the course of preliminary organizing for the pending session, grumbling arose in the conservative caucus about Stockwell's status. He was representing the Thirty-second District while residing in the Thirty-fourth. Some favored ouster or other challenge. Vivian Thorp leapt to his defense:

One is not favorably impressed with the attempts to dislodge on a technicality that veteran legislator and fine citizen S. A. Stockwell.

With all the talk of lack of reprisals, tolerance, consideration and so forth with which the new Minnesota deal has been inaugurated, such an effort to kick out Mr. Stockwell after his years of service to the state, as was promulgated by some members in the first conservative caucus, present a poor omen.

Mr. Stockwell first and foremost is a real liberal. Moreover he is the kind of liberal that Minnesota wants and needs. He has behind him many years of fine citizenship, which was publicly attested to by a very large group of Minneapolitans of all political faiths on an anniversary occasion last year.

Mr. Stockwell has served more than 20 years in the state legislature. During those years his constant efforts have been bent toward the good of this state, with strong emphasis on its conservation problems and with no emphasis on self-interest.

Most important of all, his district has once more declared its faith in him, and by its votes indicated that he is its choice for representative in the coming session. That should be enough to indicate the course the conservatives should take in this attempt to nullify his election, which, colloquially speaking, is "small potatoes," and few in a heap.

There are much more important things before the majority group in the coming legislature than this sort of thing, which, I am sure, will not meet with public approval.[10]

Political columnist Charles B. Cheney followed with a second article:

The Stockwell Case

If a contest is filed against the Nestor of the legislature, S. A. Stockwell, it will be an embarrassing question. For the House majority would have a technical case against Mr. Stockwell in the matter of his residence. He still owns his old home near Minnehaha Falls and claims that as legal residence, but has been living at 2109 Garfield Avenue, which is in another legislative district, the Thirty-fourth. There is no dispute about that. And under the state constitution, a member must live in the district which he represents. However, there has been latitude allowed in other cases in the matter of legal residence, and if ever it is to be granted, it should be in the Stockwell case.

Mr. Stockwell is now 81 years old, and began his service in the legislature in 1891. He has served in twelve regular sessions of the legislature. In the recent election, though the matter of residence was aired among the voters, they gave him the high vote. He ran some 2,500 ahead of the next man.

Since Vivian Thorp's recent article deploring the possible contest, other newspapers have taken it up. R. W. Hitchcock, who was a conservative leader in several sessions of the House, eulogizes him in the *Hibbing Tribune.*

"Mr. Stockwell has always been an insurgent," he says, "He supported the populist movement, the Nonpartisan League uprising, and has been active in the Farmer-Labor ranks from the very beginning of that organization.

"He is, however, a man of very independent mind, and has always been faithful to the principles he espouses. His voice has often been raised in the Legislature in vigorous condemnation of the action of his own party when its members have sacrificed principle for party.

"S. A. Stockwell has the respect of every member of the Legislature who ever served with him, and it is a good bet that no matter in which Minnesota district he lives he will serve out the term for which he was elected."[11]

Stockwell must have been especially gratified with the prompt display of fairness from Hitchcock, an erstwhile opponent. He did take his seat in the Fifty-first Session and was duly sworn in on January 3, 1939.[12]

All indications were that Stockwell would run for the house again in 1940, but events intervened to change his mind. Senator Andrew O. Devold of the Thirty-second District died in December 1939. On July 27, 1940, Stockwell served notice that he would not be a candidate for reelection to the house by filing for the unexpired portion of Devold's term, which extended to January 1, 1943. J. E. Foster, candidate for state senator, seized the chance to block him. The *Minneapolis Star* gave this account:

J. E. Foster, 2223 Minneapolis Avenue, candidate for state senator from the Thirty-second district, took legal steps today to keep the name of a rival candidate from the primary election ballot.

From the state supreme court he obtained an order directing County Auditor A. P. Erickson to show cause Monday at 9:30 a.m. why the name of S. A. Stockwell, veteran state legislator, should not be kept from the ballot listing.

Foster alleges Stockwell is not a resident of the Thirty-second district.

Stockwell explained today he lived at 3204 E. Thirty-first [sic] street until three or four years ago.

When he gave up that home, he said, he wanted to maintain

legal residence there "for political and other purposes" but finding that impossible, changed his residence to 3129 Keewaydin
Place, where he owns a cottage. A tenant is now living in the
cottage, he said, but he has kept some of his belongings there.

Since leaving E. Fifty-first street, he continued, he has lived
in various apartments, but despite moving around, he added,
"my legal residence, if I have one, is 3129 Keewaydin Place."[13]

On August 16, Stockwell appeared before a referee designated by the supreme court. The *Minneapolis Times* covered the
proceedings:

In a ringing voice that belied his 83 years of life, State
Representative S. A. Stockwell on the stand in his own behalf
yesterday testified it was his constant intention to maintain the
premises he owns at 3129 Keewaydin Place in the thirty-second
legislative district from which he now seeks election to the senate.

The hearing, before P. J. Ahern, court reporter for the District
Judge, Lars O. Rue, as referee designated by the supreme
court, ended late yesterday. The transcript must be ready for
presentation to the high court in St. Paul Monday morning
when arguments are to be heard.

Stockwell took the stand yesterday . . . Under examination by
Louis E. Lohman and Benjamin Drake, his attorneys, he
sketched his biography from the time he came to Minneapolis
in the late 70s. He told of his marriage to Maude [sic] C.
Stockwell in 1887, and of his activity in public affairs . . . Up to
20 years ago, he testified, he was in the insurance business.
Ten years ago he retired from business activity to "devote myself
to political and civic affairs."

The Keewaydin place premises, he testified in direct examination, he has considered as his legal residence, renting it on a
month basis to Miss Jenny A. Johnson. "She was to occupy it
temporarily," he testified. "There was no contract, no written
agreement, only my promise that she was to occupy it until we
wanted it."

Q. Has there been any change in that arrangement since that
time (1933)?

A. No.

Q. You retain a key to those premises?

A. Yes.

Q. Have you ever used the key to get into the house?

A. Many times, whenever the situation required it. I was to
have a garden there, and I did in 1936 and 1939. I kept tools
there and work clothes and they're there yet.

Q. In April, 1936, you and the Misses Johnson exchanged
residence for some days?

A. Yes.

Q. What was the purpose of this occupancy? . . .

A. To establish my legal residence.

Q. Did you wish to symbolize it as your residence?

A. Yes.

Attorneys introduced stationery, envelopes, and letterheads of the house of representatives to show that the residence address printed on the official Stockwell stationery was 3129 Keewaydin.

In cross-examination, J. J. Granbeck, counsel for Dr. Foster, brought answer from the witness that some mail did come to the 2103 Garfield Avenue address, as well as utility bills. Granbeck then directed his cross-examination to the residence exchange of April, 1938, when the Stockwells spent three nights and two days at the Keewaydin premises and the Johnsons spent the period at the Garfield address.

Q. Prior to that did you think you had legal residence there?

A. Well, I had some doubts about it.

Q. So up to April, 1938, you figured you didn't have legal residence there and so you and Mrs. Stockwell went there and spent three days and two nights. That's what you figured, wasn't it?

A. (Voice-rising)—I didn't figure anything of the kind. I had a legal residence there and no one ever heard me say I hadn't.

Q. Then why did you go there?

A. To further establish my right to that as a legal residence. I wanted to make it a rock-bottom cinch. I went there to cinch it so I would have a chance to come back at you fellows. [Mr. Drake had previously brought out that Foster knew nothing about Stockwell's residential location. Others led by J. P. Eckberg put Foster up to it. Eckberg got Foster to use Granbeck as his lawyer.]

Q. Does your going back to the Keewaydin residence depend on the health of Mrs. Stockwell?

A. To some extent. (He had earlier testified she was suffering from arthritis and there were more conveniences in the heart of the city than on the outskirts). It is my intention to go back there as soon as I can.

Q. You don't know how soon she's going to be well?

A. No. But she has made some progress in the past six months.

Q. You have no absolute assurance that at the end of the present legislative session (referring apparently to the session next January) you can move back?

A. No.

Lohmann then took the witness for re-direct examination.

Q. When you moved into the Garfield Avenue apartment was a lease discussed?

A. Yes, it was drawn up, but I didn't want to sign it.

Q. And when you moved to the Keewaydin Place premises for those three days and two nights, it was with the intent of letting it be known that you considered that your legal residence?

A. Yes.

Q. And that could be described as having publicized and symbolized your intention?

A. That's right.

"I guess that's all," said Lohman.

"No more questions," said Granbeck.

Ahern, pen in hand, looked up from his shorthand notebook with a smile and said, "Well, gentlemen, I guess now it's up to the supreme court."[14]

The record reviewed by the supreme court contained Stockwell's affidavit stating he had presented the facts about his living arrangements to the attorney general and asked the attorney general whether further action would be necessary to maintain his legal residence in the Thirty-second District. He was told it would not be necessary.

On August 21, the supreme court ruled that Stockwell was entitled to run for the state senate in the Thirty-second District. Printing of ballots for the September 10 primary could proceed. Stockwell, vindicated, said, "The decision gives me new heart. I served one generation as best I know, and I'm going to try to serve another in the same way."[15]

In the primary where two were to be nominated, Stockwell came in first with 6,757 votes, Young second with 5,173. Foster wound up a distant sixth with 1,011 votes. Young won the election on November 6, with 16,783 votes to Stockwell's 16,162.[16]

References

1. Chrislock, *Progressive Era*, p. 196.

2. Gieske, *Farmer-Laborism*, pp. 251-257.

3. Gieske, *Farmer-Laborism*, p. 256.

4. Gieske, *Farmer-Laborism*, pp. 264-268.

5. Gieske, *Farmer-Laborism*, p. 265.

6. Gieske, *Farmer-Laborism*, pp. 268-273.

7. Chrislock, *Progressive Era*, pp. 196-197.

8. *Legislative Manual, 1939*, p. 406.

9. Violet Sollie to William P. Everts, March 28, 1988.

10. *Minneapolis Journal*, November 17, 1938.

11. *Minneapolis Journal*, December 8, 1938.

12. *House Journal, 1939*, p. 3.

13. *Minneapolis Star*, August 9, 1940.

14. *Minneapolis Times*, August 17, 1940. For a transcript of the entire proceedings, see *J. E. Foster v. Al P. Erickson, County Auditor*, Supreme Court File No. 32676, 1940, Minnesota Historical Society.

15. *Minneapolis Star*, August 22, 1940.

16. *Minneapolis Tribune*, November 7, 1940.

Chapter 33

Final Days

S tassen's election marked the return of Republican ascendancy in Minnesota. The Republicans would remain dominant until 1954. But it was a new Republicanism, a brand unsettling to the old guard, that promised not to turn away from progressive and humanitarian reforms. Carrying this message, Stassen met with immediate success at the capitol. All of his proposals were enacted by the 1939 legislature, including a civil service system for state employees, a labor relations act, an anti-loan-shark law, and social security legislation. The occupation tax on iron ore was increased from eight to nine percent—not the ten per-

Governor Stassen with graduates of a naturalization class, ca. 1940. (Courtesy of the Minnesota Historical Society)

cent Stassen recommended or the twelve percent sought by the minority but nevertheless an increase. A 1939 poll showed that four-fifths of the voters approved his program.[1]

Running for reelection in 1940, Stassen defeated Hjalmar Petersen, who had at last prevailed in the primary to become Farmer-Labor candidate for governor, by nearly 200,000 votes. Stassen's popularity among voters exceeded that of Roosevelt, who led Wendell Wilkie by less than 50,000 votes in Minnesota. Already rising to national fame, Stassen gave the keynote speech at the Republican national convention that nominated Wilkie. Edward Murphy, the Democratic candidate for governor, received less than eleven percent of the vote.[2]

In 1942, Stassen again defeated Petersen decisively. John Sullivan, Democratic candidate, received less than ten percent of the vote. But, with World War II in full swing, Stassen felt another kind of patriotic duty. He did not complete his third term but resigned in April 1943 to enter the navy.[3]

Chrislock has pointed out that, in the face of contentions that the Farmer-Labor party disintegrated under Benson, it should be remembered that Petersen received more than a third of the vote in the three party races of 1940 and 1942.[4] Unquestionably, though, the Farmer-Labor party was weakened. An alliance or infusion was needed. The Democratic tide had been at low ebb for years; the party badly needed strengthening. In 1944, following extensive discussions within party ranks and with each other, the Democratic party and the Farmer-Labor merged to form the Democratic-Farmer-Labor party, or DFL. Hubert H. Humphrey was a principal architect of the merger. He and others, including Orville Freeman, who served as Minnesota's governor and then became U.S. Secretary of Agriculture, and Arthur Naftalin, historian and former Minneapolis mayor, believed that if Democrats and Farmer-Laborites could present a united front, chances of winning elections would be enhanced. Franklin Roosevelt was of the same mind. These men proved correct, and Minnesota politics now operate under a two-party system.[5]

Though the final days of the Farmer-Labor party were beset with infighting and excesses, these distressing events should not obscure the party's legacy. Russell B. Nye has acknowledged the party's lasting achievements:

> The Farmer-Labor party of Minnesota was the most successful third party in American history. It drew its strength from, and enlarged upon, the state's sturdy Populist tradition . . . Its foremost standard bearer, Olson, was unquestionably one of the

great leaders of radical political movements in the nation's history, holding together a tenuous coalition of political groups that together formed the Farmer-Labor party. The party brought about widespread citizen participation in political affairs and produced courageous leaders who crusaded for social justice. Its legacy includes not only the name of the Democratic-Farmer-Labor party but also the strong orientation of Minnesota voters toward social concerns, progressive reforms, high taxation for a high level of public services and, above all, the issue oriented and independent political tradition for which Minnesota is known.[6]

As his party faltered in its final years, so did Stockwell. Perhaps it was just as well he was not elected in 1940 to complete Senator Devold's term, which extended to January 1, 1943. He was approaching his mid-eighties, and he showed his age. His niece Eugenia Day Ganssle has recalled that near the end of his career he was too deaf to follow debate in the legislature. His constituents kept returning him to office just the same, she said. Althea Atwater remembered the time her son Pierce, a student at the University of Chicago, interviewed him concerning the role of third parties in American history. Albert gave garbled responses to easy questions as Maud sat silently by, never hurrying, never finishing a sentence or correcting him. On another occasion during a snowstorm, he fled out the front door to attend an imagined Saturday Lunch Club meeting, disappearing for hours. It was in this stage of life that he told Violet Sollie, though only once, "Sometimes I think we live too long." Sollie told the author about his despondence at one of their last meetings: "The country was at war. The League of Nations had proven powerless. The United States was not a member. Stockwell could see that civil liberties once again were in danger." In a letter, she pointed to the year 1940 as the beginning of his decline:

It was a sad occasion when Mr. Stockwell lost the 1940 election. War clouds were gathering. Mr. Stockwell no longer lived in the district, and was in his eighties, all of which contributed to his defeat. I had been discharged after Stassen became governor in 1939 and a new reorganization bill was passed which had replaced the old tax commission with a single commissioner of taxation. In the coming years I had been given space at the labor headquarters during the income tax filing season to fill out tax returns, and Mr. Stockwell stopped in to see me there occasionally. With the coming of the five day week, the Saturday Lunch Club had lost members and I no longer attended that. I remember him stopping during February or March of 1942. It was a cold day and he had lost his mittens and was annoyed with himself because he could not remember where he had mislaid them. I remember a feeling of sadness—like watching a once vigorous tree bending in the wind. This little giant, once so upright, was now helpless and showing his age. I was away in Washington when he died.[7]

Albert Stockwell died on April 17, 1943, from pneumonia after a four-month hospitalization. Close friend and longtime Stockwell family physician Aaron Friedell attended him through his illness. He was cremated at Lakewood Cemetery and thereafter, doubtless at his own request, his ashes were cast over Minnehaha Falls. A memorial service was held for him at the First Unitarian Society on April 23, Judge Vince Day presiding. Tributes were reminiscent of those made by friends on his seventieth birthday. Stockwell would have denied the kind things said of him at the memorial service as he had denied any justification for the tributes paid him on his birthday with these words:

> I am not conscious of having earned the right to be so generously lauded and commended. I have only done what I believed was right . . . I have not been born in vain if I have been the instrument in bringing together so many fine people. I thank you from the bottom of my heart. I wish it was true. I will do my best from this time henceforth to merit these kind expressions.

Stockwell, similarly, would have denied the accuracy of what Minneapolis attorney Gerald Friedell, son of Aaron, said of him. Friedell looked back at the glory days:

> Stockwell seemed to be the nucleus around which the rest of them assembled. They were the progenitors. From Stockwell and others in his group, the state, in a very real way, took its present, liberal bent.

But Stockwell always preferred to look ahead instead of back. Rather than tributes at any memorial service he would have favored recitation of the poem by Josiah Gilbert Holland that he had read to the members of the house when he moved to adjourn the 1933 session:

> Wanted
>
> God give us men; a time like this demands
> Stout hearts, clear minds, true faith, and ready hands.
> Men whom the lust of office will not kill,
> Men whom the spoils of office cannot buy,
> Men who possess opinions and a will,
> Men who have honor; men who will not lie.
> Men who will stand before a demagogue

And damn his traitorous flattery without winking.
Strong men, sun crowned, who live above the fog,
In public duty and private thinking.
For while the rabble with their thumbworn creeds,
Their loud professions and their little deeds
Mingle in selfish strife; lo! freedom weeps;
Wrong rules the land and waiting justice sleeps.
Mr. Speaker—I move that we now adjourn sine die.[8]

After Albert's death, Maud Stockwell continued to live at the apartment at 2103 Garfield Avenue, and she remained there, by herself virtually all the time, for the next fifteen years.[9] With both her daughters in Massachusetts, staying on alone to retain her independence would have been impossible without the devotion and care of her nephew Kingsley Day, eldest son of her sister, Mabel and the only one of the Day family to remain in Minnesota when the others moved to California. Kingsley was "just a saint," according to Eugenia Day Ganssle, his older sister: "He ran her affairs. No matter what he was doing, he would drop everything to help her out—to make a deposit, carry or move something, just to talk. Whatever it was she wanted, he would do." Kingsley's son, Gene, later living in Lake Minnetonka, aided his Great Aunty Maud in just the same way, she said.

Kingsley's daughter, Janet Tipton, later of Virgina, spoke of a special bond between "Aunty Maud" and her father: "He loved her very much, and they had such wonderful times together. They would talk for hours. She liked to challenge him, and he always took the bait."[10]

Maud Stockwell encountered numerous physical problems in her final years—worsening arthritis, broken bones and cracked vertebrae resulting from falls, and hospitalization for operations, including optional eye surgery when she was in her late eighties. "I may live five or six more years and I just won't face blindness," she told her daughters, who expressed concern abut the risks of an eye operation.[11] Despite these ailments, she allowed no letdown of spirit, no lessening of interest in public affairs, no abandonment of support for humanitarian causes. Her mind remained keen, and in spite of infirmities, she was always the participant, giving speeches, attending meetings, never failing to vote, seldom missing a Sunday at the First Unitarian Society, reading biographies, periodicals, and the newspaper as a form of continuing education. The lectern was ever her accouterment. In her mid-eighties, when Henry Wallace was running as the Progressive party's candidate for president (1948), Maud spoke up in public for him. But her support was critical, and she didn't hesitate to say that Wallace had been "too kind" to fellow travelers and Communists.[12] When nearly ninety, Maud was one of the leaders in a successful campaign to name a new Minneapolis junior high school in honor of Susan B. Anthony, pioneer crusader for the woman suffrage movement.[13] At age ninety-two, she gave a speech to the Minnesota section of the Women's International League for Peace and Freedom about the league's first president: "Reminiscences of Jane Addams." [14]

Maud Stockwell had scores of friends, mostly younger than she, during this stage of her life, and more than once she was heard to say how much she enjoyed conversations with her friends. Many of them belonged, as she did, to the Women's Alliance of the First Unitarian Society, its organization dating to 1881, when the society was founded. (Maud Stockwell had been president of the Alliance, 1938-1940.) The Alliance's primary objectives were to encourage an interchange of ideas social, economic, and religious, and to give service and support to the society and to philanthropic movements as might seem advisable.

Janet Salisbury, in a centennial pamphlet sketching the history of the Alliance, of which she is an active member, summarized its concerns, which matched Maud Stockwell's, in the fifteen-year period following the war:

> After World War II, the Alliance focused much effort and hope on the work of the United Nations. The 1950s brought its concern to Atoms for Peace, and at about the same time the Alliance became involved in the struggles for human rights in this country. Problems of civil liberties, the women's rights movement, and abortion rights or freedom-of-choice were in the forefront of its attention and action.[15]

Unquestionably the Alliance was a vital part of Maud Stockwell's life, particularly in her final years, by which time the society had moved to Mount Curve Avenue, not far from her apartment. The Alliance readily afforded companionship, intellectual stimulus, and joinder with kindred spirits in high calling. Maud was a beneficiary of the Alliance, and surely a contributor. One of the members, a longtime friend of Maud's, told Carl Storm, minister at the society, that she wouldn't dare stop subscribing to a current journal of public affairs because she would feel quite lost when having a conversation with Maud Stockwell.[16]

Maud Stockwell died on January 2, 1958, one day short of her ninety-sixth birthday, from complications following a cerebrovascular accident. Carl Storm conducted a memorial service for her on January 7 at the First Unitarian Society. In accordance with her instructions, Maud's body went to the University of Minnesota for whatever benefits might be derived from it for the extension of medical knowledge, thereafter to be cremated. In the course of his eulogy, Storm observed that such disposition was in keeping with her zeal for all human life and its advancement. Many years later, at the request of her daughters Elizabeth Stockwell Everts and Charlotte Stockwell Baker, William P. Everts, Jr., cast her ashes over Minnehaha Falls, freeing them from a vault at Lakewood Cemetery in Minneapolis. For Beth and Char, this made for Maud's symbolic union with their father, which "made everything right."

References

1. *Statehouse Review for 1939,* (Minnesota Legislative Research Bureau, St. Paul, 1939), pp. 135-136; Blegen, *Minnesota,* pp. 536-537; Chrislock, *Progressive Era,* p. 197.

2. Gieske, *Farmer-Laborism,* p. 295.

3. Gieske, *Farmer-Laborism,* p. 317.

4. Chrislock, *Progressive Era,* pp. 198-199.

5. Chrislock, *Progressive Era,* p. 199; *Minneapolis Star Tribune,* March 14, 1985. For a comprehensive account of events leading to the merger of the Farmer-Labor and Democratic parties, see John Earl Haynes, *Dubious Alliance: The Making of Minnesota's DFL Party* (Minneapolis: University of Minnesota Press, 1984).

6. Russell B. Nye, *Midwestern Progressive Politics,* as quoted in *Dictionary of American History,* 2: 490-492.

7. Violet Sollie to William P. Everts, March 28, 1988.

8. Josiah Gilbert Holland, *Wanted,* 1872. See Aalbu, *Minnesota Kaleidoscope of 1933,* p. 112.

9. On returning to Minneapolis from Washington, D.C., in the fall of 1943, Violet Johnson Sollie called on Maud Stockwell at her apartment and was surprised to hear her say "Come in" and to find the door unlocked. Maud Stockwell said she felt the dangers of being locked in and unable to get help outweighed the danger of an unfriendly person walking in on her. Violet Sollie to William P. Everts, March 28, 1988.

10. Janet Tipton to William P. Everts, June 27, 1993.

11. *Minneapolis Morning Tribune*, January 3, 1952.

12. *Minneapolis Morning Tribune*, May 16, 1949.

13. *Minneapolis Morning Tribune*, January 3, 1958.

14. A tape recording of Maud Stockwell's speech is available at the Minnesota Historical Society.

15. Janet Salisbury, *The Women's Alliance of the First Unitarian Society: A Centennial History, 1981*, is based on research by Mercedes Nelson. Maud Stockwell's interest in world affairs led to her membership in the Minnesota United Nations Association shortly after the war. A strong supporter of the United Nations from its infancy, she believed the United States erred in not channeling matters of import through the organization. See *Minneapolis Morning Tribune*, May 16, 1949.

16. From transcript of tribute by Storm at the memorial service for Maud Stockwell, a copy of which is in the possession of the author.

Chapter 34

Legacy

Albert Stockwell's legacy to Minnesota was perhaps more intangible than tangible. Few if any laws bear his name or sole imprint in the way TVA and the Norris-La Guardia Act are linked to Nebraska's Senator George W. Norris or the mortgage moratorium law is linked to Olson. The Stockwell power bill was never passed; the single tax is not the law of Minnesota. In the main, Stockwell's legislative achievements were combined efforts as in the case of his successful cooperative attempt to outlaw further power development and logging operations on state lands in the border lakes region. He was gifted in rallying colleagues to block measures deemed unjust, as he did upon returning to the House of Representatives in 1923 by quashing a proposal to eliminate tax-exempt bonds. And while his bill to eliminate capital punishment in 1897 was turned down, capital punishment was abolished in Minnesota in 1911. If his eloquence did not still echo in the house chamber of the new capitol building, at least the soundness of his reasoning was recognized. To take the stand and fight for its acceptance was to make a difference.

As Carl Chrislock noted, Sylvanus Stockwell has been identified with virtually every important reform movement since the 1890s.[1] With modesty, Stockwell had, upon Olson's death, consoled his friends with the assurance that "at least we could be part of the roadbed over which one day great movements would travel." But Stockwell was too humble. In truth his legacy soared far above the roadbed. His legacy was his example: commitment to high purpose, unwavering adherence to principle, absolute integrity. All men are created equal. He never gave up. He was the public servant that Josiah Gilbert Holland yearned for in the poem *Wanted.* Judge Arthur Le Sueur captured the majesty of his example in a

Saturday Lunch Club memorial resolution written May 1, 1943, for presentation to Maud Stockwell and for the records of the club:

> There was one common understanding among all who knew him—that Sylvanus A. Stockwell in his life and example was the very flame of civic virtue and goodwill to all men. He served the public good; he defended the common weal; he fought for human rights. Every cause which served the common man found in him intelligent understanding, never failing support and a compassionate sympathy. His was not the courage of desperation nor of anger, but was the courage of calm reason, based upon the sure foundation of his faith in human dignity. This faith in the right of every man to life, liberty and the pursuit of happiness never wavered. He set an example which we hope will long be remembered of the highest type of citizenship. He was a friend when a friend needed a friend—and his friends were legion.
>
> We express our sincere respect and admiration for this friend of man; this dreamer of great dreams and doer of great deeds, who during a long life had the rare courage and character to live and exemplify in his life the highest humanitarian principles known to man.

To read this resolution today is to hope that Stockwell's life may yet be an inspiring example of citizenship and public service for this and succeeding generations. It can be said with certainty he has touched some. His great grandson Robert Stockwell Everts spoke for his brothers Hamilton, John, and Ted when, on quitting college at age nineteen to work full time for Caesar Chavez and the United Farm Workers, he wrote:

> The Night Is Long, But Time Is Short,
> And There Is Work to Do.
> What is it, this thing we call life?
> Is it people? Is it love? Is it struggle?
> Can life be about men and women, and still be about napalm
>   deaths?
> Is it a universal harmony among human beings and nature?
> Or are hungry, lead-poisoned, innocent babies, and fleeing
>   refugees from a place called home, what we call life?
> Can it be both?
> Does one person, or nation of people, have the right to "guide"
>   another?
> Does that person or persons have instilled in him, or them, the
>   human right to live a better life than another, to make decisions for another?
> If nature has allowed such to happen, is there a responsibility

370

among all people, both the oppressed and the oppressor, to take it unto themselves to erase the inequalities?

Can we stand by, and make our way through life, perpetuating an unjust system, and still live the good life that it gives us, and not be condoning its injustices, all at the same time?

Can I feel love for my black, or brown, or red-skinned brother, and feel genuine support for him, and at the same time live the good life that he isn't living—BECAUSE he isn't living it, and be living with a clear conscience?

Or would this be a meaningless life of hypocrisy, a life in which I was fooling myself that I was doing my part, that I was a good human being?

Is not mere inaction a tacit approval of the exploitative policies of an oppressive system?

Will one less child starve if we simply just care?

Is it possible to be truly desirous of a more equal and just world, and at the same time reap the benefits of a society which have been harvested for us by another member of the same society?

Mustn't we all join in the harvest in order that we may all, in good conscience, reap the benefits of our joint efforts?

Can we only at times join the harvest, and the rest of the time reap the benefits, and profess to be sincere and to have done our part?

Or must we devote our lifetimes to the correction of the "mis-uses" of what nature intended this thing we call life, to be?

Will the change come if we do the caring and let someone else do the doing?

Is life about some having and others going without?

If it is not, whose responsibility is it to change the course of our present interpretation of this thing called life?[2]

References

1. Chrislock, *Watchdog of Loyalty*, p. 148.

2. Unpublished.

Searching the Boy

On June 16, 1984, I drove from Minneapolis to Anoka in a rented car, hoping to learn more about my grandfather's boyhood. Getting to Anoka was simple—too simple really. I would have preferred following Albert's footsteps at the same pace, along the old dirt road. I could avoid the main highway, and I chose instead the river road, a winding two-lane road fringing the west bank of the Mississippi. I drove below the speed limit.

What was the same and what was different from the days when Albert passed along the way? The gently rolling prairie? The clumps of elms and maples? Were there any early houses? One thing remained for sure—the Mississippi River. I crossed the Mississippi at Champlin, driving east over a bridge along the road leading to Anoka. A right-hand turn across a bridge spanning the Rum River brought me to the center of town. Main Street.

I knew my great grandparents, Silvanus and Charlotte Stockwell, were buried somewhere in Anoka, so I asked a man on Main Street about cemeteries. He thought Forest Hill Cemetery on Church Street was probably the one, so I drove back across the Rum, located the graveyard, and circled through it, peering at the names on the tombstones. There were more Scandinavian and German names than Yankee—this couldn't be it. I headed back to town. On the way, I spotted another, smaller, (Oakwood) cemetery on a rise to the left. I parked off Main Street and walked, almost as if beckoned, directly to the Stockwell gravesites:

Phoebe Stanton Bowdish
May 2, 1805-May 3, 1878

Rev. M. Mervin Bowdish
February 3, 1843-April 25, 1886

Silvanus Stockwell
March 23, 1824-March 27, 1910

Charlotte B. Stockwell
February 8, 1830-May 17, 1889

Nettie B. Stockwell
1868-1952

William W. Stockwell
1859-1925

I did not then understand precisely how all of these names were linked. But my mission was accomplished; I had looked back 150 years and was ready to move on. Next I found Jackson Street and the Catholic church, and in my mind's eye saw Silvanus Stockwell's first house. I drove to the Mississippi River and stood by the ferry landing Albert had used. I stood on the banks of the Rum, where he and young A. M. Goodrich had played—upper Mississippi counterparts of Tom Sawyer and Huckleberry Finn. Goodrich later recalled their favorite sport:

> I became acquainted with Mr. Stockwell in 1867 when he was 10 years old. I was seven. We played along the banks of the Rum River and one of the principal enjoyments of these days was playing on the logs that came down the river. Thousands of logs flowed down Rum River to the mills of Minneapolis to be sawed into lumber, and it was great sport to see who could stick on the longest when they were spinning around like mill wheels. Mr. Stockwell was pretty nimble on his feet even before he got into politics and in those log spinning operations, he sometimes went down, but he never stayed down.[1]

What was it like for Albert, a ten-year old boy in a pioneer settlement, to be looking ahead, pondering his future? What would he do with his life? What were the possibilities? The *Anoka Union* for Thursday, January 2, 1868, described some opportunities:

> According to our custom, we present in this New Year edition a review of the business, etc., of Anoka during the past year, 1867. To it we prefix a historical sketch of the town, and a description of its situation . . .
>
> The town is built on both sides of Rum River at its junction with the Mississippi eighteen miles above the Falls of St. Anthony. It is the county seat of Anoka County. A bridge costing $6,000 crosses Rum River connecting the two divisions of the town. The ground is high and undulating, thinly covered

with oak trees, of many years growth. There is room for indefinite extension. Both rivers here run clear and pure, and abound with excellent fish . . .

Being at the mouth of the Rum River, it is the natural outlet for the valley of the stream which is being rapidly settled. This embraces a splendid agricultural country and, further away, the finest and most accessible pines in the state. The product of these latter all come down the river through the town, giving great advantage to our saw and planing mills. Every foot of lumber sawed either at Minneapolis or St. Anthony must pass through Anoka on one or the other of the rivers, thus giving our lumbermen the first choice of all the logs. Besides this, our houses are perfectly safe, as was demonstrated by the experience of the past year. St. Cloud, Clearwater, Monticello, Dayton, Minneapolis, and St. Anthony lost nearly or quite all their logs in the July flood, besides having their mills and dams immensely damaged. At Anoka not a log was lost, and the 45,000 feet preserved in our boom furnished almost the sole supply of the state during the season.

This idea of the safety of our anchoring place for logs, combined with the excellent lumbering privileges, cheap shipment by railroad, cheapness of living, and the moral and enterprising character of the town, is rapidly turning the attention of capitalists to us. The logs can be stopped here, sawed and shipped by rail to Minneapolis, cheaper by several dollars per thousand feet than they can be floated thither by water including risk of loss. Seekers for investment in lumbering are discovering these facts and acting on them . . .

For Minnesota, Anoka is an old settlement. Geo. W. Branch laid his claim on the town site in 1854. The territorial road, located that year, crossed Rum River here, and his intention was to secure a good stand for a hotel. But others desiring to settle here, he was induced in 1853 to establish a town . . . The population increased continually. The dam was completed in the summer of 1853. For four successive years, portions of it were annually swept away by freshets, until 1857 a structure was attained, which has since resisted the pressure. During the war our record was bright, having responded to every call, and at its close more than one half of our voters had been in the army. The Indian massacres of 1863 did not reach this point and their only effect was to fill the town with refugees, which she furnished forces for the defense of other localities . . .

The St. Paul and Pacific Railroad runs through the place, giving easy access to St. Paul, 30 miles and Minneapolis, 18 miles east, and St. Cloud west. It crosses Rum River over a magnificent bridge with massive stone piers and abutments, erected during the past year at a cost of nearly $50,000. The Mississippi is navigable for fifty miles above, but steamboats have not run for two years owing to low water. Excellent public highways leading in every direction connect Anoka with neighboring towns. A telegraph along the line of the railroad, with an office at the depot, affords communication with all parts of the world . . .

Lines of Stages run from Anoka to Brunswick, Princeton and Sunrise, carrying passengers and mail. A rope ferry crosses the Mississippi, connecting Anoka with Champlin . . .

Anoka boasts of five elegant church edifices—Baptist, Episcopal, Catholic, Methodist, and Congregationalist. . . . With the Baptist, Congregational, Universalist and Methodist churches flourishing, Sunday Schools are connected, training the rising generation in the paths of virtue and religion . . .

The splendid new school building accommodates four schools and 280 scholars. The building is 48 x 56 feet on the ground, two lofty stories in height, with an elaborately ornamental entrance, and an elegant observatory at the top . . . Court house we have none as yet . . . Below we give an alphabetical list of persons and firms now in Anoka:

Architect—H. Covel

Attorney—M. A. Butterfield; R. C. Mitchell

Baker—M. E. Kellogg

Barber—S. C. Leland

Blacksmiths—Gray and Willard; E. A. King; Smith and Mulverhill; Cole and McGlaughlin

Booksellers—S. P. Starrett; Tichnor and Co.

Boots and Shoes—Kelly and Co.; J. McDonald, Cutter and Woodbury; J. H. Murphy and Ryan; Dickens and Boulter

Bricklayer—L. W. Hatch

Builders—Houston, Prescott and Co.; H. Covel; Remick and Burnham

Cabinet Makers—D. P. Craig; J. McKay

City Express—H. W. Sterling

Cooper—H. W. Noggle

Dressmakers—Mrs. D. P. Craig; Mrs. H. L. Howe

Drug Store—Ticknor and Co.

Dry Goods—J. J. Couchman; Dickens and Boulter; Cutter and Co.; E. S. Teller

Express Office—American; L. G. Browing, Agent

Fruit Trees—J. F. Blodgett; Lewis Martin, Agent; J. J. Valkenburg, Agent

Furniture—Sias, Pomeroy and Co.; D. P. Craig; J. McMay

Furs—Randolph and Fairbanks

Grain Dealers—Stein Brothers

Grocers—Richards and Curial; Cutter and Co.; Dickens and Boulter; Kent and Davis; D. Robbins, Morton and Co.; E. S.

Teller, Leland and Bro.
Gunsmiths—Braden and McCready; D. G. Miller
Hardware—E. T. Alling and Co.; Church and Ives
Hotels—Kimball House, J. Eastman, Prop.; Anoka House,
A. M. Evans, Prop.
Insurance—H. F. Blodgett; T. G. Jones; E. Pratt; C. T.
Woodbury; M. Q. Butterfield;
Agents—R. C. Mitchell
Lands—E. Pratt; D. Woodbury
Livery Stable—T. G. Henderson
Lumber—James McCann; Cutter and Co.; Martin Bros.; D.
Woodbury
Meat Market—Richards and Curial; Kent and Davis
Millers—Stein Bros.
Millinery—Mrs. C. Alberty; Mrs. W. W. Payne
Newspaper—*Anoka Union*, G. S. Pease Publisher,
H. A. Castle, Editor, *Anoka Press*
Omnibus—G. Henderson
Painters—S. L. Gale; G. A. Clark; Lewis Martin
Photographer—J. Woods
Physicians—A. W. Giddings; J. Perham; R. Whiteman
(Homeopathic)
Planing Mills—Houston, Prescott and Co.; Cutter and Covel
Printing Office—*Anoka Union* Job Office
Railroad Office—St. Paul and Pacific, L. G. Browning, Agent
Saddler—W. Wilson
Sash and Doors—Houston, Prescott and Company
Stoves—E. T. Alling and Co.; Church and Ives
Tailor—A. C. Frauman
Telegraph—N. W. Telegraph Line, W. H. Landis, Operator
Tubs and Pails—Cutter and Co.
Veterinary Surgeon—J. C. Frost
Wagons—S. D. Leeman; J. Miller
Watchmaker—C. J. Dunbar[2]

Did Albert read this New Year's edition of the *Anoka Union* and see the list of positions held by friends and neighbors? What did he think? Did he see himself as a pastor of the Methodist Episcopal Church? As a teacher, like his mother? As a blacksmith? He did love horses. As an agent for American Express? Possibly. That would give him a chance to communicate with the outside world. As a furrier? Too cruel. As an insurance agent? Maybe. H. F. Blodgett could help him get started. As a farmer? He loved working in the soil. Livery stableman? That would combine business and pleasure. Physician? Veterinarian? Lumberman? Would the white pine grow back? Who would replant? No—it would be more satisfying to work wholly in the public interest.

Albert may have pondered these callings with the newspaper spread before him on the kitchen table, or while daydreaming in the shade of an oak tree, listening to the whistle of the St. Paul and Pacific. Whenever, wherever, however he pondered the years ahead, Albert must have been influenced by one event occurring in 1865.

Albert had heard about the East, but in the main his horizon was the township border. Pioneers passed through Anoka on their way west and newcomers brought word of the outside, but he knew nothing of that world firsthand. Then came a breakthrough. His mother's brother, Wellesley W. Bowdish, was to graduate from Wesleyan College at Middletown, Connecticut, in 1865. Charlotte Stockwell decided to go, no doubt visiting her parents for an extended stay at the same time, and she took Albert, then an eight-year-old farmboy.

The Civil War was over, and on April 14, 1865, Abraham Lincoln was shot. He died the next morning. So beloved was Lincoln that when announcement was made that he would be buried in Illinois, every city, village, and hamlet along the route of the funeral train pleaded that the train stop on the way so the citizens could show their affection. The funeral train left Washington on April 21, 1865, with stops at Baltimore, Harrisburg, Philadelphia, New York, Albany, Buffalo, Cleveland, Columbus, Indianapolis, Chicago, and finally at Springfield on May 3, 1865. As the train moved from city to city, thousands gathered by the wayside to catch a glimpse of the car carrying the president. In Chicago, Albert Stockwell and his mother were among them.

What questions Albert must have asked his mother as they continued on their way—questions about Lincoln and his boyhood, about the Civil War, about slavery. What will happen to the slaves now that they are free? Why do people have to die? Shouldn't guns be abolished? Difficult questions for any parent. Charlotte Bowdish Stockwell did her best, as Albert continued to wonder. Undoubtedly he kept wondering long after he returned home. And if, three years later, he read the *Anoka Union*'s special edition of January 2, 1868, an article on page 2 must have raised troubling new questions:

A Nigger Speech
What a Minnesota Nigger Says
Many of our readers will recollect a nigger named Cromwell—
"Professor Cromwell" as he styled himself—who formerly kept a

barbershop on Jackson Street and subsequently flourished a few years at St. Cloud and then removed to Louisiana. It appears he is now a member of the Louisiana radical convention and recently made the following speech, which is exactly in accord with the sentiments of the nigger population, as molded by white and black niggers sent from the North.

"Mr. President—I hab listened to the readin ob de resultions for de second time. Dey is genuine doctrine. I wants dis Merican people to know dat today my race stands out in bold and graphic relief as de stanchion dat upholds de government ob dis country. I tinks we are able to take care ob ourselves. Ebery wind I har rushin in de leaves proclaims dat de black man who fought for de national honor am de equal ob de white. We is able to vindicate our cause. I'se not skeered. [Sensation outside the bar, and excitement among the police] This gobernment has carved out our future. My people has agin and agin been on de battlefield and shed dere blood for it. Dey claim dere rights upon the floor and in dis country, and let me say dat we will rule de rebels—dat loyal blacks must rule dis Government. [Profound sensation in the lobbies] De rebels who hab ruled us shan't rule no longer. Talk of war of races, we are ready for it. We will rule until the last one of us goes down forever. We don't intend to get down on our knees and beg for our rights. Gentlemens, I ask you that you will not deprive us of our rights. This government is pledged to maintain the rights of negroes. Gentlemens, much is said about an nudder rebelution. I say if we cannot gain our rights and be place on an equality wid de whites, let it come. Let de rebolution come. Equal rights I demand, and nothing else will I have. I will die fust. I acts as a man, I feels like a man, and I asks no more than udder men if dey possesses the fine sentiments of manhood as I does. We car nothin for Andy Johnson or any other man in dis Government. We are going to have our rights if it to be obtained by rebolution and blood. [Swaying to and fro of negroes outside the bar] We claim from dis convention equal liberty and equal privileges of de white man. I stand here, sir, to advocate the cause of my race—dat all de rights and dem we shall hab. I wants dem for de white man and de black man. Har in this convention dar are rebels. [Here he pointed to a representative of a New York paper who wore gray pantaloons and the badge of Thomas' old Army of the Cumberland.] Dar are secret blows again us. Let us go into secret meetings and prepar for dem. Let dem hole dere secret meetings at the St. Charles Hotel and under holes. Let dem telegraph from de St. Charles dat I, Cromwell, will demand his rights. [Hisses] Gentlemens, pardon me for dis harangue. Gentlemens, I know my rights, I demand dem. I demand dem for my race and shall endeavor to have dem embodied in de

Constitution. I demand a guaranty. Do you know what dat is? When the proper time comes, you will know what I mean by guaranty."[3]

What has happened in the past three years? Weren't the slaves freed? Aren't they one of us now? Albert must have wondered. Why should the editor of the *Anoka Union* be so scornful? Why should he call Mr. Cromwell a nigger? Why make fun of his grammar? Mr. Cromwell was a friend and neighbor. His barbershop was just two blocks away.

———

Thinking about young Albert's view of the world from Anoka, I returned on the main highway, reaching Minneapolis in about half an hour. Some months later my sister, Libby, sent me a letter Albert had written in longhand, on Saturday Lunch Club stationery, when she was twelve and he was seventy. The letter, dated January 19, 1928, described a journey Albert had made over the same ground:

My Darling Elizabeth.
It is most kind of you to write so often and not get any answers. I have intended to answer your letter but it is hard to drive myself to write letters. I notice a very great improvement in your handwriting. I am glad you have such a fine school . . . Your horses interest me. You get your love of horses from me. There is no animal I am fonder of than a horse. I had some wonderful friends in old Ned and old Jan and old Lucy. I cried myself to sleep when old Ned died and I was quite a man at that time. He knew as much as most men. I remember one night I was driving home from Minneapolis to Anoka when the worst storm I ever was out in came up. It rained torrents and one could not see his hand before him except when it lightened. The creeks were banks full. Old Ned's eyes were sharp enough to keep the road and whenever we came to a bridge he would test it out before he would cross it. I arrived home as wet as if I had been in a lake but thanks to old Ned, safe and sound. I'd give a lot more to see old Ned again than I would to see Jesus . . . Give my love to your adorable mother.

The letter made my drive back to Minneapolis seem pitifully tame.

References

1. Remarks, S. A. Stockwell Complimentary Birthday Dinner, West Hotel, Minneapolis, June 8, 1927. Goodrich had served as Thirteenth Ward alderman of Minneapolis.

2. *Anoka Union*, January 2, 1868, Minnesota Historical Society.

3. *Anoka Union*, January 2, 1868, Minnesota Historical Society.

At Home

The Stockwell homestead is now but a sad likeness of the farm I visited as a boy. A stranger sees no beauty there—no barn, no windmill, no orchard, no gracious lawn or standing corn. The lot is tiny. The sunporch, now sealed in, has been changed to an unsightly appendage. Three elm trees have vanished. The front yard, hemmed in by tacky houses, is cut in half by a driveway leading nowhere.

But I envision the dwelling and its events as in 1903, when Beth was ten and Charlotte was twelve, when life was simple, orderly, and uncluttered, and the two walked down unpaved country roads to Minnehaha and Longfellow schools.

There were no automobiles or radios but much storytelling and reading aloud. Despite her heavy involvement in the suffrage movement, Nanna (Maud) found time to make up her own bedtime stories. Two gray squirrels, Brighteyes and Nimbleheels, were principal characters.[1] As Olin had read *Uncle Tom's Cabin* to his family, so Charlotte, now the eldest, read to hers. If not Harriet Beecher Stowe, then Mark Twain or perhaps Howard Pyle, who wrote and illustrated children's books of the highest order; Pyle's reworking of legend in *The Merry Adventures of Robin Hood* is classic. Was Horatio Alger, whose protagonists were variations of the poor man's son rising to success, read aloud? What about *The Red Badge of Courage*, Stephen Crane's imaginative reproduction of the horrors of Chancellorsville? Perhaps in later years. One can be sure that dime novels, the rage from the Civil War until the birth of motion pictures, were not on the reading list.[2]

Albert's typical day in 1903 was strenuous. It started early and ended late. He rose at 4:00 or 5:00 A.M., milked the cow or cows, and did his chores. Weather permitting, he worked barefoot,

A careful dresser in his public life, Stockwell preferred the simple comfort of bare feet while gardening. (Family photo)

Stockwell gave his grandchildren—William P. and Elizabeth Everts—a ride in a wheelbarrow stacked with cornhusks in 1922. (Family photo)

a custom he followed all his life. His only hobbies were horticulture and gardening, and his vegetable garden was his greatest joy. Years later, when Stockwell family rugs were handed down, Charlotte recalled his pride in those oriental rugs "as in the straight rows of his vegetable garden." He found relaxation in gardening and found the undertaking even more fun when his daughters helped— or hindered. The Stockwells were vegetarians, so gardening also gave the satisfaction of providing needed staples.

During dry spells Albert lovingly watered the three elm trees in the front yard with bucketfuls carried from the windmill.

Sundays were special days for the family. Nanna's parents were members of the Universalist Church. She had been brought up in that denomination. But in the 1890s, she and Albert started attending meetings of the First Unitarian Society. Unitarianism became an important part of the liberal philosophy held by both—in politics and social affairs, as well as religion—and the two played an active role from the beginning. Genevieve McGraw, now the society's oldest member, recalled that when she was a little girl attending Sunday school, Albert served as superintendent:

> He didn't teach a class, but he got things started with an assembly, and then he moved from class to class. There were songs and political discussions, talks about the environment and such, all as spurred on by [Albert].

Fourth of July celebration in Anoka, Minnesota, c. 1899. (Courtesy of the Minnesota Historical Society)

Minnehaha Falls was the family's favorite place to visit, so much so that, upon his death, S. A. Stockwell left instructions that his ashes were to be scattered here. (Photo by Hamilton Everts, the author's son)

McGraw was struck by his enthusiasm and, in particular, by his encouragement of group singing. The day began with "Welcome, welcome is the greeting which this day we give our friends."

Sometimes the family took the train to Anoka to visit Silvanus Stockwell. Three generations gathered in Anoka on March 26, 1904, for example, to help celebrate

Silvanus' eightieth birthday. The family also made train expeditions to Lake Minnetonka for picnics. Nearer home they picnicked at Minnehaha Falls. Beth never forgot what fun these picnics were. Later, in Petersham, Massachusetts, she often led her own children across the pasture and down a trail to Brown's Pond for supper outdoors.

S. A. Stockwell and grandson William P. Everts in his garden. (Family photo)

Many people considered participation in sports to be a sinful way of spending time. Nanna and Albert did not hold this view, and yet none of the family pursued organized sports at any level, least of all Albert. He had little interest in sports or games. There was a pool room in the Commercial Club, to which he belonged, but he seems never to have set foot inside the door. Coasting and bicycling were all right. And there were expeditions to the state and county fairs. At the 1906 Minnesota State Fair, Dan Patch, Minnesota's beloved pacer, broke the world record for the mile. Beth pursued on her children's behalf these outings, too. The annual fair in Athol, Massachusetts, with sulky racing and all, was the high spot of many summers in Petersham.

What about the circus? That was acceptable, I think. Phineas T. Barnum (1810-1891) was the pioneer, and by 1903 the greatest show on earth, as well as less-celebrated troupes, pitched their tents in Minneapolis. While the downtown parade, the acrobats, animals, and clowns were suitable fare, what about the likes of the ten-foot-tall Cardiff giant, midget Tom Thumb, or 161-year-old Joyce Heth, the African-American woman Barnum had exhibited as the nurse of George Washington?[3] Nanna and Albert probably declared the sideshow off limits. Some

Left to right: Beth, Ruth, and Charlotte Stockwell.

were hoaxes to be sure, but to stare at abnormal persons was contrary to common decency and to a respect for the dignity of all human beings.[4]

On holidays, the Stockwell family joined forces with the Days. Nanna's younger sister, Mabel, had married Eugene Day, who became a wealthy lumberman and the owner of valuable iron ore properties in the Mesabi Range. The Days' three children were Eugenia, Kingsley, and John. Upon recalling early Christmases, Eugenia said she had "no recollection of Uncle Albert being present." Reminded that he was never able to celebrate Christmas because of Ruth's death, Eugenia remembered him at Thanksgiving gatherings:

> He was always agitating about something. I was afraid of him. He believed that the iron ore owned by our family belonged to all the people. He and my father were at opposite poles politically and philosophically. They had married sisters and both belonged to the Commercial Club, but that was all they had in common. At best their relationship was an uneasy truce. My mother and Aunty Maud constantly sought to keep the conversation on neutral topics to avoid open warfare.[5]

References

1. Nanna's bedtime stories were never published. Original typewritten copies are in the author's possession.

2. The author has from Albert's library the complete works of Mark Twain in twenty-five volumes, 1906 edition, and all of the writings of Thomas Jefferson, comprising twenty volumes, 1904 edition. My mother said years ago that "Father had a passion for sets of books and was a pushover for book salesmen."

3. Accompanying Joyce were yellowed papers, including what purported to be an original bill of sale from Augustine Washington, the father of George, dated February 5, 1727, and describing her as then fifty-four years of age. She had been coached to remember all the details about young George, including the famous cherry-tree incident, which she insisted on calling a peach tree. See *Dictionary of American Biography*, 1:636-639.

4. My mother may have been stricter than her parents in some areas of censorship. She had a particular fixation about what plays and motion pictures her children were allowed to see; she read all the reviews in sight

and took soundings with other parents about suitability. We never did see *Hell's Angels* or *Ben Hur*. I remember Bobby Neall's birthday party in particular. Ours was a double house; Bobby literally lived next door at 40 Crafts Road. The plan was to see *Heidi* on the stage in Boston in the afternoon. When Bobby's mother found out at the last minute that *Heidi* was sold out, she took us to see *Dracula*, on the stage at the Shubert, instead. I doubt she ever recovered from Mother's lambasting.

5. Edward L. Peet could understand Eugenia's intimidation. An idealistic young liberal who respected Stockwell after seeing him in action, Peet described him as a "hell raiser." Benjamin Drake added perspective: "Like [Wendell] Phillips, [Theodore] Parker, and [William Lloyd] Garrison of ante-bellum days, he was an agitator. But his agitation moved with a purpose. It was intended to promote and accomplish the objectives to which he had dedicated his life." "Tribute to the Memory of Sylvanus A. Stockwell," typescript of memorial service address, Minnesota Historical Society.

Appendix 3

Programme

S. A. STOCKWELL'S COMPLIMENTARY BIRTHDAY DINNER
WEST HOTEL, MINNEAPOLIS, MINNESOTA
JUNE EIGHTH, 1927

SONGS
Franklin Co-Operative Creamery Glee Club

W. E. LEONARD, Chairman
Letters from Absent Friends

BENJAMIN DRAKE
Toastmaster

A. W. RANKIN
Politics and Taxation

W. G. CALDERWOOD
Temperance

VICTORIA N. McALMON
Public Schools

MRS. ARTHUR BRIN
World Peace

BROWN SMITH
The Colored People

REV. J. H. DIETRICH
The Church

HON. MAGNUS JOHNSON
The State of the Country

GEO. B. LEONARD
Municipal Franchises

MRS. F. A. KINGSLEY
Woman Suffrage

C. H. LEWIS
The Saturday Lunch Club

MERCEDES NELSON
The Young People

MAURICE LEFKOVITS
The Jewish People

HAROLD I. NORDBY
Co-Operation

LINCOLN COLCORD
World Citizenship

A. M. GOODRICH
Rum River Recollections

E. DUDLEY PARSONS
Summary

HOMER MORRIS
The Degree of Honor

S. A. STOCKWELL
Response

The Stockwell home at 3204 East 51st Street, Minneapolis. (Family photo)

Visiting

In the 1920s Mother, my sister, Libby (Elizabeth), and I made several trips to Minneapolis. We took the train from South Station in Boston to Chicago. Dad would see us off. He always gave us something to read on the train, invariably, when we were older, the *Boston Transcript*. The *Transcript* was a great afternoon newspaper. It had no funnies, but I didn't mind, partly because I liked the sports section. So loyal were some readers of the *Transcript* in Boston that if it rained when the *Transcript* predicted fair weather, they didn't believe it.

Everything was fun on the train, even brushing one's teeth. The basins were deep, shiny metal, and the water swished around. We swayed to keep our balance getting to the washroom; the floor shifted sideways in the smoky space between cars; wheels hammered the rails beneath; we held on for dear life. In Chicago we changed trains. This meant going across town by Parmelee Transfer, which shuttled between all Chicago railroad terminals, from the LaSalle Street Depot to the Chicago Northwestern Depot.

The Chicago-Minneapolis leg of the trip was shorter, and it was less exciting because there was no chance to sleep in an upper berth. But the meals were still a special attraction—served on white table linens with more silverware than a boy could ever use. And I remember from those trips that Mother was especially respectful of the Pullman porters. We all befriended them. Mother liked blacks; they instinctively sensed it, they knew her feelings were genuine, and there was instant rapport. I wonder whether she knew her father was a friend and supporter of A. Philip Randolph, who became president of the Brotherhood of Sleeping Car Porters. I'll never forget the sight of Minneapolis's Milwaukee Station, with its tower and vast shed for incoming trains, the sound of rain

pounding the roof. Without the clanging, the throngs, the greetings, the good-byes, the pounding rain, the "All Aboard" and
"Watch your step," Milwaukee Station is today only a shell, lifeless
as an abandoned schoolhouse. But we arrived at the depot in her
glory days. Nanna and Albert were there to greet us. You could tell
Mother was the apple of her father's eye. Her warmth and gaiety
always lifted his spirits. Baggage in hand, we proceeded to the next
and last stop—3204 East Fifty-first Street, where Pollo, a gentle
collie, joined the reception. Whether we rode out by streetcar or
taxi I cannot remember, but of one thing I am sure—Nanna and
Albert took the streetcar to the station; they never owned a car. "I
wouldn't know what to do with one," said Albert years later.

The house was about eight miles from the Milwaukee Station. When the Stockwells built it, they were settling way out in the
country. When we visited, although there were a few dwellings
nearby and a small grocery store a few blocks away, the rural feeling remained. Three elm trees planted by Albert added grace to the
front yard. The house had a spacious sunporch on the west side,
what seemed a huge lawn, and a barn. A windmill stood in the
backyard. Beyond the windmill lay Albert's garden, which always
seemed to be full of corn, and an orchard. The house seemed enormous. So did the barn, replete with chickens and a cow.

Minnehaha Falls, nearby, were almost as dear to Albert as
his garden, and we picnicked there on every visit. The falls, on
Minnehaha Creek, which flows to the Mississippi River from Lake
Minnetonka, are the ones Henry Wadsworth Longfellow immortal-
ized as the "laughing water" in *The Song of Hiawatha* (1855):

> Where the Falls of Minnehaha
> Flash and gleam among the oak trees
> Laugh and leap into the valley.

Albert also cherished the Minnesota State Capitol in St.
Paul. I remember his showing me around when I was about ten,
introducing me to his colleagues, to the sergeant-at-arms, to the
janitors, to everyone in sight. He took pride not only in the Capitol,
but in his grandson, so the day was a happy one. Since then I have
often seen busloads of schoolchildren gathering for tours of the
Capitol. Each time I have thought, "If only Albert could be their
guide . . . he would have loved it."

Appendix 5

Travel

Albert rarely set eyes on his grandchildren. Only once did he visit them in Massachusetts, and I don't remember any trips to Minneapolis with Mother after those early ones in the 1920s. School posed a conflict between June and September, and in the summer we vacationed at different places—Petersham and Woods Hole in Massachusetts, Nelson and Lake Winnepesaukee in New Hampshire. Mother did go back for occasional visits. She attended the banquet honoring Albert on his seventieth birthday, and, along with a thousand others, the celebration honoring both her parents on their fiftieth wedding anniversary.

Trips were infrequent because there was no extra money for travel. The great depression of the 1930s ruled out spending for anything except basic needs. I am sure that Dad, a lawyer, pared down the amount of his fees. Even so, many clients weren't paying their bills at all. We had always gone to private schools—Libby to Beaver Country Day and Stocky and I to Rivers School—but he and I were slated for public school in 1933. Except for partial scholarships and outside generosity, we would have made the change.

Nanna kept in touch with us by letter and occasional visits. I realize now that her visits to us in Brookline were usually combined with attendance at some convention such as the Biennial Congress of the Women's International League for Peace and Freedom in Dublin in 1926. Undoubtedly, she stopped in Boston on the way.

My grandfather loved Minnesota. So when there might be money for travel, he preferred to give it away or spend it for a cause he believed in. It was mostly a matter of priorities. How could a man sit still in the face of injustice in the world? Such disparity of opportunity? Where was the time for idle travel? And there was that other reason he didn't visit us in Brookline—the execution in 1927 of Nicola Sacco and Bartolomeo Vanzetti in Charlestown, Massachusetts, after nearly seven years in prison. Shortly after their execution, he encountered at the first Unitarian Society his young friend Mercedes Nelson, a teacher about Mother's age. He was lonely and angry. "Mercedes," he said, "you be my daughter. My two daughters live in that awful state of Massachusetts, and I can never set foot there again."

I did call once more on Albert and Nanna in the house where they belonged. In the summer of 1936, through family connections, I landed one of the most satisfying jobs I have ever had. My other grandmother, Dolly Paine Everts, was the sister of William A. Paine, who held a controlling interest in the Copper Range Company, which owned and operated an underground copper mine on Michigan's Upper Peninsula in the town of Painesdale. Copper Range was by far the largest taxpayer in the region; the local school district was doubtless the richest. High school buildings and recreational facilities, which included some six or eight excellent tennis courts, were better than those in most colleges. My position was that of recreation director and tennis coach for children out of school in the summer. We played tennis in the sun while their fathers toiled in darkness underground. Spider Trethewey, I remember, became a particularly strong player. Albert Mendelsohn, mine superintendent, promptly took me under his wing. I lived in a boardinghouse and had a great summer.

At the end of the summer I wanted to buy a motorcycle to get myself back to Massachusetts, but Mother and Dad vetoed it. Instead I took the train to Boston via Minneapolis for what was a final visit to 3204 East Fifty-first Street. Once more Albert and Nanna met me at the Milwaukee Station. At mealtime, I noted, Albert fastened a linen napkin around his neck with a silver chain, as always.

In October of the following year, Albert and Nanna moved to an apartment at 2103 Garfield Avenue. Three years after my 1936 visit, Albert attended my graduation from Harvard College,but it was easy to tell he wasn't at home in Massachusetts. That was the last time I ever saw him.

Last Visit

I did not return to Minneapolis again until the spring of 1954. Driving a Plymouth station wagon filled to the roof with luggage and furniture, I stopped en route from Andover, Massachusetts, to Hanford, Washington, where I had taken a government job as attorney with the Atomic Energy Commission. My security clearance had been held up; this was the heyday of Senator Joseph McCarthy, and if a person or member of his family had so much as subscribed to the *New Republic* or belonged to the National Lawyers Guild, he was suspect. Dad had done both. I became impatient and headed west anyway. The clearance came through while I was on my way.

Nanna, ever independent, at age ninety-one was living by herself on Garfield Avenue. I found her somewhat more frail, but otherwise she seemed just the same as always. She was well informed about the happenings of the day, her mind remained keen, and there was no loss of zest or lessening of interest in the world's problems. We drove around Lake of the Isles, Lake Calhoun, Lake Harriet, and then on to Lake Nokomis near the old home. A lovely day of sightseeing and reminiscing it was.

Unwittingly, I literally gave her a pain in the neck. I had not taken any of our worldly goods out of the station wagon, and a cot extending slightly over the passenger's seat in front made Nanna lean sideways and forward as we drove. She never complained.

That was the last time I saw her.

Bibliography

Manuscripts

Anoka Historical Society Records, Anoka, Minnesota
First Unitarian Society of Minneapolis Archives, Minneapolis, Minnesota
Minneapolis Public Library, Minneapolis, Minnesota
      Minneapolis History Collection (Stockwell File)
Minnesota Historical Society, St. Paul, Minnesota
      Pierce Atwater Papers
      Dorothy Binder Papers
      Fannie Brin Papers
      Willis Calderwood Papers
      Albert Dollenmayer Papers
      Minnesota Woman Suffrage Association Papers
      James Peet and Family Papers
      Hjalmar Petersen Papers (Interview)
      Political Equality Club of Minneapolis Papers
      Quetico-Superior Papers
      Stockwell Family Papers
      Supreme Court Files
South High School, Minneapolis, Minnesota
      Yearbooks
University of Minnesota Archives, Walter Library, Minneapolis, Minnesota
      The Gopher (yearbooks)
Wesleyan University Archives, Middletown, Connecticut
Widener Library, Harvard University, Cambridge, Massachusetts

Interviews and Tape Recordings

In addtion to his own conversations as a young man with S. A. and Maud Stockwell, the author has conducted personal and telephone conversations with (relatives) Eugenia Day Ganssle, Charlotte Hamlet, Eugene Day, Janet Day Tipton, Benjamin Granger, and Margaret Wagenhals Day; (friends and acquaintances who knew the Stockwells in younger days) E. Dudley Parsons, Jr., Gerald Friedell, Marjorie Child

Husted, Violet Johnson Sollie, Althea Heitsmith Atwater, Edward L. Peet, Robert C. Alexander, Meridel Le Sueur, Stuart Paulson, and Thelma Selander; (members of the First Unitarian Society who knew Stockwell) Genevieve Hobart McGraw, Aino Swanson, Mercedes Nelson, and Robert Haagenson; (members of the African American community who knew and wrote of Stockwell) Raymond Cannon, John F. Thomas, Frances McHie Raines; Governor Harold E. Stassen and fellow legislators Louis W. Hill, Carl E. Erickson, Samuel H. Bellman, and Michael J. Galvin; (others who had no personal relationship with the Stockwells) Ted Hall, Totton P. Heffelfinger, Clarence Sharp, Janet Salisbury, Jack N. Birk, and Ralph W. Gurney.

From the collections of the Minnesota Historical Society:

Russell Fridley and Lucile Kane Interview, May 28, 1963, in Hjalmar Petersen Papers.

Maud Stockwell, "Reminiscences of Jane Addams" (1954 speech to Minnesota section of the Women's International League for Peace and Freedom), audio recording in Minnesota Historical Society Oral Collections.

Newspapers

Anoka County Union Centennial, 1965

Anoka Union, 1868

Boston Herald, 1927

Minneapolis Daily News, 1915

Minneapolis Journal, 1894, 1898-1902, 1904, 1906-1908, 1910-1912, 1914, 1917, 1922, 1925, 1927, 1933-1937

Labor Review (Minneapolis), 1912, 1934

Minneapolis Morning Tribune, 1949

Minneapolis New Times, 1917

Minneapolis Star Tribune, 1937, 1984-1985, 1987-1988

Minneapolis Star, 1934, 1937

Minneapolis Spokesman, 1939, 1943.

Minneapolis Star, 1940

Minneapolis Times, 1940

Minneapolis Tribune, 1903, 1917, 1925-1929, 1937, 1940, 1943, 1949, 1952, 1967

Minnesota Leader (undated clipping)

Minnesota Municipalities, 1941

New York Times, 1917

St. Paul Dispatch, 1899

St. Paul Globe, 1900

St. Paul News, 1935.

St. Paul Pioneer Press, 1897, 1925, 1937, 1992

St. Paul Post Dispatch, 1908, 1913,1927, 1929, 1932-1933

Special Materials in Possession of the Author

Primary sources in the possession of the author include the letters and writings of S. A. Stockwell, Maud Stockwell, their relatives and associates, as preserved by the family. The earliest is a talk by S. A. Stockwell's mother, Charlotte Bowdish Stockwell, given before the Woman's Foreign Missionary Society of the Methodist-Episcopal Church of Anoka about 1880. The tribute written in 1930 by S. A. Stockwell's brother Walter, *Memories and an Appreciation of My Mother Charlotte Bowdish Stockwell*, provided an excellent account of Anoka's beginnings as well as of early family history.

Among Maud Conkey Stockwell's writings are an original typewritten manuscript of her bedtime stories; her unpublished "A Sheaf of Kingsley—Conkey Family History," written in November 1947; her copies of programs for the thirty-fifth (New Orleans, 1903) and thirty-seventh (Portland, Oregon, 1905) conventions of the National American Woman Suffrage Association; and a copy of her *Some Facts Concerning Military Training at State Universities* (Privately published, 1925).

Letters to the author from persons who knew Stockwell are included in this volume in whole or in part or have otherwise served as background. Informants include (Stockwell relatives) Maud Conkey Stockwell, Charles Conkey, Charlotte Stockwell Baker, Elizabeth Stockwell Everts, Charlotte Hamlet, Eugene Day, Janet Day Tipton, Stockwell Everts, and Elizabeth Everts MacLeod; (Stockwell associates in the legislature) Samuel H. Bellman, Carl E. Erickson, and Michael J. Galvin; (Stockwell family friends who as children attended the annual cornfests) Howard B. Brin, Edward W. Harding, Harry Levin, and Gerald Friedell; (others) James M. Youngdale, Violet Johnson Sollie, Edward L. Peet, Jack N. Birk, and Carol Laseski (she also provided a copy of her paper "The Minnesota Section of the Women's International League for Peace and Freedom and the Abolition of Compulsory Military Training at the University of Minnesota," written at the University of Minnesota in 1982). The author also holds a letter from William M. Olin, Secretary of the Commonwealth of Massachusetts, to Walter L. Stockwell, February 21, 1911.

The author has inherited S. A. Stockwell's sets of the first edition of R. Watson, D. D., F. R. S., Lord Bishop of Landaff and Regius Professor of Divinity at the University of Cambridge, *An Apology for the Bible in a Series of Letters Addressed to Thomas Paine* (Philadelphia: "Printed for W. Young, Miller & Son, No. 52, Corner of Second and Chestnut Streets by W. W. Woodward," 1796); *The Complete Works of Mark Twain*, 1906 edition, 25 vols.; and *The Writings of Thomas Jefferson*, 1904 edition, 20 vols.

Other valuable sources in possession of the author include the Stockwell Complimentary Birthday Book, June 8, 1927 (a scrapbook of letters and speeches made at the birthday dinner incuding letters from Jane Addams, William Watts Folwell, Newton D. Baker, Clarence Darrow, Rev. J. H. Dietrich, and Oswald Garrison Villard, as well as speeches by

W. E. Leonard, Benjamin Drake, A. W. Rankin, W. G. Calderwood, Victoria N. McAlmon, Mrs. Arthur Brin, Brown Smith, Hon. Magnus Johnson, George B. Leonard, Mrs. F. A. Kingsley, C. H. Lewis, Mercedes Nelson, Maurice Lefkovits, Harold I. Nordby, Lincoln Colcord, A. M. Goodrich, John Lind, E. Dudley Parsons, and Homer Morris); a transcript of Carl Storm's tribute to Maud Stockwell at her memorial service on January 7, 1958; Lillian Marvin Swenson's poem dated February 28, 1918, and found in Charlotte's desk after her death; and various unidentified family newspaper clippings.

Books, Articles, and Unpublished Materials

Aalbu, R. M. *The Minnesota Kaleidoscope of 1933*. Thief River Falls: Forum Publishing Company, 1933.

Anthony, Susan, and Ida Husted Harper. *History of Woman Suffrage*. Indianapolis: The Hollenbeck Press, 1902.

Appel, Holbrook and Livia. *Minnesota in the War with Germany*. St. Paul: Minnesota Historical Society, 1932.

Benedict, William A., and Hiram A. Tracy. *History of the Town of Sutton, Massachusetts, 1704-1876*. Worcester: Sanford & Company, 1878. Reprinted 1966 and 1970 by Commonwealth Press.

Binder, Dorothy Walton. "The Stockwells of Minneapolis." *New Republic*, December 22, 1937. (A typescript copy is in the Stockwell Family Papers, Minnesota Historical Society.)

Blakey, Roy G., and Violet Johnson, "Minnesota Iron Ore Tax Valuation Problems." *Minnesota Municipalities*, February 1941.

Blegen, Theodore C. *Minnesota: A History of the State*. Minneapolis: University of Minnesota Press, 1979.

Brown, W. Gertrude. *Ten Years a Neighbor: Phyllis Wheatley Settlement House, 1924-1934*, [Minneapolis: No publisher, 1934], available at Minneapolis Public Library.

Buck, Solon J. *The Granger Movement*. Cambridge: Harvard University Press, 1913.

Buell, C. J. *The Minnesota Legislature of 1917*. St. Paul: [Buell], 1917.
_____. *The Minnesota Legislature of 1923*. St. Paul: [Buell], 1923.

Carlson, Stephen P. *The Scots of Hammersmith*. No city: Eastern National Park and Monument Association in cooperation with Department of the Interior, National Park Service, 1976.

Cheney, Charles B. *Minnesota Politics*. Minneapolis: Reprinted from the *Minneapolis Morning Tribune*, 1947.

Chrislock, Carl H. "The Alliance Party and the Minnesota Legislature of 1891." *Minnesota History*, 35(September 1957): 297-312.
_____. "Profile of a Ward Boss: The Political Career of Lars M. Rand." *Norwegian American Studies*, 31(1986):62.
_____. *The Progressive Era in Minnesota*. St. Paul: Minnesota Historical Society, 1971.

_____. *Watchdog of Loyalty: The Minnesota Commission of Public Safety during World War I*. St. Paul: Minnesota Historical Society Press, 1991.

Clarke, Mary Stetson. *Pioneer Iron Works*. Philadelphia: Chilton Book Company, 1968.

Cook, Louella B. "Tribute to the Memory of Sylvanus A. Stockwell," typescript of memorial service address, Minnesota Historical Society.

DeMille, Agnes. Portrait Gallery. Boston: Houghton Mifflin, 1990.

Dietrich, John H. *Religious Humanism—Excerpts from an Address by John H. Dietrich*. Minneapolis: The First Unitarian Society of Minneapolis, 1983.

Dictionary of American Biography. New York: Charles Scribner's Sons, 1964. (10 vols., 7 sups.)

Dictionary of American History. New York: Charles Scribner's Sons, 1976. (7 vols.)

Drake, Benjamin. "Tribute to the Memory of Sylvanus A. Stockwell," typescript copy of memorial service address, Minnesota Historical Society.

Elderkin, John, et al., eds. *Dinner Speeches at the Lotus Club*. New York: Printed for the Lotus Club, 1911.

Everts, William P., Jr., "E. L. Godkin: On Trial in the West," honors thesis, Harvard University, 1939.

Folwell, Williams Watts. *A History of Minnesota*, rev. ed. St. Paul: Minnesota Historical Society, 1956.

Foner, Philip S. *Organized Labor and the Black Worker 1619-1973*. New York: Praeger Publishers, 1974.

Foster, Mary Dillon. *Who's Who Among Minnesota Women*. St. Paul: No publisher, 1924.

Fraser, Alice B. *Twenty-Five Years a Neighbor: The Story of Phyllis Wheatley Settlement House*. Minneapolis: No publisher, 1949.

George, Henry. *Progress and Poverty*. New York: Robert Schalkenbach Foundation, 1938.

Gieske, Millard L. *Minnesota Farmer-Laborism: The Third Party Alternative*. Minneapolis: University of Minnesota Press, 1979.

Goodrich, Albert M. *History of Anoka County*. Minneapolis: Hennepin Publishing Company, 1905.

Gray, James. *The University of Minnesota: 1851-1951*. Minneapolis: University of Minnesota Press, 1951.

Greene, Mark A. "The Baptist Fundamentalists' Case Against Carleton, 1926-28." *Minnesota History*, 52/1, Spring 1990, 16-25.

Hawkes, David Freeman. *Everyday Life in Early America*. New York: Harper & Row, 1980.

Haynes, John Earl. *Dubious Alliance: The Making of Minnesota's DFL Party*. Minneapolis: University of Minnesota Press, 1984.

Helmes, Winifred G. *John A. Johnson: The People's Governor.* Minneapolis: University of Minnesota Press, 1949.

Hitchcock, R. W., comp. *Issues of the Minnesota Legislature, Regular Session 1935 and Special Session 1935-1936.*

Holcombe, R. I., and William H. Bingham, eds. *Compendium of History and Biography of Minneapolis and Hennepin County, Minnesota.* Chicago: Henry Taylor & Co., 1914.

Holland, Josiah Gilbert. (Poem) "God, Give Us Men!" (1872) in Hazel Felleman, ed., *The Best Loved American Poems of the American People* (New York: Doubleday, 1936).

House Journal, 1891, 1897, 1902 Extra Session, 1923, 1925, 1927, 1929, 1931, 1933, 1937, Extra Session 1937, and 1939. No publishing information. Available at Minnesota Historical Society.

Jackson, Helen Hunt. *A Century of Dishonor.* Boston: Roberts Brothers, 1888.

Joughin, G. Louis, and Edmund M. Morgan. *The Legacy of Sacco and Vanzetti.* New York: Harcourt, Brace and Company, 1948.

Keillor, Steven J. *Hjalmar Petersen of Minnesota: The Politics of Provincial Independence.* St. Paul: Minnesota Historical Society Press, 1987.

_____. "A Remedy Invented by Labor: The Franklin Co-operative Creamery Association, 1913-1919." *Minnesota History* 51 (Fall 1989): 259-69.

Kennedy, John F. *Profiles in Courage.* New York: Harper & Brothers, 1961.

Kennedy, Mabel Stockwell. *The Stockwell Genealogy.* Lebanon, New Hampshire: New Victoria Printers, Inc., 1983.

Laws of Minnesota (miscellaneous). [No publishing information but published after each legislative session]

"Laws That Limit Rights," *Roots* 13, No. 3 (Spring 1985):17-20.

Legislative Manual, 1891, 1893, 1897, 1901, 1903, 1923, 1925, 1927, 1929, 1931, 1933, 1935, 1937, 1939, 1991-1992. No publishing information. Available at Minnesota Historical Society.

Leonard, William E. *The Saturday Lunch Club of Minneapolis—A Brief History.* Minneapolis: Privately published brochure, 1927. Available at Minnesota Historical Society.

Link, Arthur S. Wilson, *Campaigns for Progressivism and Peace, 1916-1917.* Princeton, New Jersey: Princeton University Press, 1965.

Mayer, George H. *The Political Career of Floyd B. Olson.* St. Paul: Minnesota Historical Society Press, 1987.

McGrath, John S., and James J. Delmont. *Floyd Björnsterne Olson: Minnesota's Greatest Liberal Governor.* No city: no publisher, 1937.

Morlan, Robert L. *Political Prairie Fire: The Nonpartisan League, 1915-1922.* St. Paul: Minnesota Historical Society Press, 1985 (new introduction by Larry Remele).

Morison, Samuel Eliot, and Henry Steele Commager, *The Growth of the American Republic.* New York: Oxford University Press, 1940.

Morison, Samuel Eliot, Frederick Merck, and Frank Freidel. *Dissent in Three American Wars.* Cambridge: Harvard University Press, 1970.

Naftalin, Arthur. "A History of the Farmer-Labor Party of Minnesota." Unpublished Ph.D. dissertation, University of Minnesota, 1948.

Navasky, Victor S. *Naming Names.* New York: The Viking Press, 1980.

Nord, David Paul. "Minneapolis and the Pragmatic Socialism of Thomas Van Lear." *Minnesota History* 45 (Spring 1956):2-10.

Nye, Russell B. *Midwestern Progressive Politics,* as quoted in *Dictionary of American History,* 2: 490-92.

Olin, William M., Secretary of the Commonwealth. *Massachusetts Soldiers and Sailors in the War of the Revolution.* Boston: Wright and Potter Printing Company, 1907.

Parsons, E. Dudley. *The Integration of the Saturday Lunch Club with the Liberal Movement in Minnesota.* Minneapolis: Privately published brochure, 1951.

Rachlis, Eugene. "Sacco, Vanzetti, Hammett and Boyer," a review of Rick Boyer's *The Penny Ferry* (Boston: Warner Books, 1984), in *Rights* (July-September 1986).

Rankin, A. W. *The Minnesota Legislature of 1925.* Minneapolis: Voters Research League of Minneapolis, 1925.

Remele, Larry. "The Nonpartisan League: The Courage to Stand Up for Farmers." In *Plowing Up a Storm: The History of Midwestern Farm Activism.* No city: Nebraska Educational Television Network, 1985.

Salisbury, Harrison E. *A Journey for Our Times.* New York: Harper and Row, 1983.

Salisbury, Janet. *The Women's Alliance of the First Unitarian Society: A Centennial History,* 1981. Minneapolis: First Unitarian Society of Minneapolis, 1981. Pamphlet available in First Unitarian Society Archives.

Schlesinger, Arthur M., Sr. *Birth of the Nation.* New York: Alfred A. Knopf, 1968.

_____. *The Rise of Modern America: 1865-1951.* New York: The Macmillan Company, 1951.

Searle, A. Newell. *Saving Quetico-Superior: A Land Set Apart.* St. Paul: Minnesota Historical Society Press, 1977.

Senate Journal, 1899, 1901, 1902 Extra Session. No publishing information. Available at Minnesota Historical Society.

Sevareid, Eric. *Not So Wild a Dream.* New York: Atheneum, 1976.

Sloane, Arthur A., and Fred Witney. *Labor Relations.* Englewood Cliffs, New Jersey: Prentice-Hall, Inc., 1977.

Spangler, Earl. *The Negro in Minnesota.* Minneapolis, T. S. Denison & Company, Inc., 1961.

Starkey, Marion L. *The Devil in Massachusetts.* Garden City, New York: Doubleday & Company, 1969.

Statehouse Review for 1939. St. Paul: Minnesota Legislative Research Bureau, 1939.

Steffens, Lincoln. *The Autobiography of Lincoln Steffens.* New York: Harcourt, Brace and Company, 1931.

_____. *The Shame of the Cities.* New York: McClure, Phillips & Co., 1904.

Stephenson, George M. *John Lind of Minnesota.* Minneapolis: University of Minnesota Press, 1935.

Stockwell, Maud. *Early Minneapolis Memories.* [Minneapolis]: First Unitarian Society, 1981. Written in 1945.

_____. *Some Facts Concerning Military Training at State Universities.* [Minneapolis]: Privately published, 1925. A copy is in possession of the author.

Stockwell, Charlotte Bowdish. Speech given before the Woman's Foreign Missionary Society of the Methodist-Episcopal Church of Anoka, about 1880.

Stockwell, Maud Conkey. "Our Debt to the Seventies," typescript copy of an address given at the sixtieth anniversary celebration of the First Unitarian Society of Minneapolis on November 18, 1941, Stockwell Family Papers, Minnesota Historical Society Archives.

_____. "A Sheaf of Kingsley—Conkey Family History." Written November 1947, never published. A copy is in the possession of the author.

Stockwell, Walter Lincoln. *Memories and an Appreciation of My Mother Charlotte Bowdish Stockwell.* Fargo, North Dakota: Privately published, 1930. Copies are in the collections of the Newberry Library, Fargo, and the University of Minnesota.

Stuhler, Barbara, and Gretchen Kreuter. *Women of Minnesota.* St. Paul: Minnesota Historical Society Press, 1977.

Thurston, Harlan. *Life in Anoka—1900.* Anoka: Anoka Historical Society, 1972.

"Tribute to the Memory of Sylvanus A. Stockwell," a transcript of proceedings of Stockwell Memorial Service on April 23, 1943, at the Unitarian Center, Minneapolis. Stockwell Family Papers. Minnesota Historical Society Archives.

Trimble, Steve. "It's the Law." *Roots* 13 (Spring 1985): 17-22.

"Tracks." In *Anoka in 1889.* Anoka: G. H. Goodrich, 1889.

Valelly, Richard M. *Radicalism in the States: The Minnesota Farmer-Labor Party and the American Political Economy.* Chicago: University of Chicago Press, 1989.

Walker, Charles R. *American City.* New York: Arno & The New York Times, 1971.

Winchell, N. W., Edward D. Neill, and J. Fletcher Williams. *History of the Upper Mississippi Valley.* Minneapolis: Minnesota Historical Company, 1881.

Winston, Carleton. *This Circle of Earth—The Story of John H. Dietrich.* New York: C. P. Putnam Sons, 1942.

Index

415

About the Author

Bill Everts, born in Boston, lives in Mill Valley, California. He is a retired lawyer and teacher, having taught at Kimball Union Academy in New Hampshire, San Francisco Law School, and Hampton Institute in Virginia. *Stockwell of Minneapolis*, the biography of his grandfather, is his first book. Most of the research and writing was done at the Minnesota Historical Society in St. Paul, Minnesota. Mr. Everts relied not only on materials available in the library and the archives of the society, along with family papers, but also on his knowledge of history. He majored in American History and Literature at Harvard, graduating with honors.